What Is Heterodox Economics?

Since the Global Financial Crisis, economics has been under greater public scrutiny, revealing a crisis in the discipline. This represented a potential turning point on how economics should be thought about and taught. Heterodox economics has played a prominent role in these discussions revolving around new economics thinking and pluralism in economics. Yet, its identity, aspirations, and pedagogy remain underexplored, contested, and somewhat opaque.

This volume brings together 16 interviews with leading economists to understand what heterodox economics is. How and why does an economist become heterodox? In which way do heterodox economists see themselves as "different" from mainstream economics? The interviews shed light on what problems heterodox economists perceive in the mainstream, elucidate the different contexts under which they operate in higher education, and provide insights on their ontology and methodology. The reader will also find answers to the following questions about the nature and state of heterodox economics: do heterodox economists have particular intellectual journeys, motives, and aspirations? Is this reflected in their teaching practices and strategies to achieve social change? What is the relation between heterodox economics and the humanities and arts?

Appealing to a diverse audience, including philosophers, sociologists, and historians of economic thought, the book will be of great interest to anyone keen to find out more about the internal discussions in the economics discipline.

Andrew Mearman is Associate Professor of Economics at the University of Leeds, UK. He has previously taught at the University of the West of England (UWE Bristol), UK; Wagner College, New York, USA; and the University of Lincoln, UK. He has published extensively on economics education, the philosophy and methodology of economics, and heterodox economics and pluralism.

Sebastian Berger is Senior Lecturer in Economics at the University of the West of England (UWE Bristol), UK. He is a recipient of the Helen Potter Award from the Association for Social Economics and a trustee of the Kapp Foundation for the Humanization and Integration of the Social Sciences.

Danielle Guizzo is Senior Lecturer in Economics at the University of the West of England (UWE Bristol), UK. She has published articles on the history of economic thought, philosophy of economics, and teaching of economics.

Routledge Advances in Heterodox Economics

Series editors:
Mark Setterfield
The New School for Social Research, USA
Peter Kriesler
University of New South Wales, Australia

Over the past two decades, the intellectual agendas of heterodox econo-mists have taken a decidedly pluralist turn. Leading thinkers have begun to move beyond the established paradigms of Austrian, feminist, Institutional-evolutionary, Marxian, Post Keynesian, radical, social, and Sraffian economics—opening up new lines of analysis, criticism, and dialogue among dissenting schools of thought. This cross-fertilization of ideas is creating a new generation of scholarship in which novel combinations of heterodox ideas are being brought to bear on important contemporary and historical problems.

Routledge Advances in Heterodox Economics aims to promote this new schol-arship by publishing innovative books in heterodox economic theory, policy, philosophy, intellectual history, institutional history, and pedagogy. Syntheses or critical engagement of two or more heterodox traditions are especially encouraged.

37   Microeconomic Theory
A Heterodox Approach
Authored by Frederic S. Lee, Edited by Tae-Hee Jo

38   The Economics of Law, Order, and Action
The Logic of Public Goods
Jakub Bożydar Wiśniewski

39   Advancing Pluralism in Teaching Economics
International Perspectives on a Textbook Science
Edited by Samuel Decker, Wolfram Elsner and Svenja Flechtner

40   What Is Heterodox Economics?
Conversations with Leading Economists
Andrew Mearman, Sebastian Berger and Danielle Guizzo

For more information about this series, please visit
www.routledge.com/series/RAHE

What Is Heterodox Economics?

Conversations with Leading Economists

Andrew Mearman, Sebastian Berger
and Danielle Guizzo

LONDON AND NEW YORK

First published 2019
by Routledge
2 Park Square, Milton Park, Abingdon, Oxon OX14 4RN

and by Routledge
52 Vanderbilt Avenue, New York, NY 10017

Routledge is an imprint of the Taylor & Francis Group, an informa business

© 2019 Andrew Mearman, Sebastian Berger and Danielle Guizzo

The right of Andrew Mearman, Sebastian Berger and Danielle Guizzo
to be identified as authors of this work has been asserted by them in
accordance with sections 77 and 78 of the Copyright, Designs and Patents
Act 1988.

All rights reserved. No part of this book may be reprinted or reproduced or
utilised in any form or by any electronic, mechanical, or other means, now
known or hereafter invented, including photocopying and recording, or in
any information storage or retrieval system, without permission in writing
from the publishers.

Trademark notice: Product or corporate names may be trademarks or
registered trademarks, and are used only for identification and explanation
without intent to infringe.

British Library Cataloguing-in-Publication Data
A catalogue record for this book is available from the British Library

Library of Congress Cataloging-in-Publication Data
Names: Mearman, Andrew, 1971- author. | Berger, Sebastian, author. |
Guizzo, Danielle, 1989- author.
Title: What is heterodox economics? : conversations with leading
economists / Andrew Mearman, Sebastian Berger and Danielle Guizzo.
Description: Abingdon, Oxon ; New York, NY : Routledge, 2019. |
Series: Routledge advances in heterodox economics ; 40 | Includes
bibliographical references and index.
Identifiers: LCCN 2018053198 (print) | LCCN 2018055743 (ebook) |
ISBN 9781315188737 (Ebook) | ISBN 9781138731950 (hardback :
alk. paper)
Subjects: LCSH: Economics. | Schools of economics. | Radical economics. |
Evolutionary economics.
Classification: LCC HB75 (ebook) | LCC HB75 .M388 2019 (print) |
DDC 330.15—dc23
LC record available at https://lccn.loc.gov/2018053198

ISBN: 978-1-138-73195-0 (hbk)
ISBN: 978-1-315-18873-7 (ebk)

Typeset in Bembo Std
by Cenveo® Publisher Services

We dedicate this book to the memory of
Fernando Cardim de Carvalho (1953–2018).

Contents

Preface	ix
Acknowledgements	xii

1	Introduction	1
2	Sheila Dow	17
3	Fernando Cardim de Carvalho	33
4	William Darity	49
5	S. Charusheela	66
6	Karma Ura	82
7	Rolf Steppacher	94
8	Julie Nelson	111
9	Tony Lawson	130
10	Joan Martinez-Alier	156
11	Esther-Mirjam Sent	173
12	Gary Mongiovi	186

viii *Contents*

13 Anwar Shaikh   207

14 Victoria Chick   232

15 Edward Fullbrook   252

16 David Dequech   262

17 Ulrich Witt   275

18 Concluding thoughts   286

Bibliography   293
Index   302

Preface

The present volume comprises 16 interviews with leading economists undertaken between March 2017 and April 2018. Our intention in doing this is to better understand heterodox economics from the point of view of its leading exponents, especially how one *becomes* a heterodox economist and *how* heterodox economists see themselves as "different" from mainstream economics. The interviews also offer timely discussions of the current state of the economics discipline, the problems of the mainstream, the different contexts of higher education, and insights on the philosophy and ontology of economics.

This book has no clear creation story; rather, it is the result of individual histories, circumstances, sustained curiosity about similar key questions, common interests in philosophical approaches to economics, and trying to promulgate greater openness in economics in a discipline we experience (with some justification) as unfriendly. Immediate triggers for the book were conversations between Andrew and Sebastian while both worked at the University of the West of England, Bristol (UWE), about the nature of heterodox economics. Could it be more than a negative approach – that is, a collective rejection of the mainstream? A coincidence played a significant role. As Andrew read the article by Thornborrow and Brown (2009) on the formation of elite military identity, which inspired analogies to economists, and the volumes of interviews with mainstream economists (Klamer, 1983; Snowdon and Vane, 1999; Colander, Holt and Rosser, 2004a; Samuelson and Barnett, 2007; Bowmaker, 2010), this chimed with Sebastian's established interest in the psychology of neoclassical economists and differences to that of heterodox economists. A visit to Brazil in 2014 by Andrew then inspired questions regarding that country's pluralist approach to economics: how did heterodox economics become part of the mainstream there, and what are the implications for its self-image and identity? Danielle joined UWE and brought not only her knowledge of the Brazilian context but a Foucauldian perspective on the history and philosophy of economics. Our shared interests generated work on the reform of economics teaching in the UK (now published as Mearman, Guizzo and Berger, 2018a, 2018b). All these strands pointed towards interviewing heterodox economists to capture

x   *Preface*

their understanding of what heterodox economics is; how they see themselves, their ultimate concerns, and their directions of thought; how they become who they are; and whether they differ significantly from mainstream economists. The idea was then to collect a book of interviews, building on existing contributions, but focusing more on the nature of heterodox economics. The formation of the book can therefore be considered as the result of a series of connected, significant turning points.

The book captures a recent moment in the history of economic thought, specifically a set of individuals who might be thought of collectively. It discusses how they have created but also responded to the times in which they worked. The interviews capture a group, but they also express the thoughts of a set of leading thinkers. The book is therefore also partly a record of oral history, an autobiographic account of those leading minds. It is part of a process and a contribution to a kind of self-reflection, a taking stock and clarification that is meant to raise the level of understanding of what heterodoxy is about.

The book may then appeal to a diverse audience, including philosophers, sociologists, and historians of economic thought and science who are keen to find out more about the internal discussions in the economics discipline. More specifically, self-identified heterodox economists might find it illuminating to see how leading members of their community see it. Those in the mainstream of economics may be curious about what this thing called "heterodox economics" is: what motivates these people? How do they see the mainstream? This book might offer answers for them. Aspiring economists may be wondering which road to travel; they may want to take a heterodox route but doubt it to be possible. They may wonder why a heterodox strand exists or is necessary; they may prefer pluralism and be grappling with its possibilities. We hope that this book might offer insight to these new scholars.

Since we have chosen to write a book, we intend that it be read as such, taking in our motivations and explanation of our approach, the interviews themselves, and our interpretation of them. We hope the book is a coherent whole, and we suggest it be read in that way. However, other approaches are open to the reader. It is possible, for instance, to skip to our concluding thoughts on what heterodox economics is and the answers to the questions we have posed. Another approach is to skip our contributions entirely, given that the thoughts of our interviewees are the actual subject matter of this book. Here we are aware that some of our interviewees are extremely well known, and we understand that readers will be drawn to their contributions; however, we hope that readers will take the opportunity to consider all the interviews. The book may then offer a voyage of discovery for readers, as it has been for us.

The reader might find that defining heterodox economics is not an easy task. Heterodox economists are complex, and this reflects the sociology and psychology of the discipline. Exploring the minds of our interviewees results in a positive conceptualisation of heterodox economics: there is some

Preface xi

agreement on key characteristics of heterodoxy as well as the problems of the mainstream.

We found the conversations revealing and insightful for understanding heterodox economics better, but we were also intrigued and to some extent even puzzled by some of the responses offered by our interviewees. Additionally, we asked ourselves what these conversations mean for the future of heterodox economics as a complex community and its aspirations. The reader might notice that open questions remain and can be subjected to future enquiry. Their answers depend on further research on the topic or how future generations of economists will deal with the issues that surround heterodoxy.

Acknowledgements

As with all such projects, there are several groups and individuals to thank. We presented early thoughts about the framework for the book at the Association for Heterodox Economics (AHE) 2017 conference and received numerous helpful suggestions there. We presented findings from the book at the AHE 2018 conference and again got excellent feedback. We thank all participants for their comments. We also offer special thanks and encouragement to our colleagues (alphabetically) Andrew Brown, Yannis Dafermos, Jamie Morgan, Esther Pickering, Elke Pirgmaier, and Don Webber. Clearly, there were many others worthy of being interviewed: we could easily construct a second and third volume; alas not yet. Principally, of course, we must thank our interviewees, who gave up their time to meet with us, go through transcripts, and where necessary provide extra information. Their assistance was indispensable. We also thank Routledge for making this project possible, in particular Laura Johnson and Anna Cuthbert.

1 Introduction

Especially since the Global Financial Crisis, economics has been under greater public scrutiny, revealing a crisis in the field. This also represented a potential turning point on how economics should be thought about and taught. Heterodox economics has played a prominent role in these discussions revolving around new economics thinking and pluralism in economics. Yet, its common ground in terms of identities, goals, aspirations, and collective actions remains underexplored, contested, and somewhat opaque. Thus, the question posed here – that is, what is heterodox economics? – has a particular relevance.

What is the existing literature on Heterodox Economics?

The literature on heterodox economics may best be characterised as appearing confused; however, this may be misleading. The first point to note is that though the first known use of the term "heterodox economics" was by Ayres (1936), it is only recently that its usage has been widespread and hence its meaning debated. Despite considerable activity, it remains contested. For example, the heterodox economics directory (HED, 2016) presents a collection of short theses by leading thinkers on what heterodox economics is. A few themes emerge, which are emblematic of the wider literature.

For many commentators, heterodox economics is inherently oppositional to some orthodoxy or mainstream. That in turn is characterised by adherence to, *inter alia*, mathematical formalism, individualism, and equilibrium and the exclusion of concepts of power, political economy, and history. This list is deliberately chosen to reflect the tenets of what might be called neoclassical economics: that is representative of the literature which often conflates mainstream with neoclassical economics. As Mearman (2017) holds, this may only apply to economics teaching and mostly at the undergraduate level. In the same vein, several commentators (Colander, 2000; Colander, Holt and Rosser, 2004b; Cedrini and Fontana, 2017) have remarked, this may not capture the current diversity, or more controversially, fragmentation and incoherence of mainstream economic research. Hence, if heterodox economics is

2   Introduction

(analytically) oppositional to a diverse (and complex) mainstream, it might be expected to be diverse and complex itself. And indeed, many view it as such. For these commentators, heterodox economics is merely a collection of existing schools of thought unified only in their opposition. However, to others, heterodoxy is becoming a unified project, with both oppositional aspects as well as some positive common ground. To yet more others, heterodoxy is synonymous with pluralism: that can apply to its own constitution but also in its approach to the mainstream. In this respect, heterodoxy is necessarily non-homogeneous. This does not imply that it is incoherent.

Admittedly, that treatment may be more aspirational than descriptive. The existing literature suggests at best an emerging clarity in the meaning of heterodox economics. Until now – as is captured in the contributions to the HED (2016) – we can see numerous, often inconsistent treatments. Dequech (2007) identifies two strands of definition of heterodox economics: intellectual and sociological. The former captures all definitions which offer either a set of theoretical concepts or methodological principles which heterodox economics either accepts or, more likely, rejects. Unfortunately, as Dequech shows, these intellectual definitions are problematic. For example, if, as Lawson (*passim*) argues, mainstream economics is characterised by an insistence on mathematical modelling, then heterodox economics represents a non-insistence. As Mearman (2012) argues, though, a non-insistence is hard to evidence, and in any case there are strands of what appears to be heterodox economics which do appear to stress mathematical modelling: for instance, analytical Marxists such as Roberto Veneziani, or a group of Post Keynesians, such as Eckhard Hein, Steve Keen, Ozlem Onaran, and Engelbert Stockhammer, who do appear to at least emphasise modelling. Economists working in the Sraffian tradition may be similarly characterised.

Dequech concludes, then, that intellectual definitions of heterodox economics are inferior to sociological definitions, which denote it by the membership of its social groups. These memberships seem to offer greater coherence of definition. However, they also raise some interesting questions about inclusion and exclusion. For instance, it appears that some view Austrian economics as heterodox. According to some intellectual definitions, these do fit the heterodox label: Austrians de-emphasise at least mathematical modelling, equilibrium, optimisation, static analysis, and the like. In these senses they look very like many Post Keynesian economists, many Marxists, and Institutionalists. Yet, politically, they look rather different. This may lead to their exclusion from the "true" heterodoxy. On the other hand, many commentators associate heterodoxy with being excluded by the mainstream. From the HED (2016) contributions, for example, Denis, Hopkins, and Galbraith all define heterodox economics in that way. Wrenn (2007) similarly uses the term "marginalised" in her treatment. These approaches hint at broader sociological notions of heterodoxy as reflecting the social structures of the economics discipline and indeed the broader political economy of modern capitalism. Perhaps unsurprisingly, many HED contributors define

Introduction   3

heterodox economics in terms of an opposition to prevailing social structures and power relations within economics and within capitalism. Further, they define heterodox in terms of pro-social movements designed to achieve real change (Albelda, Elsner, Pollin and Wolff in HED, 2016).

Sociological definitions of heterodox economics may then capture better the actual composition of heterodox groups; as such Dequech regards them as better than intellectual definitions, not least for their ability to be positive. Nonetheless, Mearman (2012) argues that sociological definitions are conceptually empty: they describe who is in the set "heterodox economics" without telling us what it means. So, some combination of sociological and intellectual is necessary. He comments on "empirical" approaches to defining heterodox economics. Mearman (2011) is one such attempt. He applied various statistical analyses to survey data collected from a sample of Association for Heterodox Economics (AHE) members (i.e., self-identified heterodox economists). He found that although the group shared core beliefs that history and power are important in understanding the economy, connections between individuals reflected more closely linkages between pre-existing schools of thought; for example, Marxists agreed with each other more than they did with Post Keynesians. Further, he found considerable variation in the degree to which members of the heterodox group labelled themselves "heterodox". On average, they responded that they agreed about 85%. However, they also agreed about 20% that they were mainstream (and about 80% that they were pluralist). This evidence undermines further a strict distinction between mainstream and heterodox. However, this work misspecified the nature of the object by ignoring sociological elements of groups of heterodox economists and not looking at the "descent" of different economists. There is some evidence of such analysis as applied to heterodox economics (e.g., Lee, 2009 Davis, 2009; Backhouse, 2000; Ederer et al., 2012). Indeed, this book is partly an exploration of the intellectual lineage of current heterodox economists.

Mearman (2012) also detected two psychological aspects of heterodox economics: self-labelling and an oppositional attitude. On the former, it is well established in sociology that labelling has effects. This usually operates via the powerful labelling the powerless negatively (e.g., the "lazy unemployed"); however, in the case of heterodox economics, the label has been chosen by themselves. Indeed, when Frederic Lee set up the Association for *Heterodox* Economics in 1999, he chose that label. It is not generally used pejoratively by mainstream critics, although many claim to find it unnecessarily divisive. Rather, heterodox writers must contend with being brand-marked as "non-economists". So, it may be that something about the psychology of heterodox economists leads them to accept that label.

Second, as already mentioned, heterodox economists may adopt a critical or oppositional attitude towards mainstream economics and (aspects of) capitalism. One manifestation of this attitude is their position on pluralism. Many of the HED (2016) commentators explicitly associate heterodox economics

4   *Introduction*

with pluralism. Lee (2012) claims heterodoxy has a pluralist orientation. However, for some, this pluralism may be strategic, to create space for themselves to operate (see Garnett, 2006). As Dobusch and Kapeller (2012) argue, pluralism can involve ghettoisation, or perhaps tolerance: a decision to "live and let live". However, they argue for an "interested pluralism" in which heterodox economists actively engage with other heterodox economists and mainstreamers. This approach reflects a belief that the dividing lines between mainstream and heterodox are ragged and dynamic. This is also confirmed by Wrenn's (2007) findings on the existence of a continuum between heterodoxy and mainstream. Any individual and, perhaps, any school of thought may be somewhat heterodox, and this may change as the mainstream changes. If, as Cedrini and Fontana (2017) argue, mainstream economics is also fragmented, heterodox economics (and indeed economics, generally) may advance if heterodox economists were to work in relevant niches with mainstream economists. However, the decision whether to do this reflects a psychological attitude, personal experience, and power relations. It also often depends on whether heterodox economists can find mainstream collaborators, hiring committees, access to journals and publishers, and policymakers open enough to engage in genuine dialogue and acknowledge research that is not based on neoclassical economics. It also reflects whether mainstream and/or neoclassical economists refrain from taking ideas from heterodox economics (institutions, history, environment, etc.) without acknowledging the original sources and changing their meanings to squeeze them into a neoclassical framework. In the past this has often served to defend the status quo of the mainstream and neuter its critics.

An example of a collaborative approach may be Jo, Chester, and D'Ippoliti (2017). They are explicitly not anti-mainstream. Further, they asked that contributors to their handbook of heterodox economics try to integrate a variety of heterodox approaches. Moreover, they cite Lee and Lavoie (2012) as identifying opportunities for heterodox ideas to be incorporated into fringe mainstream areas. An aspect of this may be to engage with other disciplines. This cross-disciplinary work is a feature of contemporary mainstream thought (Dimmelmeier et al., 2017). It may be significant that several of the HED contributors unambiguously defined heterodox economics as being interdisciplinary (Forstater, Hermann and King in HED, 2016). Therefore, much depends on the understanding of inter- and intra-disciplinarity – that is, whether and how the integration of insights from a variety of scientific disciplines, the humanities, and economic paradigms can or should be going forward (here, see Kapp, 1961; Gerber and Steppacher, 2011; and Boulding, 2011).

Mainstream interview books

There is an existing tradition of interviewing economists. These interviews are mostly with mainstream authors; however, King (1995) and Ederer and colleagues (2012) do offer collections of heterodox economists. Arestis and

Sawyer (2001a) also offer an anthology of biographies of "dissenting economists". On the mainstream side, there are more but proportionately fewer. Those collections that exist also have often captured the same individuals. For the purposes of this book, we have examined in detail the interviews in Snowdon and Vane (1999), Colander, Holt, and Rosser (2004a), and Bowmaker (2010). These interviews capture several generations of economists. Snowdon and Vane's (1999) sample includes Lucas, Sargent, Modigliani, Brunner, Friedman, Solow, Tobin, Mankiw, Clower, Taylor, and Colander. Colander and colleagues' own selection of "cutting-edge economists" included McCloskey, Gintis, Frank, Rabin, Arrow, and Samuelson. Finally, Bowmaker (2010) targeted "great teachers" and included Easterly, Mishkin, Eichengreen, and Hamermesh. What do previous interviews with mainstream economists tell us about mainstream economics? This question is particularly important given the above remarks regarding the continuum between both groups, the ragged and dynamic edges between them, and the pluralism within each.

Several themes emerge from these exchanges. These interviews reveal a variety of paths into becoming an economist. Several respondents are clear that their career paths involved considerable chance or connections leading to opportunities. They fall into economics or follow the advice of a mentor or friend. For example, Clower (in Snowdon and Vane, 1999) started teaching a class in Economics as a substitute for his father, who was called to military service. Others become interested in economics inspired by world events. Blanchard (in Snowdon and Vane, 1999) is one affected by political events of the late 1960s. Colander tells how he ended up at Birmingham when there were riots at Columbia (in Snowdon and Vane, 1999, p. 208). Modigliani claims that his interest in economics first came from the motif of Bologna, a suckling pig, which his father (who died when Modigliani was 13) said "was a great expression of useful economic activity" (in Snowdon and Vane, 1999, p. 242). Binmore (in Colander, Holt and Rosser, 2004a) reports having an interest in games as a child, then found his way into economics through mathematics. The latter is a well-trodden path. Quite starkly, Frank (in Colander, Holt and Rosser, 2004a, p. 111) says: "I think of my career as a sequence of unplanned accidents". Brock goes further to claim, "It was an accident that I went to college; no one in my family had" (in Colander, Holt and Rosser, 2004a, p. 157).

Relatively few of these interviewees had a sense of purpose about being an economist. Rather, it seems that their paths may be reflective of the "aspirational selves" and hero images (archetypes) which can be found in the interviews and seem to be the nucleus of motivational energy. We tentatively identify the following: scientist, holder or seeker of truth, hero, and renegade. Strikingly, the latter bear little relation to the official rhetoric of objectivist scientists. These archetypes point to the relevance of factors which yield meaning and motivation and which are not germane to pure economic theory but rather prior to it. They also suggest a vision of the economist in

6 *Introduction*

which stories, their ongoing reshaping, and their poetic origins matter. These archetypes can be illustrated by some quotations from the interviews.

In support of the archetype of economist as scientist, we see four themes. First are proclamations of scientificity. "...Economics is a tool-driven science – absent the needed tools we are stymied" (Prescott in Snowdon and Vane, 1999, p. 260). Second, we see an ambivalence about the role of mathematics, which seems to vary across generations. Older economists lament its dominance (Clower and Solow in Snowdon and Vane, 1999; Friedman in Samuelson and Barnett, 2007). More recently trained economists contrarily associate mathematics with progress (Romer in Snowdon and Vane, 1999). Third, and related to mathematisation, some argue for close association of economics with "hard" sciences. This is captured in Binmore's assertion that "I guess I am happier to have biologists aboard than philosophers or political scientists" (Binmore in Colander, Holt and Rosser, 2004a, p. 68). That hints at a fourth strand, of objectivity. Gintis, paraphrasing Keynes, asserts that "People who are making love don't talk about politics when they are making love ... We don't have to talk about our politics when we do economics" (Gintis in Colander, Holt and Rosser, 2004a, p. 97). He then goes on to claim: "We are a more scientific discipline...".

Part of the role of the economist as scientist is to seek out and protect truth. There is clear evidence in the literature of this archetype of economist as truth-seeker. The first element of this archetype is the belief that there is a truth. For example, Gordon (in Bowmaker, 2010, p. 69) simply states, "...macroeconomic questions have answers". Further, it is the job of economists to find them: "...I confess to you that I am earnestly focused on the truth with a small t. So are most serious people" (McCloskey in Colander, Holt and Rosser, 2004a, p. 35).

Such statements hint at a heroism of the economist. Indeed, there is a clear strand of self-identification as economist as hero, saving the day. Prescott (in Snowdon and Vane, 1999, p. 268) is representative of those economists who claim they entered the subject to help solve particular problems: "My interest is in the problem of the poor countries, like India. In those countries it is important to let things happen and not protect the status quo". It is noteworthy that in pursuing these interests, Prescott sees himself as fighting established ideas and vested interests. That hints at the renegade economist, challenging existing ideas, practices, and other norms. This in some cases attracted young economists to the subject: "One of the exciting things [about the *General Theory*], of course, for a 19-year-old was the sense of intellectual revolution, overturning the obsolete wisdom encrusted in the past..." (Tobin in Snowdon and Vane, 1999, p. 92). And yet, this renegade urge can be tempered. For example, when asked if ecological economics is "terribly heterodox", Norgaard replied, "Yes, I hope so" (Norgaard in Colander, Holt and Rosser, 2004a, p. 224). But, having expressed his difference, Norgaard (in Colander, Holt and Rosser, 2004a, p. 240) maintains that he "always tries to be a constructive dissenter". In this way, Norgaard and others are positioning themselves, in Lee's (2011) terms, as *heretics* rather than *blasphemers*, that is dissent within narrow limits and without a radical calling into question.

A pertinent question, then, is what kind of archetypes are adopted by heterodox economists. Indeed, that is one of the questions driving this book. Prior evidence suggests some of the same traits. High up is the economist as hero figure, trying to make the world better. For Bergmann, tackling growth is not about some level of GDP "...it is a matter of saving the planet" (in Ederer et al., 2012, p. 30). For Bhaduri (in Ederer et al., 2012, p. 47), "What we need is a better world to live in, with a certain degree of harmony". Many others are clear that they see their role as making changes, perhaps via policy. Elson is up front that "It is important to focus on the real changes that we want to see made" (in Ederer et al., 2012, p. 68). Marglin (in Ederer et al., 2012) said he became an economist through "...a combination of policy relevance, this feeling that what you are doing is going to have an impact on the world, and the intellectual challenge of the kind of neat mathematics in which economics was increasingly formulated" (p. 133). This statement has strong resonance with many statements made by mainstreamers. Similarly, Moore's statement that "growing up as a boy in the 1930s[,] I was trying to figure out what had gone wrong and what we could do differently next time" (in Ederer et al., 2012, p. 147) resonates with Tobin's (in Snowdon and Vane, 1999) statement that "I was also very worried about the Great Depression", and Friedman's conjecture that "...put yourself in 1932 with a quarter of the population unemployed. What was the important urgent problem?" (in Snowdon and Vane, 1999, p. 125). Further, Sawyer said (in Ederer et al., 2012), "You have to go down that heterodox route because you think it offers the best insights, the best explanations of how the world works and how the world can be in some sense improved" (p. 178). While this kind of preliminary archetypal approach suggests some similarities between mainstream and heterodox economists, there is also the argument that some archetypes, such as the Great Mother, may be exclusively adopted by heterodox economists (Berger 2016). Indeed, one of the guiding questions is whether our interview-based research can corroborate archetypal differences between mainstream and heterodox economists.

Open questions, paradoxes, anomalies, and curiosities

The existing insights into the nature of heterodox economics and the interview literature raise several questions, for which our research project seeks answers. For example, what are the complex influences that shape a heterodox economist? What makes heterodox economists different from neoclassical economists, given they share some common intellectual ancestors (e.g., Keynes)? Do heterodox economists have different intellectual backgrounds? How and when do they decide to be or become – identify

8   *Introduction*

with – heterodoxy? Further, given that mainstream economists see themselves as intellectual heroes or mavericks who fight for the common good, how different is that from self-images of heterodox economists? Would this archetypal analysis break down the stylised binary to some extent? Or, does this merely expose the fact that such an approach misses what is most essential: the definition of Truth and value theory adopted by the economist; the appropriateness of their method and theory to the problem at hand; the radicalness, courage, depth, circumspection, precision, creativity, beauty, and style of thought; the alignment with powerful private-sector interests, et cetera. Do heterodox economists have different goals? And, is this reflected in their teaching practices?

The existing literature evidences commonalities between mainstream and heterodox economists, which pose a paradox. For instance, several interviews with mainstream economists critique the overmathematisation, mathematics envy, and corresponding lack of realism or relevance of economics (Friedman in Snowdon and Vane, 1999, p. 137; Binmore in Colander, Holt and Rosser, 2004a, p. 74; Clower in Snowdon and Vane, 1999, p. 191; Blaug in Snowdon and Vane, 1999, p. 322), and promote or accept that there is a plurality of perspectives (Tobin in Snowdon and Vane, 1999, pp. 120–1; Arrow in Colander, Holt and Rosser, 2004a, p. 293; Norgaard in Colander, Holt and Rosser, 2004a, p. 223; Colander in Snowdon and Vane, 1999, p. 214). On the face of it, this critique and commitment to pluralism seem to constitute an agreement with heterodox economics on an epistemological and methodological level. This could lead to questioning the accuracy and usefulness of a binary understanding of mainstream versus heterodoxy. However, it could also imply that the binary is still meaningful and useful because it is about differences in the degree and purpose of the critique and pluralism (heresy versus blasphemy). Either way, this is consistent with previous research that indicates a continuum between two extreme positions (heterodoxy – mainstream) with a fuzzy threshold in the middle (Wrenn, 2007). One interesting question, then, is about the nature of this fuzziness, the penumbra, overlap, or "middle ground". How far do the spectrum and the permissible pluralism of heterodoxy and mainstream reach? Where is the threshold, and how is it constituted? And, what are the characteristics of the extreme poles of heterodoxy and mainstream? And, how is this continuum situated within the larger dynamics and hierarchy of the modern academe with mathematics and physics on top and the humanities and arts at the bottom? Or, how is it influenced by the increasing commercialisation of science?

The existing research reviewed above indicates that boundaries of what counts as mainstream and heterodoxy change over time, in the sense that something that once was mainstream is now less mainstream. For example, American Institutional Economics went from being mainstream during the interwar period to being replaced by the neoclassical synthesis, which in turn has been replaced by other varieties of neoclassical economics. This dynamic character of the mainstream is corroborated by various histories and sociologies of the profession (Coats et al., 2000). If this is the case, then one could ask whether the boundaries are permeable or flexible with regards to heterodox economics today. A further pertinent question is whether certain segments of heterodoxy can breach the boundaries more easily than others, in the sense of being taken seriously as potential mainstream. Are they invited to discussions, and do they have access to policymakers, publications, and references in top mainstream journals? For example, can a mathematical-oriented heterodox economist dealing with macroeconomic issues cross borders more easily than someone working on philosophical issues in economics? Is it easier for a science-oriented ecological economist (see the "success" of the PhD programmes in Leeds and Barcelona) than it is for a historian of economics (see the demise of this field of economics)? How much of this is due to idiosyncrasies of the individual, such as attitude, rhetorical, personal, and political skills, rather than fundamental ideological and philosophical commitments (see the difference in "success" between Herman Daly and Nicholas Georgescu-Roegen). How much is due to the changing exigencies of the times, such as crises that lead to a search for different answers (see how mainstream economists "discovered" Hyman Minsky since the financial crisis in 2007/8).

Indeed, it is paradoxical that despite the pluralism in the mainstream of economics there is a need for the label "heterodoxy". There is a great variety of approaches in actual research and teaching practice in the profession. Some of these are incommensurable with the core of neoclassical economics, yet they are not labelled as heterodox. How is this possible? This begs the question, what disciplinary practices exist in economics that establish boundaries, define hierarchies and deviance, and necessitate the self-labelling as "heterodox"?

Moreover, "heterodoxy" in economics seems to be an anomaly in academia. Dissent about theory and method exists in various fields of inquiry whether in the sciences or the humanities. Schisms in schools of thought abound within various sciences. However, this usually does not lead to the emergence of an overall polarisation of an entire discipline. Indeed, the bipolar split indicated by the labelling of "mainstream" versus "heterodox" is quite unusual. Thus, there seems to be something unique about the state of economics. If this is not merely a leftover of the polarised situation pervading in economics during of the Cold War (Capitalist versus Marxist), then what is it?

Heterodox economics is successful despite remaining opaque. While heterodoxy is prolific in terms of research and publications, organising, group identity, attracting members, networking, providing career opportunities, funding, public attention, and even policy success, it remains underspecified, ill-defined, and not fully understood. It is intriguing that the label "heterodox" is attached to book series, organisations, and publications without there being a clear and accepted definition. Why would economists choose a label that has no agreed-upon definition? Or, is there perhaps an

10 Introduction

implicit understanding that functions as an umbrella to unite various economists (rejection of [aspects of] neoclassical economics, pluralism, social provisioning, openness)? Is its elusiveness a strength or a weakness, and is it intentional or inescapable?

It is curious that heterodox economics has so far escaped a clear definition despite its definitive label that suggests the existence of a binary difference with regard to the mainstream. Even if the notion of a binary difference is rejected – as suggested above – in favour of a difference in degree, which of the dimensions of mainstream is being opposed (partially or fundamentally)? Is it, *inter alia*, textbooks, subject benchmark statements, disciplinary practices, methods, ontologies, epistemologies, concepts, theories, definitions?

"Heterodoxy" is a consciously chosen self-label that is very different from a demeaning label assigned by a dominant group. What is this self-labelling act about? Can the historical context of its emergence tell us something about the essence of its meaning? Perhaps there was support of additional institutions to ensure this emergence? For example, Mata (2004) and Lee (2007) reinforce the role of controversies (particularly the capital controversy), institutions, and organisational support in constituting the Post Keynesian identity, including the role of key events in the 1970s that supported the establishment of new dissenting groups – for example, the establishment of academic circles and publications on Post Keynesian economics (such as the *Thames Papers in Political Economy*). Was this also the case of other heterodox traditions or specific scholars?

What kind of experiences led to this self-labelling? Is there something like a common experience or direction of thought amongst heterodox economists that can be identified? Is heterodoxy the result of a self-branding act of blasphemers who have experienced suppression and discrimination in one form or another and are in solidarity with those who have? What drove Frederic Lee to set up the inaugural "fringe" conference of the AHE (see Mearman and Philp, 2016), and what made people attend (or not)? What constitutes the appeal of self-labelling, and what are its roots in personal psychology, ethics, and attitude? What kind of person self-selects into this category, and how do they see themselves? What is the attitude behind the label: is it used with a sense of pride, spite, protest, or pessimism? What is the label used for? Is it used indiscriminately in all contexts or is it employed strategically depending on context (job applications, networks, public debates, etc.)? Is it used the same way by every heterodox economist? What is the meaning of the label? Is it understood the same way by all heterodox economists?

More specifically, why would anybody self-declare as heterodox if this can easily be (mis)interpreted and (mis)construed in a range of ways from unorthodox and maverick to abnormal, deviant, or inferior? This question is all the more interesting as it seems that this self-label could result in limiting career and funding opportunities, lead to exclusion from important discourses, and mean less overall academic and societal prestige and impact. It could also be a disadvantageous rhetorical move. Conversely, heterodoxy as a label could provide unique career opportunities within the networks created by heterodox economists and open channels to promulgate "alternative" and "better" economic ideas. If mainstream economics is perceived to be failing, then "heterodox" could be perceived as the alternative or solution. Given these uncertainties and potential for (mis)perception, is there a special level of courage, boldness, oppositional or virtuous attitude required for a "heterodox coming-out"?

Does being a heterodox economist necessarily imply membership in an overtly heterodox group, such as the Association for Heterodox Economics (AHE), and subscription to the *Heterodox Economics Newsletter*? If not, does membership in other organisations, such as the Association for Evolutionary Economics (AfEE), European Association for Evolutionary Political Economy (EAEPE), Association for Social Economics (ASE), Union of Radical Political Economics (URPE), European Society for Ecological Economics (ESEE), or the International Confederation of Associations for Pluralism in Economics (ICAPE), and contributing to their academic journals count as being a card-holding member of heterodoxy? Or, is membership policed in some other way? And how are boundaries drawn regarding the mainstream? Can anyone (e.g., Austrian economics) self-identify as a heterodox?

Does heterodox economics perhaps have the potential to become a kind of transnational thought collective akin to the neoliberal thought collective? Does it have characteristics of a political movement with a social epistemology? If so, what is it? And, what is its role, potential, meaning, and significance?

Overall, the existing literature evidences several paradoxes, anomalies, and curiosities, resulting in open questions surrounding heterodox economics. This sparks a sense of wonder, a thirst for deeper questioning and seeing anew, a sense of the yet-to-be-actualised potential encompassed by the title's question, a sense of the openness to change in the vectors of economic thinking, and an escape from tired conventionalities. Our interview questions are designed to shed light upon the somewhat opaque and complex nature of heterodox economics.

Our interview questions

Our research seeks to shed some light on the unanswered questions regarding the nature of heterodox economics. The interview questions for this research were selected based on the particular interests we have in heterodox economics, our intellectual backgrounds, and our motivations. So, it seems in order to briefly talk about our priors for making and our priors for interpreting the following questions.

Our schedule of questions is as follows:

How did you become an economist?
Please tell us how you developed your particular individual contribution.
We have chosen to speak to you as we consider you a heterodox economist. Would you label yourself as a heterodox economist?

12 *Introduction*

What do you think Heterodox Economics is?

What are the problems of mainstream economics?

What are you trying to achieve as an economist?

Do you seek to influence society, and if so, how?

What are your strategies for seeking research funding?

What do you enjoy most about teaching?

What do you seek to achieve in teaching? How do you put this into practice?

The notable economist McCloskey (1983) referred to economics as poetry. What do you think about that?

The biographical and labelling questions sprang initially from an interest in Jungian depth psychology and Post-Jungian archetypal psychology, in which archetypes, such as introjected hero images and aspirational Selves, provide motivational energy and shape ideological and philosophical commitments, theory formation, and the corresponding self-selection processes into "disciplines" and groups – largely unconsciously and at early career stages (Berger 2016). The poetry question results from interest in Nietzsche's remark that poetry and philosophy demarcate the highest human potential (Berger, 2018). The interest in archetypal psychology and poetry, then, grew into an interest in the role of hermeneutics in economics. There is thus a direct link between our questions and previous work on storytelling, rhetoric, discourse, language, metaphor, and hermeneutics in economics (Klamer, McCloskey, and Solow, 1988; Mirowski, 1990; Samuels, 1990; Henderson, Dudley-Evans and Backhouse, 1993). An inspirational model for the present interview project was then provided by organisational research teasing out the master narratives, aspirational Selves, and hero images in the military (Thornborrow and Brown, 2009). The questions on social epistemology and funding stem from an interest in prosopography – that is, research into intellectual thought collectives (Mirowski and Plehwe, 2009). This relates to an understanding of the role of the intellectual seeking power over society, which reflects on the process of theory construction (Foucault, 1972), especially the esoteric side of economics that is influenced by emotional factors.

Finally, we also ask questions about pedagogy. Can heterodox economics be defined in terms of its approach to teaching? There is some evidence that heterodox economists take a different approach to teaching, putting greater emphasis on criticality and openness and less on learning or training. Radical economic writers, many inspired by Paulo Freire (1970), have advanced such an approach since the 1970s (Bridges and Hartmann, 1975). However, the heterodox teacher faces a conundrum: because they view economics as inherently social and political, they tend to favour incorporating the social and the political into their economic analysis. They also stress critique of existing mainstream views. But they also acknowledge the role of power in economics. This should extend to an understanding of their own power as teachers. How, then, should they approach learning? It is perhaps (partly) for these reasons that heterodox economists have advocated pluralism in teaching (Freeman, 2009; Dow, 2009; Garnett, Olsen and Starr, 2009).

We do not intend, by all means, to provide a final definition to what heterodox economics is. Readers should not expect final answers from this research (the title of the book notwithstanding), which adopts more of an inquisitive spirit, aiming at best to provide playfully light and tentative answers and possible interpretations and to raise further questions. For example, the book leaves open the definition of mainstream economics. Prior to our interviews, we also did not adopt an explicit definition for mainstream economics. Rather, we left it open to the interviewees to interpret the question regarding the problems of the mainstream. As a result, we can provide a tentative picture of how our group of heterodox interviewees understand the mainstream; however, we cannot provide a final definition of the mainstream, beyond identifying that it is, like heterodox economics, a combination of intellectual and sociological elements.

Methodology and methodological issues

Over a period of around 12 months, we conducted 16 semi-structured interviews with individuals we categorised as senior heterodox economists. There are several basic methodological issues which relate to this approach: sample selection, the conduct of the interview, and the analysis of the interview data.

First, we must acknowledge that the nature of our data precludes any strong claims to generality from our data. Our sample size is clearly small. Further, the sample is purposive and therefore likely biased. Our selection is based on our collective prior judgement about what heterodox economics is. Second, the majority of interviewees were from our own professional networks of heterodox economists and based on our own particular interests and orientations. Third, our sample was expanded by the snowball technique, as contacts and indeed interviewees recommended others to be interviewed. Fourth, all of these 16 are successful senior economists in terms of impact, profile, accomplishments, research output, or leading roles in the heterodox community. This may constitute a bias as we will not have answers from the numerous "unsuccessful" heterodox economists who, for various reasons, left academia or entered positions in which they lack the resources to do research and publish. Fifth, we have defined our subjects as heterodox *a priori* but in the interviews a few of them rejected that description, which raises questions about our sample selection and conclusions.

Sixth, our sample had further purposive elements; we aimed for a distribution of interviewees in terms of four dimensions: gender, geography, paradigmatic perspective, and professional activities.

Most of our interviewees are (or were) academic economists working in universities. However, one works for governments, one is currently an elected member of a national parliament while maintaining their academic position, and one is working from outside of academia. We feel this is important to

14 *Introduction*

capture the diversity of heterodox economics. Also, we tried to ensure some gender and geographical balance; however, in Economics this is difficult given the lower representation of women in the area – 13% in the US and 15.5% in the UK (CSWEP Report, 2017 and RES Report, 2017) – and the dominance of Anglo-Saxon institutions in the discipline. Of our selected 16 economists, 5 are women. In terms of geographical balance, 5 interviewees are US-based, 4 are UK-based, 4 are based in continental Europe, 2 are based in Brazil, and 1 is based in Bhutan. Whilst this is therefore a diverse group, it does not include any interviewees from Africa or Australasia. The last group may be an important omission given the prominent groups of self-identified heterodox economists there. To ensure paradigmatic diversity, we interviewed what we considered to be Feminist, Marxist, Buddhist, Institutional, Social, Ecological, Post Keynesian, Austrian, Evolutionary economists, who – upon closer inspection – were actually found to represent a mix of several of these traditions, which speaks for there being significant commonalities amongst the different schools of thought in heterodox economics. Finally, it may be important to note that we had difficulty in finding heterodox economists from Africa that were suitable for our project. It would be an interesting question for future research to explore why this was the case: what does this say about the interconnectivity of our heterodox networks with heterodox economists in Africa and the proliferation of heterodox economics in Africa?

The interviews were either conducted in person, via Skype, or via email, depending on the preference of the interviewees and practicability of access. Particularly, language and psychological barriers had to be considered, allowing some to opt for email-based written answers with second round follow-up questions. While this does not help the comparability of the interviews, it was the only way in some cases to secure the participation of what we believed to be key figures that can provide important insights on heterodox economics. As the reader shall see, the questions were developed to tease out a variety of dimensions of the heterodox economist as a multifaceted being: a biographical angle, how are heterodox economists "made", their self-image and contribution, their views on mainstream economics, their role in society, success in funding, teaching, and poetry.

We carried out semi-structured interviews. This is a well-established method, with known advantages and disadvantages. The chief advantage is that they offer the interviewer the chance to explore emergent themes specific to the individual. The conversational format of these encounters also allows meaning to be clarified, which may avoid some typical validity problems associated with interviews. However, some researchers criticise semi-structured interviews as lacking reliability and being subject to various biases. For instance, interviews took place in a location of the interviewee's choosing. In most cases, this was their own office. This can change the dynamics of the interview; however, we felt it was justified in creating a comfortable environment more likely to elicit frank responses. We are also aware that the interview format is important. In our case, interviewees were asked the same 13 questions, and in general in the same order; so the interviews allow for some consistency and comparability across respondents and therefore a horizontal analysis of the answers. However, the interview format can lead to some deviation between interviews. Whilst this mitigates effects of question order somewhat, it can make comparison between interviews more difficult.

Weintraub (2007) notes several problems with our proposed method. First, he questions the choice of expert scientists, which he characterises as OTSOG-ery, as in *On The Shoulders Of Giants*. The problem with this is that it tends to focus on the individual and their contribution, and in establishing them as important subjects rather than seeing the history of science as a multilayered object. Second, he argues that expert scientists are keen to stress and embellish their own contribution. Given that the authors knew most of the interviewees prior to their interview, it may be that we will not subject the interviewees' contributions to sufficient critical oversight. That potential problem is exacerbated by our decision to allow interviewees to see the questions in advance and edit the transcripts, which for Weintraub means that the "economists themselves were effectively in charge of the interviews". At this stage we simply acknowledge these typical criticisms of bias and reliability because it is difficult to remedy them fully.

Even though our aim is to add and clarify open questions about what heterodox economics is and how economists classify themselves as such, using interviews to see how prominent economists understand heterodoxy can have some methodological constraints usually indicated in the literature of qualitative research methods. Besides the potential existence of *memory blocks* amongst the interviewees, which could lead to the suppression or repression of unwanted memories and affect one's answers, other methodological limitations should be acknowledged for the case of heterodox economics.

Somewhat related is the problem of *double truths* that can emerge when two truths are presented differently for two different audiences. Mirowski and Plehwe (2009) exemplify the presence of double truths when analysing the spread of neoliberalism as a collective thought. They outline two different truths. One is exoteric for the masses or for the public sphere (the libertarian ideal). Another is esoteric for the insiders who share similar political and epistemological positions (the necessity of authoritarianism to impose it). The existence of double truths can either be reflective of an instrumental view of truth as serving the purpose of persuasion, a product of a knowledge-power system, or the rejection of the idea of there being one Truth. What, if any, are the double truths of heterodox economics? How do we know that the answers to our questions contain the undiluted truths held by our interviewees? Can these at all be identified in our interviews? Or, would this require a sociology of heterodox economists that compares practice to theory and public statements?

The existence of *aspirational selves* also represents a potential methodological limitation to our examination of the constitution of heterodox economics. An aspirational Self usually portrays a self-representation as an idol of the

16 *Introduction*

imagination, or how one portrays oneself as what one should be in order to be acceptable (the heroic view), rather than what one is. This can affect the ways interviewees depict reality, as inputs into the reconstruction of facts can appear to be distorted or project wishes and desires – rather than true facts. In the case of heterodox economists, this represents a limitation given that our interview-based method cannot filter facts from the fiction of the aspirational Self. This is closely related to the problems of selective and incomplete memories and ex-post rationalisation, which may distort actual events, motives, and the character of the decision-making.

Moreover, value-free research is an unachievable ideal when dealing with socially engaged research – that is, research that holds itself ethically and politically accountable for its social consequences (Harding and Norberg, 2005). This applies to the interviewers as well as the interviewees of this research project. Understanding the nature and the image of heterodox economics is, as one shall see, a tricky task.

Our interview-based research goes beyond the interviews with mainstream economists and previous interviews with heterodox economists and historians of thought (see above): in particular, we make explicit our sources of inspirations and interests in this material. Our interviews go into several dimensions of heterodox economics (genealogy, sociology, psychology, pedagogy, philosophy), and they are comparative in the sense of asking interviewees questions about both sides of the notional continuum between mainstream and heterodox economics. The purpose of our interviews is thus also different in the sense that we aim to clarify the nature of heterodox economics, hoping to add to previous research.

2   Sheila Dow

Sheila Dow is Professor Emeritus in Economics at the University of Stirling, where she has been based since 1979, apart from short spells at the Universities of Toronto and Cambridge. She is also currently an adjunct member of faculty at the University of Victoria, British Columbia. Prior to that she worked in the Overseas Department of the Bank of England and was senior economist in the Department of Finance of the Government of Manitoba. She obtained her PhD in Economics in 1981 from the University of Glasgow. She also has degrees from the Universities of Manitoba and St. Andrews. Her main research interests are monetary and financial economics and policy, macroeconomics, and the methodology and history of economics, in which she has made significant contributions. Among these are her books *Economic Methodology: An Inquiry* (2002), *The Methodology of Macroeconomic Thought* (1996), and *Money and the Economic Process* (1993). She has also published over 100 articles in journals such as the *Cambridge Journal of Economics*, *History of Political Economy*, *Journal of Economic Methodology*, *Journal of Economic Surveys*, *Oxford Economic Papers*, and *Regional Studies*; perhaps most significant are those on dualism (1990), regional finance (with Rodriguez-Fuentes, 1997), and formalism (with Chick, 2001).

Sheila Dow was interviewed by Danielle Guizzo and Andrew Mearman via phone online in June 2017.

How did you become an economist?

I picked up economics as an undergraduate in my second year. I was doing pure maths when I met Alistair (now my husband), who was doing political economy and it sounded really interesting. I liked it because it was a nice complement to pure maths; it never occurred to me there might be any connection at all. So I continued to do the joint degree. Then I worked for the Bank of England, which had in a way been a fork in the road because I had been thinking of becoming a town planner. I got a place on a course for town planning but decided to take a different direction and followed from there.

What was your interest in Town Planning?

Well, I'd always been interested in it, though at one stage it was architecture which appealed more. I was a teenager in the age of the new towns in Britain, which I found really interesting. Also Brasilia was being built then; I thought that just sounded wonderful and looked wonderful from the pictures. But I think I came to the conclusion that town planning in practice, in the '70s, would probably mean designing roundabouts and other things which were less inspiring.

Was your interest in town planning about the aesthetics of it or the mathematics of it or perhaps the social side of it?

A combination of the aesthetic and the intellectual, as well as the social. I pursued art; I thought I might go to Art College.

You also said something about pure maths and economics being complementary; could you elaborate on that a bit?

I enjoyed pure maths from an aesthetic point of view I think, and political economy was much more about the real world. I liked being able to switch between the two. But I was told that the Professor of political economy tried to stop me doing the combination, since he thought that pure maths would conflict with political economy. He didn't succeed.

Is that combination something that you think that you've carried on throughout your work then?

Not really, no. I mean the pure maths thing was something quite separate. I do understand the appeal to mainstream economists of beautiful mathematical systems, although frankly I don't find the maths that's used in economics particularly beautiful. I mean, it was pure I was doing rather than applied, a distinction which is important for economics.

Can you tell us a bit more about the Bank of England experience: how did that help shape you?

I was there for a couple of years, and it was a really valuable experience in all sorts of ways. One of the valuable things which I think a lot of people experience in the public sector is that you learn how to write memos; a lot of trouble is taken to teach people to put something concisely on one page. I found that very useful training. But otherwise it was just *so* interesting; it was a really interesting time. I was on the Europe desk when we joined the EU (or EC as it was then), and then I was on the IMF desk when dollar convertibility was suspended. So it was interesting and the Bank was very good about encouraging people to do research. Particularly when I was on the IMF desk, I was free to write short research papers. So I developed various ideas while I was there, which I developed further in my MA dissertation at the University of Manitoba, and then many years later in my PhD thesis at the University of Glasgow.

You were at the Bank at a very interesting time, when there were some really interesting debates ongoing. Were you tempted to stay there in the middle of things?

To be clear, I was a very long way from decision-making, but it was great to be involved to the extent I was. But Alistair and I were young; we wanted to go somewhere else and narrowed it down to Canada. We both applied for graduate school and ended up in Winnipeg at the University of Manitoba, which was a great decision – a good experience.

What led you to Winnipeg?

People make decisions much more carefully nowadays. We didn't even check the climate, which is Siberian. They offered us both funding; that was appealing. Alistair had worked with his PhD supervisor, Paul Phillips, before at Simon Fraser, and he was now at the University of Manitoba. I signed up for a Master's, working with Clarence Barker, who was the originator of the idea of effective protection, although he doesn't always get credit for it. That was a great department – well, it's still a great department – but particularly then it was a very pluralist department and really encouraged a wide range of thinking. It became more explicitly pluralist later on, and the graduate programme, if I remember correctly, explicitly covered different schools of thought. In the 1970s it was less institutionalised; it's just that the people there represented a wide range of views.

So presumably at some point it became important to you to be exposed to a wide range of views in economics. Could you identify when that was?

It seemed normal from training at St. Andrews because that was a political economy programme and the tradition was to teach political economy historically. So it just seemed normal to consider a range of views, and it was only gradually that I realised that this wasn't the norm in economics.

We're interested in how you developed your particular individual contribution. Given that we were just talking about pluralism, it seemed a natural segue to your work on the Babylonian Approach. Where did your interest in that Babylonian Approach come from?

Really it follows from what I was saying earlier about what seemed normal, but which I discovered was not generally the case within economics. I became increasingly aware of what was mainstream and how that differed

20 *Sheila Dow*

from other approaches. This was after a fairly long interval because I was working for the government of Manitoba for a while. But when I went back to graduate school at McMaster, I became much more aware of the whole notion of mainstream economics. Because thinking in a pluralist way had been normal for me, I found this quite puzzling. The whole idea of Babylonian thinking was the end of what was quite a long process of trying to figure out what was going on – why did I think the way I did? It's quite a difficult thing to do really, to be truly reflective about how you think. It was through that long process that I ended up with a category which I called Babylonian. I'm not sure that's a great word, but I'd read Richard Feynman's (1965) essay where he talked about Babylonian mathematics. That really struck a chord because he was talking about how Babylonian mathematics was problem-orientated; it wasn't axiomatic. Reasoning could take different starting points depending on the problem at hand. That crystallised for me what was different from the axiomatic approach of the mainstream. We'll no doubt come on to this when we start talking about heterodox economics. But, while classifications like this are always problematic at one level, on the other hand I think they can capture something really important. If I've helped other people to crystallise their thinking then I'd be really pleased.

Let's get on, then, to that question of heterodox economics. We've chosen to speak to you because we consider you a heterodox economist. Are you fine with that label?

Absolutely.

What does it mean to you then?

Yes, it has meaning at a variety of levels. The simplest level is to think of it as a community. I remember addressing this early on in terms of trying to classify Post Keynesian economics, and what influenced me then was to consider who's talking to whom. At that time there was a summer school at Trieste in Italy which included Sraffians as well as others more obviously Post Keynesian. The fact that people were meeting and talking, and certainly arguing – but communicating – signalled to me that that was a community. Therefore, there was a category represented there where there was a commonality which allowed that communication. I would apply the same criterion to heterodox economics. The fact that heterodox economics is a community that has conferences where people get together from different traditions and are able to communicate up to a point and certainly argue – that suggests to me that there is an entity there which we can call heterodox economics. That implies also that it's a useful category because it's one which clearly draws people who must have something in common. Within heterodox economics, there's obviously a limit to communication depending on the extent of commonality. It's quite useful to have subgroups called schools of thought within heterodox economics which have more in common.

More generally, categories are loose, they're vague, they have permeable and provisional boundaries just as any open system does. Nevertheless, just in the practical terms of who talks to whom, who publishes where, which conferences you go to, it's useful to categorise by approach to economics. So, at that practical level I think we can identify heterodox economics. But then, of course, we can drill down to deeper levels in order to explain where that commonality comes from. I would trace that to the deepest level, which is ontology, that people within heterodox economics have an understanding of the world, which is shared. There's an understanding that the social world is an open system and all sorts of things follow from that about what kind of knowledge is possible, what kind of methodology is appropriate, and so on. Focusing on ontology is obviously a core critical realist way of thinking about it. But, where I depart from that approach is that, beyond that general understanding of the open nature of social systems, I hold that there are different ontologies associated with different schools of thought, and thus different methodologies. A critical realist would stop at espousal of an open system understanding of the social world; different groups are *interested* in different things but that's all there is to it. I'd say it's more fundamental, reflecting different understandings about how the real world works.

This difference in open system ontology is most obvious between neo-Austrians and other heterodox approaches. To explain my own thinking on this, it's probably due to an exposure to neo-Austrian thinking, which I think of as part of heterodoxy (whereas I think a lot of heterodox economists seem to have difficulty with that). The Professor of political economy at St. Andrews during my undergraduate degree was a neo-Austrian. I also learnt a lot from my long-time colleague at Stirling (where I have spent most of my academic career), Brian Loasby – though he might resist the label of neo-Austrianism. Neo-Austrians have an open system view of the world, and my own experience shows that there's lots of scope for communication even though there are differences in ideology and ontology. Within an open systems ontology nevertheless there is a commonality there, so I've always thought of neo-Austrians as being part of the heterodox fold.

Is heterodoxy a school of thought?

I would say not.

Because it's got multiple ontologies?

Yes, so heterodox economics encompasses a range of schools of thought within it. Actually mainstream economists, when they engage in talking about this kind of thing, show that they also have an open system ontology;

it's just that their epistemology and methodology don't fit. That's the problem. But, I see an open systems approach as allowing for incorporating mainstream economics if it's consistent at the epistemological and methodological levels. Of course that's where the problems lie between the two. It's a matter of coherence really. This is Tony Lawson's point, that mainstream methodology and epistemology are not consistent with what we as heterodox economists believe to be an appropriate ontology, which is an open systems one, which, when pushed, mainstream economists may well realise.

May we consider further the Austrians? You said something akin to that heterodox economists are not always willing to accept the Austrians as one of them. Why do you think that is?

Well, I think there is more of an ideological and political commonality among the heterodox economists other than the Austrians. So I don't think there has been active exclusion; I think it's just that political and ideological commonality has tended to drive a lot of the communication among other heterodox economists. I remember at the first ICAPE conference, a great effort was made to include neo-Austrians and I remember being surprised that anybody should doubt that this was appropriate.

It seems to me hard to define a heterodoxy partly because of the Austrians and how you deal with them. As you say, there's some commonality in terms of open systems and other things they stress, but then they're not really members of the community fully. Then there's this ideological dimension. It seems rather messy.

Many Post Keynesians will use the work of Shackle and Loasby, for example. So there is scope for cross-fertilisation of ideas. As with all categories it's a matter of judgement where you draw the boundaries, and you can see why a Marxist and neo-Austrian might not communicate too well. There is a point where the commonality is stretched a bit, and in practice it's tended to be the case that neo-Austrians and other heterodox economists don't mix a lot. I have to say I think that's a pity.

Some people define heterodox as merely "not mainstream": I imagine you do not subscribe to that view.

No, I said it once, and people keep quoting this as my definitive view.

You could set the record straight.

Well, as a matter of fact, heterodoxy is not mainstream, but I think it's a mistake just to leave it at that. It's much better to put it in a positive light and to try and spell out what heterodox economics is about and talk about its coherence.

So it's not a school of thought.

It's an approach, I would say.

If we may backtrack a little: you were saying that it would not be appropriate to define heterodox economics as something that is not the mainstream ...

Well, I think it's not very helpful.

To define it by the negative.

It's as if there is nothing else we can say about it, which is far from the case.

In your view, what are the problems with the mainstream then? Why would heterodox economists go apart from the mainstream? What is the problem with the mainstream?

The first problem is a refusal to talk about these things, to talk about methodology, epistemology, ontology, which means that there's very little explicit written from a mainstream perspective. I'm probably putting that too strongly. I mean there's a lot in the *Journal of Economic Methodology* which is obviously addressing a range of perspectives, but there isn't a mainstream tradition of thinking at this level. Heterodox economists have had to think about methodology just in order to differentiate themselves from the mainstream, to understand what they're doing, what it implies, and so on. But there's been no compulsion on the mainstream to spell out its approach. So engaging in conversation or debate about it is very difficult. You have people like Paul Romer making very high-profile statements about methodology, which really need to be challenged and have been challenged by some people but not in a way that's impacted on the mainstream discussion. So that's one part of the problem.

What follows from that is that I find mainstream economics incoherent. This is what I find so bizarre; that a system which supposedly has clarity, rigour, classical logic at its heart, consistency in classical logical sense, could be so incoherent when it comes to application. Most economists say that they're economists because they're interested in the real world and they want to make some improvement in some way or another, and yet it's in this interface with the real world that mainstream economics faces such problems. At one level, if it's accepted that the real world is an open system, then that carries implications for what could be done methodologically and theoretically which is not addressed. Of course, the obvious features of that are the compulsion to analyse in terms of atomistic individuals, rationality and full information, equilibrium, and so on, all qualified possibly in some ways. You see that in behavioural economics. There are some very explicit statements about the need to force what in many cases is a really helpful analysis of behaviour into a mainstream axiomatic framework. It squeezes the life out of the analysis but that's regarded as methodologically necessary from a mainstream perspective.

Sebastian Berger has written about the psychology of mainstream economics: he sees the problems as partly psychological. Do you see merit in that?

I think there must be a strong psychological element, although I've got no training in psychology. I read some psychology, but it's like with most things, the more you read the more you realise you don't know. So I wouldn't want to comment on the content of the psychology. But I think there has to be a psychological explanation for some people feeling comfortable with what I call the Babylonian mode of thought and others feeling very uncomfortable with it. Heterodox economists kind of self-select as people who are comfortable thinking in a particular way, which seems anathema to those who think in what I call a Cartesian-Euclidean way – whether or not you feel comfortable with hard and fast categories. We've talked about this many times, Andrew – dualistic thinking and categorisation. I think you're absolutely right in your JEM paper [Mearman, 2012] about the need for categories to be vague. Yet, often when the subject of how to define heterodox economics and orthodox economics comes up, there's a tendency, which we're kind of educated into, to want to think in terms of hard and fast categories. This is not a heterodox way of thinking in my view.

In your own training, it was normal for you to think about different perspectives: that was just how things were done. You didn't have to unlearn a different type of training in order to get to where you were; you were already there. Perhaps part of the issue with the mainstream is that its training is rather monistic and somewhat inflexible. How important is the training of economists, then?

Another thing is attitude to argument, and I think this relates to a Scottish tradition, which is that argument is normal; I don't mean fisticuffs argument, I mean debate. It's just a normal feature of social life and it took me a long time to discover that people, particularly from a mainstream perspective, took argument as an expression of hostility. That comes I think from a dualistic way of thinking about things. Obviously mainstream economists argue about things like appropriate mathematical formulation. But I think many heterodox economists start off thinking that the hostile reaction they get to argument at a conceptual level is something personal. It took me a long time to realise that it was really a different attitude to argument. It's an interesting question, for heterodox economists who are formed in a context where they are outsiders, how that affects their attitude to heterodoxy. I'll be interested to read other people's interviews to see if there's any element of that; you know, somebody who's brought up in an orthodox educational system, how that colours the way you think about heterodoxy. So, I shall look forward to that.

In another book of interviews, mainly with more mainstream people [Colander, Holt and Rosser, 2004a], many of the people in there who we might refer to as mainstream quite clearly see themselves as being outsiders at some point, that they were resisting this monolith. Indeed, the same can be said of subjects such as Milton Friedman [in Snowdon and Vane, 1999].

That's really interesting. You think of people like Krugman, who clearly thinks of himself as an outsider now. It may be that people who are willing to be interviewed are people who think about these things and, because it's not normal within the mainstream, it makes them outsiders.

Are you an outsider?

Well, this is the thing, you see, I didn't think of myself as an outsider for a long time and then I realised I was, in a way. I suppose it's made me more willing, and in some ways compelled, to try and communicate with the mainstream that I don't think of myself as inherently an outsider. I know this is a difficult subject within heterodox economics; some people feel very uncomfortable with that strategy and think it detracts from the main activity, which should be pushing ahead with heterodox economics. Personally I take a pluralist approach to strategy as to everything else, which is, some people do one thing, some people do another; we push on a variety of fronts, and trying to talk to mainstream economists who are willing to listen strikes me as an important element of the strategy.

Presumably, that partly informs your view that just defining heterodoxy as negative is unwise. You say you've tried to communicate with mainstream economists; does that mean that you've not been successful?

It's very hard to tell what effect you have really. I've been able to communicate up to a point – I've been invited to some mainstream events. They seem to listen but what they hear is another matter. I've made presentations about

Keynesian uncertainty and been told that "that was a very nice presentation", but then the discussion returns to the mainstream habit of treating uncertainty as a shock. So the effort is better than nothing; it seems to me it's worth pursuing, not least I think because it gets 'round the idea that heterodox economists are hostile. I mean, given the way many heterodox economists have been treated, there was good reason for hostility at one level. But I don't think it always helps. I think a lot of these mainstream economists who are not terribly happy with what's happening with mainstream economics must be aware that there are inconsistencies and incoherencies at the methodological level. But because heterodox economists publish in non-mainstream journals and we've got our own conferences and so on, these mainstream economists just don't know what's out there. It's a matter of trying to open a window to heterodox economics, to show that there is a whole body of work that can be explored. In any case, communications are a pluralist activity as well. Listening to somebody talking means that some things get across which don't get across on the written page, for example. So I don't do it a lot but I do see it as something that is worth pursuing.

I'd like to pursue that a little bit more but also to refer back to your previous career with the Bank. How do you see the Bank's approach to economics? Some people say, well, the Bank is a relatively open, relatively pluralist place in a way that some areas of economics are not. They cite *inter alia* Andrew Haldane's work and the recent paper on money supply endogeneity.

Yes, I would agree with that. What I'm not sure about is how far they believe in the models they use and how far in their use for rhetorical purposes. We know that central bank communication is so important and having something that's "scientific" behind it adds weight. I imagine there are differences of opinion within the Bank, but I suspect there is a rhetorical element to it because a lot of, as you say, Andrew Haldane's work fits quite well with a heterodox approach. And there is this acknowledgement of endogenous money. They took their time about acknowledging it, and they ended up saying in the end that central banks still have great influence through the interest rate, but the Bank's thinking has definitely been moving in the right direction.

The reason for this relative openness is that a central bank is at the sharp end; they have to make decisions which have real consequences, and so the academic kind of discussion isn't enough. They have to have a real feel for the consequences of their actions. So, for example, the Bank of England agents, from the different parts of the country, make presentations to the Monetary Policy Committee [MPC] on a regular basis. These reports are based on agents going 'round talking to people in different sectors about their real business experience and that's fed in to decision-making. The fan charts, that quantify expectations about the path that inflation and GDP will take, do incorporate judgement, although that ends up being quantified. But a lot of the process that goes into that is unquantified. The Bank has its suite of models, including the main model. It's not unlike a Babylonian approach, or accords to Keynes's theory about the weight of argument, that different types of evidence and reasoning feed into the decision-making. But some bits are inconsistent. If you get one of the models that has agents with full information and full rationality, that sits rather oddly with central bank uncertainty about models. Having said that, I would say that the Bank of England, particularly among central banks, is in the area between heterodox economics and mainstream.

You said earlier about economists who are trying to improve the world. They have a genuine goal of improving society, making the world a better place. Again, this is a theme of extant interviews. Is that something that drives you? Is that one of the things that you have been trying to achieve as an economist?

Yes, though it started with just finding economics interesting and I particularly found banking and finance interesting from working at the Bank and then working for the government in Manitoba. It was important to me to be working in the public sector. I liked that aspect of the work, which is more explicitly addressed to improving society than an academic position. In academia I still pursue working in money and banking, always in the hope that I might make helpful contributions to thinking in that area. In a way what's the main driving force, both behind teaching but also research, is to try to contribute to helping economists think about what they're doing – try to help clarify different modes of thought, for example. In particular, now the student movement is a wonderful development and they clearly want to think things through for themselves and anything I can do to help that, I'm very happy to do.

Have you tried to influence society?

Yes. It wasn't just at the level of content in terms of the way we think about money and banking and monetary policy and so on, but particularly also in terms of trying to contribute to a framework to help people think about how they are thinking about these things. I started with this in the 1970s and '80s when there were all these fights about the slopes of IS and LM curves which at the time seemed a bit odd: why are these grown-ups getting so worked up about this ...? It dawned on me that they were talking at cross purposes, that they were just thinking about things differently and if only everybody had been aware of that, then we could have been saved a lot of bother and concentrated on what was important, which is to debate how best to think about things and what it implies, where there is scope for agreement, where there isn't, and so on.

28 *Sheila Dow*

I was reminded of Thomas Kuhn in what you just said. When did you first read him?

It was in the 1970s sometime; I can't remember. I've always found Kuhn tremendously helpful; there's been a lot of criticism of his way of thinking of things, from very different perspectives. Some people argue that it shores up mainstream economics because it implies that we can't criticise them because we operate on different grounds. Others criticise Kuhn on the grounds that there haven't been any Kuhnian revolutions. If there haven't then I think it's a really interesting question, why not. Basically, Kuhn identified something really helpful, which was an answer to the question, why falsification of theories didn't mean they were ditched. He started the whole business of thinking about scientific communities in sociological terms but also in terms of discourse. So he talks about this Eureka moment when he was a graduate student. Aristotle was being presented as somebody who was in retrospect rather foolish and Kuhn found this difficult to accept. So he went back to Aristotle and read carefully, trying really hard to read him from the perspective of Aristotle's own time and intellectual context. And he realised that that was the key, that from the perspective of a modern understanding of astronomy, Aristotle was foolish. But in a way that's not the point, the point was that there had been revolutions of thinking since then so that we now think totally differently. Now, as with Foucault, there's a limit to how far we can read something in the context of somebody's own very different time, but we can try. Before he died he was working on incommensurability. I found his work really helpful.

You said it was an interesting question why there hadn't been more Kuhnian revolutions; so what's the answer?

Well, the sociological power of the mainstream. There have obviously been changes within economics, such as the marginalist revolution. Part of the difficulty, I think, is that people think of a revolution as something very immediate. But in Kuhnian terms I think of it as reflecting the fact that if you look at a discipline or a school of thought of one point in time and then look at it, say, two decades later, understandings, meanings, frameworks may have changed completely; that tells me that there's been a revolution. So in practice it does take a long time; it takes generational shifts, and it takes gradual shifts in understanding of terms and this kind of thing. It's not as dramatic as the word "revolution" seems to imply. But we know that there wasn't a Keynesian revolution in any fundamental sense. Economics changed because of the growth of macro and the way in which that encouraged econometrics – that was a big change but it didn't change the way we think about economics.

You've already mentioned teaching and trying to help people think about what they are doing. When you've taught, can you give us some examples of how you've sought to do that, how you sought to help people think about what they're doing? Can you think about any more concrete examples?

Well, in teaching money and banking, for example, I taught Post Keynesian theory. But because institutions have been set up from a basis of mainstream theory, and mainstream theory drives policy decisions, I would teach both. Now there's a limit to how far that can open minds, although I have to say just as an aside, I know the crisis that started in 2007 was awful in so many respects, but I'd never had so much fun teaching as when it hit. We'd been doing Minsky – and the students got so excited; even back in the '87 stock market crash, I remember it was the same thing, the students got really excited because this was theory coming to life. Sorry, I'm digressing a bit.

Where I was able I think to have more of an impact was teaching history of thought and methodology. It was just a one-semester course and I was limited in what I could do. Really, I treated it as a vehicle to help students think about economics; so, the content was in history of thought and methodology, but really the whole purpose was to help them think about economics more generally. Each time I did it the most striking thing was that, for the first seminar, I would ask students to prepare a short presentation on a piece of writing that had struck them in some way; either they loved it, they hated it, it was interesting – it didn't matter why it had struck them, just to write about it. That in itself seemed to open eyes; some students were in tune with this already but many of them said that it had never occurred to them that they could comment on a piece of economic writing, that they could express an opinion that would be treated with respect. Ideas might be criticised, not just in the usual way of "growth theory used to be like this but now we've learned the error of our ways", which is normal in conventional mainstream courses. Just the general proposition, that they could express an opinion about a piece of writing, they found eye-opening. As soon as they got that we were up and running.

You talked about teaching during the crisis. What did you enjoy about that yourself? What did you enjoy about teaching at that time?

Well, it made it so immediate. Often you can see students' eyes glaze over when you're teaching at a fairly abstract level. Even teaching Minsky during the great moderation was a bit of a challenge – "Instability? What's that?" – whereas this was something playing itself out before our eyes. It's very rare to get something that's so dramatic, where it's clear that nobody knew how

30   *Sheila Dow*

things would play out. For example, the central bank governor would say something and we could discuss whether that was the right thing to say or not. The media just made it a really good teaching experience. Students from earlier cohorts wrote to me afterwards, saying that they were now in the financial sector, and that they'd understood what was going on, which was really nice to hear.

So would you say that heterodox economics is doing a better job in providing a more "liberal" or "critical" form of teaching, instead of just instrumental teaching?

Yes, there's lots of material now on pluralist teaching, and all this started with the Paris students who introduced the demand for teaching by debate. But it's grown now so that the heterodox community has produced and is aware of a lot of material to help with the pluralistic approach to teaching, and there are several departments now which are actually implementing that. However, not all heterodox economists, I think, agree about the importance of thinking methodologically and epistemologically. There is some debate about that, on the grounds that we should "stop navel gazing and get on with it". But I think it's important because so much misunderstanding persists, even within heterodox economics, about what we're doing. And, I know it is hard to examine one's own thought. It requires quite a lot of effort, more than trying to examine thought from another perspective perhaps. It's not something we should be doing all the time, obviously. It's something I specialise in, I suppose, but I think it's really important for all economists to be methodologically aware. It's like citizens of the world should be aware of other cultures and communities, ideally other languages (many of us fall short badly on that front). These things are important; we have to do it to keep an open mind and I think it applies to the discipline of economics as well.

From your past experiences, how are students' reactions to that increased awareness?

The impression is that they really enjoyed it. It has to be said, though, that the students who would register for the history of thought and methodology class were self-selected, so they were inclined to think that way. The same applies to the current student movement – these are all students who want to be helped along this road. One thing I find interesting about the student movement is that it's so vibrant that it seems to be pulling in students who have a mainstream perspective and just want to be part of it. As well as Rethinking Economics, there are the Young Scholars Initiative networks as well, for example, which seem to be really productive. The more students who start off thinking in a mainstream way are exposed to other ways of thinking, the better. It may be that they conclude that mainstream thinking suits them best, which is fine but they've learnt to compare it with others, to work out in their own minds how to justify their choice. That's what seems to me to be most important.

You already mentioned that one of the benefits of working for the bank was learning how to write more concisely. You already mentioned about communication, and the rhetorical purpose of models, et cetera. McCloskey has referred to economics as poetry: what do you think about that?

Well, I'd have been a bit thrown if you'd just asked me that, but because it was on your prior list of questions I have been pondering that question. As with many things, I'm not familiar with theory of poetry, so this is a lay-person's answer to the question. What it reminded me of was a conversation I had with Frank Hahn many years ago, where he talked about mathematical economics as being like poetry, and indeed pure mathematics being like poetry; as I said, I liked pure maths for aesthetic reasons. Having read your question, I started thinking about what poetry is, and I think a lot of people use the word to apply to something in terms of aesthetics, as if it's something divorced from life. I'm probably getting in deep water here. But the poetic appeal of general equilibrium theory seems to me to be purely aesthetic. The poetry I like connects with real experience. To think of economics as poetry in the sense that it taps into real experience, and, having tapped into it, creates a new understanding of that experience, would be good.

Is that your attitude towards mathematics and economics in general?

I don't do mathematical economics anymore because I actually don't find it aesthetically appealing (quite apart from methodological issues).

But did you prefer the maths that, in addition to its aesthetic qualities, connects to the real world?

Not really, no. I liked it for itself.

We are concerned about the pressures on people to show their work to have value, impact, et cetera. To the extent you've had to engage in seeking research funding, what strategies have you deployed there, if any?

Not very good ones. I did keep applying for funding and was rarely successful, and I'm sure lots of that was just due to poor skills in grant applications. But the other issue which you raised is what kind of research is regarded

32 *Sheila Dow*

as socially useful, and history of thought and methodology research doesn't tend to attract external funding; it doesn't tend to require the expense of lots of data gathering and analysis, obviously, so there's less reason for raising money; it's really a matter of raising money to cover your time. I think it may be getting more promising, but I'm so detached from that now, being retired. To be frank I'm quite relieved not to need to apply for funding. I used to do it because it's obviously what one should be doing as a university academic, so I kept trying but I rarely succeeded. I am curious to know how REF works with work in methodology, because I understand that you have to provide documentary evidence of real-world impact. Well, how do you show that people now think differently?

3 Fernando Cardim de Carvalho

Fernando José Cardim de Carvalho was Emeritus Professor in Economics at the Federal University of Rio de Janeiro and a Senior Scholar at Levy Economics Institute of Bard College. He obtained an undergraduate degree in Economics from the University of São Paulo (USP) in 1975, a Master's in Economics from the University of Campinas (Unicamp) in 1978, and a PhD in Economics in 1986 from Rutgers University, supervised by Paul Davidson. Fernando worked as a consultant to both public institutions and financial industry associations, including the Central Bank of Brazil (BCB), the Brazilian National Bank for Economic and Social Development (BNDES), the Central Statistical Office of Brazil (IBGE), and the National Association of Financial Institutions of Brazil (Anbima), as well as for NGOs such as IBASE (Brazil) and ActionAid USA. He was also the chairman of the Brazilian National Association of Graduate Schools in Economics (ANPEC) between 1992 and 1994. Cardim de Carvalho's work has been published in, among other journals, the *Cambridge Journal of Economics*, *Brazilian Journal of Political Economy*, and *Journal of Post Keynesian Economics*, of which he was associate editor. He is the author of *Mr Keynes and the Post Keynesians* (1992) and *Liquidity Preference and Monetary Economies* (2015). Born in 1953 in São Paulo, Brazil, he passed away in May 2018 in Cascais, Portugal.

Fernando Cardim de Carvalho was interviewed online by Danielle Guizzo and Andrew Mearman in June 2017.

How did you become an economist?

Well, I became an economist entirely by accident, actually. When I finished high school and I was preparing to go to college, I was going to study law and journalism. I wanted to be a political analyst for Brazilian newspapers. But the way the higher education system is organised in Brazil, or at least was in the 1970s, is not like in some countries. In Brazil you have to apply to a specific faculty, say economics or law or engineering, and at the moment that I was registering for the entrance examinations I was asked what was the course I was enrolling for. Instead of saying "Law" I said "Economics". I never knew why. I didn't spend more than ten minutes trying to think

34   *Fernando Cardim de Carvalho*

why I did it, because it was too late and I was already enrolled. And that's how I became an economist. Of course, later I enjoyed it and so I stayed. But why I chose economics instead of law or, I don't know, Greek writing or something, I have no idea. Actually, even my family was surprised because I had already prepared for Law, but in the end, that [Economics] is what I did.

Do you think your family had an influence on that?

No. You see, I come from the '60s in a cultural sense. In 1968–69 my wife and I, and all my friends, we took part in the movement against the military regime in Brazil. But any organised movement against the military regime was organised by clandestine radical groups, and this shaped our views as to what to do with our lives. So, we wanted to study something within the social sciences, with some possibility of being politically active. My wife studied political science. I went to economics, though to a very conservative school that is the University of São Paulo, which was the leading economics school at that time. My professors were mostly people who were working with the military regime and so on, which I think was to my advantage because it made me very familiar with neoclassical economics, which I would probably not be if I had had a different initial training. After I finished my degree at the University of São Paulo in 1974–75, I went to a new school, a graduate school in economics that had been created in Campinas with non-orthodox, mostly Marxian economics, where I obtained my master's degree. But, mostly by accident, that was where I began to know Keynes. People didn't read Keynes at that time. You read the textbooks on macroeconomics that were a poor man's version of the neoclassical synthesis, not even Tobin or Samuelson, it was actually something very introductory in character. But I became curious about Keynes, and I decided to read it and that was it. I gradually moved to Keynesian economics, but that was more or less the origin of my generation of non-orthodox economists in Brazil. We all came from the same background. We began in, let's say, the hard left of the 1960s, and then we went to some other variations of non-orthodox theories.

And your first contact with Keynes and Post Keynesian economics, you had that in Campinas during your Master's degree programme?

Yes. Although it was not due to Campinas, actually. But what Campinas did, and that was personally the most important thing, was that you had the chance of reading the originals. So instead of just using textbooks as I had in my undergraduate years at the University of São Paulo, in Campinas you had the time and the incentive to read the original texts. So, we read Hilferding, Marx's *Capital*, Kalecki. Sraffa was not very well known in those times, and it took a long time to arrive to Brazil. This was in 1975 or 1976, almost nobody had heard of Sraffa, but of course everybody had heard of Joan Robinson. Joan Robinson was the big name in many fields for Marxians because we knew her little book on Marxian economics, although we were not very appreciative of it. Her interpretation was considered, let's say, not very precise. But we were also reading Keynes all the time. And one important reference for me was not even Post Keynesian, which was Axel Leijonhufvud's version of the contrast between Keynesian economics and what he called the economics of Keynes. And everybody was talking about this. In those years, in Brazil it was very hard to get an imported book. You had to order it, and then wait for months. But I was lucky that a friend was coming from the US and brought this book to me. So, my first contact with alternative views of Keynes actually was with Leijonhufvud's interpretation. I became very excited, so then I went to [Keynes's] *The General Theory*, and then to Paul Davidson, and so on. And, in the early 1980s, in 1981 to be specific, there was something that I think was the most important non-orthodox initiative we had in those years: the summer school in Trieste in Italy, which was organised by Jan Kregel, Pierangelo Garegnani, and Sergio Parrinello. It got together everybody who was important in the field, and I was lucky to attend the first summer school in 1981. So, my first contact was actually with Leijonhufvud, who is not even particularly friendly to Post Keynesian economics. He is much more conventional in his Wicksellian approach. Leijonhufvud rejects "liquidity preference theory", but the book [*On Keynesian Economics and the Economics of Keynes: A Study in Monetary Theory* (1968)] was really exciting. Exciting for an economist, especially if you had been trained in neoclassical economics, but terribly boring for other people. For me, in those years, it was a kind of revelation.

So, during your Master's, you already had in mind that you were going to pursue a PhD and continue in academia?

Yes. You don't have much else to do with a Master's degree in Brazil other than joining a university. The Master's programme does not train you to do anything in business. So, if you got your Master's, it was because you were expected at some point to move on to doctoral programmes. But we didn't have many doctoral programmes in Brazil in those years. We had only two or three, and all of them conventional. And we had the government's [financial] support to study abroad. This was a kind of paradox because we lived still under the military regime. But the National Council for Scientific and Technological Development [CNPq] was very open-minded. You could apply to get your doctoral degree anywhere, and if you could show that the university and the faculty was prestigious, they would support you. So, I went to Rutgers University, in the US, to study with Paul Davidson, and I had absolutely no problem at all (my background included Campinas

36 *Fernando Cardim de Carvalho*

and so on) to be funded by the government. The research council was oriented by the idea that dominated the military regime in Brazil: that Brazil had to be a power – a regional power, but a power. So, it was less hostile to some ideas they thought could strengthen the country's position – unlike Chile or Argentina, which lived under openly right-wing neoliberal regimes. So, I had this plan: to get the Master's degree, then move on to a doctoral programme, and if I could get accepted, I would go abroad.

So, your original plan was to take your PhD with Paul Davidson initially?

Well, the reason I went to the summer school was to choose a doctoral programme. I went to the summer school the year before I went to Rutgers, when I was still in doubt about where to go. I was fascinated by two debates: one debate involved Paul [Davidson], Hyman Minsky, and Jan Kregel, among others, and centred on money. This was a new thing for me. The Marxian economics I knew at the time, apart from Hilferding, was not very challenging on this point. But there was a very lively debate at the time in Italy around the labour theory of value opposing Sraffians, like Garegnani, to intellectuals connected to the Italian Communist party, such as Lucio Colletti, who was a philosopher I used to read then. I was very much interested in this discussion. In the summer school I saw both groups, because they were both part of the faculty, discussing among themselves. And there I decided that the discussion about money of the Post Keynesians was – at least for me – more attractive than the Sraffian discussion, which seemed to me too narrow. It was the liquidity preference theory that attracted me.

And when you started your PhD at Rutgers, your initial plan was to go back to Brazil and continue your career; you never considered staying in another country?

Yes. When you go abroad funded by the government, you sign a contract with the research council and commit yourself to go back for at least a period equal to the one you spent abroad. I have always been very serious about this kind of thing. In other words, I was not free to choose. I stayed for four years in the US, so I had to stay at least for four years in Brazil. So, the idea of staying in the US or moving to another country was never entertained, even though those were still the military regime years. We were trying to build something. At that time, I was teaching at the Fluminense Federal University in Niteroi, Rio de Janeiro. We were a very small university with limited resources, so they had to release me for the doctoral programme because they had the expectation we could organise something when I returned. I did not come back reluctantly. It was a kind of a professional commitment that I was not willing to break.

I have other questions on that last point. So, was your plan to go back to Brazil and to effect some kind of change on the country according to this project? Or, did you want to go back and carry on your career? What did you have in mind?

Well, I went back in 1986, one year, if my memory serves me right, after the military had gone back to the barracks. So, we had a civilian government that was, for various accidental reasons, open to new ideas. There was a chance of influencing policymaking, directly or through public debate. Some of my former professors at the University of Campinas were then in the federal government. Of course, politics is always a lot more complicated than just having good ideas. But if there was an effective chance of being heard by the authorities and public opinion, there was also the chance of creating something different at the university. The Brazilian debate in economics then – if you can call it a debate, since neoclassical groups were so prominent they didn't have to debate, as they do in the rest of the world, and the Left was usually very happy to talk to other Left only – was stale. But we had this group of 20 or 30 people, very interesting people, willing to explore new possibilities. We had the chance of shaping the debate, at least in part, because, paradoxically, our university was very small. In a big university you have to fight to get some room against established non-orthodox views just as much as it happens in orthodox schools. In our university, there was nobody above us. There was nobody that would feel threatened by rising paradigms. So, we did have the chance of creating something different. And we actually did, and we ended up having a disproportional influence on the Brazilian academic environment for a few years, disproportional, I mean, to our number of people and to our resources then. We were called to – and when I say we, it's not the majestic "we", but because we actually had a group of people. So, it did work, I think. It was the beginning of the Post Keynesians in Brazil. We had support, again, from the national research council. They supported us all the time. We had many conferences that they funded, totally or, most frequently, in part. It's something that is very specific to our research because it is in our culture. In Argentina for instance, there is a strong university community, but they don't have this central support. And we had this unexpected support from the community itself. So, we had both a public and an academic voice. But it was in the university that, I think, we sought to have a lasting impact, which I think we actually did. Was it worth it? For me personally it was worth it.

My next question is about when you read Keynes, which clearly had an effect on you. Could you elaborate a little bit more on that and why Keynes had an effect?

I read it many times through the years, and still do. The first time I read it I was still an undergraduate. I was curious because it was a footnote to some of our textbooks, most of the time to say that he [Keynes] was actually wrong, that he had the intuition but he didn't have the opportunity, or the econometrics, or the

38 Fernando Cardim de Carvalho

knowledge of economic theory, or the patience to get that knowledge, and so on. Most of the time they would say that it was a nice clue, but not really an alternative. The alternative came especially with Paul Samuelson, and to a lesser degree with Tobin, Solow, Modigliani, et cetera. In my student years, Paul Samuelson was not even the King of economics; he was actually the God of everything for everybody in the conventional sense. Milton Friedman was not as popular as Paul Samuelson. Paul Samuelson was the economist's economist, was the guy who knew everything, who wrote about literally everything, including Marxian economics. I was curious about Keynes's *General Theory*, but my English was not very good at that time. I read the Brazilian translation and I was left with the impression that there was something there, but I had no idea what, because there were so many paragraphs that were completely impossible to understand. Not because of content, but because the phrases didn't make much sense. I read it again during my Master's course, but then it was the Harcourt, Brace, Jovanovich edition [Keynes, 1964] (which I still have actually; it is annotated from cover to cover), and I was fascinated especially by the discussions in the last chapters, the chapters in which Keynes made digressions on the business cycle theory, on social philosophy, the mercantilists (all those chapters that usually people don't have much interest in). I was interested especially in the last chapter, on policies, even though it doesn't really suggest any specific policies. It discusses Keynes's "social philosophy", which he wrote was half conservative and half revolutionary, and the need for some degree of socialisation of investments. Some people, reading the text through Brazilian eyes, believe this may mean "take all companies", nationalisation. Keynes in fact had admitted this possibility, in his discussion of the coal industry in England, contained in volume 19 of his *Collected Writings*. But it was obviously far from being a central part of his thought, even though it was very provocative. And this led to a third reading of *The General Theory* when I was preparing to go to Rutgers, and at this point I had already read Kregel, Davidson, and Minsky, besides the volumes (13, 14, and, later, 29) of the *Collected Writings*, which included the papers and correspondence written in preparation and defence of *The General Theory*. And when you put all those together, then I think that was it, my fundamental view of Keynes was complete because then everything made sense. This is still basically the way that I work and I discuss and try to explore and apply Keynes's theory.

You've mentioned about all these influences, your readings on the original Keynes. Can you tell us how you developed your particular individual contribution with your works?

The first things I did of an academic nature were based on a fascinating debate I saw in the Trieste summer school around the concept of uncertainty. And it was fascinating because half of the faculty shared the view that uncertainty was central to a reformulation of macroeconomic theory, which of course involved Kregel, Minsky, Davidson, and Tom Asimakopulos, among others. The other half, the neo-Ricardians, although they do not use the label anymore, totally rejected the centrality of something so subjective. It was a heated discussion around an idea that did not seem, at first sight, capable of generating such an exchange. For us, the students, that was amazing because we were not used to witnessing heated debates like that. It is very unfortunate that the school lasted only seven or eight years. Nowadays, there are at least 30 heterodox summer schools every year, but no one is even close to the kind of faculty they put together. At the end of the school I delivered, as was expected, a short essay contrasting the views of Keynesians and Sraffians on uncertainty and time. That became the basis for my first published article, a paper called "On the concept of time in Shacklean and Sraffian economics" (1983). I had George Shackle, who had the most radical subjectivist view, and who had been a student of Hayek before switching to Keynes. He had a very subjectivist view of decision-making under uncertainty. On the other hand, you had Sraffa as read by [Pierangelo] Garegnani, in which everything that was theoretically important "happened" in the long term, and in the long term, in his view, uncertainty was just smoke, not a fire. This was my first paper, which I initially made for the summer school, and later I delivered it to Paul Davidson as a full paper during my first year at Rutgers [University]. He suggested that I work a little more on it and submit it to *JPKE* [Journal of Post Keynesian Economics], and this was how it began. And then the paper – to my surprise – was published in my first year during my PhD programme and was very well received. Well, "very well" by some people and "very badly" by some others. More or less as I expected. Garegnani wrote against it, which was an honour, to be criticised by a guy like him in your first published paper. On the other hand, Tom Asimakopulos liked it and quoted it in his own debate with Neo-Ricardians. I decided to explore the issue a little more deeply. I read Keynes's *Treatise on Probability* to understand what Keynes *actually* did in his field, his arguments with Ramsey and so on, and produced a few more papers on the issue, and this is how I landed on money, finance, and financial crises. Of course, money was the main topic of my study at Rutgers, since Paul Davidson's career was devoted to this. I was expecting that Kregel would also be there, because he was until 1981. But he had a fight with the economics department and resigned. My mentors were Davidson and [Alfred] Eichner, who introduced me to the corporate pricing systems, where he developed many very interesting ideas which unfortunately many people don't seem to remember anymore. Fred Lee was also very close to Eichner too. By the way, Fred was one of the students in the first summer school. He was my colleague in our 1981 class.

We have chosen to speak to you because we consider you a heterodox economist. Would you label yourself as heterodox? If so, why is that, or if not, why not?

Well, yes. I am not usually very enthusiastic about this kind of label because one of the things that irritated me, that usually irritates me, is the need people feel sometimes to label other people. "You are not a Post Keynesian guy",

40 *Fernando Cardim de Carvalho*

"you are not a *true* Post Keynesian", and so on, most of the time led to sterile debates and we end up meeting in very small rooms because nobody else is a reliable fellow. It is important to be clear about your assumptions, but one should keep in mind that we are (or should be) all trying to understand the real world. Economics should not be a religion. But I don't have any doubt that, at least in my mind, there is one difference, a central difference between the orthodoxy and the non-orthodoxy. When you think of Keynesian categories (and I say this here because it's my training), during the preparation of *The General Theory*, Keynes relied on the distinction between two concepts of modern economies (that is the one I still use) to distinguish orthodoxy from non-orthodoxy: one he called the "cooperative economy", where factors of production combine in ways described by production functions, and everybody gets their rewards in baskets of goods equivalent to their marginal productivity. The other type of economy is what he called the "entrepreneurial economy" (some people would prefer to call it a "capitalist economy"): there, production is organised by firms. Firms are not consumers; firms are firms. They exist to generate a money surplus, and the production and generation of this surplus – and of course the distribution that follows it – is what this type of economy is about, and this is where aggregate demand can be deficient. An entrepreneurial economy exhibits the characteristics of a modern economy, including how money is organised, the role of contracts, the role of markets, and so on. For me, "non-orthodox economics" is the "non-cooperative economy". When you get, for instance, Stiglitz's works, he says very interesting things about policies, about real situations, but he's always trying to phrase this in terms of a "cooperative economy", thus limiting its reach and depth. Years ago, he wrote a book on socialism (*Whither Socialism?*, 1994) based on the idea that the second Pareto theorem was not valid, the idea that you can support maximum welfare with a price system, and that was the extent of his criticism. So, his fundamental concept of economy is still that of an economy organised by households "growing their garden of vegetables, and exchanging their production because nobody wants to eat all the lettuce. Some of the lettuce they trade for beef or whatever, and this is how the economy is supposed to work". Of course, this has lots of problems to introduce, things like money, but these are the basics. The real world is marked by "imperfections", because reality cannot be directly described like that. You have these imperfections, but the basic logic of the economy is still that of a cooperative economy. Minsky had an ironic expression to describe that view, which he called the "village fair paradigm": every Sunday everybody would put their lettuce to trade for tomatoes and other things. It's not a capitalist economy. And this is the dividing line. If you think of an economy organised by businessmen (either Schumpeterian, or Keynesian, or whatever), the basic system being not reducible to the "village fair paradigm", for me this is heterodox. But if you think of the "village fair paradigm" and that everything else is an imperfection – it is like you were expelled from the Garden of Eden on account of market imperfections, you are orthodox even if, for some reason, you end up proposing policies with which non-orthodox people agree. This is what separates "them", the orthodox, from not them, the heterodox.

I think this answers our next question about what you think heterodox economics is.

Yes.

The "them" and "not them". But I would ask you a more specific question. How would you see the case of Brazil and heterodox economics, because we know Brazil is different when compared to some other nations, such as the US and the UK. Can you expand a bit on that?

To some extent it is a mystery how we, as "not them", got to the position of strength that we have. That is very unusual. Even in the continent (Latin America) it's unusual. If you look at Argentina, you have some very influential non-orthodox economists there like Roberto Frenkel and his group at CEDES. But the mainstream is still the mainstream. They have a political influence that is much bigger than their intellectual, or academic, influence I would say. In Brazil, we have the academic influence and sometimes the political influence, although more strongly with public opinion than with government authorities. I have thought a lot about the reasons for this situation. I have one hypothesis, which is not very strong, since it fits only our own case. If you live in Brazil, not only if you are interested in the country, but if you actually spend part of your life in Brazil, you are always very suspicious about equilibrium concepts, especially for my generation. We went through crises and high inflations and all sorts of things. The idea that "this economy will then reach spontaneously any kind of equilibrium in the short, long or forever term", is always something that sounds suspicious. But, for us Brazilians this was obviously a problematic idea. So, the experience of students who were interested in economics and were introduced to these self-adjusting properties, was to look around and to say "well, something is not working here". All the debates about economic development emerged because it somehow addresses this kind of thing. And then you have the role of influential Brazilian economists, such as Celso Furtado and the most influential economist on the continent, the Argentine Raúl Prebisch, who were both Keynesians (Prebisch was the first Latin American economist to write a book on Keynes). Furtado and Prebisch were fundamental references for my generation. So, you had some kind of natural path, which, of course, was sought all the time, toward heterodoxy, although you needed to work with mainstream ideas if you wanted to get a job and so on. Nowadays the situation is much

42 *Fernando Cardim de Carvalho*

easier, especially in the academic community. Heterodox economists face multiple options to work within their own theoretical tradition in Brazilian universities. The problem with my interpretation is why it does not fit Argentina for instance. They have a very similar history, but they don't have the same results. It's one of those things that make me think that my story is still missing an important point, maybe an accident, maybe a coincidence that at some point we got exposed to ideas like Davidson, and Minsky, and so on. I think that when we were looking for something, we were offered this alternative, but I admit it is still a mystery to me. I feel that I don't really have the key to understand why not only Post Keynesian economics but many other non-orthodox groups flourish there. This has been the situation for more than 30 years. It's not a short-lived phenomenon. This has been going on since the 1980s and heterodox economics is still there and it is still strong.

What are the problems of the mainstream economics, or "them"?

I think that the main problem of the mainstream is that its theoretical foundations are not helpful. You have very smart people practising it, either because some of them think that adhering to the mainstream is a condition of professional success or because they don't really know the alternatives. The bulk of the mainstream dedicate their time to formal games to talk to each other. Smart people are able to perceive important developments in the real world not because they were trained to do this but because they are smart. They can see things happening and explain them empirically rather than using the theories in which they were trained. So, I think the main problem is that the apparatus, the theoretical concepts and apparatus that characterise "them" is mostly useless. When you get somebody who is a good observer, he/she is always going to say interesting things. For instance, many of my friends get mad because I like to read, and quote from, *A Monetary History of the United States* [1971], by Milton Friedman and Anna Schwartz. I do think it's a great book. It has many – I would not say mistakes, but there are many points that it still takes them into a direction that I would not take, but it is smart, they looked at the data and they see things in the data that sometimes do not actually fit with what they are theorising, but they decided to put their ideas on paper and maybe someone will find the connection. On the other hand, nowadays you have a lot of people doing the Dynamic Stochastic General Equilibrium [DSGE] models, probably to get nothing useful out of it. First of all, 95% of these people don't realise it, perhaps because they don't think about what they do. If you begin with those kinds of models, you will just end up not getting much, because they just copy other models and they go through all the formal techniques. I think the problem is that most of the community is trained to be technicians, not really academicians. But they're not trained to think.

And when you have somebody who thinks, for instance when you read the columns that Krugman writes in the *New York Times* twice a week, they are wonderful because they have an impact. He also wrote a new introduction to *The General Theory* (and in 2007, the copyrights of *The General Theory* expired, so everybody could reprint it without paying any kind of copyright). So, Macmillan, which is Palgrave now, decided to reprint the edition whose rights belonged to the Royal Economic Society, but had to differentiate it somehow so they asked Paul Krugman to write its preface. It's very impressive, but it has nothing to do with Krugman's own theoretical work. The difference is that he is a very smart person, so he could see important things even though he could not construct a theory where they could fit. I think the problem is that you cannot rely on the availability of smart people to support a school of thought, because unfortunately there are very few smart people around. If you are not helped by good instruments, by good concepts, eventually the group will decay. And all the rest will just send papers to the *American Economic Review*, but they don't have any real influence on government policies; they never had in the US. There is a strict separation; academics at most get to the council level providing advice. They can advise the President, but never ever the Treasury Department or the Federal Reserve. The problem is that it is all very sterile and survives by the mass effect: you have all those people who don't know what else to do, so they have to do this because they were trained like that and so they survive by interacting ones with the others.

What are you trying to achieve as an economist?

Well, at this point I retired from UFRJ [Federal University of Rio de Janeiro] and I am basically an independent researcher. I'm at Levy [Institute] right now, but will move to Portugal this summer (of 2017) and I will probably teach in a Portuguese university. Because I am Emeritus Professor in UFRJ, I still have a connection with my former university. But professionally, I already passed it on to the younger generation. It is a very active group. We created the Brazilian Keynesian Association [AKB] which, to my surprise, is going on for about ten years now – when we had this idea we didn't expect it to last so long – and it's working very well. But I have been away from Brazil for more than five years now. I teach eventual courses at UFRJ, I supervise a few theses, but now I mostly write. I keep writing and studying because I am a researcher and I am working in a project, which is a book on the economics of austerity. The one thing that is good when you retire is that you are no longer under any pressure to write papers, so you can do things that take longer to prepare but allow you to explore things that you cannot deal with in a paper. So, being retired and not being under the pressures of publishing papers, teaching a certain number of courses, allows me to actually write books and this is my project right now.

44 *Fernando Cardim de Carvalho*

I have a couple of questions, Fernando, on that. The first one you've mentioned about influencing other generations in Brazil. We also had an interview with David Dequech...

An old friend. Formerly a student and then old friend.

It was interesting because we asked him if he had any influences, how he got in touch with Post Keynesian economics, with heterodox economics, and he mentioned your name as one of his influences as an example of somebody that went abroad to pursue a PhD and got back to Brazil. Could you comment on those influences through students?

Well, there are two things to point out. The first is that those people who had the chance to stay abroad during the 1980s would do it without a second thought. I think it's a moral point in this case because of the things we talked about before – we had a contract with the Brazilian society by which it supported us abroad in exchange for our services when we returned. I don't take these things lightly. But besides that, the year I went back, 1986, was a very effervescent time in Brazil because of a bad reason and a good reason. The bad reason, of course, was the economy, which was completely chaotic, but it gave us the chance to experiment; people were willing to hear something different. And not only in political terms, but in universities, and in particular in economics I think, which is usually "naturally" conservative. And we had a more benign period in which the community was more open to some ideas. It was a very good time to go back because we felt optimistic, we had this ideal situation in which you have something different to say when there were many people demanding something different. And [the University of] Campinas was one of these places to be. It was a very attractive school in the 1970s but it did become hostile to some of the new ideas that were emerging. I was not there at that time but we followed how things were developing at the school. In Rio de Janeiro, on the other hand, we had the chance at UFF [Fluminense Federal University] to create a group of Post Keynesian economics. In fact, we had at the time two core Post Keynesian groups, the one in Campinas being more Marxian/Kaleckian and the one in Niteroi, at UFF, being more Keynesian. We were lucky that we had something to offer when the students had a need for it. At that precise moment – and David [Dequech] was a student at that precise moment – we did have an impact in this, say, second generation. It was the people who, people who were my contemporaries and myself, who trained new generations particularly in those two universities. They became younger professors later. At this point we are in the third or fourth generation of Post Keynesian economists.

Do you seek or do you intend to seek to influence society in the past or now in any form?

Well, I worked for many years with an NGO – which we actually helped to co-found, my wife and I – a Brazilian NGO which still exists called Ibase. It was created by Betinho [Herbert de Souza, sociologist and activist]. This was around 1980–81, when Brazil had a general amnesty – people who had been persecuted by the military regime were allowed back in the country. You had people who were old members of Communist parties who were exiled since 1964, you had also people throughout the leftist movements of the late '60s, some of them which were closer to us. Many people had used this time, the last years of the military regime, to rethink not only their personal lives but also their political practices. Many shared this kind of doubt about the action of parties and about the formal political game that at this point had already become very corrupt. Then, NGOs emerged in Brazil and the first and most successful of them was created by Betinho, who advanced the idea that the people didn't need our communication but they needed information. They need access to, and they need the decoding of, hard information. So, we helped him to organise this system through which we would collect, distribute, and, when requested, explain information. We had access to social and economic information and what we needed to do was to prepare things, materials, and when eventually they invited us, we were available to discuss the content of the information and to answer their questions. We were very strictly warned, however, not to give them answers. This NGO became very influential and I think we had a strong political impact through that work, which was very satisfactory. Of course, we also have some influence on the government, through professors who join governmental bodies and so on, but, on a personal level, this was not so interesting. Most of the professors became very frustrated with the uncertainties of day-to-day politics and left the government at some point. But the NGO thing was really interesting and connected us with NGOs all over the world. We had debates about financial regulation, the environment, and gender issues, raising problems that are usually ignored in the general political debate. Other NGOs were interested in what Ibase did, so we would look for ways in which we could create common fronts. We joined Ibase in 1980 and we wrote the first work that it ever published. I loved it so much that we stayed there until the time when we left Brazil.

Our next question would be if you have (or had) any strategies to seek research funding?

No, not really. As I said before, I had continuous support since I got my grant for my PhD in 1982 until last February 2017, and it has ended because I decided to suspend it to be free of professional obligations. Besides, I am not connected to a Brazilian University except as an Emeritus Professor in

46   *Fernando Cardim de Carvalho*

Rio de Janeiro, so I thought it was unfair to other people who are still active in the country that I would keep receiving grants, especially because the support I had was a long-term grant, lasting five years. In all the period between 1982 and 2017, the National Research Council [CNPq] has never refused the support we requested. We had enough funds to fund a Post Keynesian seminar which was the first big public event we had, still in 1997. We brought people like Jan Kregel, Steven Fazzari, Nina Shapiro, and Philip Arestis. We had lots of people attending the lectures and debates and CNPq funded most of it. CNPq always consults the community, and despite the fact that we were all non-orthodox, we had the support from the community, even from many orthodox researchers. We kept our academic output high and this got us the support of the community, even from those who do not agree with us, except for the unreconstructed reactionaries that the whole community knows and are rarely consulted. But the truth is that it is a kind of network economics. The problem is how to begin. At some point if you get a mass of the community working on different traditions it gets easier to secure funds. And at some point you also have the public thing, because some of us, including myself, became known in the community so it gets harder for people to refuse support for purely ideological reasons. So, the core trick is that the community changes first and then, when you need support, there is a good chance that referees are going to give favourable reports. Unfortunately, it's very hard to export this.

What do you enjoy most about teaching?

I like teaching undergraduate courses more than graduate courses particularly at home, because in Brazil graduate courses are a kind of "elite". And they are particularly so among non-orthodox. The students are usually self-aware of being an elite, so it is important to recover the spirit of discovery, the delight of understanding. Undergraduates are usually more open to the possibility of discovery and understanding. That is why I always preferred undergraduate courses. I don't have problems with the younger students. Sometimes you have to sacrifice the depth of what you are examining, but I think the reaction is more lively. And undergraduate, it's fun. I love it.

And what do you seek to achieve in teaching and how do you put this into practice?

My idea of teaching is not persuading that this or that school of thought has all the relevant answers but that of capacitating the student to decide by him/herself which approach seems the more promising. Planning undergraduate courses isn't much of a problem – you have to follow the core thing. In graduate courses it may be a little more difficult because you need to balance the things you think people should know because they are going to be professional economists, and the things you think are really important.

It's not that you want to be eclectic or neutral, but you don't want to indoctrinate, because it doesn't last. I usually adopt a different posture for each of two types of courses one can offer in graduate school. We have some general courses like microeconomics and macroeconomics, which I always defended should cover the relevant schools of thought in a non-judgemental way. That is the way we teach them at UFRJ and at the Levy Institute. If you have to teach Real Business Cycles theory, we teach it as a person practising it would do. In the core courses, the idea was that students should be able to recognise by themselves what schools were convincing – the idea was to be as neutral as possible. And then we have the elective courses, in which people will enrol in a course because they knew that you did some work according to some point of view, in some area, so they came because they wanted to know what you as a practitioner of that tradition are prepared to say. We were always afraid of what we used to call "heterodox by default": those who tried to get into the neoclassical but could not do it, those who tried econometrics and failed, so they decided to dedicate their time to write that the future is uncertain, nobody knows what the future will bring, and so on. We cannot accept that students make a choice for reasons of this type. We want people to think about uncertainty, but who also understand probability and are able to understand, see what the concept is about. I think this is the heterodox academic mission. I think it's much more efficient than indoctrination in the long term.

I spoke a couple of years ago to Rubens Sawaya, and he told me that economics teaching in Brazil had been influenced by ideas of Paulo Freire in particular and the sort of critical pedagogy and student-centred learning thing. What do you think about that?

I guess it's not just in economics, but in university teaching is very undisciplined in Brazil. Nobody has any authority over pedagogical methods chosen by each instructor. A Director or a Dean does not tell you what to do, so it is up to the students to judge whether instructors are efficient in any sense or not. When students think the instructor is a disaster, they end up making it clear at some point, by striking or staging some kind of public manifestation of repudiation. When students do not take up this role, you can use Paulo Freire or you can just get a book and read aloud in the classroom; nobody will tell you or do anything. The behaviour of the instructor is completely – at least in the universities I know, and I do know quite a number of them – uncontrollable. If a teacher does not mind having to see a protest at his office door there is very little a head of department or dean can and will do. Faculties in Brazil don't recognise authority in anybody to demand the adoption of a given pedagogical method. If one thinks a given instructor is not performing well, one may try to exert some moral pressure on the instructor but at the end of the day the person can do pretty much whatever

48 *Fernando Cardim de Carvalho*

he or she wants. Sometimes it's outrageous. It's some kind of "default policy" which I personally think is very bad but it is how it has been and I don't see any movement toward changing the situation.

McCloskey referred to economics as "poetry". What do you think about that?

I gave a course once about decision-making in Keynes. That was an elective course based on the texts of some of Shakespeare's tragedies. I personally have been a fan of Shakespeare since I was a teenager, and I even published a paper in the *Journal of Post Keynesian Economics* a few years ago called "Decision-making under Uncertainty as Drama" [2003]. In the paper I discuss characteristics of behaviour under uncertainty using three tragedies. The first is *Hamlet*: why he didn't act, why he took so long to do something, until he was forced to, that is, when he was provoked into fighting by Ophelia's brother. The second is *Julius Caesar*, why even having the forecast that he would be killed on the Ides of March, he still went to the senate and "defied the forecast". And the more interesting play, I think, *Macbeth* because Macbeth faces a rigged game in which the witches issue confounding signals all the time. Macbeth thinks he is making decisions but in fact he is not because all of the relevant variables are manipulated to mislead him. There is one particular scene in the play, which is usually cut from theatrical performances or from movie versions, which is the one of the witches' sabbath in which Hecuba, the queen of the witches, explains how they should make Macbeth believe that he was destined to become the king of Scotland. If it was his destiny, it had to happen, there was no risk of disappointment, making him think he was invulnerable. I think it is much better reading actual situations conceived by a great poet, rather than just reading about uncertainty in economics. Theoretical texts give you the relevant concepts but they don't actually allow one to visualise what is the substantive problem of making choices under uncertainty. So, how can one better understand what uncertainty means than having a great play show you the anguish of decision-making and how the consequences of one's actions can develop in entirely unexpected ways to form situations that may be catastrophic? This type of interaction between economics and poetry means yes, of course, this is a promising way to understand economic behaviour. In fact, I think it is invaluable. The students that took the course loved it. Most of them had never read Shakespeare before, and they read the plays in English to appreciate his poetic language, which is incredibly expressive. They were absolutely fascinated with the kind of situations with which they could connect. Some of the situations in *Hamlet*, thinking about his own condition or why he could not make a decision for instance. That is Keynes, Shackle, Joan Robinson. I loved it, and the students loved it too because they told me they could not wait.

4   William Darity

William Darity is the Samuel DuBois Cook Professor of Public Policy at the Sanford Institute of Public Policy at Duke University, where he is also Professor of Economics and Professor of African and African American Studies. Previously he has held a number of other positions, including with the University of North Carolina; University of Maryland, College Park; and the Centre for Advanced Studies, Stanford. He holds a BA from Brown University and a PhD from Massachusetts Institute of Technology. His main research interests centre on inequality, race, education, segregation, and "stratification economics", including policy to address these problems. He has published 12 books, including *Persistent Disparity: Race and Economic Inequality in the United States Since 1945* (with Myers, 1998) and *What's Left of the Economic Theory of Discrimination?* (1988). He has also published over 200 articles in leading journals such as the *American Economic Review, American Sociological Review, Journal of Economic Perspectives, Journal of Economic Psychology,* and *World Development.* Amongst the most significant of these are articles on evidence of employment discrimination (with Mason, 1998), "acting white" and high achievement (with Tyson and Castellino, 2005), and social psychology and unemployment (with Goldsmith, 1996).

William Darity was interviewed by Andrew Mearman at Duke University, Durham, North Carolina, USA, in April 2017.

How did you become an economist?

If I can reconstruct the story accurately, I decided to become an economist when I was an undergraduate at Brown University. And there were two steps in this process: the first step was making the decision that I wanted to be an academic; and then the second step was trying to figure out which field I would be an academic in.

So the academic came before the subject?

Yeah. Because the assumption that everyone had made was I would become a lawyer, and I think this was partially because I was active in debate, especially in high school. But I never really had any strong interest in being a lawyer. And during my first semester as an undergraduate I took one of these mass lecture courses in political science – it was the introduction of political science. And because it was a mass lecture course we had smaller section meetings. And I just had the good fortune of having a section leader who was a graduate student at the time, who was named Ira Strauber, and then Ira subsequently became a faculty member in political science at Grinnell College in Iowa and was there for many, many years. But while he was a graduate student teaching our section, he was somewhat of a provocateur, and he would give us readings that were in some ways critical of the materials that were being presented in the mass lecture. And so I found that I really enjoyed reading materials that posed a critique. But I also found myself engaged in a critique of the critical readings. And so after some conversation with Ira, you know, I think we both concluded that I would probably be happiest as an academic where I could engage in that kind of activity on a full-time basis!

So then the question was, would I do a PhD in political science, or would I do it in economics, and so I concentrated in both areas. And I started taking economics courses because of my interest in the problem of inequality and poverty ... poverty as well. And I assumed that because economics was about money that there would be some valuable answers that I might uncover as to why some people are subjected to poverty and others are not, why there are vast disparities in income and wealth and health, and all those sorts of things. And I soon learned that basically the answer in economics is that this is all contingent on variations in human capital; and I found that to be an entirely unsatisfactory answer. And so I decided to become an economist to change the way economists think about these issues. So that's ... But I think I said in the radio interview that this is with the hubris of youth!

And so obviously, I have not changed the way the economics profession writ large thinks about these issues, but I have pursued kind of an alternative way of thinking about the sources of inequality and poverty, and I think it has some traction with some scholars, yeah.

Was the interest in equality and poverty there before?

Yeah. Again, in this radio interview I talk about my experiences growing up in the Middle East and what I observed there. And my father worked for the World Health Organisation, so we would come back to the US every two years or so. I was born in 1953, and so it wasn't until 1964 that the Civil Rights Act was passed, so essentially when we would come back we would come back to the Jim Crow South. And my ... we would typically visit my mother's mother who lived in Wilson, North Carolina, and my father's parents who lived in the mountains in North Carolina at East Flat Rock, and I was very acutely aware of the relationship between segregation and the lower level of resources that were present both among individual families but also in the community collectively, in the black community. And Wilson, North

Carolina, is one of the towns which has the classic pattern of being separated racially by the railroad tracks: this is a somewhat common phenomenon in many southern towns. Wilson is one where that was very much the case, and so ... You know, from a very early age I was very, very attuned to the existence of these kinds of disparities and some sense that there were nuances in the ways in which these disparities operated in different places, but I kept having a sense that maybe there was some general explanation for these kinds of unfairness, really. So, that was kind of always there. And so when I became a college student, this was one of the things that I was hoping I would really learn or come to understand in a strong way, as a university student.

And is that sense of unfairness still there as strongly as it was?

Oh, yeah. Yeah, yeah. And in some ways, maybe it's more acute, because I actually can put numbers on the scope of these inequities in a way that I wasn't able to as a small child – it was more a sensation that something wasn't really right about this, that I never had a sense that the folks who were in the bottom slots were folks who deserved to be in the bottom slot. So, I think that really was a critical dimension of my thinking and led me in the direction that I ultimately took.

My second question here is about how you developed your particular contribution. Thus far, we've talked about your overarching approach to work and your goals. More narrowly, what about your PhD dissertation? Can you remember how you arrived at that topic and how you started to think about it?

Well, it was actually three essays; and since I was at MIT, there was definitely an impulse to do some form of mathematical modelling.

So the other route would have been to do something that was more empirical, that involved the use of data and the like. But I didn't really do that in my dissertation – so had three different essays. The first one was a re-examination of the ... the Samuelson-Modigliani refutation of Pasinetti, where they attempted to demonstrate that ultimately in the long run in a capitalist economy that was divided between workers and owners of capital, where the workers actually were partial owners of the capital stock, that eventually the workers would own the entire capital stock. And so I did a dissertation chapter that demonstrated that the opposite could potentially happen and that the capitalists could ultimately own the entire capital stock. So this is maybe not really, really important, but I guess it was kind of ... I didn't want Samuelson and Modigliani to get away with it, and so that was the ... And actually, I took a class with Franco [Modigliani], and Paul [Samuelson] was the third reader of my dissertation; so I think he more or less accepted the proof that I had developed was okay.

52 William Darity

But ... then the second essay was an attempt to construct a three-region model of the Atlantic slave trade. And this was prompted by my exposure as an undergraduate to some books that other black students at Brown had recommended that I should read. So one of these was C.L.R. James's *Black Jacobins* [1938]; and second was Eric Williams's *Capitalism and Slavery* [1944]; and the third was Walter Rodney's slim book called *How Europe Underdeveloped Africa* [1973]. And so I tried to construct a three-region trade model that could generate some of the outcomes or results that are associated with what I think is the general conclusion of the phenomenon of uneven development out of these works. So that was the second chapter.

And then the third chapter was an attempt to formalise Ester Boserup's model of agricultural growth. So, those were the three essays, and I think the third model actually ... All of them got published as separate articles, but the third paper actually has an error in it, which was propagated into the published version of the article, but you know many years later I did a paper with William Winfrey in which we corrected a mistake that I had made. Yeah. But those were my three papers, so in a sense I would say that they shared the characteristic of my interest in uneven development and maybe inequality on an international scale or global scale. But as time went by I became more and more interested in thinking about inter-group inequality: that is, disparities between ethnic and racial groups; disparities based upon gender; disparities based upon religious affiliation and the like.

What was the motivation for the third paper?

Yes. So, partly it was motivated by my sense that Ester Boserup had developed an anti-Malthusian argument. So, the classic Malthusian argument is that the force of diminishing returns will put sufficient pressure on the supplies of food that at some point there'll be a crisis, and so there would have to be some means of reducing the population. And it might be warfare, it might be famine, it might be pestilence; but population size would have to be reduced. And so, the companion point is that population growth is a negative in some sense, I guess. So, this is very consistent with the Club of Rome's view of the world, and others who you know, who'd argue that the world's going to run out of resources because it's going to become overpopulated. And, the Boserup argument was somewhat different: although not initially something that we might necessarily view as positive. But, she argued that communities that are engaged in primitive agriculture – primitive in the sense that it's not mechanised and it doesn't rely upon chemicals – in response to population pressure will intensify their production. What this really means is that everybody engages in more hours of work. And, she also talks about changes in the type of agricultural production: so you're moving to different schemes of tillage, from an initial stage where you may essentially be engaged in hunting and gathering. And so, she talks about these transitions.

And, these transitions are associated with a greater demand for work effort from the population. So, what population pressure is doing is it's creating an increase in the food supply, but it's doing so in a way in which people have to work more. But then she argues that at a certain stage this prompts technological change. And so then each individual becomes more productive, and you can then reduce the work hours, but you also have managed to feed your population. And so it seemed like a counter-Malthusian story, and I thought it would be interesting to elaborate on it; but it also had some implications about inequalities across communities that might be at different points along the Boserupian trajectory of agricultural production, so that there was an inequality mention that was involved in that too, yeah.

And were all three mathematical papers?

Yeah, they're all three mathematical models, yeah. There's very little statistical work involved in these papers.

And did you choose that because you were good at maths, or you thought it was strategically useful? Or perhaps did you think this was what the literature needed?

So, I think I did actually have a sense that there were some things that you could reveal by going through a mathematical formalisation that you could not see if you kept the analysis at a verbal level. I'm more convinced nowadays that an oral presentation of most of your ideas can really take you quite far, and that you can see where the problems are even without putting things in a mathematical form. But, I also have a sense that there are certain conclusions that I only could have really demonstrated or found by working through the formalisation exercise, so ... I mean, I think that one of Samuelson's most famous theorems, the factor price equalisation theorem, is nonsense. But, you know, it is a logically valid inference from a particular set of conditions that he establishes, and so, then you can ask whether empirically those conditions actually do apply, but we don't observe factor price equalisation; or you can ask whether the reason why we might not observe factor price equalisation is because those conditions don't really hold. And, I think ... So, there is a kind of a value to the precision of the argument that might emerge from some forms of mathematical formalisation. So, I don't know if I've reached that conclusion mostly because this was a way in which MIT succeeded in indoctrinating me, but I actually do think that there could be a potential value in some circumstances to trying to lay out a model in a more mathematical way, so that you can look in a more exact way about which conditions, which parameters lead to certain results and which ones don't.

Do you think it gave you extra credibility as well?

Well, I certainly don't think the papers would have been published! Yeah, I guess it did in the sense that as I moved to do other things people wouldn't necessarily say it was because I was incapable of doing it that way. So, I think there was, as you put it, some strategic value. But, I also was in a period where I was doing a lot of papers that relied upon the use of differential equations, and so not just the papers and the dissertation, but some subsequent papers. There was a paper I did eventually where I believe I successfully demonstrated that Hume was wrong about the price-specie flow mechanism. People haven't really paid a lot of attention to this paper. But, I had to use a mathematical model to try to demonstrate that, that you would not necessarily end up in a situation where there was some fixed distribution of specie between the two countries – under the conditions that he posited – and so I almost had to do it mathematically to try to demonstrate that there was an error there.

That's interesting. This book is sort of partly about heterodox economics, and we've come to you because we've provisionally labelled you as heterodox. What do you think about that? Do you use the label yourself? Does it mean anything to you?

So, I think when I hear it used it signals to me that there may be a cluster of economists who I will find some sense of being simpatico with. I don't actually use the term myself. I think of much of the work that I do either in an implicit way or sometimes in an explicit way as being influenced by Marx, and I don't feel uncomfortable about saying I'm a Marxist economist, although I guess there are other people who use that label who might be sceptical about the validity of my appropriating that. But, I guess I've always felt that categories like heterodox or progressivism are terms that are viewed as safer than sort of declaring yourself! But, then there are a lot of people who are in the heterodox category who truly are not Marxist at all. So, you know, I think of an array of folks who are Post Keynesians who would say that they're a heterodox economist, and you know, I find tremendous value in the work that many of them do, but it certainly would not be in the orbit of what we might call Marxism. So, I don't use the term, but I'm appreciative of what it may signal about the folks who do use the term. So, you know, it's like finding folks who might be your friends!

That's interesting. So you wouldn't define it on a conceptual level: it's more sociological, or about people positioning themselves ...?

Yeah, because I don't think heterodox economics is one thing. You know, I think heterodoxy includes some people who call themselves institutionalist, which is a ... that's the one that bothers me a lot. But, you know, Post Keynesians; folks who might view themselves as being neo-Sraffians; you know, then folks who say they're Marxist: I mean, I think all of that falls under heterodoxy. But, that means that heterodoxy is not really an approach in and of itself, from my perspective. I mean, it just means that in some sense you're working with an approach or a tactic or a strategy that's different from what we may view as the strategy of orthodox economics. So, you could just as well call it unorthodox economics. But yeah, okay ... By doing that you're kind of privileging the ... you're privileging the empire in some ways.

What about political economy, though? What does that mean to you?

So, that term bothers me a bit, because it's also associated with the Buchanan–Tullock tradition of thinking about political processes as essentially mimicking the market, the marketplace, and so, that's what some people mean by political economy; others mean when you're trying to pay attention to politics and economics at the same time, but that can mean any number of things, it's ... So, you know, I'm a little sceptical about using that term also!

But you do use it: you published something recently, on the "Political Economy of Education".

Yeah. I didn't choose that – to be honest, I didn't choose that title! But yes, yes, it has appeared in some of my work. But ... yeah.

So does it mean anything in particular to you?

I mean, yeah, what I say I do is stratification economics, yeah. So that's, you know, what I've come to say is ... that's what I would describe as my strongest attachment as kind of a centring point, yeah.

Do you recall how you came to realise actually that that's what you were doing?

So yes, there's a paper of mine that was published in the *Journal of Economics and Finance* that was a lecture I had given, an invited lecture I had given, to the association that produces that journal. And it was in the process of preparing my lecture that I said, "You know, the sociologists make use of this term 'stratification': it's a legitimate field in sociology. But most of what we do in economics that addresses questions of inequality is the purview of the labour economist". And this kind of bothered me, because I thought there's a host of dimensions of inequality, especially wealth inequality, that has very little to do with what happens in labour markets. Okay, so I was thinking "you know, well, what else could we kind of call an approach that doesn't centre all of this on employment and labour?" And so I took the term from the field of sociology and said let's just link it to economics.

56   *William Darity*

And by calling it stratification economics I wanted to signal that we are not – those of us who are using this approach – are not, we're actively and consciously not making the argument that people who are at the bottom of the society are there because of certain deficiencies or defects that they possess, that there's a set of structural processes that allocate people along the hierarchy. And so, if you're a victim of that structural process then you'll end up at the bottom, and if you're the beneficiary of that structural process you'll end up at the top. And what we need to explore in detail is the nature of those structural processes. So that's ... I think that's what led me to say let's put a label on this. I will not make the claim that the ideas that are at the heart of "stratification economics" are entirely unique – they're not. You know, I've argued that actually Thorstein Veblen's theory of the leisure class has a lot of conceptual content that I would say is stratification economics. Herbert Blumer's essay in 1958 in the *Pacific Sociological Review* on the relationship between prejudice and relative group position to me is archetypal stratification economics. But they didn't use that language, and so I think what I've done is put a name to a body of ideas, or an approach to looking at inequality.

Does anybody ever say to you that you're not an economist?

Oh, yeah! And both from a negative and a positive point of view.

But you consider yourself one?

Yeah, yeah. I mean, I was trained as one. I think I know what economists do. And I think that this ... what I might view as the development of a new field is a subfield that I would squarely place in economics. I mean, there's long been a tradition of work that has not fit with the main thrust, or the main momentum, of what many economists are doing. But I don't necessarily think that it's any less economics per se. I mean, even if you take something like Hyman Minsky's work on financial crises, you know, that's not at the core in any sense of conventional economics – I mean, if it was, then economists might have had something to say about why the crisis took place in 2007–2008. You know, it was interesting that the vast majority of economists couldn't explain it, you know. They'd roll it out with this real business cycle theory [RBC] hoke. So there's long been alternative approaches, and I view those alternative approaches as squarely within the economics tradition. There's a serious issue about what we want to extract from those approaches, what we think is really useful in terms of giving us insights. But, that's a judgement I think we have to make. By introducing something that I call stratification economics, I want it squarely to be part of the *corpus* of economics, but it's providing an alternative approach to the way in which most economists look at these issues.

Frederic Lee [2011] distinguished between heretics and blasphemers. Heretics are those who are critical enough that they cause a bit of trouble but not so critical that they reject fundamental beliefs; they are acceptable critics. And he said people like him were blasphemers. I'm just reminded that you said that when you were an undergraduate that you were attracted to the criticisms, but you're also critical of the critics. You also said something about going against the grain of what is normal in economics. So I wondered whether there was something about being contrary that was appealing.

So, this is a comment I also made in the interview two days ago, which was why I didn't want to become a lawyer. So, it's not exclusively contrarianism. You know, in the world of debate I discovered that you can make, or you can almost always craft strong arguments to support any position. But, ethically and morally I know that not any position is valid. And so, my contrarianism arises out of my perception that what people are promoting in much of what we might call conventional economics actually gives us a false view of the world. So, it's not contrarianism for contrarianism's sake; it really arises out of my ethical conviction that we truly should be seeking the truth. Okay? And so to the extent that more conventional ways of doing a thing mask what I might perceive as the true story, or the valid story, then I'm very disturbed about that whole strategy or approach to doing research or investigations of human societies.

What, then, are the problems of mainstream economics? Does the word "mainstream" have any meaning to you?

Yeah, I mean just in terms of … If we were just thinking about the sheer numbers or proportions of folks within the economics profession who do it in a particular way, yeah, there's clearly a mainstream. I was talking earlier about being indoctrinated into doing mathematical modelling and perhaps valuing it; but there's an indoctrination that takes place into a particular way of doing economics. And, you know, we have a programme that's a mentoring programme for junior faculty who are from under-represented groups in the economics profession to facilitate their transition from being untenured assistant professors to being tenured associate professors. And, in the cohort that we had come together in 2016, there were about four or five people who were macroeconomists, and they were all doing models that had some variant of real business cycle theory [RBC]; and I kept saying, "Well, you can't explain what happened here or what happened here or what happened here with this model". But, for them to survive in their academic programmes as macroeconomists, they virtually had no choice but to do some variant on a RBC. And so, yeah, I mean, I think that there's pressure that's applied to stay within the mainstream if somebody's going to succeed. And, I think there's also a tacit – or sometimes an explicit – understanding that

58 *William Darity*

the possibility of you getting a strong recommendation as a new PhD from your senior faculty members is going to be contingent on the work that you're doing looking a lot like the work that they're doing. And so, you kind of perpetuate what I would say is actually bad research. And, it's bad research done by very clever people. Because you know, I do think that there's a large number of people in the economics profession who are really quite bright. But you know, that doesn't mean that you don't produce bad work. And this bad work gets propagated in the major journals and so on.

We've already discussed a few of the reasons you use the phrase "bad research". May we unpack that a bit more? What do you mean by bad research?

So, bad research promotes a falseness. Falseness in terms of our understanding of the world, falseness about the inferences we can draw about the world, et cetera. So yeah, it's obscuring a more accurate picture of how things are actually operating. So, I'm clearly not a postmodernist, because I don't think everybody's truth is valid – or invalid! I mean, I think there are some things that are true, and there are some things that are false, and so that really informs the way I try to do …

Right. And bad research: can that come from anywhere, from any starting point? Or are certain starting points more likely to lead to bad research?

So, I would agree that it's possible to construct inaccurate or false stories from almost any starting point, but there are some starting points that are going to lead you in a less accurate direction than others. And particularly thinking – you know, you asked about my attachment to economics per se, and there is something that's central to the way I think about stratification economics that's drawn from a long tradition of thought in economics, which is the notion of self-interested behaviour. But, in stratification economics we transfer the notion of self-interested behaviour from the individual in isolation to the social group that the individual might belong to. So, then we're thinking about self-interested social groups. And so there is a drive in stratification economics to identify what is rational about various forms of collective behaviour. And so, it departs from the behavioural economists who are always trying to look for the irrational. But it also departs from conventional economics because of its focus on the importance of social groups, which leads in turn to an emphasis on relative position as opposed to absolute position. And I think much of conventional economics is driven by claiming that utility improvements are associated with changes in absolute position. So, this is closer in spirit to Veblen and to James Duesenberry's relative income hypothesis as an explanation for the way in which aggregate consumption actually operates. You know, it's interesting that in many of the major texts for undergraduates on Macroeconomics that have a treatment of the consumption function, you know, most of them now never make any reference to the Duesenberry hypothesis, the relative income hypothesis: it has just disappeared. And so, for me, stratification economics is appropriating something that's very much at the heart of conventional economics, which is the notion that people act in their own self-interest; but it's doing so through the sociological construct of the importance of the group, the tribe, the team, and the like.

If you flip that back into the economics profession: one of the things that we've been thinking about, it's whether there's a mentality or a psychology of a mainstream economist, or whether it's a psychology of mainstream economics. What do you think?

I don't know, I don't know. I mean, now we get into the question of whether there are particular types of personalities who are attracted to economics, or … This may well be true, I just don't know, I just don't know.

The next couple of questions are about you as an economist and what you're trying to achieve – and you've already hinted at that. Perhaps you could elaborate further.

So, I'm trying to achieve a better understanding of why there are huge disparities between social groups, and I'm also trying to think in a very careful way about what types of policies we could introduce to change those conditions. And so I think those are maybe my two tasks.

And the next question is: do you seek to influence society? Seemingly you do.

Yes. I'm not sure I'm particularly successful at this, but yeah, I think yes, I'm very engaged in trying to make the translation of the research into widely accessible language and venues and also trying to literally promote some of the policy ideas that have evolved from those programmes of research, yeah.

Is that something you've always done?

No, I think this is maybe something that I've become more engaged in than in the past … Well, I'm old, so I've been at this for a while; in fact, I've been at this for close to 40 years. I would say that this desire and this capacity to be very publicly engaged is about 15 years old now, yeah.

And what changed? Was it a change of status, or perhaps did you just become more confident …?

Yeah. I … you know, it's interesting. So for many years I was on the faculty of the University of North Carolina, Chapel Hill, and I don't think that I'm fundamentally a different economist from the one that I was there. But, it's quite clear that – and I didn't realise this when I made the move here – Duke provides a different public platform for research than UNC does. And so, there's several people have said that, you know, since I made the move to Duke they've heard a lot more about my work; I've been much more visible. And so I'm not sure when I reached the point when I was just really, really conscious of the desire to try to have a public presence; but I do know that I didn't have the same capability to have that public presence until I made the transition to the other faculty.

Because of institutional support – not necessarily anything about you?

Well, I think it's partially … it may be partially that the Duke label, or brand, has a different resonance with the public at large, but it's also because I think this is an institution that places a high value or a premium on gaining a substantial amount of public attention for the work that its faculty does. And so, I think that there is … I guess the language would be public relations, but I think the public relations I've heard is stronger at Duke. I'm not sure if it's just because of resources or what exactly, but it seems to be different.

Some people change their focus or activity or they approach things a different way because of personal circumstances. For example, as people have grandchildren, they become more conscious of the future: does that apply to you at all?

No, my sons say that I'm perpetually the angry old black man. So I don't think I've changed much in terms of my passion and sense of urgency about issues. I think I … I guess they say people become more cautious or conservative as they age. I don't know that I've really changed that much. Sometimes I feel like I'm the same person I was when I was in my early twenties, although when I look in the mirror I realise this is clearly not the case!

The next question is about research funding. In an increasingly neoliberal environment, there is a lot more pressure to get money. You've attracted lots of research funding. How do you go about negotiating that or navigating that environment?

So, a lot of it is serendipity. You know, there are foundations that are committed to something quite the opposite of the neoliberal agenda. And, one of the issues that arises from the standpoint of a researcher is that frequently they are more interested in funding, understandably, funding advocacy groups, grassroots organisations, organisations that are having a direct role in trying to engage transformative change. But, there are some that also realise that those entities can't operate as effectively unless they have really good information and evidence. And so, they will on occasion provide support for the kind of work that we do. And so, there are some government funding sources that will provide support for projects that might be related: so for example, this mentoring programme that I mentioned is a programme that's funded by the National Science Foundation; but that's not a research project per se, and I'm not sure you know, consistently how easy it would be to fund a lot of the research activity through a publicly funded agency like that. You know, we try, and occasionally we're successful, but there's much more of an inclination to fund this type of work on the part of some of the private foundations, charitable foundations, particularly those that have a commitment to trying to address inequality, which is a major theme for many of these foundations at this moment.

But you know one example is the point at which the Ford Foundation had a major project on the racial wealth gap, and that led us to have the opportunity, with Ford support, to conduct a series of surveys in five American cities – Tulsa, Oklahoma; Washington DC; Los Angeles, California; Miami, Florida; and – what's the fifth one? – Boston, Massachusetts – and we did a set of surveys to try to uncover the wealth position of various more precisely identified national origin communities. The US census has categories like Asian or Hispanic, or Black collectively; or for that matter, White. But we were interested in trying to know more about the various groups that comprise those aggregate categories, and what their wealth position looked like, and to what extent there is variation among those national origin communities that come under the umbrella of being, for example, Asian. And so, we identified a set of cities where we could target those particular communities. So, for example, we chose Tulsa, Oklahoma, because we could get a significant set of responses from Native Americans. We chose Miami, Florida, because we could get a significant number of responses from Haitians and Puerto Ricans, and so on. And, the Ford Foundation was our paramount funder for this effort. We also got funding support specifically for the City of Boston from the Federal Reserve Bank of Boston. And, issuing our report on Los Angeles, we did get support from the Federal Reserve Bank of San Francisco. So, we've actually developed some collaborations with some branches of the Federal Reserve Bank, branches that are primarily ... those branches that have some strong interest in the phenomenon of wealth inequality. So, you know, I can't really make the claim that there is some magical trick that we've performed so much as there are folks out there who are interested in this kind of work and have been willing to support us, so we've been lucky! Yeah, really.

How do you advise? My impression is that for younger academics there's a lot more pressure on them to get – so in the UK this is true – to get money and to be conversant with how funding works, and ... Is it true of here?

So this is ... I don't know that this is so true in the economics profession. I think, you know, many, many folks can have successful careers in economics without ever seeking external funding, yeah. Yeah, it's a little bit different in that respect. I mean, you know, I don't have to seek external funding for the purposes of supporting my salary. But, I have a strong commitment to particular kinds of research activity, and there's a lot of it that cannot be done without extramural support. So, that's why I do it. But most of us who are in the social sciences generally are not on soft money in that sense, so we don't have to go out and hunt our salaries. That's a little bit different from folks who might be in a School of Public Health, where virtually everyone has to get grants to actually support themselves. That's not the case in the social sciences departments in most of the United States. So you'll find, especially in the humanities in particular, and in much of the social sciences, that most of the faculty members have never written a grant proposal. Yeah. So, it might be quite different from the UK on that score.

It sounds like it might be, yes, maybe it's coming.

Yeah, it might be! Who knows? But, of course, the other side of the coin is that in terms of federal monies there's some sense that we're going to experience substantial reductions in federally funded research, so I don't know. I mean, you could push people to have to seek their salaries, but if you do it at a point in which there's less funding, yeah, it's going to be quite messy.

How do you advise the people you're mentoring about this side of the profession?

So we actually do have – since it's for the programme, it's funded by the National Science Foundation. We usually have a representative of the National Science Foundation's Behavioral Sciences Division, which includes economics, come and talk to the fellows, and talk to them about the ins and outs of preparation of grant proposals and the like. So, we do actually encourage them to do this, but I'm just saying, they don't necessarily have to do it for the purposes of being successful – it's not something that most economics departments actually use for the purposes of evaluating their faculty. So, you know, my advice to folks is: if you've developed a research project that you can't carry to fruition without additional funding, or that you've conceived of that's going to require a significant amount of funding, then you do need to figure out an extramural source of funding to do it. But, I think it's got to be driven by the content of the project, not just "I'm seeking funds for anything I do", yeah.

Does the project or does the money come first?

Yeah, I think the project comes first for me, and I think also that's been important in terms of us maintaining some sense of integrity. So, we would like to work with funders who are interested in the things that we are interested in, rather than identifying a research fund and then arbitrarily trying to design something that will mesh with that. I think you don't do work that's as good, and I think ... I don't know, it's just I think you develop a better research programme if you are seeking funding for things that you are deeply interested in rather than tailoring the project to what you think the funder is interested in.

I'd like to now address questions of teaching. Have you, as many people are, been taken away from it?

No. I do. No, actually, the irony is I'm teaching three classes this semester. Yeah. I don't have to teach more than three a year, but sometimes I will take on more than that. This is a year when I've taken on more than that. But yeah, I guess the most important thing I can say about teaching is I enjoy it a great deal, except for grading – I despise grading but it comes with the territory! But, I also try to, as frequently as possible, design and teach classes that are actually in some significant way connected to the research that I do. I really like to have classes where I don't have a sense that there's some sort of divide between teaching and research. Also, I like to work with undergraduates on research projects, and I think I've published about seven papers with undergraduates – yeah – refereed papers, so ... So, that's also an artefact of having classes where the subject matter is closely related to the work that I'm attempting to do.

What are your objectives when you teach?

I think my primary objectives are to get students to think about the world in a way that I don't believe they've previously thought about it. And, in so doing, to put them in a position to have a more accurate understanding of the dynamics that are taking place. I'm an economist but I actually invest a substantial amount of time in trying to learn more about the work that's done by historians. And, I think it's vital, particularly – and I teach a course, introduction to African American studies – it's absolutely essential that I can give the students as accurate a reading on the historical record as possible, because there is so much distortion about that historical record, and I have to be able to demonstrate to them why I think one piece of evidence completely dominates another piece of evidence. We examine why one author's point of view is more consistent with real facts than another. It's not enough to say, "Well, I think this is true": you have to demonstrate why you think this is true, and I think that's vital, and that's something I place a lot of value on in a classroom setting.

And how do you do that?

Basically, I do it by laying out what the competing perspectives are and discussing what the evidence is in support of each of those perspectives and then trying to engage the students in a conversation about which body of evidence is most persuasive. You know, why should we believe this author relative to that? What is it about the way in which this author has structured the argument and has made use of the data and the evidence that leads us to think that this is a more credible point of view? So I guess in a way my debate skills are coming back into play, but not towards the purpose of demonstrating that anything is valid, but more for the purposes of trying to determine which perspective is more valid.

And how do you assess whether you've done the job that you wanted to do?

Well, I don't necessarily! 'Cause once they leave the class there's very few that you have a sustained contact with. But within the confines of the class, of course, I can assess how they're thinking and what they're doing by looking at the assigned work and seeing if there's an improvement in the critical eye that they bring to the materials as the semester progresses. But I can't really say a lot after they leave the class. There are some who maintain contact, and there are some who are college professors themselves now, and so I have a very strong sense of what they're doing. But most of my students I'm not going to necessarily see after I teach them in one class, no.

And if you could sum up what you enjoy about teaching, what would you say?

I think it forces me to – you know, selfishly, it forces me to have greater clarity, because if I can't present something clearly to others, then I don't really understand it myself. And so, there's a real pressure to have a greater degree of precision about what you're saying or how you're organising, if you're in discussion of a particular argument, or an approach to an analysis: I think that's something I really value. But also – again, this is somewhat selfish – I think there's tremendous value to the ideas that the students bring forth. Every semester there's something that – at least one thing, but usually more – that's a really profound insight that doesn't come from me, it comes from one of the students in the class, and that's really rewarding, yeah.

McCloskey and others talk about economics as poetry: what do you think about that?

Well, I don't know. I think a lot of economics papers are written in such a way, it would be hard for us to claim that they're poetic! There are some economists who write like poets in a sense – I mean, they're artistic writers.

But, frequently they're dismissed. Some of them are quite successful and prominent but still dismissed by many of the other economists. I'm thinking of somebody like John Kenneth Galbraith for instance: just really a marvellous writer, and you could say that there's kind of a poetic quality to the way he did it. And you know, his son Jamie doesn't write exactly the same way, but there is a similar kind of poetic feel. So, there's also some of that in Keynes – yeah, especially the *Essays in Persuasion* [1931].

He clearly understood the value of that sort of writing.

Yes. His objective was persuasion, right? That's so, yeah. But, I would say I'd be hard-pressed to make the claim that many, many papers I read about economics have a poetic quality!

You've never thought of yourself as a poet then?

I would love to be, but I don't think I'm that good!

Thank you very much.

5 S. Charusheela

S. Charusheela (Charu) is Professor at the School of Interdisciplinary Arts and Sciences (IAS), University of Washington, Bothell. Prior to joining IAS in 2011, she held positions at the University of Nevada, Las Vegas (2007–2010), University of Hawaii at Mānoa (1999–2007), and Franklin & Marshall College (1995–1998). She obtained her PhD in Economics from the University of Massachusetts, Amherst, in 1997. She has served as editor of the journal *Rethinking Marxism* (August 2005–July 2009), as elected member of the Governing Board of the Cultural Studies Association (2009–2015), and as elected member of the Board of the International Association for Feminist Economics (2003–2006, 2007–2010). Her research examines the relationship between gender, development, identity, and postcoloniality/globalisation. Her co-edited volume (with Eiman Zein-Elabdin), *Postcolonialism Meets Economics*, was published by Routledge in 2004. Selected other publications include "Response: History, Historiography, and Subjectivity", (2011) and "Engendering Feudalism: Modes of Production Debates Revisited" (2010, both in *Rethinking Marxism*), "Gender and the Stability of Consumption: A Feminist Contribution to Post Keynesian Economics" (2010) and "Social Analysis and the Capabilities Approach: A Limit to Martha Nussbaum's Universalist Ethics" (2009, both in the *Cambridge Journal of Economics*), "The Diaspora at Home" (2007, in *Cultural Dynamics*, special issue on Rethinking South Asian Diaspora Studies), and "intersectionality" (2013, in Deborah Figart and Tonia Warnecke, eds., *Handbook of Research on Gender and Economic Life*).

Charu was interviewed by Sebastian Berger via phone online in July 2017.

How did you become an economist?

Completely by convention. I had some sense of the fact that economics was the actual study of the economy because I grew up in India in an era where economics was the handmaiden of planning (in particular development planning), which is very different from the subsequent era when economics becomes the handmaiden of business. In the '70s and '80s that sort of economics was respected. There were development economists, people we had heard of, like K.N. Raj, like [Pranab] Bardhan and [Amartya] Sen.

I was in Delhi University – in those days it was the era of planning, so you became a doctor or an engineer. Those were the two main fields we chose. As I think about what planning did to our educational vision – I think like an economist don't I? Even when I talk about personal choices I focus on material conditions – planning prioritised infrastructure, which was engineering, and health, which was medicine. It wasn't law, not like here – so it wasn't doctor, lawyer, and engineer it was just doctor/engineer. And if you didn't want to become either of those, one of the options you did was economics.

That's what I did. I just got lucky that it turned out I liked it. I suspect I would have enjoyed sociology just as much, though at that point the kind of work that's happening in South Asian sociology right now wasn't there. The field in terms of understanding sociology as something you could also use to grasp what was happening in our contemporary societies was just emerging, since it was mainly understood as anthropology, right? It used to be understood as anthropology, it wasn't sociology you saw as the framework being used to look at developing societies.

What happened before university – was there anything in terms of in your school or in your parents, family, or anything else that played a role?

Yes, my father was in the civil service. Both my parents were born pre-independence. My father is now 87 going on 88, my mother is no more, but if she had been alive she would have been about 83 now. My father was in the government; he was in the Indian Administrative Service and worked a lot on development. His heart was in rural development and poverty and when he retired he retired as Secretary of Agriculture. My mother was in public finance; she was an academic and she retired as the first woman to be a full professor in public finance in the Indian Institute of Public Administration. So yes, economics and development was very much something I was aware of growing up, the kinds of questions people asked, and the concerns they had … Not at the level of theory or debate or anything, because it was just something your parents did, but just the idea that you would do this type of work. But, I didn't know it as a field until I went to college.

When you went to high school or university, were there any influential instructors that made you become an economist or choose economics as a doctorate, people that guided you a certain way, that maintained your enthusiasm?

In Delhi University, you would get admitted to the major. You didn't choose a major later on. When you got admitted, you would get admitted into economics or medicine or engineering and that's what I was explaining.

68   *S. Charusheela*

I didn't want to do medicine or engineering and so I ended up getting admitted to economics. It isn't like here [US], where you chose a major at a certain point.

Was that a master's programme or was that right from the start?

No. That's undergrad; that was my BA in economics in Delhi University. I went to Miranda House, which was a women's college in Delhi, and I went to Delhi because my parents were posted in Delhi at that moment and basically you went to college where your parents were. This idea of going somewhere else was not there, especially for girls, since there was a perfectly good college right where your parents lived.

What happened in the transition to graduate studies? That's interesting too.

The transition to the kind of economics I did took place in grad school. When I was in Delhi we had micro-macro. I was good at math; that was easy. I found development interesting. And, I remember very clearly that I took part in some type of debate on development. I remember prepping for the debate (I doubt if he remembers this, we were undergraduates, and Kaushik Basu came to judge the debate), and I ended up doing some independent research and I came across Prebisch-Singer. We weren't taught Prebisch-Singer in depth in college, I just came across more of their work and I was fascinated by the way in which the arguments were put together logically. I don't think I fully grasped the issues. But then, I also remember that because I was an undergrad in Delhi I would go to hear people at the Delhi School of Economics. Delhi School of Economics only had graduate courses. But, I remember that they would let us come and attend if there were people who were giving guest lectures. You would go there and hear speakers.

I also remember in Miranda there was a little library in the economics department office and it was nice, something I realise after coming to the US was unique, where we actually read Hicks, we read Studenski and Kuznets ... We were in the '80s reading the original scholars ... Sure, we had economics textbooks, everybody had Samuelson. But we were also being required to read the original writings as undergraduates (not just a few of the obvious ones like Keynes). I think that made a difference; I began to see it as a field.

In terms of going to graduate school, to be honest, I just wanted to go abroad. I was 21; I wanted to see the world. This is the 1980s; there were fewer options for Indian women. Definitely it's not like what people imagine that it's awful or anything like that, but it was like – what are you going to do? I didn't know. I didn't want to go into the management field. By that point I also wasn't sure that I wanted to be in the administrative services or the government. I went into college in '82. Until then it had been the era of development; '82 to '85 things change. The debt crisis was inaugurated just as I entered undergraduate, and by the time I'm finishing my undergraduate, development economics is pretty much a dead field. It was all neoliberal.

My father was a socialist, but that other kind of view that they had in development was dying, I think. Also '84 in Delhi it was very formative for me; we had Indira Gandhi's assassination and the rioting which killed the Sikhs. I just remember the violence in the city and I remember just suddenly feeling that something about how we were understanding what it meant to shape economic policy or national policy was off, that we were just not understanding something about how things were working.

Thinking back, there was also the Bhopal gas tragedy in 1984 – that also had a real effect on how one thought about issues of industrial development. In any case, in 1984–85 as I considered future options, between the riots, the neoliberal turn in development, and Bhopal, I was ready to rethink issues of development economics.

There was a young professor, Nandita Mongia, she used to teach microeconomics, and I was like, what am I going to do? She said, why not apply to go abroad, do a Master's? After all, if you don't like it you can always come back. For me it was an option between going to Delhi School – because anybody who gets above a certain mark gets admission into the Delhi School of Economics – or going abroad. And I thought, why don't I go abroad? I had no idea what UMass Amherst [University of Massachusetts, Amherst] economics was, to tell the truth. I had a vague sense that it was different, but I didn't really understand what the Cold War meant for the culture of economics in the US, so I never really understood how unique it was. I think she did, so she did suggest that it would be one of the schools I applied to. My parents had a lot of education, but we didn't have any money, not the kind of money that you can afford to send your children abroad. UMass gave me a fellowship, so I went there, and that's where I really dramatically began to understand myself, not just as an economist but as a heterodox economist, as someone who thought, what is the purpose of the field? What is it that one is trying to do with the study of economics? I would say until I went to UMass, I was doing what people did, which wasn't necessarily conscious. I was not deeply aware of the field; I was basically making decisions where I did what people of my gender and class background did. I went to college, I did a degree, I thought, "maybe let's do a Master's and let me go abroad, since what other way do I have to go abroad? Let me see the US." That's really all it was.

How did you develop your particular individual contribution to economics?

I think that is still an ongoing project. I still don't know whether I've really done a good contribution to the field. When I was at UMass I began to really try and think through what it was economics was. I really encountered a different way of thinking about Marx and Marxism there, with Stephen Resnick

70   *S. Charusheela*

and Richard Wolff. I encountered feminism (in the Women's Studies department). Not in the same way as when I was younger. Then I was a feminist in the sense that you were against women being beaten and hurt. I was in college, there were anti-dowry protests in Delhi and I marched on the streets – but who's *for* that, who's *for* killing women? Maybe some people are, but not as a political movement (at least in my experience back then – I know differently now). But the idea that you could theorise it, that was new to me.

I came to the US and I spent a good 10 years in graduate school. I thought I would be finished with my degree in a few years, but everything I thought was changing. I encountered epistemology, I encountered ontology, and I still remember I actually encountered postcolonial thought and subaltern studies which is from India, in a very different way in the US. I'd read Sumit Sarkar because you read his *Modern India* [1983] as part of your economic history paper in Delhi University. I'd already read some of that, and some of the debates about economics when I was an undergrad. But I didn't understand the political stakes until I came abroad.

I was trying to do initial work on dowry because in my undergrad days that was one of those issues that was being raised, and I increasingly had been feeling that the cultural explanations for dowry were not making very much sense. Because it was very alive in the lives of many of the women who went to college with me, and it was very clear to me that its monetary or economic elements were dominating their lives; it was no longer working via that old idea of cultural prestige. It was really about the money, and about accumulating wealth, and about control, and I was trying to make sense of that. I remember giving some talks and not being very comfortable with the positive responses I was getting from my American audiences. It seemed to me that their positiveness was about becoming a little bit too excited about highlighting things that struck me as orientalist rather than relevant to the question of power which I was interested in.

I gave a talk on dowry in 1989 at UMass, and Gayatri Spivak was invited to give the comment by Steve Resnick – who became my dissertation adviser at the end – and who I think thought it would be useful for me to encounter this, so he just invited her. And I had no idea who she was; I literally had never heard of her. She gave a discussion that I subsequently figured out was a public wiping out of my argument, explaining just how ahistorical it was. I didn't know enough to know that she had demolished me; that's how little I knew of the historical debates. But being a fairly confident person, I emailed her and said "I hear you had a lot of critiques. I didn't understand what you were saying. Could you help me?" She wrote back and said, maybe you should do some reading, and she gave me a reading list, so I started reading. Two years later I met her and said, I've read this and I get this. She had no reason to – she's not in Economics; she's in Comparative Literature, and she's not in my university – but she wrote back. She gave me more feedback and I shifted my work. I shifted it from being on dowry. Even though the feminist elements have always been there in the later work, that paper on dowry never got published. It's still available as a working paper and I'm a little embarrassed by it. But it's there as a working paper from the Association for Economic and Social Analysis – I never published it; it was awkward. But I changed my work – I changed it to be about the way in which our assumptions about economic subjectivity, about ontology, were orientalist.

I've continued to address this issue, particularly around questions of gender in later work, but in that earlier work it was just a question of orientalism and how you construct the concept of the developing economy. This is also when I began to hunt out things, after the incident of the talk. This is when I started reading Arturo Escobar, who was at that point an Associate Professor who had just joined UMass in the anthropology department and his book *Encountering Development* [1994] wasn't out yet. But he conducted a seminar which was about this work. I remember taking it, and after that – the economics department got a little frustrated about this – but I ended up changing my thesis in the fourth or fifth year. I ended up taking more courses; I sat in on a course on Marx with R. Radhakrishnan in the English department. I took this course with Alejandro Sanz de Santa Maria which was also about encountering development. I grew up in a family and in an era where development was going to save the nation. I'm sitting in this class with encountering development, where development emerges as the orientalist imperialist project that comes after colonialism. It was a very destabilising way of thinking of things and really made me reimagine and rethink how I was theorising.

Everything I've done since then is this constant effort to think, what are the power dynamics of what we're theorising, and what changes does it generate? To what extent does it promote control and exploitation, to what extent does it promote social transformation? Just a very different set of questions. No longer thinking that policy is the same thing as politics. No longer imagining that the only successful scholarship in economics is that which results in policy. No longer imagining that a policymaker is my audience.

That is really where the transformation came for me, which is kind of hard even for heterodox economics. We think that's what it means to be relevant – to be in the state and to make policy.

Would say that your contribution to economics came out of graduate school and the transformation across the questions that you are asking?

Absolutely. There's no doubt in my mind that for better or for worse I'm a product of UMass. UMass economics and its particular commitment to heterodox economics. I encountered Post Keynesians; I encountered Marxists, Bowles and Gintis, Resnick and Wolff. In the field of development, I encountered multiple frameworks. I encountered Latin American structuralists. And I encountered Walrasian microeconomics with Don Katzner, who very carefully took us through mainstream approaches. It really was committed to this framework where so many schools of thought talk to you *as* schools of thought, talk to you as different approaches to asking questions, different ways of understanding. I encountered questions of ontology and epistemology and began to understand how important it was to be aware of them. I would say that was definitely formative for me. Everything else has come out of that experience. Not as an "application of theory" model. That is, it's not like I learnt the theory and then I apply that theory everywhere, but more like a critical model. A way to think of what the questions should be, that was the takeaway for me.

Would you be able to pinpoint how you would label or what you would consider your main contribution?

Hmm. I would say my main contribution is to bring postcolonial feminist thought, and poststructuralist feminist theory in general, to economic analysis, especially Marxian economics. That's what I would say. Awareness of the ways in which modernism and modernist assumptions have really shaped the field of development economics. The questions we ask, the metrics through which we imagine what it means to have progress; that awareness and thinking about how that has shaped economics' activity in the sense of how we theorise – that is what I have brought. Particularly as a third-world Marxist feminist project.

It's not that everybody who does this is Marxist – for example, my colleague and co-author Eiman [Zein-Elabdin] comes from the institutionalist tradition. I really come out of the Association for Economic and Social Analysis/Rethinking Marxism tradition, while Eiman really comes out of the institutionalist tradition. We met each other at Franklin & Marshall. It was my first tenure track; we were both hired at the same time out of the same search. And we were coming out of these two different – not opposing or hostile but just very different – traditions of economic thought. We were both asking questions about development and the nature of development as a project. Both of us were picking up on this as an extension of colonial thought at the same time, but also with some differences because of different ways in which postcolonial ideas get developed in African contexts compared to the way in which they get developed in South Asian contexts. But overall, I would say it's bringing postcolonial studies to heterodox economics, that's where my key contributions lie.

We have chosen to speak to you as we consider you a heterodox economist. Would you label yourself as a heterodox economist?

Yes, oh yes! I definitely would. I will say something about that though. I think it is so revealing when I talk to colleagues from outside the field.

After I finished my third-year review at Franklin & Marshall, I ended up feeling that I needed to be in a more interdisciplinary environment, and especially in a Women's/feminist studies context. Not that I didn't want to keep engaged with heterodox economics questions or publish in heterodox economic journals – I am still very active in economics. But I shifted my actual job into Women's Studies (now called Women, Gender, and Sexuality Studies), as I decided that that's what I wanted to do – to take up the questions of gender full time through this postcolonial lens. So, I went to the University of Hawaii Women Studies Department (that's where I earned my tenure), and now I'm in the School of Interdisciplinary Arts and Sciences, a completely non-divisionised School at the University of Washington, Bothell. We offer multiple degrees, but we don't belong to any one degree area or discipline; we collectively work across disciplines. It is so fascinating talking to colleagues here, who range from biology to performing arts. And I can see that as heterodox economists, it's odd that we (economics) are the only field in which, literally, there is an entire subfield that is defined purely as an Other.

That's all it is, right? It is that we are not orthodox. It has no self-content, other than that it is not orthodox. It's an umbrella term, and it reveals something about economics which is very disturbing, which should be disturbing. Economics is not the only field that has disputes, but if you take sociology, people actually have content for the dispute. Are you a Weberian, do you follow Durkheim, are you this, are you that? There's a naming of the perspective you use. Are you a materialist, are you an idealist? There are the continental philosophy folks … But no, no you can't have that type of discussion in the majority of economics. It's absurd. That's one thing that's very revealing.

But the other thing I've been really upset at is – I know that many heterodox economists, people who were my teachers and friends, paid a very severe price in their careers. Heterodox economics was something that was penalised; people were not hired, people were not published. And now you have mainstream economists that take up heterodox ideas as if they completely invented them themselves. With zero attribution, zero referencing. And these ideas are then represented, but the way they represent it is, they remove all questions of power from it. As far as I can tell, behavioural economics has many of the insights from Institutionalism, but without the issue of culture or power.

What do you think heterodox economics is?

I would say right now, it depends on how you define it. One way to think about it would be that heterodox economics takes power seriously. But that's just me really, because not all heterodox economics does so. Some of the Austrians are all about ensuring you never take power up as a concept, as far as I can tell.

It can be a fairly diverse set of ways of viewing power. So I would also include uncertainty here, as it is taken up in the work of some of the folks who do Marx-Keynes syntheses – including in my own work – I've also contributed to Post Keynesian economics, some work on the concept of stability of the consumption function where power is a central concept – issues of power also get taken up there. It can be the more overt concept of power which I don't find very compelling, or it could be a much more Althusserian or Foucauldian concept of power, which I find is a much more useful way of thinking about economic structure.

But then you get Austrians who don't touch power, or who insist that power does not exist in markets. So, I would say that I would *like* it if power were at the centre of what heterodox economics did. But, at this point, I do think heterodox economics is an umbrella term for people who are not orthodox, who are hoping to make the field understand that there are multiple ways of understanding the economy. Longer term I think it would be better for us if we were able to go back to that moment when schools of thought had names. Where instead of saying "heterodox" we would say this is what institutionalists claim, this is what Marxists argue … and, this is what neoclassical economics is. Instead of using orthodox and heterodox economics (or just economics and heterodox economics), I think Julie Nelson is right that we need to just call neoclassical economics "neoclassical economics", and then start calling other types of economics what they are. I think that's the way in which we need to go – because I think it actually matters that we learn that this is what's happening in Post Keynesian economics as distinct from what's happening in Marxist economics. Not because they're opposed, but because there's more than one way to put them together.

It's a disservice to the coming generations if we present economics the way it was often presented to me in my early days, as a field where everybody knows what the questions and approaches are. All you've got to do is to go out and apply the model; you've got to find your data set and apply the model because the model has been done for you, right? There's no more theorising to do. But as the world changes the theory has to change. The theory, the way you understand what's happening in the world, also changes. We can't present economics as a set of pregiven theories to folks who come after us; it's wrong that we would imagine that our thoughts are adequate to the needs of future generations. I think that's not true. I do think at some point we're going to have to not just teach it as heterodox, but teach it as this is what different schools of thought say, and be prepared to be the old farts who get displaced for having asked the wrong questions, right?

Do I understand correctly that you, because of your particular biography, stay clear of these inner economic repressions against heterodoxy?

I made my career outside economics, in terms of the bread and butter of it. I didn't end up in departments that cared whether I published in a mainstream journal or a heterodox journal. I was in Women's Studies; as long as it was a journal that was highly ranked relative to outlets for the audiences I wished to reach, they were fine with it. I didn't face that repression in a career sense personally once I shifted.

Of course, I faced other repressions, because it's not as if there aren't tensions elsewhere. Women's Studies had its own tensions and polarities. The nature of these polarities is also very interesting. Where people are interdisciplinary and breaking down divisions, there's normally lots of anxieties and ambivalences about how far you go. For example, is it an interdisciplinary project inside the social sciences, or does it extend to the humanities? Is it about method or is it about framework? There's all kinds of other things going on. Inside Women's Studies when I was coming through, there were huge fights about the status of the category "Woman" and fights about whether you were Women's Studies or Gender Studies and so on.

But it is different, the way this works out in economics when we have these fights. Not only as theoretical differences, but as efforts to remove people and entire ways of thinking from the field altogether. I knew that this was an issue because it took me a long time to land my first tenure track, and we were pretty much told that we were coming out "branded" as marginal because we were coming from UMass Amherst; I remember that very clearly. My very first tenure track was in economics and it was a very friendly department. I stayed there for three years; Eiman and I were there going through the tenure process together. But we were very aware, all of us, that we were marginal to the field. You would go to the American Economic Association [AEA]/ASSA meetings, and it was almost like you were a mini-conference inside the big conference. I would go to other panels by mainstream development scholars, but you were very aware that people who lived in the mainstream were never going to attend a panel, they were never going to attend an institutionalists' panel, and you knew who the heterodox economists were. At one memorable panel with Robert Pollack at the AEA, a friend and I were sitting in the audience. The issue was something about households and labour market behaviour. She asked a question about how his assumptions and model about decision-making did not hold for some case, based on her fieldwork. And he just looked puzzled and said, that was a nice point, but surely that belonged in anthropology and not economics? He said it very sweetly, but we were basically being told, even if what you are looking at is labour market behaviour and households, which is what my model is about, and even if you are possibly right, you don't belong in our profession.

I know many of my colleagues had a lot of difficulty especially in the '80s and '90s finding a space inside economics. I also know that when I was still a junior scholar I used to hear about the way in which senior scholars were treated and it was not very good. I still remember when Julie Nelson was denied tenure by Brandeis, after having already got tenure at UC-Davis, mind you, mainly for doing feminist economics. The problem was they did not see this as really economics; it was appalling. Of course, now she is widely respected and cited, which only reinforces my point. Then, I know that UMass itself was formed by people who were having difficulty in the places

76 *S. Charusheela*

where they were and that's why Sam Bowles and Steve Resnick and others ended up coming to UMass, because of the hostility from the rest of the field. If you were in UMass at that time, you knew that your professors were there because of the way they were treated elsewhere and that UMass had been formed for that reason. When you were in grad school you found out when you applied for jobs which places would accept heterodox economists and which would not. I think that was the US formation; I'd heard that it was not so divided in Europe. Fred Lee used to say that it was more open until there had been a proactive shift in the UK in the 1990s. But that it was far less divided until then. But I don't know if that's true.

What do you think are the problems of mainstream economics?

I talked a bit about the problem with the profession as a profession, sociologically. Let me talk about it in a theoretical sense. I think one of the main problems with mainstream economics is the way in which it understands two items, which create a deep, deep limit to our analysis. The first is the way in which mainstream economics understands subjectivity, the ways in which subjectivity is constituted. It's not just a question of rational economic man, it's not just a question of individualism, it's the deep modernism. It's a lack of awareness of this Eurocentric androcentric modernism, which informs this very specific way of theorising human behaviour, which is a problem. It's not just that they have the wrong assumptions; it's also that the very specific set of assumptions they have are not wrong in a random way; they're wrong in very systematic ways that prioritise the ways in which elite people interact with the economy. They reflect the experiences of the elite and so, for example, feminist economists have shown that the way in which rationality is theorised is one that excludes emotions, excludes connections in ways that render care work invisible. There's ways in which it's very systematically problematic, so that's one thing.

The second way in which it is problematic is it also makes the mistake of confusing the quantifiable or enumerative with the empirical. This might not be unique to economics, but this is a very particular problem if you want to pick up on feminist questions about the micro-dynamics of social interaction, or some of the more nuanced dynamics of power around, say, race. Only those looking at the aspects of the world that are capturable by numbers are understood as empirical, which is very bizarre. Nobody says that there is not a quantifiable element to the empirical world. But to assume that if it is not quantifiable, it is not empirical, that does not follow. Do you see what I mean?

This is actually not theorised, there's absolutely no philosophical debate about why this would be the case … but then you hear these strange, even now to me, very strange debates about qualitative versus quantitative. I don't understand that "versus", and it's likely because I live in an interdisciplinary department now. I remember the first time I mentioned this and the folks who looked at me in complete bafflement were actually not social science people, as they had heard this numerous times going to grad school. But the scientists, biologists, looked at me in complete shock: "We don't decide whether a species exists/existed depending on the number of specimens we get." Right?

The entire species may depend on the fact that you found one item in a fossil record. Classification doesn't work that way. There's nothing scientific about this debate; it's not even clear about the scientific status of observation, it's just taken for granted. Even in heterodox economics, we fall for that view very often; we don't clarify that being empirical is not the same thing as being quantifiable. Those are the two things that mainstream economics has done to the field; these two items have left their mark on economics as a whole.

Earlier you defined heterodox economists as those who take power seriously. Would you then say one of the problems of mainstream economists is that they do not adequately address power?

Yes, the reason I hesitated when I said heterodox economists are those who take power seriously is I should have clarified that while not all who are heterodox take power seriously, I think that those who take power seriously tend to be heterodox.

But not everybody who's heterodox takes power seriously. Because there is the Austrians; I don't know about them. If they count as heterodox, then I don't think power is the definer. But if you take power seriously you are probably heterodox economist, because mainstream economics is not very good at that. There's some formulations of mainstream that take power seriously with bargaining models, I suppose. But even there, most of the bargaining model stuff that takes power seriously, it depends on the way you put someone like A.K. Sen, I guess, and capabilities. I would tend to think of him as mainstream, but I have mainstream colleagues who think of him as heterodox, so what can I say? I'm definitely for a strong feminist framing to what he does. Maybe the difficulty lies in the way the term "heterodox" is simply those not in the mainstream (as opposed to based on the content of the actual school of thought), as I had noted before.

What are you trying to achieve as an economist?

Good Lord! I used to think that I was trying to achieve something as an economist. I know of late I've been spending a lot of time thinking about what I want to achieve. I was very ambitious. I had thought "yes, I wanted the R1 tenure track" and I went to Hawaii in Women's Studies since no economics R1 was going to hire me, and I ended up hanging out with political scientists and literature folks in Hawaii who were really amazing. My understanding of Foucault and the role of Foucault in theory comes from that experience, not from my time in economics. Then I knew I wanted to come to the [US] mainland because Colin, my husband, who is also an economist, is here. We met in grad school; he's also a heterodox economist. I came to University of Nevada, Las Vegas [UNLV], and then I was editor of *Rethinking Marxism*, since I wanted to have that presence. I was also active on the board of IAFFE. But in each case, the project mattered for itself, not just for the career.

But as I started realising that I was actually doing projects that mattered for themselves I began to wonder how much of it was about building economics as a profession and how much of it was about engaging the social world? I guess right now I don't know what I want to do as an economist. But I'm interested in learning – and I'm really bad at this; I don't know how to be a non-academic writer. I'm interested in learning how to do more non-academic writing to engage not some major national-level issues or anything like that but to basically be able to engage local communities in Seattle and bring back from Marxist economics in particular some of the popular engagement, public engagement work that we used to do. Something that was initiated by Philip Wohlstetter, someone who is in the City of Seattle. He's not an economist; he's a theatre person, a socialist. He created this event, Red May, and invited me to join, and it was amazing. We went into bars to talk about economic issues. We did this walk where we talked to people about commodity fetishism and alternate frameworks. So, there's a community engagement element that I want to do now, which somehow was missing in my plans of my career until this time.

Do you seek to influence society? If so, how?

Oh, definitely. I think a lot of the interest is through my students, to tell the truth, because the other thing is, I really want to think of my audiences as no longer just my other colleagues. It's easier now. I just became full professor, and I'm starting to feel that this constant idea that I would publish and the audience was other economists receded. Now, I think of my students, I teach MA and undergraduate students, and I'm thinking about how do I teach them so that I don't imagine that my purpose is to turn them into a version of myself. That the purpose is not to make sure that they all become economists, but just teach them so that they can use this for whatever they want to do. That turns out to be surprisingly hard. It turns out I've been spending too much time teaching people as if they were planning to go into economics grad school, which is not necessarily what they want. So, I've been trying to think of that. I'm working to modify courses to make them multidisciplinary. I'm working on trying to give students a chance to do some more community engaged type of work, and I'm trying to do this project on working in the community to do more popular economics teaching. That's where I am right now with that.

But to be honest, I also think it's because I don't see the state as something that one can touch easily in the US anymore, except at the local level. I'm not seeing national-level politics or policymaking as a location. If you see yourself being able to influence policy, you're going to do something very different. You're going to publish; you're going to be doing policy analysis. The move to teaching and the move to community engagement is because I really don't see that opening, at least for me and the kind of work I do. So this move, it's not all hopeful.

What are your strategies for seeking research funding, if that is a variable at all in your career or in your university?

I have none. I do small grants. I've never got big research funding, ever. I don't do the kind of work that … it's never been part of my career.

The units I've been in are places where funding is one of the many ways in which we give you credit for work. But it's not the only way. In my School, for example, there are people who get funding for their projects. That's fine because that's the kind of project they're doing, these big demographic public health projects. But then there's also people who get funding to go off and do art, because I'm in an interdisciplinary unit. The most recent funding I got was a small grant for this course. It's called COIL [Collaborative Online International Learning], so this is part of my efforts to change how I do my teaching. I am working on this collaboration with Ambedkar University Delhi's Centre for Development Practice, which is not an economics department. It's an interdisciplinary department. It includes sociology, it includes cultural studies, it's a very different kind of department. I did it because I realised my own students were encountering the developing world mainly as an object of investigation. But they weren't encountering as many people from the third world as intellectual equals. While the study abroad course model was about taking you there to see people as someone you helped, or someone you studied, with COIL they've got their classmates in Delhi. So they're suddenly talking to the people in Delhi as fellow students, and I wanted that shift. That's what I got funded most recently.

What do you enjoy most about teaching?

Oh boy! I don't know what I enjoy most about teaching. I know I enjoy it. I know what I don't enjoy about teaching: I hate grading with a passion. Really awful. It's not that I hate grading because I can't make comments; I like the engagement of comments. It's that moment when I have to put a number on it, or a grade on it, which irritates me. It's also because I find I can't do it fast, because I still don't know, I don't know how not to give lots of comments. I just don't. But I like it. I enjoy walking into the classroom, I enjoy choosing readings, I enjoy engaging. It's not just the students,

80 S. Charusheela

it's not just about seeing them learn something, it's that their passion and their excitement renews mine. They get excited, you get excited about something then they're excited about it too, and it feeds your excitement. You're always changing. You're changing what you're reading because they come up with new questions, they raise new issues. It becomes an opportunity. Nowadays the way which I figure out a new field or a new area is to try and design a course syllabus for it. When I was a student I used to learn about a new field by taking a class; now I teach. This is the way I figure out new areas. I sit down and think "okay. I'd like to figure this out", and I spend some time thinking of what I want to know about it. You can't do that at a grad level, but undergrad level you can definitely figure out, take up a topic and figure out how to teach it, and that helps you think about it. So, yes, I love it.

What do you seek to achieve in teaching? How do you put this into practice?

I used to be more ambitious about what I wanted to achieve in teaching, in terms of a grand leader. Touch their lives and change their minds, that kind of thing. I no longer think that. For one, it's a sort of patronising of my students and I've realised that a lot of that way of thinking about it was a way for me to feel secure about myself, grandiose myself. Now I think, share your views and doubts, and they will make their decisions. A lot of my goals have become contained to the classroom itself, or the class dynamics. A lot of the bigger things about what I wish to do with teaching are at the level of curriculum, and that has to do with what do I want to make sure is offered in a degree as a whole with colleagues. We want to make sure that they don't graduate without having at least one class where they do some kind of research, that kind of stuff. Outside of that big design the rest of my focus in what happens in my class-room, what do they take away from the course in terms of what it is I sought to teach them. Then out of in a given class, if they get that, I'm happy. What they do with it later – some of them want to do something more with it. And many of them do, and they come back and they take another class with you. Three, four students will end up working on their thesis with you, and that's great. But I no longer try to teach with the idea that I'm going to try and make an entire class believe X or transform Y. If I feel that it's really important for them to understand something about how feminist economics lets them understand gender dynamics in the household, then that's really the extent of my aim. At the end of the quarter, I would like to make sure that they understand that.

The notable economist Deirdre McCloskey referred to economics as poetry. What do you think about that?

I think she is right that it is like poetry. Given who I am and given the kind of work I do, definitely it's discursive. But we're terrible poets, aren't we? If this is about poetry, our genre of poetry is very limited. We don't seem to know very much beyond the narrowest type of modernist poetry. We probably need to expand our literary genres; we need to move beyond a very particular, narrow type of poetry, which comes from a very particular part of the world, to include say, *ghazal*, the poetic tradition that I love. To include freeform verse, but even more – to include genres like postcolonial novels and biographies. So, I think Deirdre is right to say that we should think of it as a literary genre; alas, I think that we need to expand that. Yes, that's what I feel.

6 Karma Ura

Karma Ura is the president of the Center for Bhutan Studies, where he has been since 1999. He also holds or has held positions at the Ministry of Planning, as Vice-Chairperson of the National Council (upper house), at the Chief Economist's Advisory Panel (South Asia Region) of the World Bank, and on the Board of the Royal Monetary Authority of Bhutan. He obtained an undergraduate degree from Magdalen College University of Oxford and Master's in Philosophy of Economics from the University of Edinburgh. His main research interest is in the development philosophy of Gross National Happiness. He is also an avid painter. Amongst his most significant publications are *Deities, Archers and Planners in the Era of Decentralization* (2004) and *The Unremembered Nation* (2018).

Karma Ura was interviewed by Sebastian Berger via phone online in June 2017.

How did you become an economist?

Let me tell you in three short parts: one is my education, up to university; then my professional work; and then my works which are outside of my formal work. At the time when we completed our high school in this country there was no university in Bhutan. Almost all who did well in the examinations were sent abroad for undergraduate studies. I was admitted in St. Stephen's College, the best college in India – incidentally not to study economics. For some reason unrelated to my choice, I landed in the history honours department, and I studied precolonial and colonial history of India, which was a very unusual discipline for me because Bhutan did not go through colonial depredations at all. While I was studying Indian history, I was awarded the Third World Scholarship at Magdalen College in Oxford, to read politics, philosophy, and economics [PPE]. I was the first Bhutanese to go to the University of Oxford. It was a very different place in a different community than the one I was used to. I come from a small, subsistence farming, high-altitude village in Bhutan. It is a pastoral village, so the place from which I emerged was very different. In finals in Oxford I read economics and philosophy, and then after that undergraduate degree I went to the

University of Edinburgh to read an MPhil degree in economics. Looking back, my exposure to history and philosophy gave me a broader interest, but my focus was all the time on development economics. Bhutan was intensifying modernisation at that time.

Both in Oxford and Edinburgh I was also trained in statistics. Statistics was seen as a very relevant subject in those days in Bhutan because it had just begun to gather data to build its national accounts and other data systems. For example, Bhutanese national accounts estimations first started in 1985, and the first Bhutanese demographic survey took place in 1983. Economic statistics was considered a very useful subject to create accurate knowledge of the country and to support planning its future. I returned to Bhutan in 1988 to work in the government. My first job for the first 11 years, from 1988 to 1999, was to support socio-economic development planning by being in the Ministry of Planning. While in the Ministry of Planning, I was part of the team that handled the making of two five-year plans: the seventh (1992–97) and the eighth (1997–2002). That organisation is still the cockpit for socio-economic development planning in Bhutan, though it is known by a different organisational name now.

In 1999 I moved to start a new organisation called Centre for Bhutan Studies and GNH – GNH stands for Gross National Happiness. It's a government-sponsored but autonomous or independent agency in a broader sense. It is the main think tank in Bhutan. So for the last 18 years my focus has been on giving a new twist to development economics in Bhutan, and that twist has been to insert the elements of GNH into policy and planning. A lot of what we do here – to the extent possible – is framed by GNH, in keeping with the development philosophy started by the Fourth King of Bhutan. So that has been one sort of life as a professional economist.

But there is a modest additional trajectory in my life, of devoting a large chunk of my time to designing murals, iconographic paintings, and art objects, and translating and writing about old Bhutanese Buddhist texts. For example, I and my team painted some 3,000 square feet of murals and designed the world's biggest golden butter lamp, all now installed in Dochula Druk Wangyal Temple. I have to a humble extent become engaged and enriched by arts and culture of Himalayan tradition.

Was there something else in the background, whether it's family or religion, or political events, or some current that precipitated you to do this line of science rather than something else? Were there other options that you did not choose for a specific reason, and why specifically this area?

My family background would not have taken me to any of these areas: I would have become a pastoralist and a householder, looking after cattle or yaks and farming. But due to the introduction of the free education system in

84 *Karma Ura*

this country, I managed to go up the educational hierarchy. It was simply due to a chance incident that I met a research fellow from Oxford University who was visiting St. Stephen's. He – a German of immense kindness – encouraged me to apply. He advised that philosophy and economics may be a very good combination for me when I come back to work in Bhutan. Having read Indian history for two years, I headed to Oxford to study yet another field to which I was unaccustomed.

Were there important figures, economists, supervisors, professors, who influenced you along the way, that made you choose that particular orientation within economics?

Yes. Within the undergraduate course I had two distinguished tutors at Magdalen College: John Enos and Keith Griffin. Both brought me up on economics. These were the two most important people who provoked, so to speak, my interest in development economics and led me further to continue at the postgraduate level. For Western philosophy, Ralph Walker generated a lasting curiosity in the subject, in addition to Buddhist philosophy, which is also my passion.

And was there any particular institution or funding that supported this transition into this particular area at the postgraduate level or later into the full-time economist position?

My undergraduate was done under Oxford University's Third World Scholarship. And my postgraduate degree was partially supported by the United Nations Development Program, to read statistics and economics in the University of Edinburgh.

Would you say that statistics, a quantitative approach, was something that was very important for your particular trajectory as an economist? For instance, if you had not gone into statistics, would it have been much more difficult to establish the same line of career?

A journey into the world of numbers is very important. It gives a grasp of all sorts of realities, to the extent those numbers can tell you. You have to be competent in statistics to view the underlying reality through them. It is a necessary skill, more so as digitisation generates a greater amount of data. The anchoring of your work in statistics is valuable up to a level, especially when dealing with data-demanding statistics peers. So a basic foundation in statistics was in hindsight very useful. But it is not sufficient because you reach the boundaries of numerically fascinated people quickly, even in the government. Far more important is being able to reach a general audience with a meaningful narrative that most can ponder and join. A narrative drives the urge of the policy makers and general audience.

How did you develop your particular contribution as a heterodox economist?

A particular concern of this country, that is GNH, predates my joining the civil service. So it was already a kind of background that we as officials had to assimilate. The concept and measurement of GNH is a contribution of the country rather than of any individual. Amongst the individuals if there is any, the most important one was the Fourth King of Bhutan, Jigme Singye Wangchuck, who had that original idea. I got into the civil service as part of a team who furthered empirical research, development of metrics, and policy formulation. Now you might ask why did the idea of GNH come up in Bhutan. The King made broadly people's happiness as the main objective of the government. How it is measured and how it is applied in policy and programmes is quite important. Most people misinterpret it as they assume, erroneously, that those applying happiness studies to policy might be compelling people to be happy, to be docile by indoctrinating them, which itself is a very strange idea.

But the Fourth King also drew from a broader background of Buddhism in this country. Of course, the idea of happiness as a key concern of government and individuals is not at all modern. Buddhism has been here for over 1,000 years, and in Buddhist understanding happiness is recognised as a very spontaneous or reflexive aspiration of all beings, whether animal or human. As long as they have consciousness they are assumed to spontaneously have this aspiration. So he was also refining this major idea that springs from Buddhism. And Bhutan's politics and economics is heavily influenced by Buddhism. We couldn't be otherwise. So that is the broader context. Now, of course, economic theory of the classical kind, or neoclassical kind, mainly deals with the human mind and human beings; and if happiness is the key concern of all beings that have consciousness, we have to deal with it. So that is the background.

How did this project get situated, or how were you able to situate it in the academic environment of journal publications and book publishers? Was this easy in terms of developing your own particular orientation?

I think we were lucky to be living after the 1960s. As you know, 1960s is the beginning of heterodox economics, and we find that after that period there is an emergence and flowing of many new things. Broadly I surmise that it has to do with us being at a remove from wars that went on, such as the Second World War, and wars of struggles against colonialism and wars as the so-called Cold War. Putting aside these preoccupations created space for a beginning of a new kind of collective consciousness all around the world, which was not excessively focused on domination, industrialisation, and

86 *Karma Ura*

materialism as the route to living well and meaningfully. That is the general background, and against that background you would have noticed all 'round the world that there was a sort of flowering of different ideas, of peace and happiness, of freedom and rights, and many other alternative and multiple perspectives. You can trace back to that period also the rise of engagement with psychology, with alternative medicine, and with alternative economics including the very early hints of behavioural economics and so forth.

So I would say that interest in happiness on a wider scale than before belongs to this stream of collective awakening, which is unusual. It was a beginning; and being at the beginning to strike a new path is always a struggle. But if you see this as a very important issue, you have to just soldier on and expect some kind of broader impact – and it did have that broader impact: writings on happiness and well-being began to grow out of it; research institutions across the world began to kind of respond to a collective urge. Now we are in a period where internationally, multilaterally (e.g., UN bodies), and academically there is some acknowledgement of the field of happiness and well-being as important. But it has to widen and deepen quite a lot.

We have chosen you because we think you are a leading heterodox economist: do you consider yourself a heterodox economist?

I should say that this distinction that you have drawn sharply into heterodox and orthodox economists can be much clearer in the academic world and in theoretical fields of economics, but far less so in the real world of decision-making. But even in the academe, the discourse of economics, as you know, has been enriched by the contribution of heterodox economists. So even without being explicitly acknowledged by orthodox economics, they are influenced subconsciously or consciously by heterodox economics. Once you detect that people are being influenced at a subconscious level, you have made some mark. Now in a concrete sense, as you know, the heterodox theories have been recognised as very useful, and many official institutions take that on board. We can notice that the phenomena of social cost and its theory, which is a contribution from heterodox economics, has been taken on board by many governments at a country level, at a bilateral level, and at a multilateral level. That is a very important contribution. In the real world, the world that I live in, or the world other economists who are working in the government live in, we are, by the scope of work, heterodox economists. Why are we like that? Because we have to always work in the intersection of politics, institutions that contain normative directives and values, and with reality, which is far more complex than the world represented by any models in neoclassical economics. So if you ask an economist who is functioning in the government, by practice they are likely to be heterodox, always. In the academic world they could be a bit more of a purist.

Now, coming back to Bhutan, a person like me, who is an economist of a sort, we are forced to be heterodox, because the emphasis of the government of Bhutan is on the goal of being an ecological-welfarist-happiness-oriented society. These are the established goals: that Bhutan would like to be welfarist, it would like to be ecological, and it would like to be oriented towards happiness. So now on all of these major triple concerns of the government of Bhutan, neoclassical economics offer limited insights. Due to its welfarist orientation, a remarkable range of fundamental goods are on free provision. Due to its ecological goals, Bhutan has added 20% of forest cover in the last 27 years, now standing at 82% forest cover. But, of course, economic discourse in Bhutan is by no means entirely confined or limited to heterodox economics. Because there are educational institutions that teach orthodox economics, and there are global economic institutions that fundamentally draw inspiration from orthodox economics, people come out of both of these institutions with certain entrenched ideas. Major educational institutions and major global institutions are primarily Anglo-Saxon or are shaped by the Anglo-Saxon world view. That being the case, people who come out of these kinds of institutions are likely to spew forth a neoclassical, neoliberal perspective of the world. So when we come across such people, then we get into sparring with them. The dialogue with them is sometimes conflictual and sometimes helpful. But my main point, in sum, is that an economist who is functioning in the real world is heterodox by virtue of being in the real world. So, I would consider myself a heterodox economist with, however, being informed broadly by both types of economics. And I think that can make a heterodox economist more effective. I think you can be a superior heterodox economist if you are also at the same time fully informed about the other one.

What do you think heterodox economics is?

I think heterodox economics is a constructive challenge to mainstream economics; and it has posed that challenge since the 1960s. And heterodox economics is a challenge at the same time to the epistemic hegemony of the economic knowledge centred in Anglo-Saxon mainstream institutions. So it's not only a challenge to mainstream economics, but a challenge to the institutions which are embodying that mainstream economics. As you know very well, there's a major humanitarian issue at stake at the moment. Heterodox economics claims that the existing economy based on the idea of the free market does not stand adequately for what the economy should stand for, for human beings let alone other sentient beings. The other major thrust of heterodox economics is that it does not accept the fact that the market as described by neoclassical economics is self-adjusting by converging towards equilibrium. It is not only not self-adjusting but, more seriously, it is not just, from the point of view of heterodox economics. Thus, it has mounted an intellectual challenge to the neoclassical view of automaticity of an adjusting system as well as a philosophical challenge to the view that the societies can be just within the kind of economic system based on orthodox economics.

What are the problems with mainstream economics, the main problems you see with mainstream economics?

Yeah, I think there are three sets of problems, some of which are very well known in the media now. The first one, adding to what I just said, is the searching question of economic stagnation and inequality. These combined problems have attracted criticism to neoclassical economics, because they are rather big in scale, and there is no satisfying diagnosis or prediction of the future according to neoclassical economics. They are practical problems that the theory has not been able to adequately explain how they could emerge and how they will be resolved. The second problem, which has also been stated amply in literature, is the problem of neoclassical economics conjuring up universalistic assumptions and being very obsessive with formulations in terms of mathematical models. Such models come with a heavy baggage of blinding assumptions concerning rationality and set preferences of agents, methodological individualism, institutions, markets, and technology. But from my point of view there is a third set of problems. Neoclassical economics does not provide adequate ways for the evaluation of well-being and happiness on the one hand and ecological sustainability on the other. Neoclassical economics makes attempts to explain and evaluate a lot on the human–market relationship. One facet of this is the interplay of macroeconomic variables and human beings as economic agents, to which it devotes a great deal of itself. But the other key relationships are really human–nature relationships, human–community relationships, and mind–body relationships. Expanding understandings of happiness have to address all of these intersecting four relationships: human–market relationship, human–nature relationship, human–community relationship, and human–mind relationship.

One could also add that human–time relationship is a crucial aspect of happiness. From the GNH point of view, we endeavour to understand all of these relationships, as they are more important than any variables by themselves, standing alone. Thus GNH surveys and research encompasses the domains of GNH such as community vitality, psychological well-being, time use, culture, good governance, ecology, education, health, and living standards. On the whole, neoclassical economics has less to say on these than heterodox economics. If economics is to deal with larger question of welfare and well-being, it seems fairly imperative that it must explore all these points I mentioned, which lies beyond the human–market relationship.

What are you trying to achieve as an economist?

As an economist, at one level, our team's work consists of keeping track and analysing dynamics of various data sets, such as sectoral growth, productivity, labour, inflation, employment, migration, finance, banking, consumption, investment, and so forth. These are standard macroeconomic data that can be analysed to make sense of social and economic progress. At the same time, from the point of view of GNH, as heterodox economists, we can reveal the blind spots of GDP and its associated indicators, which are heavily used in standard macroeconomic management. But more interestingly, we collect an entirely distinctive set of information, which can illuminate the happiness and well-being of the Bhutanese population, by conducting regular surveys. This helps us to delve into the happiness and well-being of the Bhutanese population. There is mutual interaction between economic change on one side and well-being and happiness on the other, and so we have to study both in their mutuality.

We take the view that well-being and happiness emerges from various sources: what we call domains of one's life, or domains of GNH. Some sources of happiness are influenced by money and economy. Some factors that influence happiness are not correlated with money and economy. Understanding to what degree monetary and non-monetary factors independently influence happiness leads us to different kinds of policies and programmes. So that inspires us to study psychological, communal, social, and ecological factors, broadening beyond such factors as health, income, and educational factors. After the findings from the distinctive set of GNH data are established, we offer a dialogue with policymakers and the population in general. Government can do some things towards happiness, others by communities. A lot also depends on individuals' effort. We have to touch many strings to produce a melody. So that's what I am trying to do as an economist.

Would you then say that part of your goal as an economist has something to do with helping society, improving society, trying to accomplish a social vision? Is that something that you're trying to achieve as well?

We are trying to find and forge a path where individuals can be happy. But relying completely on the individuals to work that out while the systems we build are adverse would be some kind of perverse methodological individualism. We have to take a higher and broader perspective. What kinds of ecosystem promote individuals to be happy? What sort of ecosystem of education and health services, community and governance, ecology and culture, is best for human beings to live well and feel well most of the time? So it's a question of creating and sustaining institutions and settings for happiness, and that is what we are trying to achieve. That's what we are seeking, through various means, by influencing the society.

Do you seek to influence society? If so, how?

Yes, almost all of us are trying to influence something or other. There is hardly anybody who is not doing that implicitly or explicitly, I suppose. But it becomes a little more prominent in some jobs rather than others. I have felt that there are two overall issues in trying to influence a society: one is direction; one is speed. Overall, I think direction is far more important than speed. To sustain a direction of the journey of society, we have tried to engage on three planes. One is that we can appeal to society through the media, in the broad sense of the term – entailing publications, audio-visuals, conferences, et cetera. We have to always take into account the operation of the media nowadays. However, the media is very cacophonous, heterogeneous, and sometimes inconsistent over time: at best they are a plural force, but we have to keep on engaging with them.

The second thing we do in order to influence society is to appeal to the public through the channel of policies and programmes by involving bureaucracy and legislature. I think if we succeed to do it through them then it is a little more consistent, and systematic, rather than depending on the vagaries of the media. So, we work through the state planning organs, from the planning ministry, right up to the cabinet level. We work together. When you work with bureaucracy, it always depends on something like standard operating procedures of the bureaucracy – working norms, managerial tools, and rules and regulations, decision-making criterion, et cetera – so it's very important to offer such management tools on a proactive basis to the bureaucracy: then irrespective of the belief of the individuals in a bureaucracy, things will move on, because you have developed standard operating procedures to be applied at various levels of bureaucracy.

The third way of appealing to society is through the education system: that is to say, schools up to the universities and also think tanks. That is very important to exert sustained influence on a longer-term range and a larger scale. But, all of these ways of appealing to society I mentioned – through the media, through the bureaucracy, through the education system – are underpinned by some of us taking seriously the role of intellectual workers, who try to shift things in society in an incrementally right direction. So that's what we are doing.

What are your strategies for seeking research funding?

On research funding we have been very fortunate actually. Yes, finding funding is an ongoing struggle, but we would not be here if we had not had generous benefactors. There is a general climate in the world to support this kind of well-being research, partly I think for intrinsic reasons – for happiness and well-being is intrinsically good, to be promoted. But a favourable climate has come about partly to search for an alternative route to happy but ecologically non-degrading existence. The question is: Is there a way to peaceful, tranquil, and satisfied existence, without running down the ecology as we have done dangerously? So people are interested in finding a way of making human beings happier without so much scope for consumption, which leads to production, and ever-increasing production leads to escalation of ecological degradation. Research into well-being and happiness are progressing at many levels: neurobiological, psychological, and behavioural. In the journey of GNH, we have been able to mobilise an astonishing amount of international research funding. Our research funding needs are of two types: one is to finance a regular large-scale survey, sampling 8,000 respondents in this country of about 700,000 people. It's a very big sample with a long interview. Each interview lasts about two hours face to face. The second funding need is dissemination, which includes publication and conferences. In the past we have been able to get support from the government of Canada through the International Development Research Centre [IDRC] and the Canadian International Development Agency [CIDA], the government of Thailand, the government of Japan, the government of Brazil, the United Nations Development Program, and many other agencies. We also receive generous funding from the Royal Government of Bhutan, who, using the findings of the Gross National Happiness, want to improve policies and programmes. After all, the ultimate aim of the GNH survey and research is to really find out why people are unhappy. And what can the government do? The sources or the causes of unhappiness may be very diverse: psychological, communal, social, genetic, environmental, health, educational, and economic. Identification and delineation of causes is obviously important to tackle unhappiness, so that's why they fund it. Solutions can come in two or three ways: one is solutions may arise from the government actions, because government makes a lot of policies and legislations, and if the legislations and policies are not favourable to the individual's strivings of happiness, individuals cannot succeed. The second level of action can come from the local government and community organisations. And the last one is from the individuals themselves. In the light of information and knowledge, they can change their behaviours and habits quite a lot towards happiness.

What do you enjoy most about teaching?

I do not teach in the accepted sense of the term, but I give a lot of talks in executive trainings, universities, and international forums. It is quite frequent for me to do talks. What is teaching? Teaching is a concentrated delivery of knowledge in a scheduled time between the lecturer and the audience. What I find taxing for myself is preparing the visuals that will go with the acoustics of talk. And here I take the opportunity of being an artist rather than an economist. During preparation of visuals I take the view that an image that burns into human memory is far more effective than exhaustive monologues of lecture. I focus on the tone of colours, design of powerful imageries that will come in a PowerPoint. It always makes people shift their view as they do after watching a great film or documentary.

And what do you enjoy most about it?

Well, in my type of talks, apart from longer-term influence, we endeavour to educate people while being entertained for one hour. That's a very important emphasis! Can you imagine a lecture on happiness being boring? That

92 *Karma Ura*

is anti-happiness. So, the method and the moment itself have to be a pleasing experience to the audience. Of course, you wish to achieve a little beyond this: shifting their perspective and shifting their paradigm. Being able to achieve that is gratifying for both sides.

What do you seek to achieve in teaching, and how do you put this into practice?

We – all those who are engaged in public communication, teachers included – must be guided and abide by some norms, some purpose every time, that underpins morally the communication. In that regard I like to cite Lord Buddha: he set down probably the first criteria of public speaking. He said that you must speak only what is true, what is factual, what is beneficial, and what is timely. And it is said that the Realised One, Lord Buddha, did not speak what was untrue, what was unfactual, what was unbeneficial, and what was untimely – he kept quiet! What is true, what is beneficial, what is timely, and what is factual are very unsurpassable criteria.

Deirdre McCloskey, a notable US economist, referred to economics as poetry. What do you think about this?

I'm a bit puzzled by this; I'm a bit intrigued by it, because economics as poetry can be understood in multiple ways. Economics is part of humanities rather than physical science. Perhaps McCloskey is saying that economics is closer to poetry than to physical science by measurement of their distance from each other. She might be saying that just as poetry deals with human feelings, emotions, and experiences rather than machines and mechanics of physical sciences, economics is a bit like poetry. She might be also saying – and she *has* said that – that we have to use the tools of poetry and literature in order to further economics, to tell a very good story, to have a grand narrative of something or the other, while writing economics.

But what came to my mind when I read this question was William Wordsworth's definition of poetry, and his definition was that poetry is an intense experience of a sensory kind, which is afterwards recollected emotion in tranquillity. If you apply this definition, something is missing in McCloskey's argument. I do not think economists have such kind of powerful sensory experiences. Indeed they're mostly dealing with abstract things and data, you know! So whether they have this kind of direct feeling of sensory experiences rather than intellectual vibrancy is a question that needs attending. But economists as communicators do fulfil the second part of William Wordsworth's aim of poetry: he said that the aim of poetry should be to change a reader's mind by presenting interesting imageries and unforgettable metaphors – what he called certain colouring of imagination. In that sense a good economist who is very literary, who resorts to all the tools and techniques of literature and poetry, may be able to move people more to his side; his or her persuasion power might be higher in an economist who is aware of this sort of thing.

Since you referred to McCloskey, I should add something as an opportunity arises. She wrote an article called "Happyism: The Creepy Science of Pleasure" in 2012, in *The New Republic*, with her overall critique of subjective well-being and its measurement of happiness in interval scales from 0 to 10. In that lively article, she mentioned Bhutan as part of her overall critique. And her criticism was levelled repeatedly at something that she derisively called 1-2-3 studies of happiness: hedonism of 1-2-3 and 1-2-3 happiness. She was referring to the Likert scale used in subjective happiness studies to measure happiness, and then trying to calculate non-interval points from interval questions. She called it "boyish games" – I think she was quite acerbic in that article. She mentioned Bhutan in a fleeting way. But the overall thing was to club us together with the subjective well-being people. That was unfair. She and others who are interested in our concept and measurement of GNH might read our latest book [Centre for Bhutan Studies & GNH Research] on the 2015 GNH Survey that is available full text online on www.grossnationalhappiness.com. I just wanted to say that our concept and measurement in GNH – if she happens to read our reports she will know – does not have anything she has presupposed in her criticism. She criticised subjective well-being measurement that is prevalent mainly in the West. She praised the eudemonic concept of happiness, in which the capabilities of people and income which gives scope for people to flourish. As she praised that; and if she reads our reports on GNH, GNH values much of what she proposed.

7   Rolf Steppacher

Born in 1944, Rolf Steppacher studied economics at the University of Basel, where he obtained his PhD in 1972. From 1967 to 1971 and 1973 to 1975, he was the teaching and research assistant of Professor K. William Kapp, interrupted by research work at the Gokhale Institute of Politics and Economics in Poona and fieldwork in Kerala, India. From 1976 until his retirement in 2010, he served as senior lecturer at the University Institute of Development Studies in Geneva (now Graduate Institute of International and Development Studies). Besides this long-term position, he most of the time held complementary teaching appointments, such as at University of Bern (Ethnology, Geography, Environmental studies), University of Zürich (Ethnology, Geography, Environmental studies), ETH-Zürich (Human Ecology, NADEL), University of Basel (Environmental Studies), University of Fort Hare, South Africa (Agricultural Economics, Development Studies), and the Institute of Interdisciplinary Research in Klagenfurt. Amongst his most significant publications are the revised and extended version of his PhD dissertation entitled "Surplus, Kapitalbildung und wirtschaftliche Entwicklung – Zur Relevanz der Physiokratie und der institutionellen Ökonomie für das Problem der Kapitalbildung in unterentwickelten Ländern" (1976); his book chapters on the Keralese health paradox (1989), the relevance of K. William Kapp's economics (1996), and the issue of property, resources, and sustainable development (2008), and his publications with J.F. Gerber ("Some Fundamentals of Integral Economics", 2014 and "Basic Principles of Possession-Based Economies", 2017).

Rolf Steppacher was interviewed by Sebastian Berger in Abingdon, UK, in March 2017.

How did you become an economist?

This is both easy to answer and also not very easy. I went to a trade school, becoming acquainted with some basic economics already there. I found the subject interesting enough to continue, although I did not know then about alternative approaches to economics. The decision to enrol in economics at university resulted from my preferring it over other subjects, such as accounting and technical skills, which I found relatively boring. Another factor was my interest in exploring how society and economy actually function.

Did your family background play a role in this decision?

My father was a motor mechanic, and we were working class. Since we had such a limited horizon I had almost no background in liberal arts and humanities. My upbringing was very religious, actually sectarian. Since that way of thinking was narrow-minded, I was unaware of a broader array of options for my university studies.

Were there influences early on in university that furthered your interest?

When I began my studies at university in 1962, mindsets were still conventional although not narrow-minded in a neoclassical sense, and not so dogmatic that I would be turned off by academia. Fortunately, there was an almost universal expansion of awareness in the mid-'60s, from which I drew benefit.

How did you make the decision to do a PhD dissertation?

Firstly, this had to do with the fact that K. William Kapp became a professor at the University of Basel. Secondly, a young economist by the name of Jacques Stohler was present who integrated politics and economics – sadly, he died very young. Kapp introduced me to new "dimensions" because he reinterpreted the history of economic thought in a radically different way from what I had learned previously. This was interesting to me as I saw that interpretations obviously depend on paradigms, and there can be very different understandings of what is real. This was the first time I understood that. I felt then I had to study epistemology, which Kapp taught as well, so I understood that theory is context-dependent and value-laden. Kapp interpreted the history of economic thought as development theory. This meant that neo-classical economists could mostly be ignored, because they say nothing substantial about development. Their attitude was unlike previous schools, and other authors, such as the Physiocrats, classical and Marxist economics, Thorstein Veblen, and Institutional Economics. At the same time I was interested in developing countries, other cultures, particularly in understanding their differences from my own experiences in Switzerland. This is why I also participated in lectures in ethnology, understanding why there cannot be a universal economic theory applicable to all cultures. This was just the start as Kapp went much further by introducing Institutional Economics and ecological questions. This is how I moved from studying development economics to ecology, and beyond, such as the concept of what it means to be a human being, this being part of a broader agenda of philosophical and psychological questions.

So was Kapp a formative and decisive factor in your studies?

Yes. I became his assistant and I taught his tutorials on developing economies and also the history of economic thought. I developed these two fields into a topic for my PhD thesis by asking which theories from the history of economic thought were most relevant for the specific contexts of developing countries. This is why I chose the Physiocrats: they focused on agrarian questions and institutional economics, understanding how economic processes are influenced by the variety of different cultural contexts.

How did you decide to become an academic economist working in academia?

To explain this I must expand a bit. I was already in academia, twice as Kapp's assistant, the second time following my research in India, so this was a natural continuation. My commitment to academia was in the early stages endorsed by the enormous pleasure of participating as Kapp's assistant within a group of fine academic lines open to the exploration of new forms of integration within economics. Working under Kapp, the research seminars were a joy blessed by good relationships and a shared sense of new orientation. The tragedy was that this could not continue since three of these men died within three years. To the final years of my career some of this pleasure returned, working with Jacques Grinevald and our assistants and research group at the IUED [Institut Universitaire d'Études Developpement] in Geneva on global ecology and sustainable development. There my own fragmented academic life finally came together as a whole. This was an enormous relief that I saw as a gift.

In order to understand my progress towards an alternative perspective on economics, my unhappy and unusual experience with my PhD needs to be understood. The chosen co-supervisor of my thesis committed suicide, and the neo-classical substitute for him unfortunately had no understanding of the multiple issues of developing countries. Alas, it was he who criticised my research. Whilst Kapp wanted to give me the top mark (summa cum laude), this particular neo-classical economist gave me only an average mark. Fortunately the study of economics was still in the faculty of philosophy and social sciences. Its Dean was a world-renowned Egyptologist who had read my thesis, finding it very interesting and relevant. He rejected the mark given by the neoclassical economist, arguing that his critique was not based on the substance of my work but was instead driven by his more conventional approach to the subject.

This meant the neo-classical economist had to increase the mark. But this raised problems for me. I could not understand why he had not understood the value of my work, even from his different point of view. With no obligation to do this, but losing confidence in my own approach, I started to rework my research so that from both perspectives my work could be understood. I did not want to polarise the issue, but in practice, I actually wrote the content for a quite separate book, which could have become my professional "Habilitation" rather than an amended version of my doctoral thesis. This unfortunately meant that I lost a lot of time. Only then did I realise that it makes no sense to try to convince somebody who is following a different paradigm and perhaps does not want to understand. For example, I had taken well-reasoned arguments out of my thesis which I later discovered in one of Nicholas Georgescu-Roegen's books. This taught me that one must not accommodate ideological and unreasonable criticism if it makes no sense. During this unfortunate process, Kapp died, shortly after I was editing a volume in honour of his retirement. This mental trauma meant that I lost Kapp as the main supervisor for my Habilitation. The Research Council of Switzerland had already assigned me a second supervisor, now at the Institute of Development Studies in Geneva. This was Roy Preiswerk, a man with sympathy to my approach, who also died during the writing of my required Habilitation work. Confronted with two more deaths in my life, I was unable to complete my Habilitation, which was a disaster for me, since this was at that time a requirement of German-speaking universities. Not having the required Habilitation, I stayed at the French-speaking Institute of Development Studies, the only one in Switzerland, having then to speak French at an academic level, now being blocked from access to a career in a German-speaking university where the Habilitation is required.

More emotional shocks followed, as in finding some of the academic books by Kapp thrown to the floor by colleagues. What was I to do as everyone who understood what I was working on had died within a short period of time, and worse, my work was rejected by some of the other academics at the Geneva Institute. This experience of rejection was dramatic. But the rejection, in retrospect, was a dark gift. It meant that my teaching gave me access to students from all over the world, seeding in them the new paradigm of an integrated economics. My new approach combining Institutional and Ecological Economics was what most of the students wanted at a time when in Europe there were not yet organisations defending these paradigms.

Were there any alternative career options that you considered?

No. But it was clear to me that just economics, narrowly defined, was not enough for my life. This is why I had to develop this theme in different directions, integrating Ecological Economics, Institutional Economics, depth psychology, and ethnology.

Please tell us how you developed your particular individual contribution.

The deepening of my understanding of Ecological Economics and ethnological knowledge, which I wanted to integrate with economics, was inspired by Kapp. Based upon the whole history of economic thought, my source material included a wide range of institutional material drawn from Thorstein Veblen, Gunnar Myrdal, and others, also including a wide range of ecological sources such as Nicholas Georgescu-Roegen. All this material I developed into courses on economic development, the development in the history of economic thought, the foundations of Institutional and Ecological Economics, and also eco-development. This was the search for development alternatives based upon the value premises of the satisfaction of basic needs, self-reliance, and sustainability. I also developed critical courses on agricultural development.

I was motivated to explore still further, wanting to know why the impact of knowledge communicated is so limited. That is why I studied depth psychology, giving me an understanding of blockages that are barriers to original thinking and clearly causing irrationalities. I also thought there must also be issues of consciousness here.

Could you point to a specific publication that reflects your core contribution?

The second and published version of my thesis had already anticipated much of my orientation. Two integrative articles are "Property, Mineral Resources and Sustainable Development" (2008) and "Some Fundamentals of Integral Economics" (with J.F. Gerber, 2014).

Would you say that your work for the Kapp Foundation, the Kapp archive, and involvement in awarding Kapp Prizes was a major contribution to economic studies?

It was simply one amongst others. For me it was nevertheless in the beginning sometimes difficult because Kapp had died too early, before I was ready to continue his work. I first had to go further than him in ecological questions based on Nicholas Georgescu-Roegen, and also doing the inner work of depth psychology. It took a long time to integrate these newer elements with Kapp's insights so that I could teach all of that in an integrated fashion. When I worked on Institutional Economics there were neither Associations for Evolutionary nor Ecological Economics. It was for some time difficult to develop this alone, under pressures, and without much support.

Was the integration of depth psychology your main contribution?

It was one important contribution in my teaching. Decisive was my acquaintance with Fred Blum who introduced me to depth psychology, which I further developed with Katherine Tetlow, an English mentor. Yet, like in other new domains, I published too little. Given my experiences I was afraid and therefore blocked to write much about it due to my own unhappy record of publications and the situation at the Institute. I also never published my research on Bali.

Now in retirement, looking back on my career, I know that my best work was in the content and style of my teaching. I communicated well, mostly with a wide variety of postgraduate students, coming from many different cultural contexts and disciplines too.

I hope that I have seeded alternative possibilities which are more expansive and even more vital than the ideas of past generations, especially the conventional wisdom of those more recently teaching neo-classical and even heterodox economics. I believe that we are all living in an age of transience between old forms and new ones which will emerge more fully in the years to come. It is often true that progress moves two steps forward to every one step backwards. Sometimes the pace is even slower, going just one step forwards but two in regression. Paradoxically, time appears to be speeding up since the changes made in the past 50 years of my life are enormous and widespread, not always for the better. The issue of there being different levels of consciousness actualised in human beings will no longer go away. A better understanding of how different lenses of perception affect group dynamics, and how these gaps function within institutions, where gaps in awareness occur as different paradigms, can only help in understanding differences in the ways people perceive and act accordingly. Recognition that there is a "grid of consciousness" is a future reference point that could explain many conflicts.

I would like to have written more material, expressing more fully my alternative points of view that are admittedly only more expansive working truths. Sadly, this was not possible, not least because I was emotionally wounded by the ferocity of intellectual and emotional opposition that I experienced occasionally in Basel, and within the rigidity of a French-speaking academic institution. Too many good people of my acquaintance died too early, and this also was traumatic for me. Left without an academic mentor, I was naïve in sharing too many of my early writings with people who then published them under their own name without authorisation or acknowledgement that I was the source. My story might have been very different without those untimely deaths, but dark gifts sometimes bring surprising blessings. I hope that the next generation of students can build upon the layer that I and my allies have constructed, so that seeds sown generate new possibilities, perhaps not dreamed of, not only in Switzerland but also across the world. Ecology, cultural context, sustainability – newly defined, and an integrated approach are, I think, the key notes of my academic legacy.

We have chosen to speak to you as we consider you a heterodox economist. Would you label yourself as a heterodox economist?

This term has always been ambiguous for me as the word "heterodox" is not precise enough. Instead, I always used "alternative" economics, or economics within an ecological-social context. An integrated economics that incorporates the ecological, social, psychological, and universal questions was what I was looking for, but the term "heterodox" does not say enough about this. I do, however, understand myself as a critical economist, and thus, probably do fall under the definition of heterodox economics, meaning multi-resourced, in the eclectic meaning of that term.

What do you think heterodox economics is?

For me this term is a critical enquiry into economic reality and economic theory, seeing an economy as a consequence of ecological and social contexts that differ, whilst having universal rules that are generally applicable. The difficulty with heterodox economics is how to combine a few universal principles with the many culturally specific social conditions. For example, the economic process is entropic. But this means different things within the context of renewable and non-renewable resources. Also important is that economic decisions take place within institutional contexts. But this too is a weak statement because the context is so variable. It matters whether it takes place under the logic of private property or possession, a democratic or an authoritarian structure. This study has to be developed in detail, but the integration of economic questions within these relationships seems to me to be the real essence of heterodox economics which is not often applied.

Would you say that this is what heterodoxy should be or what it already is?

There are several versions of heterodox economics. I have said already that the essence seems to me that the economic questions have to be integrated into substantive ecological and institutional contexts. This is the main difference from mainstream economics which tries to apply its own perspective to ecological and institutional problems. Having a different paradigm without projecting my own mindset, I give priority to Ecological Economics over environmental economics.

Would you say the different heterodox approaches should coexist or be integrated?

Both are needed. Specialisation is necessary because one cannot work on everything, but this content should be integrated with the essential insights of other paradigms. It would be absurd to be ignorant of the other heterodox traditions where much work is being done. There are enough commonalities to justify a common term of heterodox economics. And, in addition, people are needed who work on this important new concern for integration. I think this second priority is what we should work on, rather than still further specialisation in each area.

What are the problems of mainstream economics?

The whole substantive content of neoclassical economics is mechanistic and impersonal. I would refer to the concept of humanity, which for the general public is unsatisfying on the level of realism, also to its overemphasis on the supposed universality of a capitalist framework. Both aspects are problematic. Furthermore, its naïvety regarding ecological problems and also its concept of society overlooks many other possibilities. The question of the unconscious is equally unsatisfying since many projections take place in the theory of consumption and on all other levels. These are the main limitations.

Are these all problems of lack of realism?

Yes, with regards to context, which mainstream economics mostly ignores. Those students who have studied in different cultures and developing countries do not understand why the neoclassical approach is at all significant for them. There is a problem of this selective perspective, which is ideologically driven. Unless it is admitted that neoclassical economics is not a God-given absolute, the core of the issue is not addressed. A simple example: we have for decades now increasing inequalities throughout the world but still ignore this in most of our economic discussions. This is not acceptable. Also bad news is the selection of indicators that we use to measure growth without this inequality. I recall those early discussions about how we can change the measurement of gross domestic product to account for social costs, and how to publish some new indicators. The continuous reduction of measurement to indicators that ignore what is central to many people is highly problematic.

Would you say that the cause of this neglect is an intellectual dishonesty? How deep is the problem?

It is an intellectual defence, probably unconscious, with which someone identifies, holding learned theories against reality, whilst not accepting certain clearer facts that would challenge their truth. Such a defence easily becomes an institutional lie. This can only be explained psychologically, specifically by depth psychology. There is a common intellectual defence mechanism, based largely upon fear, which shuts out reality. This survival technique has a personal investment in denying responsibility by maintaining the status quo against change. Such a mechanism is clearly advantageous to the ego but damaging to other classes, future generations, and many other countries in the world. It shuts down reality, obscuring those unpleasant things which threaten the security of internalised mindsets, by this means establishing an identity, even when that is not the true Self.

Would you say that the problem of neoclassical economics is a psychological one?

Not entirely; there are both social and depth-psychological factors. Support for the old paradigm might be a career decision because today you often only fulfil ambitions if you do not say those things which challenge the authority base of those holding academic power. Your career can easily become blocked if you do not subscribe to mainstream thinking.

Are you saying that this attachment to false truths could be also a psychological mechanism supporting the aspirational Self?

Yes, it has to do with an overidentification with the ego structure, having wealth in the sense of enrichment and social status, fearing to lose this by doing something deviant. Every serious critic of any system lives under this threat. It has always been like this. I do accept though that any new form must run the gauntlet of the old in order to prove its viability. This is the nature of organic durable changes.

Would you say in reverse that heterodox economists are structured differently as they can accept this threat?

Yes. They go into the risk, probably because they have an expansive "seeker" level of consciousness that tries to understand the need to take responsibility for our current conditions. We cannot easily change the status quo, but we can talk about the issues, raising some awkward questions, challenging conventional wisdom. These explorers do not close the system as the mainstream does. This is the fatal flaw of "boxed" thinking. A heterodox economist who works on these critical questions is always at risk of being ignored. One has to be ready to accept these risks, becoming someone who can deal with this without becoming the victim of institutionalised oppression.

What are you trying to achieve as an economist?

It was very important to me to influence people but not to indoctrinate them. I wanted to give students the chance to see things critically, giving them an understanding of how the economy works in ecological and social contexts and how our economic behaviour affects future generations. It was my intention always to make this as clear as possible so that one cannot become complacent, or plead ignorance, by ignoring these questions (as in the extreme case of President Donald Trump, who currently ignores everything). I wanted to create consciousness about these problems, not only for economists but also for more general public debate.

Raising consciousness, what is underlying this? Is there an underlying ontology or cosmology? What is behind this?

Essentially, I mean an understanding of creative options for alternative behaviour, which enriches people substantively. I hope that those dangers, such as ecological destruction, are being reduced, that we have political options to drive these changes so as to avoid running into foreseeable global problems. I do not simply want to improve the world. Raising consciousness does not mean necessarily to make people happy. It means to reduce illusions by an acceptance of deeper realities both in us and outside of us.

Is there a higher goal to this process?

I personally have a cosmology, seeing the soul life as an extension that we can develop further as an open process of expansion, supplying a bigger picture. I also see the dangers. I do not see that we have guarantees that we will solve these problems. The evolution of consciousness has not yet progressed that far. I would say that my work with Katherine Tetlow – although it is difficult to say with certainty – has nevertheless led me to understand that there is a divine reality and that humankind can choose to make a certain development towards it, from the basis of an integrated love, having also will and wisdom, and unifying all opposites. I have no clue how this looks, only that raising consciousness is one thing that we can do. Economics needs to make a contribution to this process of developing our consciousness, growing an understanding of ourselves, other human beings, and all sentient creatures, hence, the web of ecology through which all life is connected.

Would you say this fits into the Kapp-Wiechert tradition?

Yes. But what influenced me more was the work of Thorstein Veblen, Erich Fromm having the concept of man and psychology, and also Eugen Drewermann, who understands the power of mythology. That choice of persons could include all those who understand these inner processes of destructiveness, why institutional change does not occur, due to people lacking a commitment towards their own inner changes. This interests me, so that is what I continue to develop further. Without understanding inner processes and inner change, heterodox economists who get into power will risk acting just like mainstream economists as offenders. This is the classical offender-victim dynamic. We have to be able to hold the opposites and make them conscious, moving beyond polarities to find the new middle ground.

Would you then say there is a room or justification for neoclassical economics at all?

I see no real role for its continuation as "neo-classical economics" has not even understood the logic of private property, the money logic, and its difference to possession logic. Understanding this was the contribution of Heinsohn and Steiger, which is compatible with Veblen's insights. Neoclassical economics is too abstract and unrealistic, not being grounded in the everyday experience of those ordinary people who do not necessarily own property. The subject makes no real contribution except that markets can help to allocate resources and goods. It is already known that when all eco-social problems are solved this works well, but this is all it has to say, which is actually very little. The real cost of investment and future-oriented action, such as Goethe has shown in the Faustian bargain with Mephistopheles, is also not understood by them because they do not grasp the ambiguity in their thinking, which gives them two different masters to serve. This is a subject expanded by Hans Christoph Binswanger [*Money and Magic*, 1994].

Do you seek to influence society, and if so, how?

I consciously chose not to go into formal politics because as a social scientist I need to be free of such restrictions. As a citizen I vote, of course, in such a way that my vision for a society is well represented. I have participated in many podium discussions and have written many articles on policy issues. These have included "Does Agriculture Have a Sustainable Chance Within Switzerland?" [1999, in German] co-authored with Hans Bieri and Peter Moser. My main contribution and influence was, however, through teaching students and others. Some of these people now hold political office. I have been fortunate in teaching students from most developing countries, especially Africa, former French colonies, and Latin America. I do not know what kind of political influence they now have.

Do you see the Kapp Foundation as a way to influence society?

Yes, insofar as the Kapp Foundation has helped many students to develop their critical perspective. The Kapp Prizes have honoured research in both Institutional and Ecological Economics. We also created an archive of Kapp's work that is now kept at the University of Basel, and we re-edited and published many of his works.

Why did you not found a Kapp School?

I did succeed in securing the knowledge of Kapp and the Kapp archive so that it was not forgotten. I was teaching his work, integrating his insights, and I would like to have done more. I just was not ready after his death to accept all the invitations to speak about him that came from across the world. I personally made some publications concerning him in German, English, and French which are still available today. But I had to differentiate myself from Kapp. I could not simply repeat his work. Maybe I had not matured sufficiently in my thinking at such a young age. Having so little support left me feeling very isolated. I did honour Kapp's contribution, but it did not occur to me to found a Kapp school of thought. Even such a School as this ran the risk for me of becoming too tight a framework for my open mind. I chose to study other perspectives, different contributions and authors to arrive at my own interpretations – including the disciplines of other academic fields. This extended work prepared me to go further than Kapp on several questions. Please note that in Geneva there was no motivation to set up a Kapp School since it was an Institute of Development Studies. This some of my critics have not understood.

What are your strategies for seeking research funding?

In the beginning, research funding was not yet a problem. As a full-time assistant I earned enough to finance my doctoral dissertation. For my research at the Gokhale Institute of Politics and Economics in Poona I needed only a small stipend; my empirical research in Kerala was part of a development project where I earned a small salary. My Habilitation was financed by the Swiss National Research Fund. Unfortunately, since I had been unable to complete it, this funding was no longer accessible to me. For my research work on traditional agriculture in Bali, I just required the travel costs, otherwise self-financing. My research work on a sustainable Swiss Agricultural Policy together with Hans Bieri and Peter Moser was financed by SVIL [Swiss Association of Industry and Agriculture], an organisation working on the interaction of agriculture and industry. The Kapp Foundation contributed in the early years to a project on Institutional Economics. Otherwise I was earning money only through teaching.

Was there pressure from within the university to apply for money?

Yes, but only since the '90s. And it came for me as a surprise as before research was mainly publicly funded. My reaction to it was rather to expand teaching at different universities and departments than fundraising for the Institute. Time became finally a premium because I had so many teaching obligations. Part of it was also the setting up of a small private company called *eco-integrative* with two colleagues, with the aim of teaching personality development together with ecological foundations within corporate organisations. It turned out to become quite a lucrative and successful activity.

Were you ever tempted to change your research topic to obtain money? Did you have to sell your interest and truth for money?

I only noticed it once. It was when I gave seminars on personality development at Swiss banks as part of our newly founded consulting firm. I noticed then that I said all the things I believe in but not with the same insistence. The danger is that if you make good money somewhere, you don't argue quite so convincingly, becoming instead more cautious and moderate, perhaps to appease the client. At this occasion I noticed this tendency in myself, just as in others at the university. One has to be very careful and vigilant not to let oneself be bought. I never made concessions regarding content, but I did notice that I became more cautious in my style.

If it wasn't money at the time that threatened your pursuit of truth, was it politics?

Not by choice. I think that career ambitions are important to people, which can result in the subordination of truth to lies, but I held on to my integrity. I did lose part of my contract twice and had my hours reduced, but I never made any concessions to my premises. Luckily I immediately found alternative positions to pick up lost hours and pay. I think that everyone has to have enough faith that if one stands by one's convictions, something positive will work out. It is so important for self-respect to have trust in saying what we think and believe whilst at the same time dealing with any emotional issues emerging in the process. Heterodox economists have to work on themselves so that they are not dependent internally on maintaining the status quo for personal emotional reasons, often based upon fear and sometimes repressed anger. Otherwise they make situations worse, often creating the same double binds as in Faust's dilemma.

What do you enjoy most about teaching?

This is the best of all possible occupations. I love it because a good teacher can communicate what is important to us, and also to them, seeing young people's potential being mobilised and watching them develop. I have done this often. When someone came into a seminar wanting to do a conventional research project I invariably told them to select a topic that would expand awareness beyond their existing level of knowledge. Otherwise what is the point? Original thinking is surely to be encouraged.

What sort of philosophy or theory of human beings is behind this?

I think that all humans have potential qualities asking to become actualised. If they have an exploratory nature, young people may have had few options to develop latent potential within the conditioning of their home. It is our privilege to let such students develop under our guidance, so that which was previously unformed, if not actively suppressed, is mobilised within a supportive environment. This nurturing process of students is as important as their grades. If this awakening talent is mobilised, lots of creativity and novelty emerges, which is a beautiful experience. I find this to be the best aspect of teaching and certainly my own job satisfaction. I also like to have good content to my teaching, passing on credible views as working truths, which can be integrated into the questions of these young minds, integrated in a way that has a foundational substance for their future.

Would you say that a personal relationship with students develops here?

Yes, and this is interesting for both sides. We organised an open research seminar with Q&A where students could just come and ask any questions. This was very successful. Sadly this changed radically and was finally abandoned after the recent merger with the Institute for International Trade. Now under the Bologna system of points for modules taken, the students are required to get credits for attending seminars, forcing us to define learning goals and outcomes, formalising the process with constant assessment. This was the opposite of what our particular open-spaced seminar wanted to do, so it was dropped. The students wanted to attend, but without getting credits they could not register. Sadly, in my opinion, this introduction of credit accounting interrupted a creative process that was the space reserved for risk-taking and originality.

What do you seek to achieve in teaching?

I aimed to relate through lectures and seminars the topics that make possible a coherent world view. My intention was always to relate problems back to certain universal principles, thereby arriving at a coherent picture of the world with a picture of the archetypal human being that gives orientation to students. Look at an example from the course on global ecology and sustainable development. Principles of global ecology show easily many of the illusions held in economics and in social sciences. The confrontation with these illusions and the critique of conventional theories often produced some crisis in students until the reconstruction of alternative theories had re-established the possibility of a coherent ordering, which in retrospect the students found really interesting. Most of our students at the Geneva Institute had already a diploma and a Master's degree, so they were adults who had lots of previous education and experience. We could therefore develop advanced topics.

Quite different but also enjoyable was my experience at the ethnological seminary in Zurich where I taught students from freshman to final-year graduates. I noted that over the years of my own employment most of my students did not stay in academia, preferring to take jobs outside the university.

108   *Rolf Steppacher*

We can only surmise the reasons for this. I know some would say that current academia has become too pressurised, too mercantile, and in the case of neoclassical economics, too confined, without adequate return for energies expended.

How do you put this teaching aim into practice?

You are asking about my style. Before the lecture I always focused on the main points that I wanted to cover as the minimum substance. I spoke freely but always left a space for open discussion. These were lectures with 120 students. In the seminars students provided often astonishingly creative contributions based on combining our teaching with their specific theoretical or practical knowledge. It was often a great joy and also allowed me to constantly learn from my students.

Did you teach in a pluralist way or aim at delivering one single perspective?

My early experience that Kapp interpreted the history of economic thought in a completely different way from what I had learned previously helped me to understand the meaning of different paradigms, how value-laden they are and how limited all knowledge is. I consciously choose for that reason my last seminar before retirement once again on this subject. Pluralistic teaching seemed obvious to me. Pluralism can, however, be limited, confined to relativity with regard to mere opinions or illusions contradicted by certain fundamental truths, such as that the material economic process is entropic and not mechanistic. Where then are any absolutes? Can we offer our students anything more than the working truths of relativity, that another generation may scorn. This is the subject, of course, of much debate as an epistemological issue.

You emphasise creativity; should this be added as the essence of critical heterodox economics?

I think that if someone is creative, that person is also necessarily critical. Creativity wants to do something new, which presupposes a critical attitude towards what is. Offering a critique, meaning simply to criticise texts, or even people, in the form of judgements, is not so interesting. The ecological-development perspective in the 1970s is a good example of sound criticism, when professionals met and creatively thought about how a new alternative production system or health-care system could look. Later in the 1980s – given political reality – the critical approach towards neoclassical and neo-liberal approaches became again important in showing that such an analysis blocked creative alternatives. This important but rather limited process was not as interesting as a more radical one that could have developed creatively in searching for new ways.

Looking back at your aims for social impact, would you also include the ecological goals you mention now in teaching? Are these ecological values related to raising the level of consciousness which you stated as your main hope?

Yes, raising consciousness even within the student population allows new steps to be taken, which in ecology is very important, not least because of the pressure of time before even more destruction in nature is becoming irreversible. How can we live sustainably? This has been a major issue since the 1970s and the concept of eco-development. Now the meaning of sustainability has become an empty term and needs to be reworked, but at that time the ecological sustainability was a real project that had public interest and even commitment to changes in lifestyles. This was a legacy of the 1960s when the Space projects allowed us to see our Earth from the outside, valuing it more, and not wasting resources in unnecessary commercialism.

Which picture of society or ideal or values underlie your pedagogy?

This was made clear in my lectures on eco-development, focusing on sustainable fulfilment of basic needs, keeping development options open for future generations. Such content was not the destruction of the planet! Also important was the relations between countries, encouraging self-reliance after colonialism instead of globalisation by dominating units. The idea of interdependence behind the concept of humanity is that each person actualises who they are within the context of their relationships, which is not what they have been conditioned into as a false Self. This is the quest against unwarranted authority, towards the furtherance of the true Self that some people are ready to realise in this lifetime – if they are willing to pay the price, daring to escape from attachments to money and those other seductive structures on which they depend.

The notable economist McCloskey referred to economics as poetry. What do you think about that?

Poetry and art and economics offer different opportunities to actualise human potentials. Combining the study of them can result in useful experiences of creative expansion, or mere novelty. A good piece of art expresses human potential, mobilising unique perceptions in us that are variable for everyone, speaking to the nobility of differences in our personalities.

Real art does this. Good art speaks to human potential and furthers it. Economics and the economy have the capacity to project potential into the future via the property structure and the implementation of new projects and technologies. Creative initiatives, like artworks, can stimulate individuals so that they can live with greater risk, and fewer resources, potentially transforming their lives. In economics the effect is tied to a logic which actually reduces the amount of potential development because only the profitable options are mobilised. I repeat that this is a Faustian bargain. The study of economics opens potential gifts, but only those which are marketable and profitable. And that is dangerous. There are economic orientations which are destructive because they are against eco-social reasoning, furthering only profitable expansion for those who already have material wealth. That growth is limited to economic growth rather than human development. Economists can be artists if they offer potentials for further realisation, but mainstream economics limits this opportunity if only profitable potentials are actualised. Many mainstream economists only see art and the human being as a commodity, not engaging with it in a deep way. If they do engage they risk more than that, but such an activity is generally outside their economic mindset.

8 Julie Nelson

Julie Nelson is Professor of Economics at the University of Massachusetts, Boston, where she has been since 2008. She is also a senior research fellow with the Global Development and Environment Institute. Her prior workplaces include the United States Bureau of Labor Statistics and the University of California, Davis. She obtained her PhD in Economics from the University of Wisconsin, Madison. Her main research interests are gender and economics, philosophy and methodology of economics, Ecological Economics, and quantitative economics. Amongst her most significant publications are *Economics for Humans* (2018) and *Beyond Economic Man: Feminist Theory and Economics* (co-edited with Marianne Ferber, 1993).

Julie Nelson was interviewed by Sebastian Berger and Andrew Mearman via phone online in May 2017.

How did you become an economist?

Somewhat by accident. I was an undergraduate student and had no intention of studying economics. I was at a small liberal arts college in Minnesota that had a Lutheran church affiliation and a strong service orientation. But my impression of economics was that it was business, and business was about making money and greed, and I had no interest in economics. But, I needed to take a social science course and my adviser more or less frogmarched me over to the economics table – we signed up for everything at tables back in those days – and signed me up for an econ course. I'd wanted to do psychology but that was full so he got me signed into econ. And then, when I took my first course, I thought "well, gee, maybe this has something to do with poverty and how we could reduce poverty". At an undergraduate level there was enough there that let me continue to think this might be a useful thing to do. So I stayed in and majored.

And then you got in touch with poverty. Was that a particular class or module you took at your university on poverty?

I don't know. There was not a particular module. I'd been aware of poverty, of course, before, and we did have some sections of courses that dealt with this to some degree. I would say more just the example of the faculty. A number of the faculty there, I think, were trying to do good things with economics. I guess the closest I came was a class in Latin American development economics, in terms of showing what might be done.

And that peaked your interest and then you considered pursuing more in-depth studies of economics later on as well?

No. Well, how I went to graduate school was somewhat different. I did also take, as an undergraduate, an early "women and the economy" course. This was back in the mid-1970s and "women in the economy" courses at that point were pretty much Gary Becker's specialisation and exchange kinds of models. But it also exposed me to just basic facts about pay disparities and that sort of thing. So it started to raise some of my feminist consciousness at the time, and I realised that the models I was learning did not jive with my experience very well. But the penny didn't drop until I had finished with my undergraduate work and I heard a feminist social scientist from, I think, sociology – could have been another social science – speak about doing feminist work in a social science and I immediately thought, "economics needs that". Those models that I was using to try to explain gender disparities and household issues just did not jive with how I saw the world working and, in fact, I saw the masculinity of the model of rational economic man. So I actually started graduate school and my graduate school application essay said I want to come to graduate school to do a feminist critique of economics. The admissions committee – one of the people on it – later on told me they'd no idea what that meant but my test scores and grades and stuff were good enough to get me a fellowship anyway.

You went to grad school. Did you enrol in any particular courses then, right away, or was there a curriculum that was laid out for you, that attracted you, that you went to that particular graduate programme?

I went to University of Wisconsin, Madison, apparently because it was the university from which the person from whom I'd taken the Latin American development course had recently graduated, and it was fairly close to where I was living. I was in Minnesota at the time. I came to appreciate that at that time Wisconsin had a very strong policy focus and historically had been the major institution of American "old institutionist" school of economics. And there were still some vestiges at the time of that legacy around in terms of the faculty and the department and the approaches. There was an institute for research on poverty, for example, in which a lot of economics faculty were involved. I found the first year to be one of the most intellectually stultifying of my life. It was all problem sets. But I also realised that if I didn't get the credentials nobody would ever listen to a critique. So I slogged through all the problem sets. I did a major field in public economics, mainly with an interest in income and inequality, so again coming back to that issue. In order to stay sane we were also allowed to choose a minor field. People doing that outside the department usually did it in math or statistics. I did a kind of put-your-own-programme-together sort of minor that was essentially women's studies. I took classes in education, law, history, and I think one other graduate course in women studies in other departments.

Was this a Master's programme or a PhD programme, and were your interests nourished in that department? Were you able to find a supervisor for you dissertation topic? How did that go?

It was a PhD programme. I picked up a Master's along the way. In terms of the feminist critique there was definitely no support, but there was tolerance as long as I went ahead and did the work that they expected. I purposely did not try to tackle a lot of this in my dissertation, although my dissertation was inspired by feminist work. My original idea was to adjust household equivalence scales for time use, which still has not really successfully been done. That is household equivalence scales – how you measure income and inequality across households of different sizes. You can't just say a six-person household has the same welfare level as a one-person household with the same income. There's obviously a different standard of living, so you need to adjust for that somehow. But something that has never really successfully been put in there is time use. If you've got two people working full time to make an income, that income is going to go less far than if it's earned by one person and you have someone able to do full-time household labour. I actually didn't get that far in my dissertation because it turned out just the work on monetary measures of household equivalence scales needed a lot of help, so I ended up just doing my dissertation on that. I will be very grateful to Gene Smolensky who became my PhD adviser and who was very intent on seeing me get through. He was very supportive in that way. He made me show up every week and show him what I'd done and gave me the pointers to get through. I finished the dissertation. My first publication out of the dissertation went into *Econometrica*. So, that was a credential.

114 *Julie Nelson*

How did you manage to transition into the job market? Did you have support through networks? Did you target any particular schools or employers that peaked your interest the most? How did that process work?

It was greatly complicated by the fact that it was a joint job search. I had married one of my classmates by that time, and we were looking for two jobs in the same geographic location. I wanted an academic job where I could design my own research. Because of the joint job search issue I ended up at the US Bureau of Labor Statistics, which was very disappointing to me but probably actually helped me in the long run. I had inside access to US consumer expenditure survey data and was able to get out a number of additional publications in *Review of Economics and Statistics* and such journals during that period. I started to write on feminism and economics at the time. I just privately circulated working papers in which I had to put a large paragraph disclaimer that even though I was working for the federal government nobody there gave any sort of approval. A long legal disclaimer. I also did that on my own time, outside of my workplace.

How did you then transition into the academic world from there?

After two years my then-spouse and I got jobs together at the University of California, Davis, and so we both went into the economics department there.

Can I ask, do you think there was a moment when you decided to become an academic as opposed to something else? Do you remember when that was?

Actually, another part of going into graduate school, besides doing a feminist critique, was wanting to do my own research. I'd been working for a sort of advocacy group up until that time. I was using the results of other people's research and when it didn't jive or I couldn't tell where they got the numbers from I found it frustrating and I wanted to do my own work. Wanting to do my own research was always part of it. I didn't really want to be working for the government because I wanted to be able to design my own research project rather than follow one I'm given by the job. I was given quite an amount of leeway there, not to do the feminist work but to do basically anything using US consumer expenditure survey data and along theoretical lines relating to that. But I wanted to do the feminist work.

You mentioned equality a few times. Were those issues of concern to you for a long time even before college? I'm interested in where that came from.

From the time I was a child I always knew that there were some people who really were not getting what they needed to live and that this was unjust and should not be tolerated.

Is there any family background that had anything to do with your decisions to go to college or graduate school or to become an economist?

Well, I would say in terms of this desire-to-make-the-world-better orientation, as I said, I went to a liberal arts college that had a service orientation. It was associated with the Lutheran Church, and my father was a Lutheran minister. So, I was raised with the idea that I should be of some service to the world. I think that got in under my skin quite well. In terms of becoming an academic or an economist, no. My mother had a bachelor's. My father had a bachelor's in divinity, which then retroactively became a Master's. I have one cousin who has a PhD and he and I, out of a massive, a fairly large family, are the only ones with advanced degrees.

How did you develop your particular contribution to economics?

I suppose it depends on which bit you think of as being my particular contribution. I feel like I've contributed some in empirical analysis, some in methodology areas, mainly in feminist work, but also somewhat in Ecological Economics and ethics. But I guess I'm most known for the feminist work, so let me talk a little bit about that. The feminist work that I've done some work on includes caring labour and pay rates and that sort of thing, but I particularly did not choose to go into labour economics when I was in graduate school because there was already a kind of tendency of thinking of women as only doing labour economics. I didn't want to fall into that, and that also wasn't my main area. I was more interested in what I would call economic theory. The grand social theories of economics. How do we think about the world, and what kind of tools do we use to think about the world? I guess that it had become obvious to me early on that the particular set of tools that economists were using were pretty inadequate for a lot of the things that we were trying to look at. I think that some major breakthroughs came for me from reading, particularly, some of the 1980s scholarship on gender and science. People like Evelyn Fox Keller and Sandra Harding and others were writing about how a certain notion of science is based on mathematics and detachment. It really showed a particular kind of bias that might be attributed to a fear of connection, a fear of engagement, an idea that other methods of investigation are squishy or soft or somehow more sissy than this tough mathematical physics-like stuff. I've heard, I think, it was Margaret Schabas who calls it "physics envy" going on in economics. We ended up with this bizarre methodology which confuses science with math, or objectivity with math, that somehow the more mathematical something is the more rigorous it is, even though it may never touch down to any reality. That's where I started working and I realised that I needed to take apart a lot of these binaries that economics was

116 *Julie Nelson*

constructed around. There's hard science, and there's soft science. The hard stuff, the economics side, was obviously better than the soft stuff like sociology. McCloskey – at the time Donald, now Deirdre – had also written her work on the rhetoric of economics, and she came up with a table which I and a couple of other people I think at the same time pretty much independently came up with, which was what aspects of reality did economists choose to highlight and, in highlighting those aspects of the world and those aspects of method, what did they leave out? Neoclassical economics highlights the individual, so we forget about family and social ties. We highlight rationality, so we try to supress anything about emotion. We like quantitative analysis, so we really put down qualitative analysis. We highlighted autonomy of agents. Again the social ties are all thrown way. And if you go down this list, what's the gender association of everything economics chose? It tends to be a masculine sort of world view. And what's the gender association of everything that it rejects and supresses? Those gender associations are feminine. Then I started to think about … I did not like the idea, which you still see sometimes people say, but okay, men are destroying the world so now it's up to women to save it by flipping the charts, going entirely from one side to the other. That never seemed satisfying to me. That seems like playing with half a deck. Neoclassical economics plays with half a deck. But if you think we have to get rid of all the math only to use qualitative analysis and study cooperative societies or something like that, it seems to me you're just playing with the other half a deck. We need to take into account *all* of this. So that's how I got started on that and what I wrote early on. I also read George Lakoff and Mark Johnson's *Metaphors We Live By* [1980]. McCloskey had written about how economists really tell stories using metaphors. My first major publication in feminist economics was in *Economics and Philosophy* called "Gender, Metaphor, and the Definition of Economics" [1992] about how the shape of economics was based on this metaphor of science and manliness.

Would you consider that your major contribution, or is that something that others attribute to you as being your major contribution? Do you feel comfortable with that, or out of the other things you mentioned would you consider those as equally major contributions, and if so, how did you develop them?

I think the idea of looking at the sexist biases in the definition and methods of economics is probably the major thing I've done. I've taken that in a lot of different directions since then. I've got about 12 different areas I could talk about. I guess I got into Ecological Economics looking at particularly issues of climate change and again reading some of what conventional economic analysis was doing with that issue, which still tends to be essentially discounting away the future and saying that somehow this is scientifically rigorous and objective and the sort of methodological – I backtrack here; I'm not being very organised – but as opposed to thinking about mathematics as supplying rigour and objectivity, what is much more appealing and has come out of a lot of philosophy of science and scientists who understand what they're doing is that objectivity and rigour really mean passing muster with a wider community of scholars and people looking into the question. I don't think people a couple of generations from now are going to look back at using a market rate of interest to discount their lives as being a particularly objective point of view.

I'm intrigued by what you said about your early publications being in places like *Econometrica* and *Review of Economic Statistics* and places like that. When you were working on that, were you conscious that this was for a strategic reason, that you already didn't really believe this stuff perhaps but you thought "well, I better do it" and you already had something else in mind?

Some of them were very consciously building those credentials. I also got into some work which led me back into quantitative work that got me back into looking at basic assumptions and again how hollow standard analysis could be. I did some empirical work on aggregation. I was using consumer expenditure survey data, and while microeconomics says we've got "quantities", we've got questions. In the real world what is the "price of butter"? It's going to be different at your convenience store, versus your supermarket, versus different brands, versus different times, versus everything else. I was working with data and when trying to actually do something with the data you realise that when aggregating anything into "butter" or "dairy" or "food" or whatever level you're aggregating at, you're getting rid of some things. One of the things that prices tend to reflect are also the quality of the good. You say "price of meat". Well, is that bone, or is it prime rib, prime filets? It got me looking even more at the sort of assumptions of the theory – the way that the very elegant mathematical theory really doesn't touch down to reality. I got into what I think of as some interesting issues. I've recently come full circle on that. Just in the last few years I did some work on, I guess, pretty much an issue of aggregation, which has to do with how people talk about people in social groups. There's a lot of literature that uses the words "women are more risk-averse than men" and essentially that's using aggregates – that kind of putting all women in a group of women and all men in a group of men. It turns out that the empirical work that underlies that in no way justifies the statement. The statement is usually understood as referring to essential categories of men and women and in fact what you have is a quite small difference in means of risk-aversion measures calculated over overlapping groups. I'm still kind of a nerd in terms of really wanting to dig into what numbers mean.

Can we pursue this thing about credibility just a bit more? Just going back to the kind of thing you were just talking about, Julie, that you're able to talk about these things with some people who can't dismiss you very easily perhaps because of that early work and your early training and perhaps even the job working for the BLS.

Well, they still do, but I think it makes them a little bit less credible. I should mention, while this is coming up, that I was tenured at UC Davis, which is a top 30 economics department in the US, and then for personal reasons I moved on. I was married at that time, and my then-husband didn't want to stay in California. I moved to Brandeis University, taking a tenure-track job as an associate professor with a short tenure clock. I was then denied tenure on the basis of inadequate research at a university that had a very small, very new PhD programme, didn't rank anywhere – after having gotten tenure at a top 30 department. So this research idea was pretty spurious, and also I continued to publish in good places since then. So I had a sex discrimination complaint with the state which was eventually "resolved to the satisfaction of all parties" – what the lawyers tell me I can say about it. But being denied tenure when you've got two small children and are in the middle of a divorce was not a good time. So, yes, I have paid for doing the feminist work.

But you ended up moving to Massachusetts?

I moved to Massachusetts from Davis, got the job at Brandeis, got denied tenure at Brandeis, and had a couple of visiting things. I had a fellowship at Harvard Divinity School for a while. I did a year of visiting here at UMass Boston. I had a research job at Tufts, which is where I worked on the curriculum materials. I then came back to UMass Boston and am now a full professor, tenured here. What I think happened at Brandeis was they knew I did feminist work but they didn't actually read it until I got there. They thought I was doing women-in-the-economy work, applying regular economics tools. They didn't realise that I was actually critiquing economics until I was there, and then they came up with some excuses.

So you think that your work and your particular orientation within economics has something to do with being denied tenure?

Yeah. The man who had just gotten tenure the year before me, his highest-ranked publication was in *World Development*. I publish in *Econometrica*, *RE Stats*, *The Journal of Economic Perspectives*, *The Journal of Political Economy*, *American Economic Review Papers and Proceedings*, and they denied me tenure on the basis of inadequate research.

We have chosen you because we consider you to be a heterodox economist. Do you consider yourself to be a heterodox economist?

Yeah. Considering heterodox to be an economist who is trying to use social science methods to study the real world but is going beyond neoclassical orthodoxy.

What do you think heterodox economics is? You've kind of answered that with social science method.

Well, I mean, anybody who's wanting to study the economy and is not in the neoclassical orthodoxy I would say is heterodox ... and there's many different varieties of that.

It would be good to explore what else you think it means because we've looked at this and talked about whether it's associated with particular theories or particular methods or a mindset perhaps?

Well, I don't think that there is a thing called heterodox economics that all heterodox economists ascribe to, except that neoclassical orthodoxy is too narrow a view for studying the economy. So, it's not that we agree on ... we have a common enemy more than we have actually agreed on things among ourselves, I would say. I also call myself a feminist and some people have a lot of problems with that word. When I teach a class we have to talk about that, why do people like to think it's man hating and blah, blah, blah, sort of silliness there.

You talked earlier about playing with half a deck, and you talked about trying to avoid that and play with a full deck. So, I guess, borrowing from both sides perhaps. And, I guess what strikes me is that some people think about heterodoxy as being oppositional, as an act of rejection of something, as opposed to taking more of a broader view.

Well, I actually think of not so much a broader view as a more radical view, using the word "radical" in terms of getting to the root of things. I think our brain likes binaries and oppositions to make life simple, but often too simple, and to really find out what is going on we need to dig under those binaries and see what is happening in the world. For example, one of the things I've been working on the last maybe 10 or 15 years now is looking at the theory of the firm. That is, neoclassical economics tells us that firms maximise profits and they are just entities and their reason for being is maximising profits. It turns out economists invented that. If you look at a longer history of business and corporations, businesses were about running businesses. Making a profit is part of what's going on, but creating employment, adding to a community, a lot of good things could be part of running a business. With the separation of a certain management class now, maximising CEO salaries has gotten to be a big competitive sport, one that shareholders are pretty pissed off about. But I find it interesting that both people on the right who say "firms maximise profit and then the magic of the market will make that work for good" and a lot of people on the left who say "firms maximise profit and therefore they're the epitome of greed and we need a socialist revolution", have at root bought into the same theory, right? They're both saying the economy is mechanical, that firms have no choice but to do this, et cetera. There's this myth going around that corporate charters talk about maximising profit. No they don't, because they're about running a business. So I was looking into the law and history of a lot of that, and so I am pretty sceptical of binaries. It seems to me that there tend to be a couple of major camps in economics, one of which says "government is bad, business is good, we're on the right-wing side". And then on the left-wing side, "business is bad, government's got to come in and whip them into line". I think both of those have failed to notice the strengths and weaknesses on both sides.

And does that work reflect the Institutionalism that you encountered at Wisconsin?

The old institutional school was very influential in US New Deal policies. This was coming into play during the period of the robber barons and the last big peak of American inequality – unfortunately we have now re-created that – and at the time there were communist revolutions going on in Europe, which made capitalists in the US a little nervous, and union organising, everything going on, and so you had all of this industrial strife. The people doing the New Deal, they were informed by people like John R. Commons. A lot of the old institutionalists were saying "what if we get everybody together and try to figure out a way through this? How can we share the prosperity so that the capitalists are still doing well and the workers are also doing well?" And I think they created a deal that lasted for a number of decades in the US, pretty much until Reagan, by bringing together the various interests and not treating one side or the other as beyond the pale.

What are the problems of neoclassical economics?

I'd say it's very inadequate. I think there are situations in which parts of the theory can give you a little bit of insight. It's not that I am against the theory, per se, as against the *hegemony* of the theory. I actually think supply and demand analysis can be a useful sort of heuristic device for some things. Where you get into problems is where you start to believe there are actually supply and demand curves out there in the real word and firms actually draw marginal cost curves to come to their decisions. Then you're starting to take that a lot too seriously. In the curriculum materials I worked on – people are kind of under obligation to teach certain sorts of things in introductory courses, but I think it makes a big difference whether you treat something as "this is the way the world works" versus "this is the way some people have thought about explaining how the world works". So, neoclassical theory is one of these tools – I often summarise my views as "broader questions and bigger toolbox". I think economists should be dealing with things like inequality and climate change, the big questions, and use a bigger toolbox to do that. Neoclassical theory can play a role, can be one of the things in one of the compartments in the toolbox, but it's clearly inadequate also for a lot of other things like deciding at what rate we should combat climate change. Basing that on a mathematical model and a market interest rate is stupid.

Is it an intellectual problem or is it a sociological problem or a psychological problem? How would you categorise it?

I would say at base there's two things going on. There's a really bizarre belief and then there's "why has that bizarre belief been maintained?" The bizarre belief is this idea that our mathematical models give us some kind of objectivity. It's just a very strange notion of what science and investigation are about. I think science is open-minded, systematic investigation. You can't get a lot more dogmatic than neoclassical orthodoxy. "You look at things this way or get out of here" is essentially the message you get from neoclassical orthodoxy. And then I think there is more of a sociological and political explanation for why that belief has been allowed to persist when it's so bizarre. Some of it has to do with images of masculinity, that somehow this is more tough. The economics profession continues to be male-dominated. Most people in the profession don't even notice the sort of masculine biases in the definition and methods because fish don't know they're swimming in water; it just seems normal when you're there. There's also a political reason for this, which is that if you can keep people at their desks doing DSGE models retroactively explaining the 2008 financial crisis you can keep them from studying inequality and rattling the cage and creating problems for people who want to stay wealthy and in power.

What are you trying to achieve as an economist?

Yeah, I am trying to, in some kind of general terms, make the world a better place. I think, in terms of specific things, that the recent work I did on gender and risk aversion is trying to prevent bad science and bad economics from reinforcing stereotypes about women and men and also reinforcing stereotypes about things like risk-taking and finance. Risk may be considered to be a good

122 *Julie Nelson*

thing or maybe it's not. The work I was doing on theory of the firm, one of my projects there is to try to help convince management schools to stop teaching so much economics when they're talking about the firm. Do some actual research about firms instead of teaching so much Micro. Or, Ecological Economics; I think economists need to face up to the ethical demands of living in a society where the economy, and particularly a fossil-fuel-based economy, is leading already to great suffering and possibly to great catastrophe. I'm not solving all of these problems myself, but I guess I'm at least trying to prevent some of the damage I see being done by stupid economics. I say stupid economics lightly there, but sometimes it's very smart people. They just haven't stopped and stood back and looked at what the assumptions are and what they're doing.

Would you say that there are enlightenment concerns of justice and equality in the background?

Well, I wrote a piece actually for *Ecological Economics* where I talked about the original enlightenment being the enlightenment beta version, and I had some problems. We need to move on. Some of the problems with the enlightenment beta version were this great faith in reason and this great faith in the individual. I wrote that piece particularly in light of climate-change issues where really we have to pay attention to the fact that we're all in this together. We have to start working together more. The individual that became so central in the first enlightenment is not so useful anymore. We need to pay more attention to our emotions and care. I think I gave an example – is it in that paper? Somewhere anyway – there is a book by an author who ecological people would know, Hans Jonas I think, about ethics and dealing with climate change. It's got chapter after chapter dealing with philosophical issues – Kant versus ... I don't know. He's got Rawls in there too – but all of this kind of ethical philosophy. And then he's got a paragraph in there that, I wish I could quote, but it's essentially that our obligations are demanded of us, and we see that most clearly looking at a newborn baby. That newborn baby demands of us that we take care and make a world for them. And you're not going to get that out of enlightenment individualist philosophy. You're going to get that out of going beyond that, looking at our social ties, looking at the way that we really need to relate to each other.

Would you say, then, this beta and alpha, or maybe alpha and beta, new version of enlightenment, has anything to do with Postmodernism? Is that something you would align yourself with, with this sort of Po-Mo movement?

I read a good deal of postmodernist theory back quite a while ago. I'd be postmodernist in the sense of trying to criticise, break down, look at the underpinnings of modernity and question those assumptions. But, at the end of the day, I'm a social scientist, and you might say I'm a do-gooder. I want to actually do high-quality research and use it for something that's of use. It seems to me that a great deal of the postmodernist literature just kind of stopped at deconstruction and never got back into "so, what do we do next?" And so I found that out.

Do you seek to influence society? If so, how?

Well, I wrote a book entitled *Economics for Humans*, that I wrote for a popular rather than an academic audience. I'm supposed to be revising that this summer and expanding it for a new edition. We will see if I get to my five months of research I had planned for my three months of summer. I give a number of talks around. The other thing would be the curriculum materials that I worked on, the *Microeconomics in Context* and *Macroeconomics in Context* that I worked on while I was at Tufts at Global Development Environment Institute. Again that's trying to reformulate the introductory curriculum in such a way that it's a bit of a compromise – teaching what people feel like they need to teach but without the brainwashing aspects. Highlighting the aspects where it could actually be useful for the world, why this should be useful. But also bring in, for example, in the chapter on consumption we teach budget sets and that kind of thing but then also go into the rise of the use of credit and the environmental effects of consumption. Again, like I said, to the extent we teach the theories, we teach them as *a* way, not *the* way. A way of looking at the economy rather than the way the economy works. I've taken on some editing responsibilities. I was an associate editor of *Feminist Economics* for a long time. I'm now a section editor for a section on economics and business ethics for the *Journal of Business Ethics*. It's where I'm trying to do this "don't listen to economists about the firm", which is also a way of saying let's actually hold firms up to having social responsibilities and acting ethically. We just give them a free pass if we just let them say "oh, the system made me do it". It's an excuse. And I'm co-editing a special issue on sustainability, ecology, and care for *Feminist Economics*.

Do you do political work? Are you associated with political parties, rallies?

Not directly. I'm an active citizen, but I wouldn't say that I have used my economic expertise to advise any particular groups. I guess that I mentioned I had done some work on economics of caring labour. I wrote a commissioned piece for a foundation working on childcare, and I know that piece was used by advocates in an organisation in the state of California working for higher wages for childcare workers. So I've contributed a little bit here and there, but it's not my major focus.

124   *Julie Nelson*

Do you deliver your research sometimes to research institutes that have a particular political orientation?

No. I've known people in and I've used research from places like the Economic Policy Institute and Institute for Women's Policy Research. I was on an advisory board for Institute for Women's Policy Research for a while. But in terms of actually doing research that becomes part of their work, except for this one childcare foundation, I don't think I could say that I've done that.

Do you recall what inspired you to want to write the *Economics for Humans* book for a popular audience?

I'll go back to another formative point for me. Back probably in the early '90s or so I think I was thinking of a lot of the sort of work I was doing in economics from a feminist perspective as trying to change the economics profession, which I think needs doing. I was having dinner with somebody and they said "how about doing an end run?" Talking about the fact that philosophy departments, for example, used to be pretty much the whole university if you go back a few hundred years, and now philosophy departments have their own little corner. What if we got things like public policy schools and health policy programmes and other groups like that to do the real economics, the real hands-on useful economics, and we got the management schools to do the real analysis of businesses, markets, and that kind of thing. Maybe economics departments could become this little rational choice corner over there in the university, and we could have real economics being done otherwise. I guess a lot of the curriculum material work I've done and the more popular writing is to get people to stop listening to mainstream economics and start looking for good economics wherever it might be.

Can you think of any other good examples of that kind of work out there?

There is certainly some good work done by very smart, very informed journalists on a lot of issues. I'm thinking of Yves Smith's book on the 2008 financial crisis. Very accessible, very well informed, actually gets to the real important issues going on and yet not written by someone who is technically qualified as an economist ... Let me just stop with that example. I could think of some more if I'd spent time on it. It's ironic there are good ... what was the movie I saw? Oh, shoot, I'm blanking on the name of it, but I saw a movie that had a better analysis of what it's like to be a working-class American today than I'd seen coming out of a lot of economics. So when the people writing fiction are doing more research and coming up with greater realism than the people who are supposedly doing social science, you know the world's gone a little crazy.

What are your strategies for seeking research funding?

I have been involved in that world here and there during my career. I had a two-year National Science Foundation grant for consumer expenditure survey work when I first got to UC Davis, so that was my one big grant. I haven't needed it for a lot of my other work. I did actually need it for that because I needed to do a whole bunch of data work at the time when computers and stuff were still pretty primitive. I actually needed to buy equipment and hard storage drives of half a gigabyte – big things! Anyway, so I needed funding for that data work. I didn't do so much at Brandeis. The years I was at Tufts University it was all soft money. Fortunately, Neva Goodwin raised most of that. There was some Ford Foundation money, and there were some other donors, I think, contributing into that. I had some input to grant writing, but I was not the major grant writer there. I've had a few smaller grants since then. The grant from, I think it was, EcoTrust for some of my ecological work. I had an INET grant for my work that ... some of the work that was on Ecological Economics and also the work that turned into this gender and risk-aversion research. So the INET grant was my last bigger grant.

Was your textbook, the in-context Micro and Macro textbooks, was that supported at all by grants, funding, external?

Yeah. That was what I was ... I was on salary at Global Development Environment Institute (GDAE), and my salary came out of grants that they got, a number of which were tied to the writing of those curriculum materials.

What do you enjoy most about teaching?

If you remember my earlier comments about going into graduate school, I really was more inspired by the research and wanting to do my own research. I wish I was one of these fabulous teachers that would inspire students and all of that. I'm afraid I'm not. I'm a good teacher but I'm not as good as I would like to be. I enjoy the students where I can see a light bulb go on and they start to think and see things in a new way. It doesn't happen as often as I would like. I enjoy teaching at UMass Boston for some reasons and I find it incredibly frustrating for others. University of Massachusetts, Boston, has a very diverse student body. It's kind of the gritty urban commuter campus of the University of Massachusetts system. It used to be 80% first-generation college students. I think that's dropped now. I think it's now more around maybe 65% or something like that. A lot of immigrant students. A lot of people that are a little bit older than usual. They've been out working for a while. People with families. People of low economic means. Big racial diversity background. I like teaching here in the sense that students who come from relatively disadvantaged backgrounds can get a really good education here and can really move up. We see some of those students coming through and it's inspiring. I taught one semester at Harvard and I also taught at Brandeis and did a visiting thing at some other elite schools. Getting up in the morning to teach the children of the elite to be the next elite does not inspire me. I like to be able to teach in a place where it maybe helps some people move up in the world. The other side of that is that our enrolment services looks at students as cash cows and is willing to let in anybody whether they're really prepared or not. So, we have lots of unprepared students which really reduces the quality of classroom interaction and I think does the students themselves a disservice. They're paying, they're getting into debt, and they're utterly unprepared for doing college work. That is the sad part of what I'm seeing.

I was just wondering, you said your current student body is diverse and a bit older and presumably they bring experiences with them, and I'm just wondering whether you found them less receptive to some of the more obscure or arcane bits of economics?

No. We get some students here that are ready to think critically. We get a lot of students who are not. We get a lot of students who are treating this not as an opportunity for learning but an opportunity to get a certificate and get a better job and so, yeah, the mind is pretty closed off. They memorise something only to write it on our tests, which is a good chunk of students anywhere you go, and certainly a big chunk of students here. Also, they're coming from different backgrounds. The ones that are a little bit older I think sometimes I do see more of the critical aspects, but we also get a lot of the 18- to 22-year-olds, and if anything some of the diversity in background leads maybe to even more reticence to critique. Some of the students from more entitled backgrounds feel entitled to challenge instructors more than some of the students from less privileged backgrounds. The good side is that they value education, they value the system, and they respect their instructors. The bad side is they may respect their instructors or their textbook too much. So, overall no, it does not help, I would say, in terms of getting students to think critically about economics.

You use the phrase "good teacher" and describe yourself as a good teacher. I think inspiration is one facet of a good teacher.

Well, inspiration is part. I think I'm best at teaching the students who are already engaged. What I see some people being able to do that I have not figured out the knack of is being able to inspire and engage students that come in not so inspired and engaged. I wish I could do that. I wish I had more of that knack.

Okay. Inspire and engaged them to do what?

To learn. Open their minds. To question. Actually, just basically doing things like reading. The number of students that actually read assignments, assigned readings, and who actually engage with the text is very low. I have tried this last semester teaching ... departments are required to offer a certain number of what are called freshman seminars, which are supposed to be fairly small groups so you're able to get to know the students. They're supposed to introduce the students to critical thinking and critical writing. All the rest of this. I was interested to see if intervention at that stage could help students. I think probably it was not a huge success. I think I moved along students that were moveable and again I had students that were not only not reading critically, they just were not reading.

You say you use a textbook. Is that something that's necessary?

Okay. That book by Ha-Joon Chang that is an intro to economics: *Economics: The User's Guide* [2014]. It was written at a college level. The students would probably have preferred that I assign some eighth-grade reading level kind of work they would have been more comfortable with, but I was trying to challenge them to actually expand their vocabularies and read more difficult texts.

I just wondered, we talked about the bigger toolbox. Is that something you're trying to get students to develop? Or, is it just to get them thinking about that bigger question?

In all the classes I've taught, I've been trying to equip students with skills and tools and generally go beyond what would be standard in an economics course.

Do you start with a problem and then say "how do we solve this problem? We need these tools"?

I use different techniques in different courses. I can't say that I have a particular ... I don't use a particular case method or field study method. It's more of a readings-based standard term paper kind of thing but trying to draw on careful reading and evaluation of the quality of arguments and evidence.

What are your goals in teaching, and how do you want to achieve them? You've already said quite a bit about that, unless you feel like adding anything?

No. I would like to be able to achieve more in that area, but I do what I can do.

128 *Julie Nelson*

McCloskey referred to economics as poetry or economists as poets. What do you think about this?

I guess there is a germ of a metaphor there. In what way are they poets and in what way are they not? In terms of a sort of creativity we might say they are poets, because it's certainly not something that's based on tangible sort of things. If they're poets they're pretty bad poets. The way that good poetry can really latch on to some larger truths and give you insights I would say economists are pretty bad poets. But in terms of coming up with things out of their heads you might say it was poetry.

Do you ever consciously encourage the students to explore poetry when they're in the classroom?

I try for basic things like complete sentences. I would be satisfied if more of my students had some of the rather more basic tools. I think the language issues are important and not just for my students. Let me tell you this again, and kind of on the two levels. One is I teach a class in which I have mostly seniors, and a lot of them find it extremely difficult to read a table and write English-language sentences that correctly state things like percentages and proportions. I am frequently getting statements on term papers of the form "98% of women are nurses". They looked at a table. They saw "women, nursing, 98%" and they write "98% of women are nurses", which is obviously wrong. It's supposed to be "98% of nurses are women", but they can't seem to handle the language and the numbers together at that level and I've recurrent problems getting them to do that. That is not so unrelated to the problem I was pointing out about the statement about "women are more risk-averse than men" because I looked into the linguistics of that. Some of the people who write that kind of statement they do some research, they run an experiment where they're asking lottery questions of men or women and they get some statistically significant differences between men and women on that lottery experiment. They write "women are more risk-averse than men" and then they go on to make policy conclusions such as "well, women investors should be advised by women investment advisers so they get the advice that fits their risk preference style". Clearly what they're thinking about is that those numbers go into that policy. Well, it actually goes from the numbers *to the language* to the policy. The numbers actually say that there might be a statistically significant, but perhaps ridiculously small, difference between the *means* of two distributions. I looked at a lot of this literature. Men's and women's distributions on a lot of these questions about risk preference nearly always overlap by 80% or more, and sometimes there is 98% overlap between the distributions. There is a statistical difference between the means, but we're talking about two distributions that lie almost on top of each other. But when that's summarised as "women are more risk averse than men", people immediately think of two distinct categories and then they go on to make policies based on categorical differences. So, this inability to go from what a statistic means to state it in correct English and understand it correctly, it happens at the PhD level, published economists' level as well. I actually documented that in some of my recent work.

It would seem that the language in particular, given your feminist background and focus on linguistics and then slash poetry, that that would be something that is probably quite important to your concerns?

Yeah. But again, I don't just want to go overall into language. One of the problems I see is the way that people try to express math in language and get entirely bollixed up in the procedure. Then there's also, like I said, the first piece that I wrote about gender, metaphor, and the definition of economics was a lot about language of these metaphors. I've come back to that over the years. But yeah, I mean language is how we communicate with each other, and we screw it up a lot.

9 Tony Lawson

Tony Lawson is Professor of Economics and Philosophy at Cambridge University, where he has worked his entire career. He holds a degree in Mathematics from Queen Mary University, London, a Master's from the London School of Economics, and a PhD from Cambridge. He has published extensively, predominantly in the philosophy and methodology of economics, mainly elaborating on realism. More broadly he has influenced critical realism with his work on abstraction, contrastive explanation, and retroduction. His books *Economics and Reality* (1997) and *Reorienting Economics* (2003) have had considerable impact on the Economics discipline, as did his earlier book on the methodology of Keynes (with Pesaran, 1985). Furthermore, he has made several interventions on the nature and future of economics, most notably his articles on heterodox economics (2005), neoclassical economics (2013), and relating the economic crisis to a crisis within the Economics discipline (2009).

Tony Lawson was interviewed by Andrew Mearman at Cambridge University in August 2017.

How did you become an economist?

I'm tempted to say, "am I an economist?" I changed to economics from mathematics, and I did so because I got the impression, listening to people debating around the various university common rooms, that economics was a more interesting subject to study. By the time I got to my third year of being an undergraduate, there were only about eight of us left on the course (of about 150) who were specialising in pure (rather than applied) maths, and the other seven didn't really want to debate mathematics. I got involved in student politics. I was interested in the way the world was and could be. Everyone else seemed to be too. I decided to change to economics. That's the short story.

So maths wasn't very interesting because people didn't want to debate ... ?

It was interesting conceptually, I enjoyed it, and quite possibly I should have stayed in mathematics; but no, it wasn't the sort of thing one debated, at least it wasn't the sort of thing most people debated. Just theorems and proofs, presented as theorem 3.1 and lemma 4.8, and their proofs. *En route* I covered results like Gödel's incompleteness theorems – not named as such, but presented merely as theorems 5.2.1 and 5.2.2 or some such – but they were not the sort of thing that engendered discussion amongst the eight. I only ever saw the other mathematics students in the lectures anyway. When I went to a general common room of the university, the topics under debate, the issues that people were getting worked up about, did not concern the nature of mathematical proofs. It was how to change the world, which, at that time, seemed much more interesting. In truth, I had very little understanding concerning the workings of the social system; I was familiar with mathematics and had always found it fairly easy, and at that moment it seemed less of a challenge than understanding the social, and fairly isolating in its study.

Was it something about the content of the debates in economics that interested you?

I am referring to other students debating issues in economics in common rooms. When I formally took up economics after completing the mathematics degree, I went to the LSE and I was bored stiff. There, it was all about mathematical modelling. In the lecture halls there was almost no debate or critical thinking. I was disappointed. I concluded I'd made a bad decision going to economics, and I was pretty determined I wouldn't stay in economics.

What attracted you to economics in the first place? Elsewhere [Dunn, 2009], you cited being involved in student politics as an influence.

Yeah, student politics. I felt economists mystified a lot with their jargon. I couldn't understand what they were talking about half the time, but they also had loads of interesting questions. Like "what is capitalism, and how does it work?"

Let me step back a bit. I come from Somerset, Exmoor, Minehead; I knew very little of how society worked. It was not an option of study at my school. I knew lots about daily affairs in the countryside, but I knew nothing about money and banks, or corporations, or the basic mechanisms of capitalism. I thought I'd learn about that if I changed to economics. But I didn't. I learnt about IS-LM curves, Robinson Crusoe, and lots of silly little things that facilitated modelling for its own sake. I regretted changing.

Then I went to Cambridge, met up with an old friend, things happened, I went for a walk, ended up at the economics department. Someone spotted me and said, "what are you doing?" I pretended I was interested in a PhD. Finding I had a good degree in mathematics, they offered me a PhD grant on the spot. So I took it. That's the short version again. I was not really interested. But I thought a year in Cambridge, after a number of years in London, would be a nice change, where I could sort out what I really wanted to do.

132 *Tony Lawson*

Strangely, I became interested in economics here because there were lots of debates, lots of argument, lots of things going on. I became interested. So, I thought I'd stay here a bit longer than a year; that was about 200 years ago.

Perhaps it wasn't the mere fact that it was debate, it was the debate about something that you found relevant, important.

It was relevant. I didn't have a particular question, but I was very aware that coming from my background, I knew so little about everything and I really loved discovering things. When I first left Exmoor for university in London, I especially discovered things like varieties of music, different cultures. It sounds a bit sad maybe, but it really was all new to me. By the time I arrived in Cambridge, I was keen to understand better how economy and society worked. Moreover, I was quite puzzled by this stage at what academic economists thought they were doing. That got me involved in endless debates with other Cambridge research students. Whereas I kept arguing that the dominant activities of economists were largely irrelevant to understanding, there were others that seemed to feel that any concern with relevance was passé anyway. I was informed that postmodernism was the orientation to embrace, wherein people just did their own thing, each constructed their own truths, and the rest of it. From this perspective, mathematical modelling was just one practice; its justification was merely that economists chose this path. Relevance was not a legitimate or meaningful concern. I wasn't convinced.

In [Dunn, 2009] you said that at some point you realised that the models that you saw or the methods being used made the wrong presuppositions about the world. When did you realise that?

From the moment I entered an economics faculty, my intuitions were immediately that this is just a totally wrong approach, in effect a misuse of mathematics, a naïve orientation to it. It wasn't that I was opposed to any particular assumptions. I just couldn't see how any assumptions that would allow those methods to gain tractability would be relevant to the world we lived in. Of course, at that time this was just a feeling. When people said to me, "well, what is the nature of the world that these methods don't fit with?", I didn't have ready answers. I didn't know words like "ontology" or use categories like open systems or others that I use today; it was just, to me, as obvious as someone trying to cut the grass with a feather or something. It just seemed a clear mismatch.

But you just knew that it didn't fit.

That was my very strong feeling, yes.

At that stage you would not have said there was any fully formed set of ideas; it was just an intuition that the practice wasn't right?

It was a bit confusing. At that stage, remember, I'm still fairly young, early twenties. From the moment I arrived at university in London I'd experienced having my eyes opened and my preconceptions challenged and changed. So, I was kind of quite used to being surprised by things. So, although this was my initial reaction, a bit like thinking the emperor's got no clothes, yet I worried that I might be wrong, because I had been about other issues first encountered at university, and because few others appeared to see things as I did. Even so, I was fairly convinced because mathematics was one form of practice – unlike many others that I engaged in at university – that I had long been familiar with.

That all said, I was not the only one, of course. Notably, I had made friends with another student, Mary Farmer, on the same course, the economics master's course at the LSE, who held the same sort of view. She had a degree in sociology. She intended, the following year, to embark upon a PhD in sociology on what she called "the economics tribe". She was spending a year in the tribe gathering material for her future research. So, we were both sat there thinking what a strange way of proceeding. But I was wanting to make sense of it because I wanted to use economics. Mary was more an anthropologist taking it in, as I say, for her later research.

How much of it was that you simply weren't impressed by the maths?

Well, I think that's true too, but I'm not sure I ever could have been, given the context. As I say, from then to now, I have never thought that social reality is the sort of thing that can be usefully dealt with using the sorts of mathematical tools that economists employ. I formed that view the moment I came to the discipline, and I have seen nothing since that has challenged that initial assessment. Rather the contrary is the case. In particular, explanations by economists as to why they adopt the practices they do makes it clear to me that they really are very naïve, that they have no good reason; mostly they merely lack criticality. A remarkable aspect of all this is that although the last 60 years is a history of failure of mathematical modelling to provide any insight, the modellers continue with their practices regardless. You look as though you wanted a different answer.

We're leading into the next question: how you developed your contribution. What do you think your contribution is?

That presupposes there is one! Well, I've realised that people are writing things about me suggesting that I've helped put social ontology on the map, so maybe that's a contribution. That certainly started right from the start. For the immediate assessment of there being a mismatch, that economists are using inappropriate tools for their tasks, is an ontological claim, even though I didn't know it as such at the time. To defend the assessment of a mismatch, it was necessary to elaborate the nature of social phenomena and show they were not of a sort as could be illuminated by way of mathematical modelling, given the conditions of relevance of the latter methods. Somewhere along the way I realised that what I was doing was called social ontology. But I started doing ontology probably the first day I came in to economics, not knowingly, subconsciously. My question was always "why do people think these methods can work, what do they think they can achieve with these methods?" I used to ask everyone that. I guess that helped make ontology an explicit concern. Is that a contribution? Maybe. If so, it is not one that many are very pleased about.

But you had another strand to your work. You worked on the Cambridge Growth Project and related projects, and there is also the labour relations or labour process side to your work. So you could have gone one of various ways. You could have gone much more into depth in that area where you're looking at actual businesses, industries, actual structures; instead you've ended up going down a more philosophical, less concrete route. Was that a conscious decision?

No specific undertaking was consciously formulated in advance. In fact, my idea of "planning" is keeping options open; it's an obvious orientation in the face of an open system. I seem just to go along with the flow, adapting, adopting a route from any options that appear in front of me. I'm surprised you know about the labour process stuff; not many people do. That also happened when I was a PhD student. Although I was interested in philosophy I had no inkling I would spend the next 40 years doing philosophy. I was in the economics department, and so I was thinking that substantive issues in economics were going to be a prominent focus. My understanding of social reality, rudimentary as it then was, included the notion that social relations were pretty important to social life. I and a number of other research students started a kind of reading group on stuff connected to industrial relations, the labour process. Eventually we evolved into a little research group. We used to study local firms, go into them, go to the local library to read up on them, and get together and talk about our findings. We met up about once a fortnight. We took it in turns cooking a meal for each other, alongside our discussions. So, it became a social thing. I wrote a paper that came out of it on paternalism at Pye, a local firm, but it was a social thing. It was the one area of economics that seemed accessible to me, that seemed relevant. At that time, I was still searching for relevance in the existing literature. I'd read papers on micro, macro, econometrics everywhere, and I couldn't see anything that I thought provided insight. So this group became a way to relevance. Ever since then I have found the relevance is best achieved by way of forming research groups whose activities are extracurricular.

Did you not seek relevance in any of the existing heterodox traditions?

Well, again, remember that I was new to it all at this stage, and I didn't know much about the different traditions. I'm not even sure how many existed then. I am not sure any did in Cambridge. There were Marxian and Keynesian, et cetera, economists about, of course. But I think I mainly read the people who became the figureheads of the alternative traditions, rather than participate in the latter. I read Marx and Veblen and Keynes, his *Treatise on Probability* [1921] especially. I've no idea when I heard the term "Post Keynesian". I think it was a lot later. In Cambridge there were quite a significant number of students and others who labelled themselves Keynesian, who identified as such almost entirely by holding the view that effective demand was important. They were involved with "The Alternative Economic Strategy" of Kaldor, Francis Cripps, and the New Cambridge School; the focus was very much on ways of solving problems of the British economy. I was much more interested in Keynes's *Treatise on Probability* [1921] and *Treatise on Money* [1930]; unlike most Cambridge Keynesians, I found Keynes's views on uncertainty and money and use of methods to be more fundamental.

So, I guess the suggestion in your question is right; I even felt the need to get involved in groups that were alternative even to the existing heterodox groupings. That said, this was a long time ago, and I can't be sure whether that's the way I felt it had to be, given the state of the discipline, or my personality is such that that's the way I prefer to operate. Looking back, I seem to have got involved with the realist workshop, the ontology group, and other sorts of groupings that were outside the mainstream, and outside the traditional heterodoxy, and set up just to facilitate different directions. It seems to have always been the case.

I can understand now, given the current context, which is much more mainstream, why those groups need to exist, but I'm surprised that they needed to exist back then when it was, if anything, a much more radical environment.

It *was* a more radical environment, but still the main group were the mathematical modellers. This building we're in now has got four floors; back then the top two were designated the "department of applied economics", the bottom two floors constituted the "faculty of economics". The top two housed researchers. They were more radical by and large than faculty members, but unlike the latter they didn't do any teaching. All the teaching was down at the bottom two floors, and that's where all the mathematicians were. So, most of the activities oriented to students, through teaching, were modelling based. I should add that not all in the faculty were mathematical modellers; it included the likes of Ajit Singh, Bob Rowthorn, Alan Hughes, and others. However, even this group did some modelling, more than I thought was reasonable. Moreover, these alternatives were largely policy oriented. There was always a need for groupings that took philosophical/methodological issues seriously and recognised a need to do relevant theory for its own sake.

In [Dunn, 2009] you discussed working with the Cambridge Growth Project. Its members were paid to provide analyses, predictions, et cetera. You come across as slightly wary about what was going on there – that it wasn't necessarily the purest academic or intellectual exercise.

Eventually, yeah. The Growth Project was the first full-time career job I ever had. My supervisor was Angus Deaton; he was on the Growth Project. He left to take a chair in Bristol, I think it was. One way or another they offered me his job. Interestingly, he's just got a Nobel Memorial Prize. My next supervisor was Oliver Hart; he's got it too. I wonder if they know I supervised myself eventually.

So it's in the post.

It's an extrapolation of a correlation, so it must be. Anyway, I took the job on the Growth Project. I could never really understand the point of it. I don't want to say negative things. My colleagues were great and all were very intelligent and interesting in their own ways, but the overall project, I just couldn't share the enthusiasm of the other members. There was another group, the Cambridge Economic Policy Group, or "New Cambridge" along the same top-floor corridor. In many ways I found them easier to understand. They always maintained that the reason they did the modelling was because it gave them the legitimacy to say the things they wanted to say and would have said anyway without the modelling. So it was in large part a question of strategy: I can see the argument, but I have never wanted to do things on that basis.

Although you've probably benefited from that yourself, having the credibility of having a mathematical background, you can't easily be dismissed.

Well, yes, is that credibility or strategic? I certainly didn't study maths for strategic reasons. Nor do I use it as an easy way to win an argument. It did make it easy to stay put when most of my heterodox colleagues succumbed to pressure and moved to the Judge Business School. As this place became more and more mathematical, there was a sort of mass exodus to the business school. Finding the maths to be not especially difficult, I just stuck with it; I couldn't be bothered to retrain as a business economist. Before the exodus I was kind of in the middle. For, there were those that thought of themselves as mathematicians on one side of me, and the policy-reforming left on the other, and they opposed each other. Because I had credentials in both camps as it were, and mostly did my own thing, I was largely left alone to do my own thing. However, once all the alternative, the left, the heterodoxy, whatever, had gone I became public enemy number one with those that remained. And I've only ever taught maths here; if I'd gone to business school I might be able to teach more interesting things. It has its positives and its negatives. I like maths; it's the mismatch that I have a problem with, not with maths. So the outcome has been mixed, but I am not sure that much of it has been the result of using my mathematics background strategically.

Do you find Mathematics beautiful?

Yes, though not what economists do in the name of mathematics. The pure maths I did at university certainly is. I was going to do a PhD in group theory, which I found especially elegant. There is also an aesthetic sort of pleasure that comes with grasping difficult ideas and proofs. Where would I get that in economics? Actually, in ontology I can get it a lot.

In [Dunn, 2009] you discussed how you found the mathematics and the jargon in economics somehow serving to mystify. Some people might say that ontological terminology is fairly mystifying as well. How have you managed to deal with that?

I think that in the interview you're referring to, I was again talking about my early days as a student. I spent a year being president of the student union, so I was heavily involved in student politics. The economists used to come to all the meetings and use a lot of jargon. I'm not sure I used the word "mystification", but I personally found it a pain because I often didn't know what they were talking about. That was one of the reasons why I changed to economics, to understand what they were talking about. That obviously required a significant investment of my time. I guess I recommend that if people think talking about ontology and realism is puzzling, but relevant, they too should invest in it and find out what it all means too. The difference between ontological and (mainstream) economic jargon, I think, is that getting on top of the former is very worthwhile. That said, there is no excuse anywhere for not seeking to be as clear as feasible. If the intended or actual audience is new to a subject matter, then I think it is sensible and polite to elaborate any terminology whose meaning may not be self-evident; any author has an obligation in this regard.

138 *Tony Lawson*

I was also struggling with that other comment. I don't know whether you've come across the *Econocracy* book [Earle et al., 2016], the book published by the post-crash students in Manchester. One of their arguments is that economists have created this language, this structure, which is detached from not only reality but from everybody else; it's become impossible for other people to understand, leading to a democratic crisis.

To understand the world in any discipline you need a language. Nuclear physicists talk easily of quarks, and neutrinos, et cetera, categories required to make sense of the world in which we live. But they don't just make up their categories without any reference to anything beyond the models. A problem of economics is that this is all that happens. Think of categories like "natural rates", "rational expectations", "social welfare functions", and "economic equilibrium". The problem is not that economists use categories or terms but they're silly ones. Irrelevant ones.

Physics is a good example, isn't it? There's lots of sort of "wacky" stuff in there, isn't there?

Yeah, but it's the world that physics deals with that's wacky. The idea that we're all made up of excitations of quantum fields is wacky. Mind you, so is the idea I defend that money is a social relation, so that the capitalism itself rests on a set of social relations. That's pretty wacky, but I think it's good wacky, it's right, it's wacky and right. But utility functions, production functions … ? They are not even wrong.

In physics some of those advances have come because somebody's taken a creative leap and they've jumped well ahead of whatever the evidence suggests.

Yeah, but the creative leap usually comes through resolving puzzles, in dealing with contradictions between explanatorily powerful theories and forms of evidence. For example, the best theory of particle physics bares the conclusion that particles had no mass. It seems to follow that being composed out of particles then we humans and all other material objects also have no mass. And yet mass seems to be everywhere. So, it's a puzzle to be resolved. Someone took a creative leap which led to the Higgs-Boson theory. According to it, particles take on the appearance of mass when passing through the Higgs field. It is a bit like running into the sea, whereupon we appear to get heavier. The point is that the creative leap is a response to a real-world anomalies or puzzles. Economists live with anomalies. They show little interest. Economists merely shift from fad or fashion, seeking new domains to model. They don't even address that finding that ought to be treated as a puzzle, that their methods provide no insight. And you don't hear academic economists sitting 'round asking "where do profits come from; how can profits exist", and such like. It's a refuge of the scoundrel to suggest that modern economics might be justified because the making of its absurd, silly, assumptions is creative.

How does this happen then? I've read lots of interviews with quite prominent mainstream economists, and many of them say what motivated them to get involved in economics was to address real-world problems. So, assuming they mean it, how do they end up where they do?

I suspect their intentions are good. I tend to think most damaging practices everywhere are honest mistakes. I suspect mathematical modellers suppose that it's desirable that economists be scientists, but naïvely suppose that that means always using mathematics. My experience is that economists are not very good at mathematics; they are rather in awe of it and would like to be considered as mathematicians. Unhappily, in using mathematical modelling methods where they are inappropriate they are proving that they are not. So, I don't doubt their statement of original intentions – merely their competence. The uncritical, and ultimately inappropriate, use of mathematics is a form of cultural blinkering. It's so widespread that it is treated as a common-sense thing to do. The absence of criticality in the economics academy is the problem. Progress requires the reintroduction of philosophy, and specifically ontology.

One of the questions we've got on here is what are the problems of mainstream economics, and we've addressed quite a few of those.

You know my answers.

Some of what we have discussed concerns people making mistakes; some of it is something about the sociology of profession as well. In [Hirsch and DesRoches, 2009], you said an overconcern with prediction in an open world might represent deep psychological traumas. One of the things that we're trying to investigate is whether there's a sort of psychology of heterodox economics that might be different from mainstream economics. Is there a psychology of mainstream economics?

Okay, well, your question is not only what is the problem, but what explains its persistence? Most immediately the problem is that the discipline is irrelevant. It has no bearing on the world in which we live; it generates no insight.

140 *Tony Lawson*

Any insights are brought in and put there; it's not generated in academic economics. What's the cause of that? I think that is pretty clear; it's the emphasis on mathematical modelling. It's a mismatch of tool and object of reality. The ontology that's relevant for those methods to work doesn't fit the nature of social reality. So, the next question is what explains the repeated emphasis on mathematical modelling despite a record of sheer failure. That's where psychology comes in, as one possible cause. There's all sorts of causes. These include psychological factors, the belief that economics must be scientific combined with a misconception of science, institutional factors, and so on. So, there is a range of explanations.

But you ask about psychological trauma. I think a relevant psychological factor is that many of us, studies suggest especially amongst those of those of us that are gendered male, hang on to notions of a world being closed, controllable, and predictable, as an unconscious coping mechanism in the face of the open world and our own mortality. It provides a modicum of security. We do so the more difficult was the separation of ourselves from the initial primary carer and the psychological trauma that that induced. It varies according to gender because the primary carer is usually a gendered woman. And this results in the reaction to separation being different for gendered boys and gendered girls. It's a long story. It is clearly not the only factor. For, if mainstream economists adopted similar methods and assumptions outside the academy as within in it, they would not last for long. So, there is much else going on, some of which is specific to being located in the economics academy.

One additional factor, already touched on, is people just think that because mathematics is so successful in so many disciplines, so many people just think it's the essence of science and that's how you're meant to do it, but for many others it's the way economics has become. It's the institution; if you want to be appointed, make progress, be promoted, then one should do mathematics. It becomes a selection device. Of course, the really intelligent ones recognise all this and change disciplines.

So, you stayed as an economist because you weren't intelligent enough to go off and do some other subject? That's a good headline.

I guess so. I probably wasn't even worldly enough to think of it. I got to university for two reasons: I could do maths and I could play football. After my first degree I could do more maths, but I still hadn't done any philosophy, sociology, or anthropology, et cetera; I was indeed quite ignorant of all these fields. I just picked them up, in my student everyday activities, but not through formal study. It was a big step for me to change to study economics, and I was disappointed. If I'd been to the sort of school that provided some lessons in philosophy or sociology perhaps I would have changed out again very quickly, but finding an additional discipline didn't even enter my head. I was, though, considering an offer to return to mathematics.

And so having entered economics you became, in a sense, stuck?

Yeah, although, having acknowledged that, I've had a fantastic life and career. It's not the sort of career path you apply for: "Wanted: someone to spend your life criticising economics and studying social ontology". But I have enjoyed it.

So, your younger Self would have been surprised to see where you are now?

Yeah. Though I never had any specific expectations, so anything would have been a bit of a surprise. Perhaps I expected things to be more difficult, given the sort of world we live in, most become alienated through work, et cetera. I have been lucky; it has mostly turned out to be an enjoyable doddle really.

Specific academic advantages of taking the path I have is that I haven't had to compete with many others, just because few others took the same route. I look at mainstream economists around me especially; they suffer. They have to endure such competition. What they do is mostly cobblers. But that applies to it all. So, to get anywhere with it they have to publish in those journals that those with the power have an advantage in positioning as core or prestigious; and it's difficult for them. Almost everyone is trying to get papers in those journals. When the goal is relevance, it takes as long as it takes; curiosity is the drive, and getting somewhere is its own reward.

Is that why people become heterodox economists then?

I guess a prior question is what is it to be a heterodox economist.

Are you one?

Am I one? I guess I am, though I'd have to define my terms; and my understanding of heterodox may not be agreeable to some. I don't mind the word "heterodox". I know a lot of people get bothered by the use of it. But "dox" just means a doctrine, and "orthodox" means a doctrine held as true by most within a relevant community. "Heterodox" just means rejection of one or more doctrines held as true by a majority. The fundamental doctrine held to be true by most in the academic economics community is that mathematical modelling methods are the appropriate or proper tools for addressing all economic questions. Mainstream participants are rather dogmatic in insisting on the use of these methods as the only serious approach. So, in rejecting that particular dogmatic doctrine, I am heterodox. This I think is the only coherent interpretation that can make sense of the complex situation of modern economics, though once more a long story.

142 *Tony Lawson*

Okay, but obviously one of the reasons people don't like that term is it could just be a negative thing.

It is a negative thing in that it indicates a united opposition to a specific dogmatic doctrine. But there are always positive reasons for this opposition, and this is where those involved spend most of their time. There are named groups opposed to war, fascism, oppression, et cetera. Being a part of such movements does not imply those involved do not also have positive projects. It is just that any positive interests will be more varied. Those interested in the progressive change involving ending the oppression according to gender may be first and foremost part of the feminist economics project; those interested in studying change and stability in a relevant way may be institutionalists. Heterodoxy is a project to unite those so differentiated groupings who share an interest in removing obstacles that stand in the way of a more relevant, emancipated, and emancipatory economics. That's all. In the past I have been quite positive about the heterodox project; recently less so.

In what ways?

I think it's changing in the sense that people are now claiming the heterodox label for themselves whilst allocating much of their time to mathematical modelling. Modelling has become a methodological ideology; economists who have known nothing else do not think of challenging it. Many modern economists view its use as a matter of common-sense approach. They have no capacity of criticality at the level of methodology. Rather, they think they are being radical, even heterodox, if they take a policy stance that is a bit alternative to that pursued at the level of government. They don't even realise that in the academy, there is no orthodoxy on policy or substantive issues. Indeed, economists in the mainstream mostly don't care; the only principle adopted is that economics be done mathematically. So heterodox contributions have become increasingly weak and of little relevance to the real world. Perhaps I am too pessimistic in this assessment. I hope so.

Just to take one example, there's quite a lot of "Stock-Flow-Consistent" modelling going on, particularly in Post Keynesian economics. What do you think about that?

I'm not a fan of any of it. I don't necessarily want to pick on any people or group. But obviously, if the ontological presuppositions of the methods do not match the nature of social reality, then it has little relevance. And all the approaches I've seen of the sort you mention presuppose the usual mainstream ontology of atomism and closure.

It's interesting that that approach comes from Godley's work, doesn't it? And he was famous for actually looking at the economy, albeit in a sort of spreadsheet form.

Godley himself didn't model. His associates took his insights and tagged them onto models. Sometimes he even asked me to explain modelling parts he didn't understand, when there was no one else around.

But, although Godley was not a modeller, and derived his insights independently of others attaching them to models, the basic point is right. So many groups that claim the label "heterodox" are really about modelling and so are misleading with their self-descriptions. That's what bothers me.

I don't know if you saw, I wrote a paper on neoclassical economics a while back. I pointed out that Veblen coined the term "neoclassical" precisely for people who have a vision of the world as open processual, or evolutionary, as he called it, but use methods that presuppose an ontology inconsistent with that vision. He introduced the term "neoclassical" to express that inconsistency. I suggested in the paper that we should drop the word; it's a bit uncharitable to define a school in terms of a basic contradiction that those so described have no idea underpins what they do. But it seems to me a lot of people within heterodoxy are becoming increasingly neoclassical in Veblen's sense, and it's ironic too because their favourite term of abuse is "neoclassical". They are the new neoclassicals in effect. Just as important as dropping the term "neoclassical" is perhaps that modelling-dominated projects give up the term "heterodox". They increasingly are not.

Just to explore that a bit more. If one were a "Stock-Flow-Consistent" modeller, one might claim that their starting point is Godley's approach. In turn, his starting point was to understand the economy as it is and then derive principles based upon this observation and understanding of the economy. Thus, we've built this modelling approach. Surely that's got to be better than starting from a general equilibrium-type approach, and therefore lumping them together is unfair.

You're interviewing me I know, but I'm tempted to say to you, in what sense better?

Well, rooted in reality.

However rooted, modellers are always faced with the problem of using something like the feather or the hammer to cut the grass. Rooting doesn't get around that problem. If you're using an inappropriate method to address claims rooted in reality, then it is all rather inconsistent, and the results can only be irrelevant.

144   *Tony Lawson*

I think the attraction of Keynesian or Post Keynesian modelling or whatever sort, is that people who are concerned with truth, the way the world is, think that these models get conclusions that are more relevant or truer. It's probably right, but it's worthless all the same because the methods are just irrelevant. The methods force you to use assumptions that conform with closed systems of isolated atoms – assumptions that are false and usually silly. The fact that there is enough flexibility to allow manipulations that generate results that are considered true in advance, and aimed for, just renders their derivations a waste of resources. All polar bears are white. That's probably a better or a truer theory than the claim that all polar bears are red. But if I can get the result by assuming, say, that all polar bears eat snow, everything that eats snow turns white, I've merely manipulated false assumptions to derive this truth; I have contributed absolutely nothing to understanding. I've not enlightened the world. I've achieved nothing. I've just manipulated assumptions that generate what I think is already the truth. Modelling necessitates false assumptions. It is no big deal to then manipulate them to reach a desired conclusion. No support for that conclusion is so provided. It is all a waste of time.

Of course, much mainstream modelling does not even dress itself up as seeking truth. Many of those modellers don't care about what they're generating; they just want to prove theorems or take a model that already exists and generalise it or get the same result using fewer assumptions. Brilliant. From where I sit, the two approaches are equally irrelevant.

Okay. So you've said you're happy to call yourself a heterodox economist in the negative sense of rejecting that orthodoxy as you define it?

I'm located in an economics department. I'm interested in issues of economics, like the nature of money, the corporation, gender, whatever, and I reject the central doctrine, the orthodox doctrine, that mathematical methods are the one proper and necessary way to do economics. So, in that sense I'm heterodox. I live amongst economists, I'm surrounded by them, a part of the community, but I reject this particular central doctrine of the discipline, the only doctrine that the mainstream participants seem all to accept.

But, you're still an economist because you're interested in economic things.

Yeah, money, the corporation, capitalism, value, gender, technology, social relations … However, the kind of ontological stuff I do leads me to the conclusion that there's really a legitimate basis for only one united social science. That is, if we divide up the disciplines according to the sort of stuff they deal with, as we do in distinguishing physics and biology, et cetera, then sociology, economics, politics, anthropology, et cetera, are all dealing with the same stuff, albeit viewed from different angles. I think the idea of separate departments of economics is arbitrary and unhelpful. But we start from here. We define people according to how the world has in fact been divided, however unhelpfully. So, I'm an academic economist of sorts. My colleagues might not accept that designation. But that's probably consistent with my being heterodox. Actually, my formal title has "economics and philosophy" in it; that's my actual job description.

You're happy with that presumably?

Yeah.

Can I ask you about Austrians? In this discussion about heterodox economics they always come up, and it's difficult to know what to do with them. I think your instinct is to say "yes, they're better than the mainstream, and in some ways they're heterodox".

Well, yes. Remember that for me, but not for many self-identifying heterodox people, the only coherent way to define the mainstream or orthodoxy is by their adherence to and insistence upon methods of mathematical modelling. Heterodoxy, when coherent, is any approach that rejects that mainstream approach and so doesn't prioritise mathematical methods in the same way. I don't think there are very many things in common with the various different figureheads of the Austrians (i.e., Menger, Hayek, Mises). But one thing that does unify them is their support for methods that are relevant to the task before them. They were all methodologically aware; methodological texts were written by Menger, Hayek, and Mises. You don't get mainstream economists writing texts on methodology as opposed to technique. Hayek explicitly rejected the use of mathematical models as scientism. So, in that sense, yes. Certainly, I'm more sympathetic to the Austrians than are a lot of other heterodox commentators. But, the latter usually make the mistake of thinking heterodoxy implies a political stance. That's just naïve; as I say, it presupposes a shared political stance by the mainstream. Most such participants do not even have one. Politically, I think Hayek, say, got things wrong, of course, largely because he lacked a notion of objective human needs. But Hayek was relevant; he was just wrong. I have no problem with people being wrong. I have a problem with people doing things that are irrelevant. Those in the mainstream know at some level that what they do is irrelevant and they're still doing it and excluding others who want to be relevant. That's a problem. That's not how I see Austrians.

146 *Tony Lawson*

If we tried to summarise heterodox economics, there's this negative definition but within that then there's lots of different traditions. How do you see things evolving? I'm not asking you to make a prediction here; I'm asking you to just imagine the future. Do you see the strands coalescing or do you see them staying separate? Do they find their own areas of interest, areas of focus?

I don't know. I was more optimistic 20 years ago. You may or may not remember that in contributions like *Reorienting Economics* [2003] I tried to argue, and I truly believed, that heterodox groups were divisions of labour in the same project, and I thought what divided them was mainly their concerns, their questions. This project, I argued, was one that recognised an ontology of openness, relationality, process, and so on. I saw openness underpinning the uncertainty that was the interest of Keynesians. I saw process as underpinning the evolutionary concerns of institutionalists. I saw relationality underpinning relations of care and oppression being central concerns of feminist discussions and of those of Marxists too. But just as I saw divisions of labour, I observed a lot of communication between the different groups. I went to many heterodox meetings in those days and realised it was the same people at feminist groups, or Marxist groups, or Post Keynesian groups, or at least there was a large overlap.

Now I'm not so sure there is a unifying project or sense of purpose and concern to prioritise relevance. Now I look at the journals of all the groups I have just mentioned, and I just see modelling exercises each detached from all others. The whole orientation to research seems often very superficial to my mind. Much of it is now technique for the sake of technique. So, I'm less optimistic. What I think has happened is that although the mainstream control of the institution of academic economics now for the last 40–50 years has led to absolutely no explanatory insight, they have managed to foster the idea that a reliance upon mathematical methods is common sense, the obviously sensible way to proceed. Students have seen little else. I myself have had to spend my whole career teaching mathematics, at least within economics. My faculty would allow nothing else into the curriculum – which is why most of my contribution has been off curriculum. In Cambridge this was possible, but it isn't always. In general economists have been trained such that even when they're unhappy with the state of economics the only alternative they can think of is more modelling, different type of modelling. It seems to be that Soros's INET, the students' Rethinking [Economics] group, all of them, there's just so much emphasis on the alternative being an alternative type of modelling. Economists, even the more critical ones, seem to find it difficult to think outside that box. The normality of modelling has been ingrained in them. And, of course, they have been selected and rewarded for their conformity.

I suppose this is an odd way of answering your question. I'm not sure I'm answering your question anymore. I worry more about what used to be classified as feminist economics and Post Keynesian economics and institutionalist. It seems to me that too many are getting away from the ideals or influences, et cetera, around which they formed. Post Keynesians are getting further away from Keynes, institutionalists further away from Veblen, and so on. Many of them don't even associate with a heterodox tradition but just label themselves heterodox pure and simple. What they mean is simply that their models are simulated to produce totally different policy conclusions to others labelled "standard" or even "neoclassical". Indeed, the term "neoclassical" is used as a term considered derogatory and arbitrarily attached to any results considered fundamentally different to their own.

In [Dunn, 2009] you said you'd like to reclaim the term "political economy".

The mainstream uses it for the study of voting behaviour. Reclaiming it may well be confusing. But if projects that are relevant adopt that term, that will help.

There is this alternative initiative in which people like Ben Fine have been involved, the IIPPE initiative, do you see that as promising?

Yeah, I do, I think it's a great project. Developments like that are important. I don't want to be all negative. I hope I'm not coming across like that. There's lots of initiatives going on. I guess the PE at the end is for political economy. Good. That said, I can't help but notice that many involved, like Ben Fine himself, are even older than I am. People who have been around for a long time share the same understanding of terms like "political economy" as I do. But it is not how so many young people use such terms. Indeed, ideas as presented today are regularly trivialised. Take Keynesianism. In Cambridge there is a whole massively sponsored INET [Institute for New Economic Thinking] Keynes institute – I forget what it's called but it's all mathematical modelling. I wonder if a single person involved has read anything by Keynes. But they are now viewed as the Cambridge Keynesians.

Of course, you see Keynes as a philosophically oriented contributor. You formed this view back in the '80s, at the same time or slightly before some of the other people did. I am thinking of people like Anna Carabelli, Rod O'Donnell, John Davis, and other people. Weren't they and you here at the same time?

Well, yes. I arrived here in '75. Life was very different then. I remember going into the library and there was a drawer in which I found Keynes's unpublished philosophical papers just lying around. No one else seemed

148 *Tony Lawson*

interested, So I just took them out and took them home. No one cared. So, I had early and easy access. These days of course they are in the archives and gaining access is like entering Fort Knox. They still haven't been published.

Oh, that stuff still hasn't been published.

Not Keynes's philosophical writings. I think Rod O'Donnell has the copyright to it and we're all waiting for it to come out. Richard Kahn took control of publishing the collected works of Keynes and just didn't think his philosophical stuff was worth bothering with. For me it's the best stuff. I was looking at that stuff quite early on, but as you say, Carabelli was here and Rod O'Donnell, they were here as research students, and interested.

Another term that sometimes gets used in different ways, but which you have regularly employed, is "dialectics", and I'd be interested in exploring with you what you mean by it.

What do I mean by it or what do I defend?

Both I suppose. What role might that play in a heterodox economics or a political economy or ... ?

Then it's epistemological, Hegelian-type dialectics. I think it's an appropriate method for an open system. A big question very often put to me is: "All right, you reject mathematical modelling, what might we use instead? After all, we have to simplify, make false assumptions, the rest of it". I don't think we do need to employ claims held to be false at all. But in any case, the starting point, the orientation, can't be assumptions, deductions, conclusions. Rather the starting point is very often a puzzle. Puzzle resolution basically is dialectics. Dialectics, schematically, is a process whereby something happens, or comes to mind, that contradicts an accepted understanding, and the aim is to resolve the contradiction and thereby gain a better understanding. Some people like to summarise that as thesis, antithesis, synthesis, although that's a bit trivial. The second stage is the contradiction; that's the puzzle. So one starts from a puzzle. But one is only puzzled if/where there is already an understanding, the first stage. The third stage is to resolve the puzzle. So, if we saw a cow fly past the window, we'd probably both be puzzled, even if we don't know very much about cows; the one thing we probably have both picked up on is that cows don't tend to fly. So we may look out the window to see what's going on. Clearly this is a silly example, but that's kind of dialectics. You start with a puzzle. You start from your own understanding of where the world works. If you think capitalism is wonderful, you might be puzzled by economic crises or wars, et cetera. If you think it promotes fairness, you might be puzzled that gendered men get paid twice as much for doing the same job as gendered women. What puzzles any individual depends on current understandings, orientation, and context, but it's a starting point and then the aim is to resolve the puzzle; and then we move on. We may discover something new in the world, or simply that existing understandings were erroneous in some way. But we can make progress. We don't need a closed system for that.

You said a few things about this. You've talked about realism and the realist project and others have asked you about dialectical critical realism. I think one of your responses to that is that critical realism has always been, all along, dialectical. So there's nothing new in that sense there.

That's another story. I think there's a desire by some participants in critical realism to talk up the importance of later stages of the project. But to my mind this mostly amounts to talking down the early stages, rendering it far more rudimentary than it was. I didn't start out doing something called critical realism; I started out doing my stuff. A point was reached where I was aware that people were doing similar stuff in geography, Andrew Sayer; in sociology, Margaret Archer; in Law, Alan Norrie; we all came together, with Roy Bhaskar, and fell into calling it all critical realism. We didn't start out "oh here's critical realism let's learn about this". It was an amalgamation of all that. And in my case the shared beliefs that encouraged me to join with the others are notions that some consider to be new. I went along with it because for me it was a project that encompassed all that's now held as good in critical realism. To me it's a misrepresentation to suppose that it was ever otherwise.

But you see dialectical as epistemological.

Well, the way I just described it, yes. We can have contradictions in reality too; I mean you do. I found that the state of modern economics is a problem at the level of methodology. The project of identifying alternative methods was then more pressing than addressing contradictions in the broader or underlying social process. More and more, however, I'm turning to the latter. It's the current emphasis. But that acknowledged, I was in effect looking at dialectical contradictions in the nature of social reality even in an industrial decline paper of 1980.

But presumably that wasn't your reason for focusing on the nature of the discipline.

No, that was my puzzle. I come into economics, I thought "what on earth's going on, why are people doing this?"

You've mentioned teaching a couple of times and you said that you only ever taught maths and we've talked a lot about maths and your views of it. You're not anti-maths but you've got your strong reservations about its relevance in economics. My subsequent questions are going to be, well, how do you then go about teaching mathematics, how do you reconcile yourself to what you're doing? I suppose you just have to do it, but how do you go about doing that in a way that's not sort of completely alienating?

That's a good question. I have taken the courses that focus on the mathematical topics in as pure a way as possible. So, for example, handouts piled up on the desk next to you are labelled introduction to methods of linear algebra, to calculus. I try my hardest not to get into applications. I believe in maths, obviously. I'm happy to talk about the nature of functions, that can have some real-world relevance, but not Cobb–Douglas production functions. That's when I start sighing. People tell me I sigh a lot in lectures; but I'm happy to talk in the abstract about functions, about complexity, about continuity, about integration, about more advanced mathematical properties. I enjoy maths and maths as a tool has lots of uses, obviously. As a parallel, I'd be happy to teach someone to play the violin but not to teach them to use it to hammer nails in. I'm happy teaching the mathematics bit. It's just examples of its use in economics that I get bothered by.

I've often asked myself should I be telling the undergraduates of my reservations. I decided not to for many years just because I was not sure it was good for the students. They come to university to get an education; most of them struggle anyway to follow the courses. To have someone at the front telling them it's all a waste of their time just didn't seem to me to be psychologically facilitating. Instead, I have encouraged those that want a critical perspective to attend the Cambridge Realist Workshop.

That said, every now and again I have told them my views. I remember I did about 10 years ago. Perhaps I had just had a bad night or something. But in the middle of a lecture, I just stopped and started telling them I thought it was all a waste of time, and more importantly why. The reaction was interesting. The room went quiet. It was the most attentive audience I think I had experienced. Two or three of them in that group have since told me that it's affected their whole lives, the courses they've taken since, the paths they have taken, their outlooks, et cetera. I tried it again in recent years. But the situation is now different. High fees are charged. More students are from overseas. The students just want a certificate that allows them to go somewhere else that is well paid, et cetera. They are less curious. Indeed, I can see it upsets students to hear things that they do not want to believe or even to know. In addition, our students increasingly are trained little but in mathematical modelling/economics in school, so they're self-selecting. It was different, even 10 years ago. It has changed over the years.

Of course, when I was a student, when I arrived in Cambridge, it was very different indeed; there were economists giving out leaflets everywhere. Same at the LSE. The leaflets promoted one Trotskyist group or a Maoist group; everyone was trying to get you to sign up to their political party. In Cambridge, when I arrived, it was notably the Sraffians that were very active; everybody seemed to want me to become a neo-Ricardian. But, that's all gone. And the more time passes the more accepting the bulk of students seem to become. There are exceptions, of course, most obviously the Rethinking Economics group. I don't know what the reason is. I'm talking off the top of my head here because I've not thought of your question recently. But, my impression is that students didn't want to hear of my criticisms. So, in most of the years I've not ever let on. I have kept the focus mostly on maths per se, rather than applications.

I have, though, throughout taken a distance in presentational style. I say things like "economists assume this" or "economists do that". I don't say "we do this" or "this is how it is done".

However, there is one qualification to add to all this. It's almost, but not completely, accurate to say I've only taught maths. This last year is the one year I've taught a bit of social ontology. That did come about because of efforts of the Rethinking Economics group, or Cambridge's own group, the Cambridge Society for Economic Pluralism. The opportunity arose because universities everywhere, and Cambridge not least, are taking more and more notice of student evaluations. What's clear across the board in every university everywhere, I think, is economics comes out pretty much bottom in student evaluations. Students find the subject narrow and mostly irrelevant. In this university it comes out bottom in all subjects and does worse even than economics departments in other universities. The students always say we want a greater variety of options. They ask for courses on methodology, philosophy, history of thought, heterodox economics. So, under pressure from the university authorities the economics faculty was more or less compelled to institute an alternative course this last year. It was started up a year ago and it's gone quite well I think. It's mostly a history of thought but with two sections, one on general philosophy and one on social ontology. That was different.

What level is that taught?

To second-year undergraduates. I can honestly say at the undergraduate level this is the first time in 200 years of teaching within economics that I've been enthusiastic. I've been able to set up a website with additional reading, with debates. My heart's been in it. In a sense I feel it's been a waste of my life and their lives to use me to teach mathematical modelling for 40 years. I like teaching, but you need to believe in something to put your heart and soul into it. I put infinitely more time into preparing resources for this course this year than I have for anything involved with teaching mathematical economics.

So, what were you trying to do with the maths then? Were you just trying to get them to learn it?

Yeah. So I gravitated towards first year and I basically taught first year most of the time – first-year maths and econometrics. Focusing on methods, not applications. Stuff that I could do without feeling too guilty.

I suppose it's to their advantage that they know the language, they know about this stuff.

The courses here are all mathematical. If they're going to stay in economics here then go on and do Master's, PhD, they have to do mathematics. So, yeah, somebody has got to teach it. I had to teach something. I've been controlled over the years. Funny enough the powers that be are getting more relaxed now, probably because they've got control of everything and it's a different group of colleagues to those who fought to change it all over the years. I've just not been given any choice. I've had to teach these courses and the content of the courses were determined not by me but by others. So, I've just done it. As I say, it's a shame; I think it's been a waste of time. Certainly, to the extent I'm a teaching resource, I have been wasted. The upside for me is that it's taken very little effort, so I've been able to get on with research and other things that I probably wouldn't have done if I'd been more involved with teaching. Although having said that, the downside is that I have spent a lot of time doing additional voluntary teaching. I have spent hours teaching courses on social ontology at other faculties. I still do in gender studies at the business school. I have taught previously in sociology, human geography, law, criminology. I suppose, if I think about it, I have spent too much time teaching.

The workshop and the ontology group as well are a sort of extension of teaching, aren't they?

They're seminar groups. They've taken a lot of time certainly. So I've been lucky to be in Cambridge because there are opportunities to be had outside the faculty group. I was a Director of the Centre for Gender Studies for two years. I've been involved with other projects too – an advantage of Cambridge being a very decentralised, interdisciplinary oriented university. So yeah, personally I've survived okay. It's just a shame I haven't been able to teach economics students much that interests me or that I think is useful for them.

In [Dunn, 2009] you talked of Cambridge being on the heterodox map. Do you think that's still true?

I suppose less and less. But heterodox scholars do still visit for the archives. People do still come here to read about Dobb or Sraffa, to go through their papers. The Sraffa library has just been opened up. Dobb's papers are still not published. People come for that reason. Some even come just to attend the realist workshop, and sometimes from quite large distances. Others travel up from London every Monday night. Others visit the ontology group for a term or a year. So things do still go on.

The *Cambridge Journal of Economics* as well, obviously.

Yes, there is the journal. Although, if you look at the journal board, I'm the only editor in an economics department; increasingly as people have left we've replaced them by lawyers and sociologists, et cetera.

Possibly poets ... ? What do you think about the idea of economics as poetry?

I don't know. McCloskey said that? I do not know what McCloskey said. I'm guessing she meant something like you can communicate in poetry as in fiction, without being totally realistic with lots of fantasy thrown in. I have no idea.

We have got this notion of poetic economics, that economists actually reach their conclusions in different ways to the ways they officially do; that economists do not view themselves as pure scientists but have a self-image perhaps akin to heroism. The sort of things we talked about seem to chime with that. So, for example, we talked about aesthetics and we talked about intuition.

I guess I'm suspicious. Part of the problem with defending economics by likening it to poetry, for me, and I hesitate in saying this on the record because I know I'll come across as a pleb, is that I'm not a huge fan of poetry. However, I realise that very many people are, and I suspect when poetry is brought into this conversation, people are thinking of poetry in a positive light. Therefore, by saying that economics works in the way poetry does, I suspect those doing so are seeking yet another way to try and defend the indefensible. That was McCloskey's aim in calling economics rhetoric. The aim is to find a way of presenting it all so that despite the obvious absurdities and irrelevance of the discipline, it after all emerges as somehow okay and desirable and worthy and the rest of it. So, it's a form of apology for a bank-rupt practice, I'm guessing.

Okay.

Of course, there is a question of what is poetry, but that's ontology and quite interesting. Probably best not to go there now though?

154 *Tony Lawson*

That's probably a good moment on which to end then. Let me just see was there anything burning that I wanted to ask you. I think we've covered everything really. There's one question about whether you try to affect society. I think we've covered that.

Have we?

Unless you wanted to say more about that. You said something very early on about getting into economics because you wanted to make the world a better place, et cetera.

My view of the world and human life is that it is not something to be controlled or predicted using models. I'm a fan of human beings; I think human nature is basically good. The goal is a world of human flourishing, and there are constraints that get in the way of that; for example, structures that allow/encourage the oppression of one gendered group by another, some immigrants by indigenous people, the poor by the rich, et cetera. The only thing we can do is try to identify the conditions of these constraints and seek to remove the latter.

One of the constraints is the state of modern economics – the emphasis on mathematical modelling. Almost all the operative constraints hindering flourishing, I think, are forms of blinkers, naïvety, misconceptions. So the goal basically, and that's where being in the academic world is important, is to try to clear the ground, to produce knowledge, to remove blinkers.

Ultimately, I believe it is mostly because people are blinkered that they do things like vote for Brexit or Trump or carry on with mathematical modelling techniques. It's not because they're nasty, conspiratorial, or uncaring. I don't believe in evil. It's just that people get things wrong, especially when they are relentlessly confronted with narrow-mindedness by equally misguided souls in the media or with power. So all my goals are about changing how we see the world, about removing blinkers and most importantly allowing everyone to develop capacities of critical thinking for them or ourselves. Social reality depends on us. That's the starting point of social ontology. So the way it is, whether it's organised as capitalism or as anything else, depends on how we see it, on us and our practices. So, fundamental to it all is our understanding.

What's the role of power in that?

Power? It's a long story, there's power, power, power, and power.

I'm just reminded of Keynes's quotation about "ideas not vested interests" and by what you just said.

Okay, even vested interest is based on understanding. Too many people misguidedly spend their lives trying to become rich, make money, accumulate, be a Donald Trump. I just think they're very sad. They have a basic misconception of what their real interests are. They are as inauthentic and alienated from their humanity as any. The real interest of all of us, I have long argued, lies in caring and creating conditions under which we all flourish. This sounds assertive, I know, but I have defended the case at length elsewhere. It is not a difficult case to make. Where we don't recognise that our real interests lie with caring rather than greed, which, when leading to money accumulation, inevitably involves exploiting others, we've got blinkers on. So, in my book the most enlightened people are people like nurses and teachers and librarians ... So we are presented with theories of general vested interests, localised contingent interests, interests of the employer versus those of workers, and so on. But at the end of the day I think we've all got the same basic interest in getting rid of all structures that are oppressive and replacing them with others that are emancipatory. This is a long story and not especially about heterodox economics.

Quite poetic.

If you say so. It's the sort of stuff I'm working on now, under the heading of *eudaemonic bubbles*, subcommunities in which a greater degree of flourishing is feasible. Heterodoxy might be considered a bubble. The Cambridge Social Ontology Group, the Cambridge Realist Workshop, the National Health Service, can be considered as such. All are environments in which we can be truer to ourselves than outside them. I think we all form such bubbles all the time. I'm sure you do it with your partner, your friends, subgroups within your business school, et cetera.

10 Joan Martinez-Alier

Joan Martinez-Alier is Professor Emeritus in Economics and Economic History and senior researcher at the ICTA, Universitat Autonoma de Barcelona. He is also currently working on a five-year project funded by the European Research Council: A Global Environmental Justice Movement: the EJAtlas. He has also held positions with many universities, including FLACSO (Ecuador), Stanford, and Yale, and is a founding member and past president of the International Society for Ecological Economics. Prior to that he was a researcher at St. Antony's College, Oxford. He obtained his PhD in Economics from the Universitat Autonoma de Barcelona in 1976. His main research interest is in Ecological Economics, social metabolism, and the environmentalism of the poor. Amongst his most significant publications are *The Environmentalism of the Poor: A Study of Ecological Conflicts and Valuation* (2002) and *Ecological Economics: Energy, Environment and Society* (1990).

Joan Martinez-Alier was interviewed by Sebastian Berger via email in March 2017.

How did you become an economist?

Lorenzo Pellegrini did a long interview with me a few years ago in *Development and Capitalism*. I explained at length that I took a degree in Economics at the University of Barcelona in 1956–61, then I left, realising that the Franco regime still had many years to go (lasting until his death in 1975), and I studied agricultural economics at Oxford and Stanford in 1961–63, with scholarships. In my year at Stanford I was lucky on several grounds: I learnt about the economics of food consumption (calories, protein); I also took some courses on Marxist economics with Paul Baran, and I met Verena Stolcke, who was not yet an anthropologist. I had no idea of what the future would be for Menlo Park, Palo Alto, and the booming informatics industry. No inkling of it.

In 1963 I was again lucky and I got a three-year appointment at St. Antony's College of the University of Oxford to write a thesis on land and labour issues in Andalusia. I proposed the topic myself. Some years later this research became a book in Spanish (1968, in Ruedo iberico, a Spanish exile publisher in Paris) and then in English, *Labourers and Landowners in Southern Spain* (1971). It is about the "relations of production" in the large landholdings of Cordoba province. I did fieldwork talking to both landowners and landless labourers. I lived in some of the farms (with Verena Stolcke); we slept and ate there, did some manual work when the labourers had to do piecework.

The best economic part of my book was a theory of "sharecropping as piecework". This became an article in the *Journal of Peasant Studies* – I am very pleased to see this journal doing so well now under the editorship of my neo-narodnik friend Jun Borras. I have been associated with this journal since its beginning in 1973. In my book on Andalusia, there are many other parts on politics (living in fear as agricultural labourers under Franco) and on technological modernisation, on migration to cities. There was nothing yet on ecology, although my friend J.M. Naredo already in the mid-1970s showed how technological modernisation, or if you wish, "the development of the productive forces", meant in energy terms a deterioration of the energy efficiency, a decrease of the EROI of agriculture as we would call it today.

From 1975 onwards, already back in Catalonia as a professor of economics and economic history, I worked on energy in agriculture, mainly after reading Podolinsky's accounts of 1880 on agriculture as a system of transformation of energy. This work by Podolinsky was not well known, despite Marx and Engel's correspondence on it, and despite Vernadsky's enthusiastic praise for it in his book of 1924, *La Géochimie*. We published the first article on Podolinsky's accounts in English with Naredo in 1982 in the *Journal of Peasant Studies*, and before this in Spanish, in 1979, in *Cuadernos de Ruedo ibérico*. This made of us "ecological economists" some years before the word was used.

I often joke that I am a lapsed economist, although I have recently been recognised as an economist by being awarded the Leontief Prize. I would like to get a prize also in human ecology. I do not consider myself mainly as a heterodox economist. I am something different, an ecological economist and a political ecologist. I belong to the environmental social sciences (Fig. 10.1), together with the industrial ecologists, environmental historians, and other students of the changes in the social metabolism in the long run (Marina Fischer-Kowalski, Helmut Haberl), the ethno-ecologists and agroecologists (Victor Toledo), the urban ecologists in the tradition of Patrick Geddes and Lewis Mumford.

When I started, neither Ecological Economics nor political ecology existed. Major figures of proto-Ecological Economics have been Nicholas Georgescu-Roegen (1906–94), K.W. Kapp (1910–74), Kenneth Boulding (1910–93), and then other (dissident) economists (as Herman Daly, Dick Norgaard, Clive Spash, or myself). Major figures in Ecological Economics have been also human ecologists (like several of H.T. Odum's students). They knew about systems ecology (i.e., the flows of energy in ecosystems). There is also an overlap between Ecological Economics and industrial ecology, with R.U. Ayres who was initially a physicist.

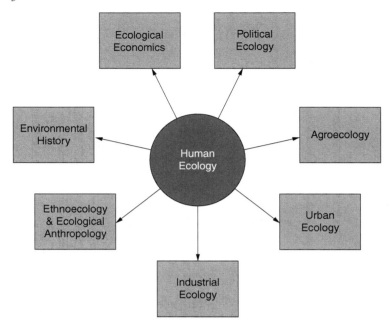

Figure 10.1

In political ecology, an early foundational book was *Land Degradation and Society* edited by Blaikie and Brookfield (1987). Later, both fields acquired international societies and their own journals, and many textbooks and handbooks; they organise conferences. I am one of the main authors in both fields, trying to bring them together.

To clarify, why did you decide to study economics as an undergraduate? What got you interested?

I remember when I was 17 years old telling a cousin of mine, five years older and studying agricultural engineering, that I wanted to study sociology, and he told me you should enrol in Economics because there is no Sociology (yet) at the University of Barcelona. I really had no idea. My father had died many years before, and my mother (of a bourgeois family) was clever but had not been to university. She regretted this. Economics was new in Barcelona. We had a normal curriculum: calculus, microeconomics, macroeconomics, and we self-taught ourselves by reading other books published in Mexico by Fondo de Cultura Económica. There was repression under Franco and a great intellectual void in Catalonia with so many people gone into exile or expelled from university teaching. We had interesting teachers in economic history (Vicens Vives), analytical philosophy (Sacristán), economic policies (Estapé). In our group of students we were asked to translate the first-draft reports from the World Bank [WB] on Spain, in 1960–61. This was when Spain joined the OECD. Quick economic growth started. I remember that the WB recommended giving up the railways and building instead new motorways. I was not yet mentally equipped to have an opinion on this.

Please tell us then how you developed your particular individual contribution.

Before coming back to Catalonia, I remained at St. Antony's College until 1973, as a research fellow, doing research on agrarian issues, first of all in Cuba (on the sugar cane planters, 1934–60, and on the land reform after 1959). In Cuba I read also about the economic debates between the orthodox members of the old Communist Party and Che Guevara. I was interested in the economics of socialism and in the revolution in Latin America but at some distance. Then I went to Peru (coming back to Oxford from time to time, and going also to the UNICAMP, in São Paulo, where Verena was working after 1971; she was teaching there and also doing research on coffee plantations and women day labourers). In Peru I did research on the "relations of production" in the highland haciendas, mainly those breeding sheep. The papers (business and confidential correspondence, accounting books) of these large haciendas (of 30,000 hectares, 50,000 hectares) became available after the Peruvian land reform. I wrote a short book, *Los huacchilleros del Peru* (1973), on the indigenous shepherds. In the 1930s, 1940s, the companies owning the haciendas wanted to get rid of the *huaccha* flocks of livestock belonging to the indigenous shepherds, because they "contaminated" the new imported breeds. The shepherds did not want to leave; on the contrary they wanted to stay put while the indigenous communities surrounding the haciendas (to which the shepherds themselves belonged) wanted to invade and take over the haciendas for good. Of course, they had been there, in a way, from before 1500. There was very good documentation on such struggles, which also showed the persistent colonialism and racism. I remember reading a letter from a young engineer, Rigoberto Calle, an expert on sheep breeding who imported stock from Patagonia and New Zealand. The letter said that there was some insubordination in the hacienda Laive and that as a matter of course *al indio xxx le metí su pateadura*.

So, in Peru the situation was very different from Western Andalusia or Cuba where there were landless proletariats threatened by unemployment and wanting assured wage work or land of their own (*tierra o trabajo*). In Peru the issue was the defence of communities by an indigenous peasantry claiming also the neighbouring land appropriated over the centuries by haciendas, and refusing to be displaced. I became more narodnik. I met Eric Hobsbawm; we went together to Huancayo looking for hacienda papers. He wrote an article on land invasions in highland Peru. I also met the anthropologist and historian John Murra (he had fought on the Republican side in Spain). It must have been 1971 – he explained to me the different meanings

160　*Joan Martinez-Alier*

of the word *huaccha* (or *wakcha*); we were sitting in an office of the Instituto de Estudios Peruanos. He was studying non-market exchanges among human groups at different altitudes: exchanges between ecological levels in the Andes by reciprocity and redistribution but not by markets. So, I became aware of Karl Polanyi's economics and the debate on substantive or Institutional Economics against the formalised analysis of markets using the economists' methodological individualism.

In Peru around 1970–71 I also learnt about the history of guano (Juan Maiguashca from St. Antony's College and Heraclio Bonilla had written on the economic and political history of guano exports from 1840 to 1890). Guano and Justus von Liebig figured later very often in my work on Ecological Economics and environmental history in the 1980s. Liebig studied biogeochemical cycles; he was an agricultural chemist, with a famous book on this topic published in 1840. He was quoted by Marx. He became an "ecological moderniser" promoting artificial fertilisers, fearing the day that guano imports would not be available. I also learnt in Peru about El Niño and the collapse of fishmeal exports when it struck. Fishmeal exports from Peru were at the root of Georg Borgstrom's concept of "ghost acreage" – the saving of land in European countries by importing cheap protein, an antecedent of the "ecological footprint" from Bill Rees and of "ecologically unequal exchange" from Alf Hornborg and myself.

The early 1970s was also when Marshall Sahlins's *Stone Age Economics* [1972] made "Chayanov's rule" so easy to understand and to teach. So, I became very familiar with economic anthropology, peasant studies, and also with ecological anthropology. I knew Teodor Shanin. I read *Late Marx and the Russian Road* [1983]. I also read Roy Rappaport *Pigs for the Ancestors* in 1971 or 1972 (with energy accounts of the shifting cultivation and pig rearing of the Tsembaga-Maring in Papua New Guinea), and when I went back to Catalonia in 1975 as a professor at the UAB, I taught introductory economics for some years (using Joan Robinson) and also an optional course on "comparative economic systems", which was 50% economic and ecological anthropology and peasant studies. I then published *Haciendas, Plantations and Collective Farms* in 1977, on Cuba and Peru, and stopped being a "Latin Americanist" for ten years. There was no possibility in Barcelona of doing Latin American rural studies. I went back later to the Andes from 1985 onwards. In 1994–95 I spent one year in FLACSO in Quito. This was much later and it was very fruitful.

Was this the origin of your contribution to Ecological Economics?

In 1975–79 I started to write on energy and the economy, not only on Podolinsky. I was a bit depressed at that time because of the very slow end of the Franco regime in 1975–79. I spent time or perhaps wasted time writing political tracts in *Cuadernos de Ruedo ibérico* against the absolute lack in Spain of what we now call "transitional justice" (as would later be applied to some extent in South Africa or Argentina). The Francoists proclaimed a self-amnesty and the parliamentary Left agreed. I still get angry, or at least agitated about this. They have not even counted properly the number of people killed by Franco, and their whereabouts are not always known. Like Federico Garcia Lorca's – one of perhaps 120,000 in Andalusia and Extremadura who were killed and buried anywhere. And there was no land reform in Andalusia after Franco's death. One of the causes of the Civil War of 1936–39 had been to stop a land reform in southern Spain.

I also wrote articles (with Jordi Roca) on the unions and on incomes policy in Spain after the change in political regime. These were still the years in the 1970s when "corporatist" incomes policy was in fashion in Europe. I criticised the top-down Moncloa Pact of 1978 that undermined the strength that the unions (mainly the Communist Party union, Comisiones Obreras) had gained with illegal struggle in the last years of the Franco regime.

At the time I collaborated regularly in a political-environmental journal, *Bicicleta*. Probably it had a negative impact factor. And I taught three or four large courses at the UAB every year. In *Bicicleta* in 1978 or 1979 I wrote a long review of Ursula Le Guin's *The Dispossessed*. Quite independently, Giorgos Kallis and Hug March have recently written on this utopia of the society of Anarres, linking it to today's debates on degrowth that we have at the Institute of Environmental Science and Technology [ICTA] at UAB. As so often, my review was in Spanish, and I did not bother or had no time or stimulus to do it in English. Le Guin's book is good for teaching anarchist-ecological political economy. Much later, around 2005, I became the adviser of Claudio Cattaneo's doctoral thesis on Can Masdeu, an occupied house in Barcelona; he did the energy accounts and he also explained the internal governance system. "The Moneyless Life of Barcelona Squatters" is the title of one of his articles. A small Anarres. The Research and Degrowth collective in Barcelona sometimes do a retreat in Can Masdeu.

Another side effect of my sympathies for anarchism (that come from Ruedo ibérico in Paris in the mid-1960s) was the doctoral thesis by Eduard Masjuan on the feminist "neo-Malthusian" movement of 1900. We have some articles together on the Spanish and Latin American followers of this grassroots social movement, like Maria Lacerda de Moura, who wrote a book entitled *Love One Another (More) and Do Not Multiply (So Much)* [1932]. Ecological economists worry about population growth. The Verhulst curve (1836) belongs to the ecology of populations (in biology) and also to demography.

At the end of the 1970s, particularly after Georgescu-Roegen (the author of *The Entropy Law and the Economic Process*, 1971) visited the UAB for a few days in 1980 and when I went to Berlin for the academic year 1980–81 at the Freie Universität, I began to write steadily my book *Ecological Economics*, which was first published in Catalan in 1984 and in English in 1987 and then in some other languages. I got help from Klaus Schlüpmann, a physicist. I corresponded regularly with Georgescu-Roegen and sent him chapters of the book I was planning to write. In Berlin the green movement was strong

162   *Joan Martinez-Alier*

in the 1980s. In the USA I already knew Herman Daly. In 1986 I met Bob Costanza and Ann-Mari Jansson, who had been students of the ecologist H.T. Odum. We founded the International Society for Ecological Economics (ISEE) with Bob Costanza as president; the first issue of the journal came out in 1989, and the first world conference took place in Washington in 1990.

I met once Bert Bolin, the first head of the IPCC [International Panel on Climate Change], and Ann-Mari Jansson showed to me the statue of Svante Arrhenius in the University of Stockholm. The theory of climate change because of excessive emissions of carbon dioxide was firmly established in the 1890s. Arrhenius reckoned there was 300 ppm in 1895; now we are reaching soon 410 ppm. He calculated the increase in temperature when doubling or tripling the carbon dioxide concentration in the atmosphere. Why did the enhanced greenhouse effect not become an international political issue until the 1980s?

My book was the first one with the title *Ecological Economics* [1990], with the subtitle *Energy, Environment and Society*. It analysed contributions from the late 19th and early 20th centuries by chemists, biologists, physicists who criticised economics because economics did not pay attention to the use of energy. This followed from my work on Podolinsky's energy accounts of agriculture. Central figures in my book were Patrick Geddes, Frederick Soddy, Otto Neurath. I read the whole published correspondence of Walras and also that of Jevons (also their books) looking for traces of interest in energy flows in the economy. Both were protagonists of the "marginalist" revolution (i.e., neo-classical economics). Jevons had earlier published *The Coal Question* in 1865, which had little to do with marginalist economics. He died young and had no time to write on the intergenerational allocation of exhaustible resources. In my book I noticed the "Jevons paradox" or rebound effect – the increased efficiency of steam engines could lead to a greater demand for coal. The most original part of my book (apart from Podolinsky's accounts and biography) is that I understood that the socialist calculation debate of the 1920s was related to the debates on what we now call the social metabolism (flows of energy and materials in the economy), through Otto Neurath (inspired by Popper-Lynkeus, Ballod-Atlanticus). This part of the book was picked up by John O'Neill, the philosopher and Professor of political economy at Manchester University who has written often on Otto Neurath and incommensurability of values.

We have chosen to speak to you as we consider you a heterodox economist. Would you label yourself as a heterodox economist? What do you think Heterodox Economics is?

No, I am an ecological economist, and Ecological Economics is certainly not a subdivision inside Heterodox Economics. I like heterodox economists in general, but many of them remain fixated on economic growth or economic development. They are not trained in human ecology.

What are the problems of mainstream economics?

Some problems are shared with heterodox economics. The main problem is to consider the economy as a system that can be explained by itself. Most mainstream economists also use the approach from methodological individualism in microeconomics. But even institutional economists of the old style who see the economy as directed by social institutions and rules that determine our choices forget about the social metabolism in terms of flows of energy and materials. They do not see the economy in terms of human ecology. This is different from Ecological Economics. And most mainstream economists do not consider political power as a factor to be taken into account. They often end their papers with naïve recommendations for policy changes directed to "impartial" state or international authorities. Heterodox economics and political ecologists focus instead on how power influences the use different classes of humans make of economic resources and also of the environment. For instance (drawing on Blaikie and Brookfield, 1987), poor peasants thrown onto the slopes by rich landowners monopolising a fertile valley are likely to increase soil erosion.

Is then "incommensurability of values" one main difference between Ecological Economics and mainstream economics?

Yes. Ecological economics, instead of resorting to a single unit of account (money), includes the biophysical aspects of economic processes and can also include social indicators like life expectancy or whatever. We criticise cost-benefit analysis (where everything is converted into money) and prefer multicriteria evaluation. We criticise GDP accounting and also the more inclusive Human Development Index because it leaves environmental aspects aside. Ecological economists look at economic processes in a way similar to the way ecologists examine ecosystems: their approach is fundamentally metabolic, meaning that the economy is seen as a subsystem of a larger global ecosystem. More specifically, the economy is regarded as open to the entry/exit of materials and energy, for instance in the form of raw materials (entry) and solid or liquid waste and greenhouse gases (exit), and economic processes are regarded as entropic and thus irreversible. The economy is not circular; it is entropic.

Ecological economics is not a branch of economics; it is transdisciplinary. Herman Daly and myself (as also Frederick Soddy) like to quote Aristotle, who famously distinguished *oikonomia*, the art and science of the material provision of the *oikos*, from *chrematistics*, which we now call economics and which is the study of market price formation for the purpose of making money. Karl Polanyi wrote about this, of course. Otto Neurath and Karl William Kapp are crucial authors for Ecological Economics between the 1920s and the 1970s. Otto Neurath became in the 1930s a founder of the Circle of Vienna of logical positivism and a theorist of the "orchestration of

164 *Joan Martinez-Alier*

the sciences" when we had to explain historical events and changes. All this is in my book of 1987.

Later in life, I "discovered" a book review by K.W. Kapp in the *American Economic Review* (1955) where he explicitly defended the incommensurability of values as a follower of Neurath. He complained that the controversy initiated by Neurath, von Mises, and Max Weber in the 1920s (the socialist calculation debate) had become sidetracked in attempts to calculate the prices of productive factors, as in Oskar Lange's elaboration of a theoretical model of "competitive" socialism. The real debate had been, however, on the importance of comparing alternatives in physical and social terms (without economic prices), choosing options democratically while faced with incommensurable values. This is not how the socialist calculation debate was taught to students of economics.

What are you trying to achieve as an ecological economist? Do you seek to influence society?

I am a well-known ecological economist, having been asked to co-edit two handbooks already, one with Inge Ropke and another one with Roldan Muradian. There is a proliferation of handbooks on all topics. I have also co-edited a textbook in English, *Ecological Economics from the Ground Up* [2012], and co-authored with Jordi Roca, in Spanish, *Economía ecológica y política ambiental* [2015], which is now in the third edition. I have also written on environmental history, co-editing books such as *Naturaleza transformada* [2001] with Manuel González de Molina and *Rethinking Environmental History* [2007] with Alf Hornborg and John McNeill.

In all those books what I want to achieve is that readers learn to do the calculations of the social metabolism, and at the same time realise that political power is essential to economic and ecological distribution. "Equity" cannot be a charitable afterthought as usual among neoclassical economists.

What we have added to Ecological Economics is the notion of "ecological distribution conflicts" [EDC]. I first wrote about this with Martin O'Connor in 1995–96. The economic values, which non-traded and traded environmental goods and services, or so-called negative externalities, might be given, depend on the distribution of political power and income and wealth. Moreover, economic value is only one type of value. To value something means to give importance to it. The dimensions of such importance are varied: livelihood needs, ecological, cultural, or religious ...

I think that in very few textbooks of economics if in any at all you would find yet this notion of "ecological distribution conflicts". They would talk of "externalities" but not of systematic "cost-shifting" and environmental liabilities. The rule of the capitalist system is never to acknowledge environmental liabilities. There are a few exceptions like the oil spill by BP in the Gulf of Mexico a few years ago. But not Shell in the Niger Delta or Texaco-Chevron in Ecuador. Notice that the COP21 [2015 United Nations Climate Change

Conference] agreement in Paris of December 2015 has a clause imposed by the rich countries explicitly denying liability for climate change.

What we teach is that the fundamental clash between economy and the environment comes from the growing and changing social metabolism of industrial economies. Energy cannot be recycled. Therefore, the energy from the fossil fuels is used only once, and new supplies of coal, oil, and gas must be obtained from the "commodity extraction frontiers", as Jason Moore called them. Similarly, materials are recycled only in part, and therefore, even an economy that would not grow would need fresh supplies of iron ore, bauxite, copper, and paper pulp. The industrial economy is entropic. Meanwhile, permanent "funds" such as aquifers, forests, and fisheries are overexploited, the fertility of the soil is jeopardised, and biodiversity is depleted. Thus, the changing social metabolism of industrial economies (including waste disposal such as the excessive production of carbon dioxide) gives rise to growing numbers of ecological distribution conflicts that sometimes overlap with other social conflicts on class, ethnicity or indigenous identity, gender, caste, or territorial rights.

The term "Ecological Distribution Conflicts" was coined to describe social conflicts born from the unfair access to natural resources and the unjust burdens of pollution. Environmental gains and losses are distributed in a way that causes conflicts. We were inspired by the term "economic distribution conflicts" in political economy that describes conflicts between capital and labour (profits versus salaries), or conflicts on prices between sellers and buyers of commodities, or conflicts on the interest rate to be paid by debtors to creditors. The terms "socio-environmental conflict" or "EDC" can be used interchangeably depending on whether the framing of the same event is socio-political or economic. The term "EDC" stresses the idea that the unequal or unfair distribution of environmental goods and bads is not always coterminous with "economic distribution" such as, for instance, rents paid by tenant farmers to landlords, or the international terms of trade of an exporting economy, or claims for higher wages from mining or plantation labour unions opposing company owners.

EDC is then a term for collective claims against perceived environmental injustices. For instance, a factory may be polluting the river (which belongs to nobody or belongs to a community that manages the river – as studied by Ostrom and her school on management of the commons). The same happens with climate change, causing perhaps the receding of glaciers in Bolivia and Peru or sea level rise in some Pacific islands or in the Kuna islands in Panama. Yet this damage is not valued in the market and those impacted are not compensated for it. Capitalism does not and cannot pay compensation to future generations for the sixth great extinction of biodiversity, or for the loss of tropical forests, or for climate change and ocean acidification. Or for damage to rivers by dams almost everywhere (and hence movements such as the MAB in Brazil, MAPDER in Mexico, Ríos Vivos in Colombia). Unfair ecological distribution is inherent to capitalism, defined by K.W. Kapp (1950) as a system of cost-shifting. In environmental neoclassical economics, the preferred terms are "market failure" and "externalities", a terminology that implies that such externalities could be valued in monetary terms and internalised into the price system. If we would wrongly accept economic commensuration and reject incommensurability of values, then "equivalent" eco-compensation mechanisms could be introduced.

Instead, Ecological Economics and Political Ecology advocate the acceptance of different valuation languages to understand such conflicts and the need to take them into account through genuine participatory processes in natural resource management. Who has the power to accept or to reject valuation languages such as sacredness, livelihood, rights of nature, indigenous territorial rights, and ecological or aesthetic values in their own units of account? Who gives mainstream economists the power they have?

Ecological Economics is doing relatively well, but in the 1980s our "enemies" in the profession were not only the Keynesians who believed in economic growth after Harrod and Domar turned Keynesianism into a doctrine of economic growth, where investments were needed in the short run to complement effective demand but also produced additional capacity which required additional consumption, and so ad infinitum. Our main "enemies" were the reinforced neoclassical and neoliberal economists, the market fundamentalists. It was again Von Mises against Neurath as in the 1920s socialist calculation debate, and the neoclassical and neoliberal had become very strong politically with Reagan and Thatcher. Thus, to come back to Latin America, the old ECLAC [United Nations Commission for the Economic Development of Latin America and Caribbean, or CEPAL in Spanish] of Raul Prebisch could have adopted our doctrines in Ecological Economics of "ecologically unequal exchange"; they could have done the accounts of material and energy flows involved in external trade as we did after 2000 or so with the members of the Institute of Social Ecology in Vienna, but already by the 1980s the CEPAL economists had been trained or indoctrinated only in mainstream economics. I have often written articles on Ecological Economics with Latin America in mind. I am a member of the school of critics of "extractivism" (with Eduardo Gudynas, Maristella Svampa, Alberto Acosta), and I have published on the terms of trade of primary exporting countries from an economic and ecological point of view.

I know well the new head of the Division of Natural Resources at the CEPAL, Dr. Jeannette Sanchez, a former student at FLACSO in 1994–95, and a minister in the government of Rafael Correa in Ecuador between 2007 and 2014. We shall try to do something together on social metabolism, international trade, and perhaps ecological distribution conflicts.

Economics is always at the service of social interests. I ask myself for whom are we doing Ecological Economics? We do it because we think it has a higher truth-content than neoclassical or Keynesian economics, but where is our social clientele? This is why I started to work with activists. From the 1980s I already thought and wrote that there would be a strong agro-ecological, pro-peasant movement (the Via Campesina was in the making) paying attention to the social metabolism of agriculture and also defending the value of agricultural biodiversity against "biopiracy" (a word from Pat Mooney of 1993) and against monocultures. I write now often with the global environmental justice movement in mind. Their members use slogans such as "tree plantations are not true forests", or "water is more valuable than gold", against open cast mining. They do not mean that water is more expensive than gold in money terms per unit of weight. They do mean that water is more valuable in a different, non-monetary valuation language.

Going back to the 1980s and early 1990s, I met in California the Marxist economist James O'Connor in 1989, and we launched together in 1991 in Barcelona (with Editorial Icaria) a Spanish edition of his journal *Capitalism, Nature, Socialism*. We wrote for eco-socialists. It is called *Ecologia Politica*; it comes out twice a year; it has reached issue 53 with a positive influence in the consolidation of political ecology in Latin America. I started to consort with activists mainly in Latin America but also to some extent in India. With Ramachandra Guha (who has become such an important political historian of India) I wrote on the "environmentalism of the poor" from 1990 onwards. He was writing on India, and I was writing on Latin America. His book on the Chipko movement was published in 1989, on the historical defence of communal forests against state-owned tree plantations in Uttarakhand. I met him in person for the first time in 1988 in a meeting in Bangalore. I helped to found the Indian Society for Ecological Economics as a branch of the ISEE and have regularly attended its meetings every two years. In 1997 with Ramachandra Guha we published together the book *Varieties of Environmentalism*, and before this I had published an article in *Ecological Economics* debunking the usual idea among economists that the environment is a "luxury good" with high income-elasticity of demand, and the parallel sociologists' and political scientists' notion (with Ronald Inglehart) that appreciation for the environment was a "postmaterialist" value. This was wrong because Western environmentalism was very materialistic in some of its main manifestations (concern for DDT in Rachel Carson's *Silent Spring* of 1962, concern for radiation in the anti-nuclear movement in Europe and the US even before the Three Mile Island accident of 1979). It was even more wrong in the South, where Chico Mendes's death while defending in Acre, Brazil, the Amazon forest in 1988, and Ken Saro-Wiwa's (and his companions') deaths defending the Ogoni against oil extraction and pollution by Shell in the Niger Delta in 1995, were a consequence of their very material fights for local livelihoods.

I was at the time involved in developing new concepts with other ecological economists (such as "strong" sustainability versus "weak" sustainability) and in my case already trying to combine Ecological Economics and political ecology, something that I did at book-length in 2002 in *The Environmentalism of the Poor – A Study of Ecological Conflicts and Valuation*. This book owes much to the women activists of Acción Ecológica in Ecuador. My classification of different types of environmentalism in this book is often quoted: a) the cult of

168 *Joan Martinez-Alier*

wilderness (conservationism, supported by conservation biology); b) the gospel of eco-efficiency (supported by engineers, industrial ecologists, neoclassical mainstream environmental economists); and c) the mantra of environmental justice and the environmentalism of the poor and the indigenous (supported by political ecologists and many ecological economists). I wish there was an alliance between conservationism and the environmentalism of the poor.

What are your strategies for seeking research funding for this type of research?

It depends on what you want or need to do. For my main two books, *Ecological Economics* and *The Environmentalism of the Poor*, what I needed was a sabbatical year paid for, good libraries, and congenial company. In 1984–85 I had one more year at St. Antony's College in Oxford. I wrote a lot though rather isolated because Ecological Economics was still a mysterious topic at the time. Mark Elvin was kind to my work, also William Beinart – both are environmental historians. Nobody was interested in Frederick Soddy's economics in Oxford. Then in 1999–2000 I wrote *The Environmentalism of the Poor* at Yale University, in another sabbatical year sponsored by Jim Scott ("everyday forms of peasant resistance"). We have known each other for a long time. At Yale, I had very good company at his program on Agrarian Studies and was subject to benign neglect by the famous School of Forestry and Environmental Studies. I had a brief discussion with Nordhaus on the economics of climate change and the discount rate, in a seminar.

So, to sum up, the answer to your question on strategies for research funding is that you need a good idea, you need motivation, and you need persistence, and if you are lucky you will get the necessary funds and good company. Then, in the last ten years I have moved away from research outcomes in the form of the single book and publication of a few papers to the coordination of three large European projects, all of them based on academic-activist research on socio-environmental conflicts, CEECEC (2008–10), EJOLT (2011–15), and now EnvJustice (2016–21) (www.envjustice.org), spending money. Altogether, it will be nearly 6 million euros between 2008 and 2021, giving contracts to doctoral students and postdocs, commissioning papers, producing books and articles, also documentaries, and in particular bringing forward (with Leah Temper and Daniela Del Bene and many other collaborators) the laborious Atlas of Environmental Justice (www.ejatlas.org), an exciting inventory of EDCs which will reach 3,000 cases by late 2019 including China and all other countries.

How many EDC are there in the world? No one knows, but there is no doubt that there are many of them. The EJAtlas aims to collect the most significant cases from the past 20 or 30 years through a collaboration methodology involving both academics and activists. The cases identified are incorporated into the interactive atlas and accompanied by a five- or six-page informative file on each conflict. We can do some statistics. There are currently 260 cases identified – a little over 12% of those registered – in which "environmental defenders" have been killed (one or more people per case). The majority are found in Latin America and Southern and Southeastern Asia. This data is only partial; the atlas still does not have enough information on some other areas of the globe in which similar killings may have occurred. The atlas also allows users to identify successful cases, in which opposition to an investment project (mines, dams, palm oil plantations, incineration plants, etc.) helped to overturn the plan. The map currently includes 360 cases deemed to be "successes" in environmental justice, which corresponds to 17% of the total. We can also calculate, for instance, the rate of participation of indigenous populations and whether this goes significantly together with higher rates of "success" in environmental justice.

So, if you ask yourself what are EDCs, here you have a very large sample from around the world. This allows doing comparative political ecology on a large scale, either focusing on countries or regions, or with a thematic focus (conflicts on coal-fired power plants, or waste incineration in cement factories, or on oil palm plantations around the world, women environmental activists killed around the world …). We also collect photos, banners, documentaries, slogans from this movement. I am impressed by the success of T.M. Krishna's Carnatic song in 2017 in defence of the Poramboke (the commons) in Ennore Creek, north of Chennai, threatened by coal-fired power plants and chemical industry, with fly ash everywhere and the mangrove forest already destroyed. The fisherfolk complain. I visited it in January 2016. We have this case in the EJAtlas. An environmentalist, Nityanand Jayaraman, wrote a long essay on the issues and this was turned into a powerful and beautiful video song. This belongs to what we call "the vocabulary of the global environmental justice movement". Another remarkable piece of this vocabulary would be paragraphs 51 and 52 of the encyclical *Laudato si* (2015) on the ecological debt from North to South on account of ecologically unequal trade and excessive disproportionate emissions of greenhouse gases and also on the environmental liabilities of investors in the extractive industries.

I want to show that there is a movement for environmental justice born from the reactions to the increased and changing social metabolism particularly at the "commodity extraction frontiers". This movement, if successful, might help to make the economy less unsustainable. In 2016 we published a first article with results from the EJAtlas in the *Journal of Peasant Studies* with the title "Is There a Global Movement for Environmental Justice?" European-funded projects in the environmental social sciences have been essential for the members of the European Society for Ecological Economics [ESEE], including myself. The strategy to get money for research in Europe, including the generous ERC [European Research Council] grants, is to have a new idea, to be enthusiastic about it, to praise yourself enough but not too much, to write clearly, and not to mince words in your application. The evaluators, I understand, are all academics more or less in your own field. They are keen to approve some projects (10 to 15%), dish out the money. They do not want to be bored.

Do you feel like you ever had to change what you write or want to research as a result of seeking funding?

No. I like the phrase in English of "having the courage of one's convictions". I would add: "having the courage and the brains". I believe it is better to be very explicit when you write a research project. You have to surprise the evaluators with something new. So, you have to have new ideas. Not only because of the money but because you enjoy them and because they are needed. However, with some "targeted" European projects you have to use ritual words. For instance, if they ask for research on the circular economy, I would not start by saying "this is total nonsense", although I believe it is. But I could start, "the industrial economy is not yet circular; it is still entropic". I would not say, "the damned capitalist economy is not circular; it is entropic", would you?

Have the pressures to seek funding increased? And has this changed what you do?

The pressures have increased in the sense that unless you get external funding, or unless you get master's and doctoral students with their own funding, your life as a researcher would be very limited indeed. We have had at ICTA UAB a series of good Marie Curie postdocs who came attracted by Giorgos Kallis and myself; we had to do very little to get them. In my view, you need time outside of undergraduate teaching. I did not start teaching really until I was 36 years old and had published two books on agrarian studies. The pressures to seek funding have increased, but the possibilities to get funding also increased, at least in Spain and until 2009 and for me also with European funding. Socio-environmental research has been well funded in Europe, although it was more difficult for environmental historians to get money than for ecological economists, political ecologists, or industrial ecologists. And I try to escape being evaluated by economists. For this, you have to choose the right calls, the right panels. This takes time. You need good advice from administrative specialists at your own research institute as regards European projects. At ICTA we have improved much on this line. We have several ERC-funded projects which are like the top prizes.

Your academic career seems to have been a great success story. Do you feel your heterodox orientation within economics has ever been suppressed or discriminated against?

On the issue of professional success, I might have gone into politics if there had been a different, more radical political transition in Spain after Franco. In 1990 I was a very unsuccessful candidate to the Spanish Parliament from Barcelona for the Green Party (which was full of internal fights). I was really engaged with Ecological Economics at the time and often travelling to Latin

America and India, so in a way electoral failure was a personal relief, although it was also a bitter experience.

On your question on discrimination against heterodox economics, you might stumble now and then on a politically motivated evaluator and then you are done for. It happens at the European level. It happened to me once in 2000 when a relatively small Spanish project on the topic of international environmental liabilities was refused. One evaluator literally wrote that he read in last week's *The Economist* that the famous environmentalist Lomborg had declared that there was too much ado about climate change, which was in fact a secondary issue compared, for instance, to malaria. I lost the funding for two doctoral students because of this fellow.

What do you enjoy most about teaching? What do you seek to achieve in teaching? How do you put this into practice?

I shall be sincere. It depends of whether students are undergraduate, or master's, or doctoral students. Teaching large classes and reading what they write or should write is tiring. I taught large classes at the UAB between 1976 and 2006, except when I managed to get away on sabbatical for one year every five years or so, and revived again. I had to teach large classes on my own; somebody has to do this in a large state university; we all did it. It was not Oxford. By "large" I mean from 50 to 100 students. Not a good method. I started with introductory economics, economic history, and my (small) course on "comparative economic systems".

But already in the late-1980s, after an internal fight, I managed to teach Ecological Economics (under the name of environmental and resource economics), and then I taught also another large class: introduction to the environmental sciences to keen first-year students in the Faculty of Sciences after 1992. I used Jean-Paul Déleage's *History of Ecology* [1991], an excellent textbook that had been a doctoral thesis in Paris which I myself had examined, and also, of course, *Environmental Science* [1986] by G. Tyler Miller and *Ecoscience* [1977] by Paul and Anne Ehrlich and John Holdren. From the late 1980s, therefore, I taught mostly what I was very willing to learn at the time or writing myself. I had a chair in economic history, but I was teaching courses on introductory human ecology and Ecological Economics to undergraduates. The students remember me more than I remember most of them. If you try to make students of a large class write frequent essays at home or answer written questions in class, and then you correct and give back their work, you really get tired. I did this in Barcelona to a greater extent than I would have done it elsewhere. I felt patriotic, I suppose. Also, I was paid to do it.

At master's and doctoral level, advising students (especially if they are rebellious and with independent minds) is a memorable pleasure. I have helped bring to fruition about 35 doctoral theses in Ecological Economics,

172   *Joan Martinez-Alier*

Environmental History, Political Ecology since 2000 in the graduate program at the UAB, which I precariously started with Giuseppe Munda in 1997 (with help from Silvio Funtowicz) and which is now solidly housed at the ICTA with luminaries such as Jeroen van den Bergh (economics of climate change), Mario Giampietro (societal metabolism), Giorgos Kallis (Political Ecology and Degrowth), Isabelle Anguelovski (urban political ecology), Victoria Reyes (ethno-ecology), Esteve Corbera (ecosystem services), and others who are also ecological economists or political ecologists.

The notable economist McCloskey referred to economics as poetry. What do you think about that?

On Deirdre McCloskey's "economics as rhetoric", I think it was a refreshing book. I glanced at it. I should read it carefully and see whether she engaged with human ecology. Her main points were against the gospel of model building and then calibrating the models with data, and then testing hypotheses for statistical significance. This is a method that I learned as an economist, and sometimes it is useful. I have not written much in this style. She favoured the accumulation of information on particular topics and building arguments, as social historians often do. I agree. In the EJAtlas we talk about "repertoires of collective action" in socio-environmental conflicts, a concept from social history. However, how does McCloskey relate to Ecological Economics? Does she discuss the economy as a system of social metabolism? Is she in favour or against this framing? Social metabolism refers to quantified flows of energy and materials, how they change with economic growth. There are, of course, some issues of contention in such measurements, but they give a perspective different to mainstream economic history. Is there "relative" dematerialisation? Is there even "absolute" dematerialisation of the economy? To say yes or no, we need some statistics and some tests of significance. Would she find the question relevant? Would she object to the method? Did she confront or agree with Georgescu-Roegen's critique about the "arithmomorphic" excesses of economic theory in *The Entropy Law and the Economic Process* of 1971? I would have to read more carefully her book again before answering your question. For instance, in economic statistics we find numbers on the "production" of oil per country. The geologists would call this "extraction", instead, because production happened millions of years ago. The economists' terminology reveals their metaphysical standpoint. Of course, using the word "metaphysical" as a nasty word is pure rhetoric.

11 Esther-Mirjam Sent

Esther-Mirjam Sent is Professor of Economics at Radboud University, where she has been since 2004. She is also a member of the Senate of the Netherlands, the Social Science Council of the Royal Netherlands Academy of Arts and Sciences, and many advisory boards. Prior to that she obtained her PhD from Stanford University and held a tenured position as associate professor at Notre Dame University. She is a recipient of the Joseph Dorfman Best Dissertation Prize and the Gunnar Myrdal Prize. Her main research interests are behavioural and experimental economics, history and philosophy of economics, and economic policy. Amongst her most significant publications are *Science Bought and Sold: Essays in the Economics of Science* (co-edited with Philip Mirowski, 2002) and *The Evolving Rationality of Rational Expectations* (1998).

Esther-Mirjam Sent was interviewed by Sebastian Berger via phone online in April 2018.

How did you become an economist?

I decided to become an economics major because I wanted to go into politics. It's something that is deeply ingrained in my family history. But then when I started economics it became quite clear that economics was not very well suited for my purpose because economics was so far removed from the real world, so abstract and focused on modelling that I had difficulties in envisioning how this would be combined with a career as a politician. So, I decided I wanted to study some more – I went to the United States for my PhD, and there Thomas Sargent was one of my instructors, and he would write three equations on the blackboard and he would say "this is the economy. I am not going to talk to you about *how* this is the economy, *why* this is the economy, *in what sense* this is the economy, but I am very happy to help you with the mathematics, with multiplying matrices, so on and so forth". And that is when I decided this is not going to help me as a politician. What I needed to find out first is where does this positioning of economics come from? Where does this arrogance of economics come from? Where does this authority that people ascribe to economics come from? And that is how I ended up specialising in history and philosophy of economics, and writing a PhD dissertation on Thomas Sargent, who was one of my instructors at Stanford, as I said. So, that is a long answer to a short question of how I became an economist, and for a long time I was not a proper economist, but I was a historian and a philosopher of economics. Over the course of the history, because this history spans from 1985 until now ("1985" is when I became an economics major, and "now" is when I do combine economics and politics), over the course of this history economics has changed and has become more pluralistic, and this has enabled me to make a gradual switch back to economics and has enabled me to combine my academic career with a political one, which I do as a professor of economics and as a member of the Senate in the Netherlands.

You said you have a background of politics in your family, so you went into economics. Were there any assumptions when you made that decision, that economics is a particularly good field to know if you want to become a politician?

Well, to the extent that I was able to figure this out as an 18-year-old, my image of economics was a science that was rigorous, that addressed the issues that were relevant for society. We had just gone through the Oil Crisis, a period of stagflation in the Netherlands; there were questions about our competitive position, and it seemed to me that studying economics would enable me to understand these significant economic developments and would help me in designing policy responses to these developments.

You said that you transitioned from studying with a rather mainstream professor in the US and then becoming a historian and philosopher of economics. In that transition, what difficulties did you encounter, if any, and how did you find support to engage in this transition of becoming a philosopher of economics? How did that come about?

As many things come about by coincidence, I did my PhD at Stanford University and struggled for two years figuring out what to do with the economics I was being taught, how this would help me in my career as a politician, and trying to understand how this fit with the authority that is ascribed to economists. By coincidence, a Dutch friend of mine studied at the University of Notre Dame, and I talked to him on the phone and he mentioned that there was a very supportive environment at Notre Dame, that Philip Mirowski was there, and it was a very intellectually stimulating environment. I ended up contacting him, and I was able to spend one year at Notre Dame (that was in the fourth year of my PhD studies). Over the course of that year I also had to find a supervisor at Stanford, and Kenneth Arrow was kind enough to think this was something to be supported, to nurture somebody who is willing step outside and be critical, ask questions that other fellow students were not willing to ask. In my fifth year I finished my PhD at Stanford, and I had a wonderful defence with Arrow and Mirowski, spending most of the time discussing with each other as opposed to me defending my PhD dissertation.

And how did you then envision becoming an academic economist in terms of teaching and publishing? Or, was the vision still that you wanted to go into politics?

No, the political dream was completely out of the picture with the focus on economics as a curious discipline that was really not able to help me as a politician. My entire focus was on academia and on developing a profile in history and philosophy of economics. Upon graduating, I obtained an academic position at the University of Notre Dame, spent ten years there. I went through the assistant professor-renewal-tenure process and ended up obtaining tenure, so the whole "publish or perish" and academic career track was my focus for ten years, and also when I moved to the Netherlands initially it was. But then gradually my old interest in politics re-emerged, and in 2011 I was elected as a senator in the Netherlands.

So, it was this interest that emerged during your PhD studies with very intellectually stimulating supervisors that got you interested in an academic career, and then later on you became more interested in politics again?

Yes, that is right.

Please tell us how you developed your particular individual contribution.

My particular contribution was inspired by the concern about the classes that were being taught at Stanford, inspired by a wish to understand what motivates these economists, where do they get their authority, and that is how I ended up developing a research line along the lines of sociology of scientific knowledge, trying to understand economists in their own terms, and in some sense also modelling economists as economic agents. A criticism of my work is that it often focuses on the individual economist, and sociologists would rightly counter that this is only part of the story – that you have to situate economists within their context and look at the group processes. To some extent, I followed the "representative agent" inspiration in modelling some economists as representative agents. It was never a clear track. I stumbled from one thing to the next, much like the person on whom I focused later on in my research, Herbert Simon. His research is on bounded rationality and how we

176   *Esther-Mirjam Sent*

search and use heuristics, and one of the dangers of an interview like this is you get post-hoc rationalisations, and that's also a danger that I encountered when I interviewed Sargent as part of my thesis – that you're always tempted to offer post-hoc rationalisations, making a clear, well-designed path with a goal that is in the present or perhaps in the near future. But if you had followed me along, then perhaps this story would not have been as crisp as you are getting now in this interview.

That is a good point; we actually speak about that in the introduction, as being one of the potential limitations of the information from the interviews. If I may go into a bit more detail about developing your particular contribution, if you could flesh that out a little bit: were there any challenges in the networks or groups of people that you were in? Was publishing easy in this niche of economics? I'm interested in the group process of you developing your contribution; were there any collaborators that helped you along the way, senior economists who you worked with at the time and published with you? Was it easy for you to get access to academic journals in the field, philosophy and history, or the sociology of economics?

I was helped tremendously by Kenneth Arrow and his willingness to supervise a curious PhD dissertation, especially when you look at the typical PhD dissertation at Stanford. He felt a certain freedom because he is not a historian of economics, but he is such an important part of the history of economics. Because of this authority he felt the freedom to encourage non-traditional dissertations, so that helped tremendously. John Dupré was also on my dissertation committee as a philosopher of science and he was very encouraging, and then obviously Philip Mirowski in allowing me to spend a year at Notre Dame and working with me as a junior colleague when I was at Notre Dame was tremendously important, and there was a whole community of historians and philosophers of economics with Wade Hands, John Davis, Roy Weintraub, Neil De Marchi (who was also my thesis supervisor at the University of Amsterdam; it was through his encouragement that I moved to the United States for a subsequent PhD). Publishing was never really an issue in history and philosophy of science and in history and philosophy of economics journals; of course, I had my share of rejections, but it did not seem asymmetric. And at that time I was very fortunate that Notre Dame had an economics department that was very encouraging of non-traditional approaches, history and philosophy of economics, so when the renewal came up and my tenure decision had to be made economists in my area were consulted; historians and philosophers of economics were consulted and looked at my file. So, for a long time I felt very safe in that community.

Craufurd Goodwin played an important role in getting my book published at Cambridge University Press. I won an award for my dissertation; I won an award for my book. And after I got the tenure things slowly turned at the University of Notre Dame. While I was away on a sabbatical, the department got split in two: with a Department of Economics and Econometrics, including the neoclassical economists, and another Department of Economics and Policy Studies. We had a long debate about whether it should be "Economic and Policy Studies" or "Economics and Policy Studies", and we managed to maintain the "s" to signal to the world that this was also a proper economics department. For a while the Department of Economics and Policy Studies with the non-neoclassical economists survived, but several years after my move to the Netherlands the department was abolished and the non-traditional, non-neoclassical economists were spread out over political science, poverty institutes, labour institutes, and other parts of the University of Notre Dame.

Would you consider building a pluralistic economics department in the Netherlands or introducing heterodox economics into politics your individual contribution?

Yes. In the Netherlands, I am in a department that carries the label "economics plus", that finds pluralism very important, and I spent a lot of effort in the last 14 years making sure that History of Economics, Institutional Economics, and Philosophy of Economics remain part of the curriculum. In our Master's programme I teach a pluralisms in economics course that is required for all our students; we spend a lot of time on behavioural finance, behavioural economics. I am chair of my own group within the department and for a while I was the department chair, and we've always labelled ourselves as a pluralistic department and we've been proud of doing so.

Did that emerge with your return from the US, or did that exist prior to your arrival?

To some extent it was there prior to my arrival, and it is partially because the economics department is situated within the school of management science, which has also business administration, political science, public administration, human geography, spatial planning, and environmental studies. So, it is not a typical economics or business school. To some extent there was this focus already, and I think this is what made them interested in my application. While there has been some pressure to become more neoclassical, we have countered this and at present there is a pride in being pluralistic at my university. It could be also that the Catholic character has something to do with it, the University of Notre Dame is a Catholic university with a strong focus on social justice and matters along those lines, with the peace institute, the labour institute, and the same is the case for the university at which I am

178   *Esther-Mirjam Sent*

teaching at the moment; Radboud University is also a Catholic university that wants to position itself as more broad and encouraging critical thinking, so pluralistic economics fits into this critical perspective very nicely.

We have chosen to speak to you as we consider you a heterodox economist. Would you label yourself as a heterodox economist?

No, I would not. I would label myself as a historian and philosopher of economics and as a mainstream economist. And here I follow the definition of Colander, Holt, and Rosser (2004b), who define "neoclassical" economics as the orthodoxy, as a school that is backward-looking and intellectually defined. They define "mainstream" economics as the research frontier in economics, as mostly a sociological category, and they define "heterodox" economics as anything that does not fit into the orthodoxy and mainstream. And to some extent I think it is a strategic move to position yourself as a mainstream economist, because that is when you can have an influence on the course of events within your discipline, and I see "mainstream" economics as encompassing behavioural economics, experimental economics, Institutional Economics, evolutionary economics, computational approaches, feminist economics, neuro-economics, and at present it is not clear in which direction it is heading, and you can see the glass as half full or half empty. The "half empty" would be, well, behavioural economics is neoclassical economics *plus*, with a twist but still very neoclassical; you can say New Institutional Economics is neoclassical economics with a little bit of institutional flavour, but I much prefer to see the glass half full with possibilities of redesigning the core of economics through a collaboration among these various mainstream perspectives.

What do you think Heterodox Economics is?

There again, I follow the line of what Colander, Holt, and Rosser said, as "heterodox economics" being anything that is not mainstream – that is, not part of the sociological research frontier as considered by most economists – and that is not part of the intellectual orthodoxy that is more backward-looking, and you have heterodox economics as the remaining category. There, I think it is also important to look at the research of John Davis, which I like a lot, and he argues that these categories are fluid through time, that something could be heterodox at some point and become mainstream later on, or it could be mainstream at some point and become heterodox later on. I think he offers some good illustrations; for instance, the older institutional approach, at some point it lived side by side with neoclassical economics, and at a later point it was kicked out when neoclassical economics became dominant. The same thing with Keynesian economics at some point being part of the mainstream or the orthodoxy, but no longer with the events of the 1960s and 1970s. So, there is a fluidity when different approaches are categorised, and of course these approaches themselves change as well.

So, you follow a sociological definition, if I'm correct. Would you say there is anything besides that, any intellectual common foundations or roots of the various heterodox paradigms? And which paradigms would that be for you now?

I am not the main expert on heterodox economics, but it is interesting that you interviewed me for your project as I would not label myself as a heterodox economist. I would label myself as a historian and philosopher and a mainstream economist. For the most part I really try to see all of us as contributing to one project, that is much more pluralistic now than it was in the past, and I think heterodox economists hurt their chances of participating in the discipline when they define themselves on the outside. It would really help your opportunities of participating in the conversation of influencing economics or influencing politics if you position yourself strategically as part of the mainstream, and neoclassical economics as being part of the older orthodoxy.

The main reason why we were very interested in interviewing you was that for some of us that think that history and philosophy of economics could be considered heterodox in terms of its position within the field, slightly marginalised, slightly underrated, with few job openings in it, and if you ask the kinds of questions that a typical historian or philosopher of economics would ask, then traditionally a neoclassical economist would not be very pleased with that, or would not be willing to engage in the conversation, or would perhaps have a defensive reaction. We were thinking that philosophy and history would fit within heterodox economics. Would you disagree with that?

It is important to note that history and philosophy of economics has undergone a transition. In the past, history and philosophy was very much concerned with telling economists where they were wrong – we would take Popper, or Lakatos, and we would say "you're not doing proper science because you are not falsifying your theories", or perhaps even Kuhn and something about "you're part of a paradigm and you should be aware of its anomalies and it's time for a paradigm shift" – that is the traditional approach to history and philosophy of economics. This specialisation has made a transition towards more of an interest in understanding where does economics come from; what inspires economists; what makes them different from other sciences; where

180   *Esther-Mirjam Sent*

do they seek their alliances; how do they position themselves. It is more of a move from traditional philosophy of science to applied philosophy, or a sociology of science approach, that is the transition that the field has undergone, and in that transition I think it has become less of an opposition to traditional economics and has more a focus on trying to understand it because we do not have any standards by which to feel superior to economists, for these standards have been undercut by the research that is being conducted in the sociology of science.

I wonder if a mainstream or a neoclassical economist would recognise it as such? Because it seems they would normally associate economics, or "good economics practice" with mathematics, econometrics, statistics, and empirical work. Would they recognise this philosophy or history of economics the way you describe it, as part of what they would consider economics? Or would they sociologically rather put it in another category?

Yeah, I think I am biased in the answer that I give, and the bias is that I have always been in nurturing environments. While I was at Notre Dame it was considered of the utmost importance that our students would be educated in history and philosophy of economics, and awareness of history and philosophy was crucial for the economists that were working at Notre Dame. Then, when I made the transition to the Netherlands to Radboud University, I encountered the same situation and I still do. And even more so now in light of the economic crisis. The crisis makes it obvious that we need to reflect on our practices as economists, that we need to be aware of our position in society, that we need to be aware of the history of our discipline and the lessons that need to be learned. History is also of interest in and of itself, and I am surrounded by colleagues who think that this is important; I am surrounded by students who study at my university because they know that this is something they are going to learn. There may be a bias and maybe it is also that I prefer to see the glass half full and prefer to see the positive side of my position.

What are the problems of mainstream economics?

It depends on how you define mainstream economics. I would define it as the pluralism you see at the present, and I would define neoclassical economics as the orthodoxy. And then the problem of mainstream economics is: what are the advantages and disadvantages of the pluralism? And there is always a tension. It is a tension I encounter as a politician: on the one hand you want to embrace the richness of the world and want to offer different perspectives on it, a philosophical perspective, an institutional perspective, a psychological perspective, but then as a policymaker and when I look at a law and a new policy I want to know what is this going to do and I don't want to get "on the one hand, on the other, and depending on the assumptions and depending on which perspectives", and this is always a tough balance we as economists have to consider. For the longest time we leaned towards offering clear answers that were entirely inaccurate, and now we lean more towards uncertainty, various dimensions, various perspectives. That's what makes economics peculiar: this positioning close to politics and the desires that policymakers have.

What are you trying to achieve as an economist?

I am an economist four days a week and a politician one day a week. And, the economist in me seeks to enrich economic thinking by focusing especially on bounded rationality, on preconceptions that people have, on gender for instance. The philosophy and history perspective is something that I still have as well, so by critically evaluating, for instance, gender research that is being done and in what sense are we essentialising matters and labelling something as female where social context matters a lot. So, the economist in me offers critical contributions to economics and a critical meta-perspective on the field and then the politician in me tries to incorporate richer perspectives than the traditional neoclassical perspective that for the longest time dominated much of the policy debate. At least in the Netherlands we have the Central Planning Bureau, and it makes predictions, it calculates the programmes that political parties have, but it is all based upon very questionable assumptions, a model that presumes that people respond rationally to incentives. So the policymaker in me tries to make politicians aware of the limitations of the predictions that we get, the limitations of the clear-cut recommendations we have when it comes to incentives, offering a broader perspective.

How do you deal with the uncertainty that comes from a plurality and more broad-minded perspectives?

You cope with it by focusing much more on experimenting and allowing for different policies to be enacted in different parts of the country because perhaps in a border region it will work out in one direction and in a big city it will work out in a different one. So there is no one-size-fits-all and there is also no certainty as to the exact outcome. So, experiments in policy are much more important and evaluations obviously, learning from the sense in which things work differently from the way you expected, and by focusing more on narrative, less on the hard figures which turn out not to be that hard anyways, working with margins as opposed to several numbers after the dot. So, those are matters which I try to bring into the policy debate. For instance, one example, our government always presents its plans for the new calendar year in September. And, in the past we would only have the economic predictions along with those plans. So, the economists of the Central Planning Bureau would calculate what the effects are of this policy on the budget and economic growth. Now, what I have introduced with some of my colleagues is more input from other bureaus, from the social and cultural planning bureau, from the environmental planning bureau, and not clear calculations but narratives, elaborating what does this do to discrimination, what does this do to inequality. We need to look at a broader indicator of our well-being than GDP. So those are ways in which I try to enrich the debate with new insights from economics.

Do you seek to influence society? If so, how?

Certainly, I am a social democrat. I am in the government for the Labour Party and I became an economist because I wanted to influence society. Then I learned that I could not do this as an economist. Subsequently, I tried to influence economics by means of history and philosophy of economics, learned that I could not really influence economics because all the traditional perspectives were being questioned. But then slowly, fortunately, it came together for me with the transition of economics towards a more mainstream approach and with the possibility of joining the Senate in the Netherlands.

What are your strategies for seeking research funding?

Fortunately, our research is funded by the university, and obviously there is always the wish to generate more funding. I have tried the Dutch Science Foundation without any luck. And most of the additional funding I get is by collaborating with companies and firms and by offering public lectures. So, it is in the consulting/lecturing area that I generate my funding. The more traditional money streams have been less forthcoming, but that is also because the competition is just so strong. In the US we were successful. Phil Mirowksi and I obtained funding for a conference we organised from the National Science Foundation because we positioned ourselves in the field of philosophy of science, as in economics there was just no space for what we wanted to do.

So, not receiving funding from the Dutch Science Foundation is not an ideological problem, or a problem of being perceived as non-mainstream?

Not at all, no. In fact, the reason for this is that in funding in the Netherlands economics is not a separate category but is included in the social sciences and humanities, which is one category. All the applications in that category are considered by psychologists, by business administration researchers, by economists, so since you are categorised in this area you don't suffer from orthodox economists arguing that what you do is not proper economics. In fact, in my chair group I have a sociologist who got a very prestigious grant for research on labour relations, and we were so excited by that that we hired her and she is now a professor in my chair. So the boundaries in the Netherlands are fluid because of the way the funding organisation is designed. But at the same time the competition is so fierce and chances of obtaining funding are rather slim. Lecturing and consulting are more likely to generate funds.

Do you think your political career helped to obtain funding?

Certainly. Visibility really is what helps to generate funding. And visibility is also how I ended up going into politics. After the crisis there was a call for explanation, for clarification. So, for three years in a row I won a media award for the professor of my university who was in the news the most. Since the Netherlands is a small country, one thing leads to the next. Once you are in the card deck of the TV and radio programmes, they think you know about everything that has to do with economics. It was this visibility that triggered my party to ask me whether I was willing to join the Senate. And this visibility also helps generate other requests, for lectures, for participation in research projects. It also hurts me to be a female economist in the sense that there are biases. But it helps me in that we are trying to overcome these biases and there are not many female economists. So when there is an explicit goal to have diversity in a consulting team, given the fact that there are not that many female economists, I am often the go-to person for such things.

Does your political position in the Senate come with any access to research resources?

No, not at all. In fact, I have to bring in my own money to get help with the research that I need to do as part of my work as a politician. While there is a scientific bureau of the party, this bureau has three employees. We have only one intern for the eight Labour Party members in the Senate. So the Dutch are very frugal in politics. Regrettably that does not open any channels at all. But it is the visibility and the authority, the Senator, the Professor, that helps generate funding.

What do you enjoy most about teaching?

The enthusiasm of the students, the willingness to engage with new ideas, the openness of the students, the fact that they are young and have a long career ahead of them. I truly enjoy giving them a good start in this career. It's wonderful when they come back and elaborate how being at my university has helped them in their careers. Indeed, teaching is much more rewarding than research as teaching is instant and research takes long, with rejections and criticisms. However, I have quite a big administrative position at my school. I am Vice-Dean of Education, and that means I only get to teach one course per year, which is the pluralisms in economics course that is required for all our Master's students. What I like as adviser on educational matters

184   *Esther-Mirjam Sent*

is to confront teachers with the changes in our student population and the new developments in technologies that are available. Because as teachers we tend to teach the way we were taught. And as teachers there is a risk of losing touch with the students that have a different way of learning that don't come into our university the way they did in the past. They are inspired by different things; they have different backgrounds than we were used to. So I find it a challenge to make sure that the teaching wishes and teaching offerings are matched in my job as a Vice- Dean of Education and bringing in new ICT in education possibilities to do so.

What do you seek to achieve in teaching? How do you put this into practice?

The motto of my university is "change perspective", and that is what inspires me. I want to raise critical thinkers that are willing to change perspective, to be aware of preconceptions, to be aware of various perspectives that one can have when considering an issue. So my course offers a different school of thought in every class meeting. And it is not a matter of me telling students what they have read but almost the entire meeting is about discussion, about students bringing in what they have learned in other classes and how it relates to the readings they have done, and to reflect critically amongst themselves. So it is really a course in critical thinking, more so than a course in learning things that you can read in books anyway or you can find on the internet anyway. And I think that is the best way to position our students when they enter the job market. Knowledge is not so important anymore. It is the creative skills that are much more important. And that is what I focus on in the pluralisms course.

How do you put this into practice more concretely?

We have a class debate, and in preparing for the debate the students write short summaries about their readings and how this relates to what they have learned elsewhere. They come to class well prepared. Assessment is by means of short essays, comparing and contrasting perspectives on a matter and elaborating what the relevance of this contrast is for their own area of specialisation, as with game theory there are enthusiasts and critics, or with neuro-economics there are enthusiasts and critics. But I ask the students to compare and contrast and to weigh in their own specialisations, illustrations, to come to a conclusion as to which they find more compelling.

Do you provide them with the readings or do you ask them to do their own research?

For the class discussions I provide them with readings, one pro and one con. For the essays they have to find additional readings on the pros and cons. And also readings that relate the issue to their own area of specialisation.

Is critical thinking the ultimate goal or an intermediate goal for yet another ultimate goal, such as educating democratic citizens?

Yes, of course, the secret agenda is to create mini-versions of me but better mini-versions of myself, but that is not something that I can tell the students. But in the end indeed "Bildung" as they say in German is very important and part and parcel of an education.

Is there a particular concept of the human being that underlies that reference to Bildung in education?

The deeper layer is mostly inspired by Herbert Simon's bounded rationality that we all have and with which we participate in society. It's a humility; it's an awareness of the complexity of society.

The notable economist McCloskey referred to economics as poetry. What do you think about that?

I think of economics as a social phenomenon, a narrative, playing a role in society. I have a hard time envisioning a societal impact of poetry. Thinking of economics as poetry would in my opinion not help the position of economics; it would limit what economics does too much. By limiting I mean that I don't see power in poetry; I don't see money in poetry. Perhaps my picture of poetry is too limited and because of that I have a hard time seeing economics as poetry. I miss the power, the politics, the authority, the influence, the sociological perspective when economics is associated with poetry.

12 Gary Mongiovi

Gary Mongiovi is Professor of Economics at St. John's University, New York. He holds a BS in Finance from St. John's, an MA from New York University, and a PhD from the New School for Social Research. He was, for almost 20 years, co-editor of the *Review of Political Economy* and is active in a number of other associations. His main research interest is the economics of Piero Sraffa, but he has written widely on economics and its history, also writing on the thought of Keynes, Marx, and Ricardo. He has published extensively in these areas. A theme of his work is trying to examine connections and distinctions between thinkers and schools of thought. Among the highlights of his work are his edited volumes (with Petri, 1999) *Value, Distribution and Capital: Essays in Honour of Pierangelo Garegnani*, and (with Koppl, 2012) *Subjectivism and Economic Analysis: Essays in Memory of Ludwig M. Lachmann*, and (with Ciccone and Gehrke, 2013) *Sraffa and Modern Economics*. His articles on interpretations of Marx (2002) and the relationship between Sraffa and Marshall (1996) are also significant contributions.

Gary Mongiovi was interviewed by Andrew Mearman at the Manhattan Campus of St. John's University, New York, in April 2017.

How did you become an economist?

Well, it was not my intention to become an economist when I went to university. I think that would have been the last thing that I'd end up being, but I had a good Principles teacher in my first year. He was a mainstream guy but an old-fashioned kind of mainstream economist – the kind of mainstream guy you saw in the early '70s – someone who was anchored to good practical mainstream work, who saw the utility of basic neoclassical tools and applied them in a sensible way. He was a good teacher and he was funny so the course was engaging to me and then I subsequently became a finance major. I was not sure what I wanted to major in, but I did have a good teacher who was doing her PhD at the New School for Social Research, so she was a non-mainstream person, and I saw that there were some interesting debates going on and this was an interesting topic.

When I graduated the only thing I knew, even though I had majored in finance, was that I did not want to wear a suit to work every day and be a banker. So, to kind of get into a holding pattern, I entered the Masters programme at New York University, thinking, "well, if this works out, maybe I'll go on to do a PhD, but let's see", and that was a very good experience. I had one terrible, small-minded neoclassical micro guy in my first semester. He was dreadful. He saw microeconomics as an ideological weapon that you could use to smash anyone who wants to actually advocate policies to make the world a better place. I remember once asking him in class: "but what about power – doesn't power influence outcomes in the market?" And he said to me in the obnoxious, dismissive, cutting way that he had with students: "well, I think that's a very naïve way to think about the economy". I thought to myself – you know, I was 21 or 22 years old, I didn't know anything; but I knew enough to realise that if this guy thinks I'm naïve for asking about power, there's a real problem with the way he's approaching his subject. So he was the one bad experience I had at NYU. My other professors at NYU were terrific. I had a Micro course with William Baumol. He was brilliant; it was a real privilege to study with him. And I had History of Economic Thought with Israel Kirzner, the Austrian school guy, who was excellent. I did a Master's thesis with him and James Becker, the department's token Marxist, as my supervisors; they were great, really, really interesting and supportive and helpful.

The thesis was on the professionalisation of American economics, so it was concerned with that period of the formation of the American Economic Association when there were all these debates going on about whether economics should be mainly a "science" or a tool for the improvement of society. What's the proper balance between them? How much should your ideology inform your professional outlook and the approach that you take to your work? Those kinds of issues. Obviously, James Becker and Israel Kirzner had different perspectives on all this. I leant more towards Becker's point of view, but Israel was really supportive and helpful, and I got interested in the Austrians then. They were an interesting bunch of people in that department. NYU had an Austrian programme at that point that really had some heft in the department. Shortly after I left, the department declared war on them and essentially tried to whittle that programme down to almost nothing now. I liked Israel and thought he was a smart guy even though I disagreed with a lot of what he had to say about how markets work.

The critical course for me at NYU was a summer seminar on general equilibrium theory that was taught by Harvey Gram, who at that point was just finishing up a book that he had written with Vivian Walsh called *Classical and Neoclassical Theories of General Equilibrium* (1980). The book basically contrasted the neoclassical versus Sraffian perspectives on general equilibrium theory. Harvey was responsible for the technical aspects of the book, so he was presenting these linear models, and I was fascinated; I thought, man – this is really nifty stuff! It was technically challenging but not so challenging that I was overwhelmed at that stage in my intellectual development, so I got really engaged by this idea of models having structural similarities but making different assumptions about how you close them, [with each method of closure] reflecting a different understanding about how the economy works at a fundamental level – I thought that was fascinating.

So, I wrapped up things at NYU and transferred over to the New School to finish my PhD. When I was transferring, I went to the Director of Graduate Studies at NYU, who was a very nice man named Jonas Prager who taught Macro. He was a monetarist, a terrific teacher, and an open-minded person, and I asked him for a letter of recommendation because I wanted to transfer to the New School for my doctorate. He was flabbergasted because he could not believe that I would want to transfer from NYU to the New School; he started to talk to me about why I should stay at NYU and one of the things that he said was that they were in the process of transforming the department; they were going to try to transform it into a place that will be in the same league with Columbia and the University of Chicago, and I said, well, now I *have* to leave! My basic feeling was I'd gotten what I could out of this faculty and it was terrific, but let me transfer and see what else is out there; the New School was closer to my orientation anyway.

I'd thought I was going to focus on Institutional Economics, but I got there the same year that John Eatwell had joined the faculty. John was teaching the core Macro and Micro PhD courses, and I took the Micro first and then the Macro and they were terrific courses. So he taught me more about Sraffa and introduced me to the Post Keynesian perspective. I also took courses with Edward J. Nell, who is wonderful and brilliant. He's a really inventive intellect, always thinking outside the box. He was the person who taught me not to be afraid to push the envelope and take calculated intellectual risks. You know you may fall flat on your face, but that's how you advance understanding. I had a couple of courses with Thomas Vietorisz, who liked to work with these linear models like the ones Harvey Gram had taught me, and those were good, useful courses.

That first year I sat in on a seminar at NYU that was taught by the Austrian School economist Ludwig Lachmann. That was one of the best seminars I ever attended in my life. He was fascinating. He wanted to talk about Keynesian versus Austrian perspectives, and he just came in every week and talked about whatever was on his mind that week. It was not structured, but it was always very interesting. He was very thoughtful, and I would say that we disagreed about almost everything, but he always took my arguments seriously and tried to respond to them in a thoughtful way. We used to have debates every week, and it was fascinating hearing him talk about all of the people. He knew Hayek. He knew Keynes; he knew Sraffa; he knew Joan Robinson and [Richard] Kahn. Out of that seminar partly came some of the research I did on Sraffa and his critique of Hayek, so that was exciting (see Mongiovi 1990).

I did my dissertation with Eatwell and Nell. They were my main supervisors, and Harvey Gram was the third reader. The dissertation was on Keynes and Sraffa – and the rest is history.

I got very interested in Sraffa when I was in graduate school. I liked his style of thinking – his way of approaching a problem, not taking anything for granted, questioning the premises and the foundations. I think that was what I found fascinating about him. So that is how I became an economist. I was lucky to land a job at St. John's, and they have been a good employer for thirty-something years, very supportive. I have never had any difficulties over the fact that I'm doing non-mainstream work, that my publications are on Marx or are critical of mainstream theory; it's a nice supportive environment.

Was there anything about you before you did this stuff that predisposed you to that way of thinking? Is there anything in your profile pre-college that influenced you? At what point did you choose finance, for instance?

Well, I'd been through a few majors. I had majored in communications, thinking maybe I would like to do something in film. It turned out that that did not engage me as much as I thought it would. I had been working in a marketing research department at a bank part time and I thought, okay, well, let me try marketing, and that was totally uninteresting. What next? I was working in a bank, so let me try finance, and that's what I ended up with because at that point there was no time left to change majors again; it would have cost me another year in school. So I finished up with finance.

I've always been a little bit left of centre, though I grew up in an Italian American household in Brooklyn, so I was definitely not inclined towards revolution. I found the Austrians interesting because they were thinking a little bit outside the box, but I always had these qualms about the ideological conclusions that they drew that just didn't seem right to me, and I didn't know why. It just didn't seem persuasive to argue: leave the market alone and you're going to get good outcomes.

So not right intellectually as opposed to morally, for instance?

Yes. My position about the Austrians is that by and large they want similar things to what progressive left-of-centre economists want. They believe in human freedom. They want the economy to be designed to promote prosperity and economic well-being. They want people to have autonomy and control over their economic lives and to not feel always up against the wall by economic circumstances. You know, when you make a list of what they would like to see the economy providing for people, it's not different from what you or I would like to see the economy provide for people; so I don't

190 *Gary Mongiovi*

think that morally there are any issues there. There's a profound disagreement about how you get to that desired place, and I think they are absolutely wrong about almost every aspect of that except for the law of unintended consequences. You and I have talked about this a little bit. As someone who is fundamentally an interventionist, I want somebody standing next to me saying, "you know, if you try and do that, here's what's going to happen: it's going to get all messed up for this reason or that reason". You still might want to go in that direction, but you're going to go a little bit more cautiously; you're going to be mindful of the need to stop once in a while and see where you stand and see if maybe you need to change direction a little bit or fine-tune; and we need to be prepared to say, "that didn't work out. We've got to go back to the drawing board". So I think that's a useful thing, and I've always had good conversations with Austrians about stuff like that.

In what you've talked about there is an interesting mix of societal goals or political goals, and then some of what has driven you is your intellectual curiosity.

Yes, my research is mostly motivated by trying to understand things that puzzle me. So here's an argument – let's say the Keynes-Sraffa-Hayek debate. I'd read the literature and of course the first time you read that stuff it is absolutely baffling. And yet, your professors are telling you that there's something important and fundamental and crucial there. Okay, well, I'm willing to believe my professors, but now I have to go and see what that crucial thing is. One of the publications of mine that gets cited a lot is that piece I did for the *Cambridge Journal of Economics* on Sraffa's critique of Marshall (Mongiovi 1996). There too I didn't feel like I understood the nuances of that polemic adequately, and I just spent three or four years trying to untangle Sraffa's argument.

Most of my papers have long gestation periods. I mull them over. I sit on them. I leave them aside and then I go back to them, and then when I'm happy with them I send them out into the world, and I would say of most of them, when I look back on them, I'm still pretty happy with them. That Sraffa paper – the 1926 critique of Marshall – really helped me to understand something about Sraffa that I had not understood before, which is that in fact he is a very, very practical-minded theorist. What was bothering him about Marshall's theory, which in the early 1920s was the only game in town really, was that it was not well designed to deal with real-world phenomena like increasing and decreasing returns. These are real-world phenomena, and here you have the theory that everyone's using, it's the textbook theory, yet it cannot deal with these crucially important real-world phenomena. That bothered Sraffa, and in the process of trying to sort that out, I think he got closer to the idea that the solution is to abandon neoclassical theory and look back to the Classicals – basically, detach the theory of output from the theory of price and distribution.

You've said lots of things about mainstream and neoclassical economics. You said you disagree with it, but you haven't sort of talked about dismissing it or ditching it.

Well, I *would* ditch it. But I would not dismiss it or be dismissive of the people who advocate it. Once I felt I understood what Sraffa was doing, to me that seemed like the way to go and it still does. While I was working on my dissertation, Pierangelo Garegnani was spending a lot of time as a visiting professor at the New School and I, at the time, was working on this dissertation on Keynes and Sraffa and he was very, very generous with his time. You know, I think about the conversations I had with him and the questions I asked him and the positions I took, and I am always grateful that he took the time to, and had the patience to, sit with me through those questions.

Yes, I mean things like – I had trouble getting away from the idea of a downward-sloping demand curve, [the idea that] the demand vector for outputs should be systematically connected to the price vector, [that] price is what determined quantities demanded. [At the time I felt,] well, that makes sense.

I'm not going to reject the idea [that price changes affect demand], but that doesn't mean you have to conceptualise that relationship in terms of downward-sloping demand curves or behavioural relations that can be mathematically modelled. It's much more subtle than that. So, even though I was prepared to reject neoclassical economics, there was still – it's what Keynes [1936, p. viii] talks about – this process of escaping from received habits of thinking. That was one that was hard for me to escape from – the idea of downward-sloping demand curves. They appear to make perfect sense: who could argue with that? But now when I teach undergraduates, I tell them there's a problem with it. In fact, there are a number of problems with it.

So yes, I do think that the Sraffian approach is the way to go, but I'm not sectarian about it and I don't think most Sraffians are. The nice thing about the Sraffian approach is that it's open-ended in lots of ways so that you can bring in insights from Institutional Economics; you can bring in, possibly, insights from behavioural economics as a way of talking about demand behaviour and so forth.

One of our interests in this book is about what heterodox economics is, how it could fit together, and whether the single approach is possible. What do you think heterodox economics is?

I don't like the label "heterodox economics". I don't recall if we've talked about this, but I think the label is a form of self-ghettoisation. The idea of drawing a distinction between orthodoxy and non-orthodox thinking goes back, I think, at least in the tradition of modern non-mainstream economics, to Joan Robinson who in the '40s started to emphasise the distinction between orthodox economists and the Keynesian or the non-orthodox school. That was a way of, in a sense, disparaging neoclassical economics. It's a way of saying, well, it's a stuffy, stodgy, old-fashioned, not-very-useful approach, whereas we're the cutting edge. And, that was probably not a good way to win friends and influence people. But, temperamentally she could be a difficult person. Nowadays many economists have embraced the mantel of heterodoxy, and I don't think it helps. I discuss this in more detail in a paper contained in a collection of essays edited by Fred Lee and Marc Lavoie (Mongiovi 2012).

You use labels as a shorthand so that when you're writing about the Austrian school or the Marxian school or the Sraffian school, you use that label as a way of giving the reader a sense of a collection of ideas or an orientation. But when you start having debates about who's a real Post Keynesian? Are Sraffians Post Keynesians? Who's a true Marxist? What's the difference between mainstream economics and non-mainstream economics or heterodox economics? – all of that is probably symptomatic of a crisis of some sort. People are reacting to being marginalised by trying to close ranks. Solidarity is a good thing, but it very easily spills over into sectarianism, and that I think needs to be paid attention to. One of my favourite quotes – I'm paraphrasing – is from the Italian economist Maffeo Pantaleoni; he said there are really only two schools of economics – the first is comprised of people who can reason sensibly about how the economy works and the second school is comprised of people who cannot do that. That's the way to think about schools of thought, and that includes heterodoxy versus mainstream economics.

I'm an economist, and I want to have conversations with other economists who have useful and sensible things to say about the economy. I have serious reservations about the analytical approach taken by mainstream economists, but I still want to talk to them. And that means I don't want to call myself a heterodox economist, because then these other people think "well, why should I talk to him? He's not doing the stuff that I'm doing. He's not interested in the kinds of – he rejects everything that I think is sound science". I think it makes it harder to have conversations.

So what do you do when you are marginalised? Well, you have to call yourself something, and I suppose "heterodox" is as good as anything else. I don't have a solution to what we should do to self-identify. Some days I call myself a Marxist. Some days I call myself a Sraffian. Some days I call myself a Post Keynesian. I don't see that there is much difference among them; there's a lot of overlap in terms of how all those traditions approach the way the market works.

What do you think those areas of overlap are?

I would say the principle concept is rejection of the idea that income distribution is regulated by a set of substitution mechanisms that manifest themselves as downward-sloping factor demand functions. This is the main thing

I got from Garegnani. Orthodoxy, or mainstream economics, is grounded in this idea that the distribution of income is regulated by the interaction of price-elastic factor supply and demand functions. Non-mainstream work is sceptical of that and that scepticism encompasses a whole bunch of traditions – from Post Keynesianism to Sraffian economics to Institutionalist economics and Marxian economics. So that's what binds these non-mainstream traditions together, and I think it's a good starting point for a dialogue, not just among ourselves but also with the mainstream, because it identifies what we fundamentally disagree about.

Now, what kind of conversations can we have [with mainstream economists], given that we don't see eye to eye on this one basic issue? But there *are* useful conversations we can have with mainstream people. For example, I know you work on environmental stuff. I think that William Nordhaus is doing interesting, useful work on the environment. Cost-benefit analysis is not perfect, not immune to criticism by any means, but it lays out a framework for having a constructive dialogue about how to approach environmental problems. For me one of the main issues that non-mainstream economists have to deal with is how to get back into the conversation of mainstream economics, and that's part of the reason why I think the heterodox label is not always helpful.

There are progressive mainstream economists. William Baumol is a good example of that, Paul Krugman, Joseph Stiglitz and Nordhaus and Samuelson and Solow, Modigliani. Pigou was to the left of Keynes; Pigou was a Fabian socialist. They get demonised by, I don't know if I want to say many, but enough on the Post Keynesian side of the divide that it becomes difficult to start having conversations.

Some people (for example, Tony Lawson) argue that the difference between mainstream and non-mainstream is methodological. Do you agree with that?

No, I disagree strongly with Tony Lawson on that; and I don't want to speak for Tony but I detect in that a desire to marginalise mathematical non-mainstream economists who are doing Sraffian-type work. And, this is partly what happens – people argue that the Sraffian-type models are variants on neoclassical economics because they're grounded in equilibrium. I think that's just a misunderstanding of the tradition. I know of no Sraffian who would say that the only interesting questions are questions that can be addressed within the context of a multisector linear model. Questions of dynamics, questions of structural change – these are all part of the story from a Sraffian perspective. And then the question is "well, what's your anchor? What's your anchoring viewpoint?" Well, okay, it's this way of understanding the interconnections between prices and distribution. You don't like that approach? Well, okay, that's fine; we're not talking about that now. We're talking about a process of growth, and here's another model that tries to address that process of growth.

194 *Gary Mongiovi*

Let's talk about that. We all agree that income distribution is not regulated by a supply-and-demand mechanism, so that's a starting point. Now let's see what the consequences of that initial premise are for growth, and there I think you can have conversations on policy issues.

I have had many disagreements with Paul Davidson and Vicky Chick about the interpretation of Keynes and how to model macroeconomic processes, but on policy issues, there is very little light between us. I think Paul is extremely good on policy questions and Victoria too, yet they would condemn Franco Modigliani and Paul Samuelson and Robert Solow. I think the models of Modigliani, Samuelson, and Solow are problematic in serious ways, but when they talk about policy issues they're not so far from Post Keynesians. They see an important role for demand stimulus. They start from the idea that there's a tendency for wages to gravitate towards the marginal product of labour, but they also recognised that there are a whole bunch of institutional impediments to that happening. So that means these guys can start talking about the differences between their models and Kalecki's model, which starts with a given wage, and why they get somewhat different results – and also why they come to basically similar policy conclusions about the need for the state to manage demand.

So far in your discussion of the non-mainstream, you have not mentioned the Austrians. You have worked with them, studied under them, you've said nice things about them, but you didn't mention them as non-mainstream. I wondered how you would classify them.

Well, it's because I have the same – I'm puzzled about that question in the same way that you are. They don't like equilibrium analysis, so in this sense they are of a piece with some non-mainstream traditions – the Institutionalists, some Post Keynesians – and yet when they talk about what regulates prices, it's some kind of supply-and-demand mechanism. They don't necessarily talk in terms of – well, they don't write out the demand equations. They don't draw the demand curves and the supply curves, but the mechanism that they describe presumes that there is a factor substitution process going on and that it is essentially a neoclassical kind of mechanism, that there would be a systematic tendency for capital to be replaced by labour when the wage falls and vice versa, and that this leads to – not optimal outcomes because they reject that terminology, but to better outcomes. You can't say "best" because that word implies optimisation. What they argue is that markets process information more effectively than planning, and that's a useful argument. It's something that non-mainstream economists who favour intervention need to engage with, but I'm not persuaded that the premise is sound.

This is where Lachmann is kind of interesting, because one of the things that Lachmann always used to say is that information has to be interpreted, and I think this in some sense is the Achilles heel of the Austrian approach.

There is no reason to think that information will be processed in a way that generates better outcomes. You know, people make systematic mistakes and make those systematic mistakes for a long time. And, if you're starting from a premise that's untrue, which is that factor substitution regulates the distribution of income – if you're starting from that hypothesis, then it is, in my opinion, always going to lead you to wrong insights about how the economy works.

It used to be that Austrians had a hard time finding their way into academic positions at good universities. I'm not an Austrian, and I don't follow this as carefully as others, but I think because the mainstream of the discipline has moved so much in the direction of seeing economics as a study of how economic actors process information, that's opened up space for the Austrians and they've found ways to fit in better. And of course Elinor Ostrom's Nobel and Coase's helped them a lot in that respect. It opened doors for them. It opened space for them in mainstream departments that probably was not available before that; they're giving Nobel Prizes to economists who are not doing heavily mathematical work, and that has worked out all to the good for the Austrians.

Are they mainstream or not? I don't know. I do know that it's easier for me to have a fruitful conversation with someone like Roger Koppl or Peter Boettke than it is to have a conversation with a Stanford University–trained mathematical economist or somebody who works on Dynamic Stochastic General Equilibrium models.

You've stressed that open-mindedness is a quality you admire. You've talked about conversation a lot. You've made some objections to mainstream principles but not to mainstream economists. However, the last thing you just said suggests there are some people that are harder to talk to. What makes it harder to talk to person x than person y?

Okay. Well, first of all I don't think the point is to win the argument. The point is to have both people walk away from the conversation saying, "that person gave me something to think about. I have to go back and, maybe not rethink my whole argument start to finish, but rethink aspects of it". Because I want to persuade them, and maybe they're pointing out something that I haven't paid attention to. And the Austrians I hope think the same way when they engage with Marxists or Sraffians.

So, what's wrong with mainstream economics? I'm guessing that you've interviewed six people for this project already. How many of them start by saying "let me count the ways" or something like that? Well, we've talked about the main difference, the big mistake, which has to do with the theory of distribution. But I think now the real problem is a little bit different in 2017, and that is that you can't talk to mainstream economists because they are by and large very narrowly educated. I was going to say 50 years ago, but you don't have to go back 50 years. When I was an undergraduate 35 years ago, mainstream economists were trained in a way that exposed them to alternative traditions. So, if you were an undergraduate in any decent university in the early 1970s, there was this idea that you had to know who John Kenneth Galbraith was; you should know who Joan Robinson was; you should know a little bit about what Marx's theory was about and how it's different and how we, as mainstream economists, think it's wrong – that kind of thing. And over the decades that has been weeded out, so the education of economists focuses very much on the technical stuff. Yes, it's broadening out in the sense that behavioural economics is part of the toolbox now, and that's all to the good.

But you don't have to know who Sraffa is because, you know, "we had that debate in the '60s and we sorted it all out and we all agree it's a non-issue", so nobody studies it. Same with the debate over the Marshallian theory of supply: "okay, Sraffa had that critique [in 1926]. It was debated. We came up with the theory of monopolistic competition and oligopoly, and it's all been sorted". So people who go through a doctoral programme in economics now, they are no longer required to take history of economic thought. It may be in the curriculum, [but it's seldom a required course] and it's not always taught by somebody who has the kind of breadth you'd like someone who teaches that kind of course to have. Graduate students are discouraged from taking it: "well, you can take it if you have room in your programme, but you know, it's very important that you learn the technical stuff". So people end up leaving graduate school and what they know are the four models they learned in graduate school and in particular the ones they explored in their dissertation. So how do you have a conversation?

There are language barriers to engaging with people in the discipline now, and that's a little bit scary because if the main task is to get back into the conversation, how do you get into the conversation with people who have a very limited range of competencies? It's a narrow range of technical models. They can't talk to you about Kalecki; they can't talk to you about Sraffa.

My next point follows on from that. In the 1960s someone like Joan Robinson or Alfred Eichner could get published once in a while in a top-tier mainstream journal, and that is barely possible now, and that's problematic. It used to be the case that you had a neoclassical mainstream who were working on their particular models, and then you had other people who are doing other things. Kalecki, let's say, submits something to a mainstream journal. Whatever the referee thinks about the appropriateness of the approach, he sees here a useful argument that makes an interesting point: "yes, okay, the author's assuming fixed wages and mark-up pricing. Not what I would do, but let's see what the implications of that are". Now when someone submits something like that they get a one-line rejection that says "where are your micro-foundations?" I don't think that's ideological; I don't think it is deliberately intended to close off debate. But, I think it's a by-product of what has happened in the training of economists. The reaction is: "this model makes no sense to me. I've not seen it before. It wasn't in any of my textbooks in graduate school. Why should I pay attention to it? Submit it to the *Cambridge Journal of Economics*; submit it to the *Review of Political Economy* or what have you. That's where it belongs". Well, maybe it belongs in those journals, but explain to me why you're not interested in it. You should be interested in it, yet you've not made a coherent case for why this approach has nothing to say to you.

If, as you say, you don't think it is either ideological or reflects an intention to exclude – how and why did the narrowing happen?

That is the difficult question, and I think here's a project now for the sociologists of science and intellectual historians, because you start seeing this happen towards the end of the 1970s. This is when it really becomes different. Jan Kregel and Alfred Eichner (1975) got something into the *Journal of Economic Literature* on Post Keynesian economics in the mid-1970s, and then a few things are appearing – maybe into the early 1980s, and then it pretty much stops. So why is this? Well, I think there is a generational dimension to it for sure, but that just poses another question because all of these [younger mainstream economists] were trained by people who knew better. So you go to MIT, get your doctorate in the mid-1970s, by the late 1970s you're refereeing for the *Quarterly Journal of Economics*. Your Professors – Samuelson and Solow and the rest of them – were quite open-minded. They knew that to be a good economist you had to know something about intellectual history, you had to know something about philosophy, you had to know something about political theory. And now the generation of students that they taught are somehow unwilling to accommodate anything that is not within the narrow technical bounds of the latest mathematical modelling techniques. I don't know why that happened.

But you use the word "unwilling" there – unwilling to accommodate.

I did. Perhaps I did say "unwilling". I don't know whether they were unwilling or incapable or disinclined – strongly disinclined, powerfully disinclined – and the question is why? It possibly has something to do with the idea that to be scientific you need to be mathematical. It's a kind of a confusion about what "scientific" means. I said it's not ideological. I don't think it's *primarily* ideological, but of course there is an ideological dimension to everything. I don't think it's entirely coincidental that you start getting real business cycle models and rational expectations models coming into play just when Reagan and Thatcher are redefining the terms of ideological discourse.

Still, these are people who've been through graduate programmes at good universities. A stupid person cannot fathom those models and do the kind of technical stuff that you need to do to get through that kind of a programme. Why anyone would choose to narrow their intellectual scope to focus entirely on these kinds of technical models [is beyond me]. I get students occasionally who want to do PhDs in economics and I always sit them down and I tell them "the first thing you need to realise is that everything about economics that you find interesting is gonna be put onto the back burner in graduate school. Those interesting things – the debates, the issues about ideology and politics, the conflictual issues, the political science and the political economy dimension to it – that's all secondary to learning the technical material in graduate school. If you're a good student, you can grab the interesting nuggets out of that, but you're gonna have to work to see it". And, I don't know why that happened. It's a sad thing for the discipline because, again, it makes the problem of discourse across subdisciplines and across traditions difficult.

But behavioural economics got in? Why did that get in whereas others did not? If you read Simon's work, it is quite radical in many ways. Now there's debate about whether modern behavioural economics has got much to do with Simon. But clearly it's growing in prominence in academic circles and in Government. How does that fit into the story?

I don't know. One of the things that you see getting played out in the textbooks is this issue of whether behavioural economics is a challenge to mainstream economics or is complementary to it. I think the way it fits in is that the bottom-line feature of mainstream economics is that all explanations have to be grounded in atomistic choice, some kind of a theory of atomistic choice and choice at the level of the individual agent, and it's in that sense that behavioural economics fits in with the framework. This is an idea that has been developed by John Davis (2014).

Personally, I think that behavioural economics casts serious doubt on some pretty fundamental aspects of neoclassical economics, beginning with the concept of a demand curve. Think about the assumptions that you have to make to justify the construction of the demand curve. The axioms of choice – completeness, transitivity, and convexity. You know, stylised facts are one thing, but these are stylised *fake* facts. If they're not true then you can't construct that demand curve, and then what happens to your theory of choice? Well, if that theory of choice is not present, then [you're missing one] of the building blocks of the substitution mechanisms that ground the theory of distribution. I think that's really problematic.

But even Marshall had a sense of the limitations of the theory. He would argue that the coherence of the demand curve is only justifiable in the neighbourhood of equilibrium. If the price changes enough to bring you far from the equilibrium point, then you've got this problem of the ceteris paribus assumptions being violated: the assumption that all of the other prices in the system have to be constant breaks down, and when that happens your demand curve is gone. If all those other prices are changing because the price in this market has changed, then the demand curve in this market is disintegrating. So I think the theory is problematic in a lot of ways.

Is history of thought important to you?

It is. I always come at things from a historical perspective. I think you can get insights into modern problems from looking at the intellectual history. And yes, I think it's intrinsically an interesting question to ask what a great mind like Sraffa was getting at. What was he really trying to say? Or Keynes, or Marx? Particularly people like Marx and Ricardo who were writing before there was a generally accepted language of discourse in economics. They were using the same words that we use. But the word "demand" means something to a modern economist and has a whole bunch of associations that it did not have for Marx or Ricardo. So trying to figure out what they're getting at is not always easy. And the other thing is that because they're great intellects, they're constantly questioning their own thinking and they're growing intellectually. They're learning, their understanding is growing, so they're also revising their thinking as you're trying to understand it. So it's a moving target to some extent when you're talking about an intellect that is active and willing to question his own preconceptions like both of them were.

You've talked about *inter alia* open-mindedness, active thinking, et cetera. I'd like to talk about teaching. I believe you teach Principles of Macro and Micro, and Marxian economics.

The Marxian economics course is pretty new. We added it to the curriculum about five years ago, and that has proved to be a pretty successful course. Economics majors sign up for it and they generally have a good experience, from what I've heard.

So, what are you trying to do when you make a course like that? What are the objectives you have?

Well, you never try and convert anyone. That's always a mistake. What you try and do is to get people to stop and say, "I never thought about it that way before". If you can get people to do that then they'll think about it a little bit more. If the issue is important to them, they'll think about it enough to either change their own mind, if they're gonna change their mind, or decide "well, I've thought it through and, you know, I think the way I understood it before is probably a better way to go".

The point of teaching, I think, is to get people to recognise that there are lots of different ways to come at a question. And your Professor has his particular point of view, across the hall there's another Professor who has perhaps a very different point of view, and what you've got to do is listen to these different points of view, reflect upon the issues that are under discussion, and draw your own conclusions. So what I try and do when I'm teaching economic principles is to teach them the mainstream stuff, and then I try to raise questions with them about the aspects of the mainstream argument that are questionable, weak, open to doubt, and so forth.

I have to say that I definitely prefer teaching macro over teaching micro principles, and that is because in a mainstream Macro Principles textbook you get a coherent story that says by and large pretty sensible things about how the economy works. You can quibble about this or that, but I don't feel when I'm teaching the Keynesian cross model that I am conveying misinformation; whereas almost from start to finish with the Micro course, I feel like I am misleading them about how the world works. I've been teaching thirty-something years, and I still wrestle with this. I just don't know how to make Micro useful or how to reconcile myself to the fact that I think these models are totally useless for understanding things like price. I do go through it with the students. When I start out, I talk a little bit about different kinds of assumptions – you know, this distinction that Alan Musgrave (1981) makes between heuristic assumptions and domain assumptions. There's nothing wrong with heuristic assumptions: you're trying to lay out the logic of a model so you assume no international trade or you assume no taxes. Figure out the logic, then introduce those things [i.e., relax the assumptions] and see what happens. And then there are these domain assumptions where if you make a domain assumption and it's not true, then your whole argument falls apart. And it seems to me that Microeconomics is just shot through with domain assumptions. [For example], you can't construct a supply curve without assuming perfect competition. When I was at university, you know, you could point to agriculture and say "okay, well, there's that one example of perfect competition out there in the real world". Now it's 2017 and agriculture is dominated by Monsanto and Archer Daniels Midland, so you don't even have that one example. And yet, economists draw supply curves left and right all over the place, but the theoretical grounding just isn't there.

This is a problem for the students now. I'm tortured because I'm teaching the textbook stuff and I'm trying to decide how much doubt students can handle about what's in their textbook and because I don't know whether I'm just confusing them or irritating them. I probably irritate, because they paid 120 bucks for the textbook and I'm telling them, well, you know, there are some problems with the argument. The textbooks are terrible, even when they're written by people who are quite good. David Colander's Micro Principles textbook is one of the better ones, but he knows what these problems are and he does not call them out, I think, with adequate vigour. You know, all of the textbooks, when they talk about minimum wage or rent controls, they have a little inset, a little box, where they talk about the Card and Krueger (1994) findings that cast doubt on the empirical connection between unemployment and an increase in the minimum wage. Baumol and Blinder have moved it out of the supply and demand chapter; they've moved it to the chapter that describes the scope of macroeconomics. What was happening was, here you have the story about supply and demand curves regulating price, and then right in the middle of it you had a box that says "well, it doesn't work like that in the labour market". So I'll tell my students, you know in the United States the labour market accounts for about 60% of GDP. If *that* market doesn't work the way your textbook says it works, to me it's "game over, man!" – why are you even talking about supply and demand theory? But again you present this to a first-year undergraduate and they don't know what to do with that. I'm trying to say, well, these are contentious issues and your textbook is conveying an oversimplified and in some respects misleading story, but they don't want to go there because then the question is "well, what's the right story?"

The other thing that I've been thinking about recently is that even when the authors are themselves fairly progressive like Colander or Baumol and Blinder, the imagery of the supply and the demand diagram is a very, very powerful ideological instrument. I don't think this gets emphasised enough – that you can have that box explaining the Krueger and Card results, but what students take away is the supply and the demand curve mechanism, the two curves crossing/intersecting at the equilibrium point. And then if there's a minimum wage, you are imposing a policy that prevents the market from getting where it's supposed to be. You're preventing that wonderful invisible hand from working its magic. That's what students come away with – even when you explain to them "but here's this problem".

Why do you think students are attracted to that?

Well, this is something for people who specialise in how the brain works to investigate. It's a cliché – a picture is worth a thousand words – but yes, I think images embed concepts in people's brains a lot more securely than words do. The problem is even worse with the discussion of rent control. It's just treated as a simple price ceiling. But in no municipal area in the world are rent controls imposed the way they are described in a textbook. They're always much more flexible. Rents are allowed to rise but by measured, regulated amounts. New buildings are usually omitted from rent regulations in New York City. The main argument against rent control is it prevents new housing from being created; it's a disincentive to constructing new housing. But in fact, if you put up a new residential building in New York City, you're exempt from rent regulations, so that disincentive argument doesn't make any sense. There is no discussion of the market power of landlords relative to the tenants and so on and so forth. But what students take away is the picture, and the picture says that if you try to impose a price ceiling you're gonna fuck up the way the market works. I don't know how you fight that.

Have you considered just not teaching that material?
Are you bound to by a curriculum?

No, no, I could leave that stuff out and I do think about leaving it out. And then I think, well, but at some point they'll be having beers in a bar with their co-workers and they might want to say something about how they're in favour of rent regulations or in favour of raising the minimum wage. And some smartass who got his degree from Harvard is gonna get in their face about how those policies mess up the operation of the invisible hand, how any intervention in the market process generates an inefficiency. So I'd rather explain to them the [conventional] argument, tell them why I think it is seriously flawed, and then at least they're not going into that kind of a conversation unarmed. And yet I am very much aware that they walked out of my classroom with me having explained what's wrong with the textbook story, but to the extent that they have understood anything, it's mainly that the equilibrium price is the "efficient" price and if you interfere with that, you are introducing inefficiencies into the system and that's no good.

So, I would like to not have to teach undergraduates until they were at least sophomores. Our kids get Principles classes in the first year, and I think that's a big mistake. They're trying to adjust from high school into college. They're used to textbooks being straightforward: "here it is; here's the story. This is the way it is". And in that first year, while they're getting their bearings, to introduce them to the idea that there's a scientific dimension to economics but it's also a form of ideology, it's a way of embedding ways of thinking in your brains that reinforce the power relations of the system that we live in. And, sorry, to an 18-year-old – that just sounds too weird to them. It's hard for them to get their heads around; they don't know what to do with it.

I don't say the textbooks lie, because I don't think they're lying. But there's some nuance here [that needs to be conveyed to students]. We're always being bombarded with messages that reinforce the power structures of the system that we live in. That's something that a 19- or 20-year-old can start to see. I don't think it's so easy for a first-year college student to see. So I always wrestle with that.

How do you know whether you're going to achieve what you are trying to? How do you assess that?

Well, every classroom has a vibe and when students are asking questions, answering questions, when they're engaged, that's how I know I'm getting things across to them. I certainly don't assess it in terms of exam performance or how many of them become economics majors or things like that. When students come up to me after class and say "you know, I was thinking about what you said and I've got this part-time job or I'm an intern and my supervisor was saying such-and-such and I think it might relate to what you were saying in this way", then I feel like the gears are turning in that person's brain and he or she is drawing connections and trying to build up the scaffolding that is going to help them to make sense of the world.

And would you say that that's what you enjoy about teaching? Is it that moment?

Oh yes – when you can see that some student is taking the ideas that you've put in front of them and is running with them in a certain way. You know, even if they're running in a direction that seems wrongheaded to me, when I'm having a conversation with them I'll say, "well, that's not the implication I would draw; here's how I think about it. But let's talk".

There is a theory that students will seek higher grades by following the professor's opinion: there is an implicit incentive to take that opinion as the correct answer. How do you ensure against that?

That's kind of interesting because in point of fact I don't see that problem too much, particularly with the freshmen. Here's one thing I do at the start of every freshmen semester: I talk about the definition of capitalism. We live in a capitalist system; that word gets thrown around all the time. What does it mean? Can you define it? And they raise their hands and it's always "the free-market system" or "no government involved in the economy". And then we have a little conversation about that: "do you know what percentage of US GDP is comprised of government spending? And would you say that there is no regulation in our economy?" So we go in that direction and I give them a definition of capitalism: (i) most economic activity is organised through markets; (ii) the means of production are privately owned; (iii) and there's a large wage-earning working class. And we will say that any economy that has these three characteristics we're going to call capitalism. Then we talk about how capitalism comes in lots of different flavours. We talk about, say, the share of GDP spent on healthcare in Canada versus the US. We talk about number of paid vacation days that employers are required to give their workers. I've got charts for all that stuff. So I do all that and then I tell them "I'm going to ask you on the exam for the definition of capitalism and I'm looking for some variation on these three characteristics". So I give the exam and I would say a good 25% of them will say it's a free-market system where people can get rich if they work hard and play by the rules and the government doesn't get in the way.

In the more advanced classes, I always tell them "look, I'm not asking you to agree with my point of view". I always ask them on the exams to outline this or that model – explain the basic logic of the model, and then they can decide whether they agree with it or not. In the Marx class some people will not find the idea of class conflict being the driving force of history persuasive,

204 *Gary Mongiovi*

but they do find interesting the idea that there's a logic to history, a way of conceptualising our understanding of history in terms of a set of mechanisms that drive a system in a certain direction. And Marx's idea of internal contradictions they also find interesting, whether they agree with how it plays out. In the Marx class in particular I talk about the fact that Marx would have been flabbergasted to see capitalism still in existence at the beginning of the 21st century, so his predictions were not always on target.

We've talked there about what you're trying to achieve in your teaching. Is this the same as in your intellectual work more broadly?

Here's what I'm trying to achieve in my teaching and in my intellectual work. I think that it's important for people to write and speak clearly about economic issues, so what I am always striving for in my own work is to arrive at a clear understanding and then convey that understanding with clarity. One of the things that I enjoyed about being an editor when I was co-editing the *Review of Political Economy* was helping people to say what they wanted to say as clearly and as forcefully as possible. So, even when I found the argument a little bit fishy – "I'm not buying this. I would approach the problem in a different way" – what I liked doing with authors was to say "you know, this argument that you're making here I think is distracting the reader from what you really want to say. And this aspect here probably is not as strong as it could be because someone will counter it with what about x, y, or z, so why don't you say a few words, even if it's just in a footnote, to at least indicate that you've thought that through a little bit?"

If people strive for that then we get back to this idea of conversations and discourse. Everyone's having a better conversation because they understand the other person's point of view more clearly. Then you can see where the fundamental differences are. And some of those you can't get past. Some of those are, you know, they're axiomatic on some level. This idea that Marx has that what fundamentally drives economic processes is class conflict – there is no way an Austrian school economist is ever gonna be on board with that. But if everyone understands that this is really what the difference is – this is what divides us fundamentally – then you can talk around and understand what the other person is saying within the context of that other person's starting point. So, I try and do that in my own work. This is one of the reasons why I got interested in the Austrians, right; because here I am a Marxist/Sraffian/Post Keynesian and I've had all of these disagreements with Lachmann and Israel Kirzner, but I see that there are things in what they are saying that are useful. So, let's see how close we can get; let's see how far we can go towards a meeting of minds. And, when we've got as far as we can get, then we have to say "okay, let's agree to disagree and move on to a different conversation".

I think it's the same with students; you want them to be able to think clearly about these issues. Not that you want them to think this way or that way but just to understand, you know – here's the logic of the problem, here are the issues. People start from different premises and they arrive at different conclusions because of that, and that's fine. But, you can't really have a constructive conversation unless you've thought through what your own premises are and made an attempt to understand what the other person's premises are. Occasionally, I've been asked by students "does that mean that the middle ground is the way to go?" and I will say "emphatically not! No, I am a person of the left and I am strongly committed to the things that I believe and I'm strongly committed to the idea that there are serious fundamental flaws in conventional economics. But that doesn't mean I can't have a good conversation, a productive conversation, with somebody who comes at problems in a different way from the way I do".

And that leads us nicely into our question about poetry. Many of the things you've been talking about here concern conversation. That reminds me of McCloskey's work. You also talked about a picture saying a thousand words; so perhaps the power of the word is also important. You've acknowledged that you pay a lot of attention to language. So what do you see as the relation between economics and poetry?

Well, I think poets are usually a lot more mindful of stylistic issues than economists are.

I have mixed feelings about McCloskey's point of view on this. I think she is right when she says that what you're trying to do as an economist is put forward a point of view. You have thought about an issue, you have analysed it using the tools that economists use, and then what you want to try to do is persuade other people to come around to that point of view. In order for anybody to take it seriously, to recognise that they have to rethink their own positions in light of the argument that you are making, in doing this you should be mindful of the fact that we use metaphors and language and that there are effective ways to use metaphors and language and that there are ineffective or less effective ways to use them. I like the fact that she talks about the terms that economists use as metaphors; for example, the production function is a metaphor. When an economist puts up a model – let's take the Keynesian cross model – you'll say something like this: "let's consider an economy that is characterised by this consumption function and this investment function". And when I read McCloskey I think, well, wait a second. That's not "an economy"; there is no economy there. That's a set of equations that are meant to stand in for certain aspects of a hypothetical economy that one hopes has some sort of relevance to the real world, that those equations have some sort of relevance to what goes in a real-world economy. I think economists need to be mindful of that when they are writing. I think non–mainstream economists tend to be more mindful of that when they're writing, but that's because they also bring to the table an understanding that you need to pay attention to history, you need to pay attention to the political and the institutional context in which these equations that you are talking about are going to play out. So in that sense McCloskey is onto something. She's right that we should pay more attention to that.

I do wish economists paid more attention to the quality of their writing. Language is a tool, and our discipline has a history of many wonderful writers. Keynes was a great writer. Paul Samuelson is a terrific writer; he's always interesting to read. I have to say that Sraffa's 1925 article on Marshall's supply curve, the original Italian article, is one of the greatest pieces of prose writing I have ever read; I love that piece. I generally think that Sraffa is a very good writer. He was very terse; he chooses his words very, very carefully and I think that's something that people should pay attention to.

But I also think that using this metaphor of poetry is also a little bit problematic, because it can be understood – or *misunderstood* – to mean that we're just trying to convince people, as opposed to trying to explain scientifically how the world works. You can put up some equations and there's a lot hidden behind them that's not always transparent, and you can use that as a way to make a point. But what kind of a point are you making? Is it a valid point? Is it a useful point? Is it something that if it were translated into words, people would find credible? You know DSGE models are elegant – they are mathematically airtight I suppose – but are they saying something useful about how a real-world economy works? You would have to be delusional to think that this kind of a model is shedding insight into what happens in a modern economy in 2017, and yet economists do that all the time – they draw conclusions from it, including policy conclusions.

I seem to have drifted a little bit away from McCloskey and rhetoric.

No, no, that's fine. It sounds like a good place to actually conclude.

Okay. Very good.

Thank you very much.

13 Anwar Shaikh

Anwar Shaikh is Professor of Economics at the Graduate Faculty of Political and Social Science of the New School University. He holds a BSE from Princeton and an MA and PhD from Columbia University. He was a Senior Scholar and member of the Macro Modelling Team at the Levy Economics Institute of Bard College from 2000 to 2005. In 2014 he was awarded the NordSud International Prize for Literature and Science from Italy's Fondazione Pescarabruzzo. He has published extensively on international trade, finance theory, political economy, econophysics, US macroeconomic policy, the welfare state, growth theory, inflation theory, crisis theory, national and global inequality, and past and current global economic crises. His most recent book is *Capitalism: Competition, Conflict, Crises* (2016). Other books include *Globalization and the Myths of Free Trade* (2007) and *Measuring the Wealth of Nations: The Political Economy of National Accounts* (with Tonak, 1996). In addition, he has published significant articles in journals such as the *Cambridge Journal of Economics*, *Metroeconomica*, *Physica A*, *Review of Radical Political Economics*, and the *Review of Economics and Statistics*.

Anwar Shaikh was interviewed by Andrew Mearman in his office at the New School University, New York, in April 2017.

How did you become an economist?

As with many things in life, it was an accident. I was an engineering undergraduate and I accidentally got a job teaching social science in the Kuwait American school, where I happened to be living with my father who was posted in Kuwait – he was in the Pakistani Foreign Service. And I realised I liked social science. I also taught physics and math there, so I enjoyed that too. And I met someone at a party and he asked, "what do you plan to do next?" And I said, "well, I don't know, maybe psychology". And he said, "well, I think you should look into economics", so I did and I applied to graduate school at Texas and Columbia and I ended up at Columbia. I'd no real direction except that I was motivated by a question: why do things work so badly for most people of the world? I came from Pakistan where I could see the abysmal poverty and yet great wealth also. I was living in Kuwait where for once there was no problem of money since there was no budget constraint for the Kuwaitis and still you could see poverty. I was working in the desert myself alongside workers from all over the Middle East and India and Pakistan in searing brutal heat and they were paid minimally. And as an engineer you think: well, things could be done much better. So I thought that economics would have an answer as to why there was inequality and poverty and all that, answers to them. It seemed to me that that's what I should study. When I got to graduate school I realised that economics doesn't even have the question let alone the answer. That was a big shock.

How long did it take you to discover that?

The first few lectures in microeconomics with Bill Vickrey and later with Gary Becker's course. The foundations of economics as it was constructed there seemed to me absurd, and so I found myself still trying to answer the same questions but already rejecting the standard tools. And of course at that time, there was the civil rights movement and the feminist movement and the anti-war movement and I happened to be living and working in Harlem at a school for young people who had been kicked out of city schools as being "unteachable". So reality weighed heavily upon us all, and the unreality of economics was thereby even more bizarre. That shaped my path away from the orthodoxy. But the questions that I had in mind still seemed to me ordinary questions.

Can I ask about the engineer in you? Does that still influence the way you do economics, think of economics?

Yes, I think my recent work has really – what I think of is a sort of expression of that side. I could have used my engineering training to do mathematical economics, but the question is what do you apply the math to? I have a great respect for math, but do you apply it to these absurd issues like general equilibrium and optimality, which is where clever people use their abilities? And that didn't make any sense to me. But then the question is "where is a good foundation so that you can use tools if they are appropriate?" And that took me a long time to come to that. It essentially became a search process at first. First looking at people who are critical of the orthodoxy, but I also read anthropology. I took a course or two at Columbia as what I remember in economic anthropology and another one with Marvin Harris. I read books, and so I was looking for a place to start. And anthropology is a very good place to start because if it's done properly it's about how societies actually function. And then a question – how do you move from there? And at that point I had not read Marx but I had read about Marx and so history of thought was the other logical place. And at Columbia there were good, interesting teachers. I had a teacher named Alexander Ehrlich whose work was on the Soviet industrialisation debates, and so I learned about the struggles that Russia had to go through, the Soviet Union had to go through, at the beginning to try to develop. There were other courses on China that I took with Carl Riskin, so I was looking for understanding of the actual society. And where the engineering part comes up is that you really cannot talk about how to make something better if you don't know what it is in the first place. So reading history and anthropology and economic development helped me get a sense of what the question was. And I continued to work on that, and I read Keynes. I read Kalecki. I actually did my MA thesis on Kalecki at Columbia. My teacher, Alex Ehrlich, who was also in the industrialisation debate, was a great fan of Kalecki, coming from Poland. So I got exposure to alternate points of view and the politics helped too, because we were talking about real-world issues. And I always thought that economics should be able to analyse those issues. I mean, I held that out as a hope, and I didn't give up.

So, in a sense the book that I've just finished called *Capitalism* [2016] is that synthesis of these different things, the different cultures I encountered growing up as my parents moved from one country to another, my own culture, the fact that my father was a Muslim, my mother was a Christian, and that right from the beginning my best friend was Zoroastrian. I mean, it just made sense to me that people have differences and anyway none of these people have behaved the way that these absurd models in economics [imply]; that led me to ask, "well, how do we do that? How do we start from what we know to be true and have understood from history and *still* address the same issues?" And then I encountered Heilbroner's book, which was taught in the business school, not in the economics department – *The Worldly Philosophers* – and I was blown away. I understood right away, okay, I'm not the first person to ask this question and nor have I asked it very well because others have asked it much better before. And that got me into history of economic thought. Not as a "Dead Poets Society" thing but as actually a source of much better economics than what I was being given. And there inevitably you read Smith, you read Marx. I mean, I read Ricardo and then you hit Marx, and Marx is a giant. And so that's how I came to Marx also.

And what were the things about Marx that grabbed you or appealed to you?

I think the sense that he spoke for the downtrodden. I mean, the emotional aspect of Marx is very important. I love the analytical rigour but I didn't understand that as well then as I did later. But I remember reading about the working day in capital. Now the beginning of Volume I on value is always puzzling and mysterious, and it took me a while to get my mind around that, but the length and intensity of the working day, to this day, and the development of machinery and the factory system and the question of what regulates a system that appears to have no central planner or regulator and yet has strong patterns, the fact that Marx lays out for you the idea that here's a system in which there are patterns but they are not dictated by authority. They're dictated by a system. I found that mind-blowing, as many, many people have. And that led me to study Marx and teach Marx for very many years as an enterprise of understanding the actual system. The emotional content is there, and it's very important, but you can't let emotion substitute for the question itself. And I've always emphasised, for instance, that among economists there's no greater proponent than Marx of the working class. I mean there are obviously other proponents, but being a proponent does not lead Marx to believe, for instance, that if you made workers richer then everybody would be better off. So that's the other aspect, understanding class and conflict as being inherent in the system. That was pretty obvious to me living in Kuwait and Pakistan or Nigeria and Malaysia. And a system in which this was built in from the start – that sounds to me like a sensible foundation.

So it sort of resonated with ...

Resonated with the reality I saw that class is an inherent part of some societies. And what I appreciated very much about Marx is the idea that class is not so natural. It's a social construction, and that made perfect sense to me and it also made sense of the historical and empirical and personal experience that I had. My father being a diplomat in the foreign service, we were largely associated with the ruling classes in different countries, so I didn't need to be persuaded that there *were* ruling classes. Ruling classes always know that they exist. It's only the academics that don't know because they think that they're just as equal. But in real life and in every society there are layers of power, and these people are top. They know perfectly well that they are at the top of a power structure, and I like that about Marx, that this was a scientific aspect of his analysis. And that's different from saying that the exploited should be freed, all of which also resonated with me. But the kind of logical intensity and character of Marx's argument for me was very important. I was not drawn so much or primarily by the fact of the exploitation of labour but that this was part of a system in which it was necessary for its existence. And that's something, a very important proposition to which I hold to this day.

Did that appeal to the engineer in you – the idea of system?

Yes, the idea that there is not only a system but there is a logic to it that helps shape people's views of themselves. And you could argue that engineers understand that different parts of a system have a role to play, and when they are put in their role that's the role they play. If they don't play it properly then they are removed or repaired, so to speak, so that made sense to me. And biology has the same thing. Different organs have places and all that, and of course human beings can change their places. But that in itself doesn't change the system. They change their place, but if they don't change the fact of the system then someone else takes their place, and that always made sense to me. That also shaped my view of the feminist movement and the civil rights movement. From the very beginning I always sided with those people who said "well, yes, we do need to integrate, we need to change the place of women and the place of blacks and people like myself, Asians". But, for me the other side is: "are we talking about changing the structure or there should be an integration of inequality from top to bottom?" And there is an element to many of these movements which is that the groups they represent want to get their share, but that doesn't mean they particularly want to do anything more. And coming from Pakistan and seeing the ethnic conflicts that I come from, Sindhis who are themselves split into class and landowning classes and all that, as an ethnic group complaining of being discriminated against, which is a fact, but it doesn't mean then if you have a Sindhi Prime Minister, as we did, that this person would somehow make the society more equal rather than to bring in more Sindhis, so that we're equally represented in the distribution of power and inequality. So, ethnicity never persuaded me as an end in itself but only part of this bigger movement of changing the pyramid of power.

Previously you have mentioned Veblen as an influence as well. Some of the themes that you've discussed are those he shares with Marx. But would you put Marx above Veblen in terms of influence?

Absolutely, yeah. I mean, Veblen I came to very late, and to be honest I think him more of an American whereas I think of Marx as a universal, and that's a big difference. Veblen had many interesting and good things to say about Western society, but I don't see Marx that way. I see Marx talking about intrinsic patterns of social structure and then the specificity of capitalism, which is not the same thing as specificity of Western society. So that's why. And that's not to say that I don't understand that Marx himself was a Westerner, and profoundly Western, but science transcends the origin of the scientist in some fundamental way. I've been reading about Kepler. He's a very interesting person because he was a Protestant in a Catholic Europe, and at that time Protestants were frequently brutalised by the Catholics. Sometimes they did the same thing to Catholics, too. In any case this was a time where religion and science were mixing. Kepler himself as a Protestant believed that God had made laws that humans could discover and that in the heavens there were his clues to the laws and it was the job of humans to figure this out. But Kepler as a scientist had a difficulty that the church had said that orbits of our planets had to be perfect circles because Aristotle had already said a circle was a perfect shape and God would not make an imperfect shape. So Kepler struggled like all astronomers with the fact that the data didn't fit. And he rejected the device which some astronomers adopted, which is to make each

212   *Anwar Shaikh*

circular orbit imperfect slightly by shifting the centre so to speak and adding an imperfection so that the orbit sort of fit the data. And Kepler believed that there was a pattern there, a set of laws. He didn't reject the idea that there was a law of God, but he rejected the imperfections approach. Now, as an economist, that resonates tremendously. The minute I walked into class as a graduate student I was presented with this law of perfections, and what every clever student did was to try to come up with appropriate imperfections in order to explain the lack of fit. My visceral reaction was, no, that's the wrong place to go. It's not about imperfections. It's about actually perfections but a different perfection. Capitalism does what it does very well. And then you read the Communist manifesto and there's Marx saying to you, this is the system that is going to crush all others because it is the best, not for the future, but it's the best for the present because it is capable of vanquishing the others because of its intrinsic power and logic. And just as Kepler himself arrives at that moment when he sees that the orbits are ellipses, and that's an astonishing, astonishing insight and mathematical proof, in that same sense Marx gives us this insight that capitalism works but not the way they say it does. And so that's motivated me throughout. I believe capitalism works and it does what it does very well, but we should not reduce it to an Aristotelian perfection. And therefore, what we consider imperfections are not imperfections; they are what it does. Growth, rising standards of living, but also inequality and environmental damage – these are all its "perfections". It's like saying to me that a dinosaur has imperfections because it is too large, but a dinosaur is a dinosaur and if we were biologists our job would be to understand how dinosaurs work, not to accuse them of being inadequate to our idealised representation of dinosaurs. The orthodox approach doesn't make any sense.

And this is very much the theme of your book, isn't it?

It's very much the theme of all my work, and that's the engineering side. The engineering side comes from saying, what is the thing we're trying to analyse? Engineers don't have the liberty, as mathematicians have, of exploring the beauty of some purely logical analysis. Engineers ultimately have to know how the thing works, and they have to understand that that is itself a theoretical task to which experience and knowledge adds. I was an aeronautical engineer. There is no way you can understand how a rocket works by just trial and error because you encounter issues along the way. You can build a rocket by trial and error, but you can't really be effective that way because a modern rocket is very sophisticated. The physics alone is very complicated. Imagine going from here to Mars without physics, without astronomy, without the laws of orbits, without all that stuff. Just shooting a rocket off into space, what would that give you? Failure. Engineers understand that science is the foundation for engineering and science has to have a real object. So, for my book the real object was capitalism and really for my project the real thing. And, this in retrospect is easier to say than in prospect. I was trying to figure out how to understand the world. But, when you hit Marx, and actually you hit Smith also and Ricardo, you'll see already the laws of political economy. It's political and it's economy and it's ordered patterns. And that is the thing that became the theme of my life, to see these ordered patterns and to see them as coming out of a small set of operating principles. I mean that's the beauty of many sciences – Darwin's biology and Newton or Einstein's physics. There are a few sets of operating rules, and these produce an amazing number of results. When you add the concrete factors and the number is uncountable. And that's where I see the beauty of it.

The beauty of reality?

The beauty of seeing the order in reality and seeing the patterns of reality and seeing that you can understand them empirically and theoretically. That's Kepler's joy.

I'm struck by you using the word "beauty". In a previous interview with Marshall Auerback [2016], quite early on you say that you don't find [mainstream] economic models beautiful.

No, not at all. Because beauty comes not just from the inner fit but the simplicity and the power of the explanation of the world. Their models are beautiful if you think that ideology is the right thing to do. I mean, many religions are beautiful in that sense, but if you're a biologist, creationism is not beautiful – it's ugly. And for me orthodox economics is ugly in that sense, that its claim to coherence is an internal claim rather than in reference to a real object. As soon as it reaches a real object it has to shout out "you're imperfect, you're imperfect". And surely that fault is not in the real object – it's in the orthodox theory itself. Darwin does not accuse reality of being imperfect, nor Newton, nor Einstein, nor Kepler. They look for the beauty in the pattern that you see. And that, from an engineering point, you can see why that makes sense and from a physics point also. The beauty comes from understanding how the thing works and not in saying it doesn't work the way I thought it did.

Is mainstream economics a science?

I don't think so because if science is something that attempts to explain a real object then I think mainstream economics is heavily contaminated with ideology which is an attempt to glorify the object. That's not to say that the left doesn't sometimes do that in its own way. But then we have to say, if we see something that results from our understanding and we don't like it for whatever reason, we can't reject it because it's not the right answer from our prior. We have to understand what's wrong with our reasoning. I can give you a concrete example. Marx is very clear that labour is exploited and that a higher wage would make workers' lives less miserable without removing the exploitation per se. But he doesn't think, therefore, that a higher wage will make the system operate better or indeed even make workers as a whole better off. In fact, in the discussions of this in "The Reserve Army of Labour" he argues something quite striking given his political view: namely, that if workers get into a better situation to the point that the reserve army of unemployed labour shrinks and the wage begins to rise *relative* to productivity, then the wage share rises and the profit rate falls. If the profit rate falls, accumulation slows down, mechanisation speeds up, the import of labour becomes more feasible, and the system re-creates the reserve army of labour. So, now you have a situation where the success of labour leads to the undermining of that success – from the internal logic of the system. Many people, many of my friends who are Post Keynesians, argue this is not true, because if workers' wages are higher, consumption demand will be higher, then demand will be higher, and capitalists will hire more people. I think that's not true as a general proposition because of the limits I described. I would like it to be true, but for me you cannot, you should not, persuade yourself that something is true because you would like it. The real difficulty is if you want that result within capitalism it imposes very strict limits on that space. It's not to say that wages don't rise – I mean, historically workers' wages have risen tremendously, but so has productivity. I've argued in a different book, *Measuring the Wealth of Nations* [1994] that in fact from Marx's point of view, the rate of surplus value has actually risen. That is to say wages have not risen as fast as productivity when you measure it in the classical way, including the approach of Ricardo and Smith and so on. So that's the limit the system poses. And if we're going to talk about how what we wish to do has an impact on the system, we have to understand how the system reacts.

Could I ask you about Heterodox Economics?

Yes.

In your interview with Marshall Auerback but also in an autobiographical piece you did for Philip Arestis and Malcolm Sawyer [2001b], you talk about a unified framework. And you've talked about Marx and Kalecki and Veblen and Keynes; however, they don't all necessarily fit together easily.

No, they don't. In creating a unified framework, you have to look for the fundamental principles, and of course there are aspects to any kind of argument that is not necessarily there in the original argument. Had Marx lived and had he had the life of Ricardo or Keynes, who knows what he would have done with the six books that he planned to do. But, we know that he did what he could under extremely difficult conditions and left most of it unfinished, and what we have is what Engels put together for Volumes 2 and 3 of *Capital* [1967]. So, I studied those in order to see the logic of the argument. And particularly, when you get to Volumes 2 and 3, the logic is implicit because frequently it's stated but it's not fully worked out. Even if it's not stated or even if it's stated and it's incorrect, once you attach to the logic then you have to follow the argument all the way through. Well, how do you know it's a useful argument? It's not sufficient to know it's logical; neoclassical theory is logical too. You have to have that object of investigation that you are studying, which has to be capitalism. So, Marx tells us a lot about capitalism, but there are other people who tell us about capitalism also. There are other people who explain certain aspects of that logic. So, I tried to extract a small set of principles, which are easily recognisable in the classical tradition, but then to add to those the things that you need in order to understand the system. Capitalism also changes. It's not a constant system. But the underlying logic doesn't change in my opinion. Profitability, exploitation, wages, money and its role and changing roles, those are simple basic principles. So when I was teaching Marx, which I did for very many years – roughly, I'd say, 15, 18 years – I tried to show the coherence of the logic of the arguments in Marx including parts that people don't normally study, the theory of rent and so on, and its implications for the theory of competition, theory of money. But then you come to a point where you can't rely on what Marx intended to do or did because it's not there. I don't know, it's quite possible that someday we will find in Marx's archives everything, I don't know. Marx was not a prophet. He was a person working on a scientific problem which absorbed a good portion of his life. For example, when we come to Macroeconomics, we already know that what Keynes was trying to understand was what actually was taking place. I mentioned in one of the interviews that Keynes was very deeply concerned with actual mass unemployment in the 1920s, and he says at one point, "look, if governments would just drop money, people will pick it up and then spend it and that would create jobs and then so on". So he's already got this idea of deficit funding or printing money stimulus. Now in Marx there's a resonance in the sense that Marx clearly understood this in his own discussion of money. There he refers to the fact that Tooke finds that the huge amount of gold that was discovered in California doesn't just simply increase prices in the same degree. A quantity theory of money would say this huge influx of gold should increase prices in proportion. But in reality the price increase is relatively small compared to the quantity increase, and Tooke has trouble understanding that. And Marx says, "well, that's obvious, capitalism is always underemployed in some fundamental sense, it's very flexible, so that huge stimulus was met by an expansion of output". Well, that's a very interesting point. It is a passing statement by Marx within the analysis of money, but for me it gives you an idea of how the level of analysis already developed implies something else. And this is Keynes's problem, is the issue that Keynes wants to address. We already know that Hitler solved Keynes's problem before

216 *Anwar Shaikh*

Keynes because within one year Hitler goes from massive unemployment to full employment by printing money to finance deficit expenditures while at the same time keeping wages down so that the reserve army of labour effect of a rising labour share doesn't take place, and also keeping prices down so there is no serious inflation. Because you didn't mess with Hitler: you want to raise your price, you have to deal with him or his minions. Hence that structure, the imposition of these rules on top of the normal operations of capitalism led to a massive expenditure of output with an expansion of profitability and price stability. Keynes already knew this. Indeed, many people have called this the first instance of military Keynesianism. But, I think that calling it military Keynesianism is missing the key point, which is how is it that the system was able to absorb this? And for me there's another question which is crucial in my book: why did Keynesianism then cease to work in the 1970s when it wasn't military Keynesianism? What limits did it run into? What were the problems? And I think one very important lesson from actual military Keynesianism was the suppression of the wage share (i.e., the keeping of real wage growth below productivity growth) because it prevents the reserve army of labour effect, which leads to the profit rate falling relative to its trend. It seems that Sweden did that early in its development: raise wages but raise productivity more. Different countries have done it. But, that tells you that there are limits, and this idea of limits is very fundamental to my understanding of economics just as it is in engineering and biology. You always have room, but the system provides the reaction and these reactions provide limits and if we don't understand the limits we run the risk of failure. In social science you don't normally get punished for being wrong; you just write another article. But, the people who might be affected by what we do, they are the ones who pay the price for our being wrong. So, I take it very seriously that you have to proceed carefully. You have to look at historical examples. You have to look at puzzles and paradoxes. You have to look to see where the catch is so that you have some reason to believe that the argument you are making has many ways of explaining things that other people can't explain and explaining things that have not been noticed before. I took a lot of time writing this book for that reason.

And you're aware of the impacts that economic ideas, policies, that you're going to have on the real world. Is that something that you're seeking to do, to change?

Yes, I am, but I'm also aware at a personal level that, as Keynes said, we are all dead in the long run. I have no particular reason to believe that my hope that this book of mine will have the desired impact will be validated. It may happen in my lifetime, or when I'm not around, or it may never happen. History does not say that just because you've discovered something that you think is true that it will be accepted by other people. And it may be suppressed. It may be thrown aside as being wrong. There's no way you can know – you have to do the best that you can. That's the only thing I can say. I did the best that I could, and I took a lot of time to do it carefully. I'm gratified that the book has done well so far. I just gave a lecture at the Bank of England on Tuesday because of the book. Now that was a surprise for me. I never expected my book to be noticed by the Bank of England! I talked about what they did and how my argument and application provide a different path and different limits on what they want to do. Evidently, the Bank of England did not change its policies in response! But people were listening. I am also aware that much of what I have to say goes against the current even on my side of the divide. Most heterodox economists are opposed to what I'm saying. And I was aware of that from the beginning, but all I can do is to try and persuade people – which is what I'm doing. The Bank of England was my 40th talk on the book in the 14 months since the book came out in February 2016. And I have been talking to a variety of people, but whether they're going to pick up this thread I don't know.

From the various comments you have made, my impression is that you see problems with both orthodoxy and heterodoxy. Do you see yourself trying to replace or supersede both?

I'd like to propose a third alternative. If only Tony Blair hadn't so devalued that word! But I would like people to understand, and I'm working on this now obviously. I would like to have a second version of the book which is shorter, more accessible. The current version is 1,024 pages in small print, so I can understand that it is intimidating. But I would like to say what we say to graduate students at the New School (which is one reason I've stayed here my whole life): "look, we want you to study Neoclassical Economics, Micro and Macro, and all that stuff, and we want to study it rigorously. We also offer you the chance to study Post Keynesian economics, which departs from this tradition and has a major macro component to it. But there is also a third path, which does not have to start from a perfectionist story and then add imperfections to it, as both neoclassical and most Post Keynesian (Kaleckian) economists do, because left and right branches from the same root end up preserving the root as the point of departure". I want to say "look, we could have Micro and Macro in a perfectly sensible way consistent with anthropology and sociology and all that. We can derive all the principles of micro, all the basic patterns, downward-sloping demand curves, and I show that in Chapter Three of my book (which by the way builds on a path initiated in 1963 and then abandoned by my teacher Gary Becker). So, the patterns we see can be explained without having to start from, even as a point of departure, the orthodoxy". The problem for me is that the bulk of the heterodox tradition is deeply invested in "imperfections". From my point of view, it is therefore always tied to the framework that it says it opposes, and I don't think you need to do that. Many progressive church-going people are taught that reality doesn't correspond to the ideal, so they have to speak about imperfections of humans. These progressive people have sometimes devoted their life to good causes, so it's nothing to do with their motivation. Darwin does not start from an ideal form, but rather from the logic of actual evolution. This is a different beginning. If we're going to approach economic life in this manner, which is the way I thought Marx was approaching it and indeed Smith and Ricardo, they're not approaching this from imperfections, they're approaching it from the logic of the system, and it's a different logic than that what's been portrayed. That's the beauty of it also.

So would it be fair to say that you locate yourself in the heterodox camp but somewhat uncomfortably?

Yeah, I mean, everybody in the heterodox camp says they don't like that term and it's not clear what the alternative term is, but if I were to try to construct a term I would say something like the Classical Keynesian synthesis. And the reason, as I argue in the book, is that Keynes is actually speaking of a micro-foundation for his macroeconomics, which has to do with competition. He rejects the idea of imperfect competition, for instance, as proposed by Joan Robinson and Chamberlain, who were his juniors. But, then what is he speaking of? Although he talks about perfect competition, in the next sentence he throws it out. So I try to argue in the book that what he's really speaking about is the theory of *real* competition embodied in classical tradition. I try and show in the book that the argument that he actually makes on effective demand follows very naturally, in fact necessarily, from the classical theory of real competition. And that in turn leads to the limits to Keynesian policy I discussed previously, because the micro-profitability dimension puts limits on the macro effective demand dimension. And for me there's a beauty in showing that, even though the limit is something I don't necessarily like. I would love to see a solution to Greece which was to just give everybody high wages and print a lot of money, but I don't think that would work. I don't think exchange rates work in such a way that if you have your own currency you'd be fine. I think that's false. Many people who are on the left adopt some aspects of the standard framework even as they reject other aspects, and I think we need to examine these hybrids critically. Even where there are things which are accepted as true by all sides, they might have to be located somewhere else.

I was just struck by the similarity to Keynes talking about a long struggle to escape ideas and you seem to be suggesting that people haven't necessarily escaped.

Yes, I think we all face that when we try – I was lucky in some way because I was already primed to reject the theory just by culture, by background, by personal experience. Engineering helps, too, because you don't have to believe something just because someone says it's true. You have to look at the thing that you're examining. I was also primed by the politics. But I was never drawn to that aspect of left politics, in which the opposition to capitalism is the defining element. To me the understanding of capitalism was the ground for the opposition to it. And you need to understand it not just negatively but positively. You need to understand how it works.

But is the purpose to understand it, or to change it, or both? Or do you do one before you can do the other?

You'll also be the engineer. You don't need one before the other. Many people change the world without understanding, but there are consequences of not understanding it, too. I have done my share of demonstrations and marches. I was a founding member of the Union for Radical Political Economics [URPE] also. But it seemed to me that providing a space for people to oppose capitalism is not the same thing as providing a framework in which this opposition can be located and which the consequences of opposition can be located also. And some of those consequences are consequences people on the left don't like to hear. They don't like to hear that Keynesian policy cannot just provide full employment. Well, I happen to believe that capitalism will not sustain full employment and that's an uncomfortable belief. But I can't reject it merely because I don't like that outcome, so I have to deal with the fact that if that's the case then that's the limits of capitalism. Where can we go within those limits? And then it also leads you naturally to ask where do you go beyond capitalism, even though my work is not about that. But it seems to me that understanding the limits helps you think about the fact that you can't go beyond those limits without leaving the system because these are system limits, not human limits.

Could I go back to Gary Becker, because you've discussed him here and elsewhere? You have spoken about going into class one day and his saying "oh, we could prove all these results without making any of the standard assumptions", and that seemed to have struck a chord with you.

Yes. The thing is that in this long project of mine I've been sort of like a theoretical squirrel. I see nuts and I take them and I bury them and I dig them up later when I need them. And so as I read, I read Veblen and I read anthropology and Becker, I saw things that I could see would be useful but I hadn't necessarily got the framework in which they would fit, and Becker's argument was one of them. In the beginning, what Gary Becker showed is that different types of behaviour, radically different from the behaviour we were being forced to absorb in his class and indeed in Vickrey's class before that, would give us the same results. So this immediately struck me as fundamental and for many years – this was 1969, I would say, maybe '70. I sat on it for a long time because as I was building the theory of real competition and the theory of macrodynamics, I knew that I also wanted to show that there was a path for consumer microeconomics which didn't have to go through perfections/imperfections at all. Becker's path (which he abandoned) made that possible, but I didn't actually write about it until near the end of the book. I waited till then because I needed to also show how it fit with all the rest. One can think of this path as stochastic microeconomics based on structural factors. Here people behave the way they actually behave, in a variety of ways – one person is tempestuous, the other arbitrary, the third pattern-dependent, and so on: we don't have to require people to be any one of those. They can move from one to the other. Nonetheless, ensembles of such populations have stable patterns even if the elements underneath are shifting, and they produce a determinate set of outcomes. Nowadays, we call this "emergent properties" and all of that, but that's an age-old understanding. So, this particular argument of Becker was about stable emergent properties of a whole even though the individual parts of it are complex and variable. And while writing up this thing, by coincidence, I happen to have picked up a book by a physicist, Robert Laughlin, who argues that that idea that the aggregate is different from the sum of its parts is not just an old aphorism but rather true of all sciences, especially physics. Especially physics. And I thought, okay, this is my point of opening for the Becker story because Becker was essentially showing that you can derive the same pattern from four different and contradictory behaviours. And Laughlin was saying "look, every physicist knows this, that the interaction of individual components can produce a stable pattern even if the components interact in complex ways that we don't necessarily even understand". And I think for me that was very important. And it also allowed me to derive all of the observed demand curves and all of that. The one thing I changed from Becker's approach, which I think is a very fundamental thing, is that people have minimum levels of what they can consume. There is a minimal level of necessary goods, which is socially and culturally variable and depends on your social location and all of that. Mathematically this generates a non-linearity due to a threshold for necessary goods. This turns out to be quite important in deriving some particular observed patterns such as the difference between the income elasticity of luxury goods and income elasticity of necessary goods. I had already sketched this out right after I first heard Becker's lecture, but I sat on it for a long time. When the book was nearing its end I published the argument in a working paper just so I could get it out. I had zero feedback! Nobody was interested! Nobody. But I think it's a very important aspect of the argument because it tells us how individual human behaviour still produces stable patterns even though we all insist that we are unique and we do what we do for complicated reasons and we can change at any point if we want, in the aggregate the ensemble is quite stable and predictable, quite predictable.

In your interview with Marshall Auerback, you suggested that Becker recognised that what he was saying at this point was radical but that he didn't want to go there.

I think that's right. He got attacked actually by Kirzner, an Austrian economist. First, of the grounds that this approach undermines rational choice and utility maximising, which is the foundation of orthodox consumer microeconomics. For me that was actually a great benefit of Becker's argument, since I believe these aspects of microeconomics are wrong anyway. But Kirzner also argued that you can't get a theory of the firm from this – which is right. In my book I make the argument that the structural consumer microeconomics is not the same thing as the microeconomics of the firm because firms have different motivations. The idea that one must have the same operative principles for the firm and the consumer is peculiar to neoclassic economics. Surely Smith doesn't believe that. I mean, that's easy if you read Smith. Nor does Ricardo and surely not Marx. So, that's why I waited until I had the rest of the story, the microeconomics of the firm and the macro implications of that well laid out before I, so to speak, dropped into place this piece of the jigsaw puzzle. It had to fit with the work I already knew to be true and it turned out to fit very well.

One of our questions is about the problems of mainstream economics. We have addressed that at length already. Could I ask why it does not change?

Well, first of all it does change. I know that because when I went to graduate school Keynesian economics was still dominant. Micro was taught but it was taught with a certain degree of hesitancy because it didn't fit well with the macro part. So micro and macro were taught as separate partitions, and the attempt to sort of bring Keynes back into micro was still germinating and didn't really take root I think until later. I think I lost the question here. What was it?

Well, I asked you why it doesn't change and you've challenged that.

So, it did change. It did change. So, I saw in my time macroeconomics being replaced by so-called micro-founded macroeconomics based on increasingly absurd notions such as rational expectations and representative agents and all that as a way to rescue the story. So, I saw this as the last ideological stand of neoclassical economics. But, I must say that like many people I didn't appreciate how powerful this ideological stand is, how much it satisfies the need to say that we can ignore the details. Yes, we know that you can't take utility functions and aggregate them up to a single utility function, but it's a first approximation so we're going to assume there's a single individual. Same thing for the representative firm. We can take that as a first approximation. But, I didn't want to spend my time fighting about whether the aggregation was valid or not. I wanted to make the argument that the problem was *not* in the difficulties of moving from

222 *Anwar Shaikh*

standard micro to a representative agent as very excellent people like Kirman and Hildenbrand had done, but rather that this beginning itself was false. And for that same reason I didn't want to go from that false beginning to imperfections because that was a better way to resolve that. Otherwise it becomes a debate whether the imperfection approximation or the representative agent approximation is more accurate. It seemed to me that the problem was that you need to go backwards to the root of the question: how do people behave and how is that consistent with the observed empirical patterns of micro consumer behaviour? For the firm I had considerable confidence because I'd worked on that for 20 years of teaching and reading in classical history of economic thought, classical political economy. And here, I didn't believe in the notion that monopoly was the general condition and that also set me apart from my fellow heterodox economists because that is a tradition I think is based on an evasion. If you start from perfect competition, you run into the difficulty that the world does not look like that. One simple way to deal with this fact is to say that the world used to look like that when competition prevailed but does not do so anymore because now monopoly prevails. So the world was perfect before, but now it is imperfect: monopoly as the original sin. I was astonished to read, for instance, that the Marxist *Monthly Review* school now says that Marx's theory of competition is the same as Friedman's theory of perfect competition, the trouble being that Friedman believes that competition still prevails, but the Marxists believe that now it is monopoly that rules. I discuss this in the book. I cannot see how one could read Marx and think that the viscerally antagonistic competition that he's talking about is essentially the same thing as perfect competition. It's politically easier to argue that monopoly power runs a system because then monopolists stand in opposition to all people who are not monopolists, which includes small firms and workers and peasants. And there's some truth to that. Obviously, the big firms have power, but as I argue throughout the book, they don't have power over their fellow combatants. And, so the struggle of the big against the big implies outcomes which are in fact the outcomes that Marx is talking about, competitive outcomes. And that sets me apart again from heterodox economists from oligopoly and monopoly schools.

You've said before that you thought that around the time of Jevons and the marginal revolution, the big shift in economics was to abandon conflict.

I think that's right.

Does this also apply to heterodox economics?

Well, heterodox economics displaces the conflict onto the idea of monopoly. And by the way, perhaps I mentioned in one of the interviews, but a group of us, four people, Howard Botwinick, Mary Malloy, Katherine

Kazanas, and myself engaged in a project, which we completed but never published, which was to study the economic analysis, economic theory implicit in the politics and political positions taken by US Left parties: Socialist Labour Party, Socialist Workers Party, Communist Party, a series of other parties such as the Revolutionary Communist Party, Progressive Labour Party, et cetera. We were interested in asking not what causes them to differ, not about whether Mao or Lenin was correct or whether the leadership in this period was better than leadership for the next period, but what was their economic analysis of modern capitalism? What we found is very surprising (that manuscript is mouldering somewhere in my basement): almost all of them relied on this idea of monopoly power and monopoly pricing because this was the dominant theme in the Marxist and the political left in general.

When was this?

When did we do this? That's a very good question. I would say mid-1980s. A long time ago. And, one reason it got abandoned was because I felt that having established what their underlying commonalities were was not sufficient; we needed to show how real competition could explain the same reality. And that explanation took me another 30 years, so that was the difficulty. I didn't want to just say "Marx said this" because that wasn't the issue. The issue was how does the system operate? Nor did I want to say that they had an incorrect understanding, which is the usual trope for showing why your Party is better than the other Party. And I didn't think we had enough to understand how the system works particularly in respect to the place of large scale in the theory of competition. Large scale is not the same as lack of competition. Some of the clues were already there. I mean, I'd already found various squirrel items here and there. An article by Jim Clifton in the first issue of the *Cambridge Journal of Economics* [CJE] where he wrote about how large-scale enterprises are actually more competitive because they don't really give a damn if they operate – they make donuts one day and they make steel parts another day; it's a question of where the rate of return is higher. So, they'll abandon one or both in a shot if they can find something that does better. That was an important thing. That's exactly like the Becker insight into consumer behaviour. I saw that and I thought, okay, that's something I have to squirrel away and bring back later. And little by little that turned into a full-fledged theory of real competition, but there were a lot of other things that still needed to be developed. What about the theory of money? What about interest rates, about bank credit? And to put all of that in an integrated framework in which to discuss – I'm not even saying criticise – the commonalities of the bulk of the Left despite of its differences on concrete issues. This is part of what this book does, even though that is not its main focus.

At what point did you become conscious that you were engaged in a very long-term project?

Well, it mutated over time. I began by trying to understand what Smith and Ricardo and Marx were talking about. And there certain issues popped up right away. For instance, I was very taken with Ricardo's idea that prices would be roughly equal to direct and indirect labour times. I don't say "labour values", Ricardo doesn't use that term, but total labour times. As an engineer, that struck me as a very interesting proposition. I used to teach international trade theory and therefore I had to teach about the so-called Leontief paradox in reference to the Hecksher-Ohlin model of neoclassical trade theory. I was preparing for classes once when I started studying the data in the back of Leontief's famous article. I found it very puzzling that the numbers in the data appendix were roughly of the same order of magnitude. And I couldn't understand that. What does that mean? What do these numbers mean? Well, it turns out, to put it in Ricardian terms, these are the ratios of market price to total labour times in each sector. And since prices were in dollars and labour time in hours the fact that the ratios seemed roughly equal magnitude to my eye, I thought that's got to mean something. So I thought, okay, I'm going to graph these. The problem is that the New School didn't have any computers at all! When I moved from Columbia to the New School I had to give up my Columbia account. So, I went to the New School Dean's office and I said "these are my computer punch-cards". I still had them somewhere, these little cards that we ran through the system. And "here are my computer tapes, where's the computer?" And they said "what do you mean?" I said "computer? You know, computer?" They said "we don't have a computer" and I said "well, how do you do empirical work?" and they said "well, you know, we do it in the old German historical tradition. You look at some data and you tell a story about it". So a friend of mine, Sheldon Danziger, was then a graduate student in economics at MIT took the data that I had, which I put into computer cards I couldn't run here, and he ran it through the MIT computer, and I got this beautiful pattern of the relation between prices and total labour times. I had the ratios from the article, as well as actual market prices, so I could calculate total labour times, and by plotting them I saw that the scatter was very close to a 45-degree line. And I thought, that's what Ricardo was saying! I wrote some articles on it, but I didn't stop there. I needed to move to the rest of the story. What about price-value deviations, the transformation problem? How do we deal with the math of that? What is the empirical evidence? So that absorbed some time and I became more and more confident that what Ricardo said was right, that what Marx said was actually right, empirically, even in modern capitalism. But, then the question was to show how and why. It's not enough to say that it works. You have to explain from within the basic foundations why, and that took some time. When I went back to Sraffa I saw here is a tool, a powerful tool. I've taught a regular course on Sraffa for roughly a dozen years, and it's always fascinating stuff.

But I was doing it in order to understand the reality. For me always that was the question. Not necessarily what Sraffa thought he was doing but the powerful tool which he produced. So, that was another nut that I squirreled away and nibbled on. And little by little these things began to come together so what I had was a path from the theory of the firm to the theory of relative prices. Through Ricardo's proposition I found that Adam Smith had made a similar argument, so that was another thing. Marx's transformation problem, how does it work, what are the empirical implications of that? And, little by little, I had a strong coherent argument all the way through. And then the question of the equalisation of profit rates arose. It is not sufficient to just say that Marx assumed it. So, I began to ask myself, how do we know they're equalised? I mean, what's the evidence? So, of course, I read the empirical evidence. Willi Semmler was my roommate at that time and he wrote, based in part on our intense discussions every day, a survey of the empirical evidence. This was very important for me because it showed that the evidence was consistent with the classical tradition. But there was another difficulty. Data on industry profit rates seemed to indicate they were not equalised: they had persistent differences over time. I found also that the average profit rate in the corporate sector was very different from the rate of return in the stock market, which is exactly what led Robert Shiller to argue that the "excess volatility" in the stock market was due to irrational exuberance. Eventually, it occurred to me that in the data on the stock market the rate of return on stocks is memoryless in the sense that for a given company an old stock certificate and a new stock certificate have the same price regardless of the dates when they were issued: the market does not care when a stock was issued. But that is not true of plant and equipment. And then it hit me like a lightning bolt that the classical argument about equalisation of profit rate was equalisation of profit rates on investment, on *new* plant and equipment. And once I saw that I realised that this was really also the argument in Marx given that in Volume 3 he abstracts from differences among the technologies of firms: new investment is like old investment at that level of abstraction. But actual data we had was the average rate of profit on all capital, new and old, each representing different technologies. This led me to a way to measure the rate of return on new investment, which I called the incremental rate of profit (irop). And then later I saw that that is actually what Keynes calls the marginal efficiency of capital, and later still I saw that my measure was what Kaldor had proposed for the rate of return on investment. But what really floored me was when I compared Shiller's data on the rate of return in the stock market and my measure of the rate of return on new investment in the corporate sector. I remember to this day that when I put the two up on this little computer screen I had at the time, I saw immediately that they moved together. This dissolved Shiller's claim that the two rates are different and that the stock market rate displayed excess volatility: *there was no excess volatility.* Over the postwar period the two rates had the same mean, the same volatility, and, therefore, the same coefficient of variation. They were not exactly equal because there were periods in which the stock market over- and undershot the rate in the real sector, so that bubbles and busts were there too. Now I went on to the next problem. How do I extend this investigation to the actual profitability of individual industries? Much of my work has been done in conjunction with students because I could seldom get funding for my kind of research (the Levy Institute of Bard College and the Initiative for New Economic Thinking notable exceptions). Here my student George Christodoulopoulos did a path-breaking dissertation in which he measured the incremental rate of return for OECD countries, and he found that it equalises in the expected turbulent manner. And again, that was something I stored away. I had it. And I could see that. I investigate it again on other databases, and over time other students did dissertations on that. Ed Ochoa did a great dissertation on the relation between sectoral total labour times and market prices and even calculated prices of production in the US, and many years later Ed Chilcote did the same for OECD countries. So I was building up a map and at some point I had a lot on relative price theory and the corresponding empirical evidence. Then I returned to another issue that I had investigated earlier in the early 1980s, the theory of international trade and its implications for exchange rates. In neoclassical economics the fundamental theorem of international trade is that real exchange rates will move to make nations equally competitive. This means that the balance of trade should fluctuate around zero on average. This is the point of departure for both orthodox and heterodox analyses of trade. The only problem is that it's never been true empirically. I had already shown that the key question was about how competition operated on an international scale. But now I needed to specify what exactly determined the exchange rate. Once again, the Marxist literature pretty much went with the standard argument except to say that nowadays monopolies or nations interfere and all that. So again I'm separated from the heterodox tradition on this issue because I happen to think that exchange rates are still determined by competition. But how do I show that? It took me a lot of reading, and I remember to this day I found a book on Empirical Studies of Exchange Rates, and as I read this I got that feeling as I always do in these moments: that this is it, this is the clue that I'm looking for. I didn't know exactly how to put it together yet, but I worked on it and out of that came the formulation that real exchange rates were merely international relative prices so that, like all relative prices, they would be dominated by the underlying real costs of the commodities. And for the empirical application, which for me was always the necessary aspect of the theory, I had to understand the principle but then I had to go to the empirical evidence. And that led to a series of papers. Again, many students were involved in that; Rania Antonopoulos, for instance, worked with me on that issue for her dissertation and we subsequently published a joint article on this. This is my research methodology. I've stayed at the New School all these years because I had these wonderful people who understood the question and were willing to work jointly on this. And, at some point I had the theory of real competition. I had the theory of relative prices. I had the theory of exchange rates. I had the theory of the stock market but not the bond market or the theory of modern money, so I began to work on those. In filling these in, the structure you have in mind when you're doing it is not necessarily the structure that emerges. Ideas have their own voice and their own integrity and I had to move things around as the story began to take shape. And, as I always did, I gave lectures on the subject. So, as the lectures got more dense in the sense that I had more and more material, I could see that I had the theory of the firm, the substantial body of it. The hardest part then was the theory of the interest rate and bond prices because I didn't know that much about it. So I read, as I always do, taking notes, and every once in a while you see something and you say that's it, that's the clue you're looking for. It's just like a murder mystery. You see something and you feel that this clue is important but you don't know yet exactly how. And that's pretty much how I pursued it. Macro was the same. Keynes was there, looming large. But what's the link? And then I began to think of his marginal efficiency of capital which drives his theory of investment and hence his theory of effective demand. Well, that was my incremental rate of return, which I discovered had been proposed by Kaldor as a measure for Keynes's rate. By now it was all linked. I knew the story of profit, where it comes from and how it varies. I knew how the wage rate and the length and intensity of the working day stood behind it. I knew that if wages go up, profit goes down. So now I've got the closure for the macro part, and that helped resolve a lot of issues in macro, including some major empirical and theoretical puzzles. And when I saw that, then I thought, okay, I've got enough, and I began writing. Basically I began writing 15 years after I had enough material and then I began to write. And, the Macro part got deeper as I wrote because I studied macro practice too. I apprenticed myself to Wynne Godley at the Levy Institute in order to understand how macroeconomic models worked; we co-authored a paper, and some years later I became part of the Levy Macro Modelling Team. As always, the important thing for me was to connect the theory to the practice. I remember finding in my friend Ahmet Tonak's library the book *Modern Macroeconomics* [2005] of Snowdon and Vane. And when I saw it there was another bang – that's it! This is a book that explains the history of macroeconomics clearly and lays out the theoretical and empirical connections of orthodox economics. That for me was very important. I work hard for such moments.

And the genuine sense of excitement still comes over.

Tremendous excitement. Yeah, excitement in the pit of my stomach. I see, I feel there's a problem. Of course, to be sure it doesn't always work by the way! But you see a problem and when you're looking at the problem you're looking for a solution and then suddenly you hit it and it just – I remember being thrilled. I mean, there's no other way of putting it. I remember telling undergraduate students that when I saw the equalisation of profit rate between the stock market and the real sector, I was high for a couple of months. And they said, "you were high?" I said, "not that way, but yes, I was high". Every day I would go look at it and say this is beautiful, this is really beautiful. And that's what I mean about the beauty of it.

And you try these ideas out in your teaching or you hone them?

Always both. I repeatedly refine and hone the arguments, try to simplify them, get the essentials connected to one another. And I always try them out in my teaching. My poor students have been my experimental subjects and not necessarily happily so! But I've been lucky that I got hold of a space and I fought to keep it. It wasn't given to me. I fought for it and was able to maintain at least some of it over the years. I felt that it was important to teach the history of economic thought as a source of ideas *better* than those now dominant in both orthodoxy and heterodoxy. There was a time when my two-semester PhD course in Advanced Political Economy had 90 students in its heyday. Over time, as the neoliberal mentality took hold, many people shifted to game theory, econometrics, and DSGE modelling, and all the other things that gave them currency in the job market and in the eyes of the orthodoxy. At its nadir my course was down to six people. But in the meantime I was teaching the main history of economic thought graduate course and some undergraduate courses. There were always people who were interested in something more, and eventually the reaction to neoliberalism and its tropes began to turn things around. The incoming cohort is much smaller now, but even so my advanced course has over a dozen people. I'm hoping the book will persuade people that it's exciting to understand how the system works and that we have a framework that doesn't require us to keep dipping, even if by way of negation, into orthodox economics.

In your interview again with Marshall Auerback you expressed the hope that this book could be the foundation of a new curriculum?

Yes.

So how would you see that happening and working?

Well, that's tricky because, as I said, the resistance is coming really from people on the left. The right doesn't give a damn. I mean, they're not going to be interested in our curriculum anyway. But the left is kind of specialised in imperfections and now increasingly focused on gender and race and environmental issues. These are critical issues, but all too often when these require some reference to the underlying economic factors the left falls back on oligopoly, monopoly, imperfections, game theory, et cetera. Or else it shifts the focus so as to avoid economic factors altogether. I believe that we need to take back that ground. We need to say "look, we can explain this in a unified manner". I try to teach these ideas in my Advanced Political Economy sequence, but this reaches only a few graduate students each year. However, thanks to the generosity of the Henry George School of Economics and its President, Andrew Mazonne, my lectures were videotaped and are now available via my book webpage (http://realecon.org). Andy was a friend and supporter who died tragically just recently. His goal was to create a video record of discussions with heterodox economists, in which our history, hopes, and intentions were recorded. Our written work is not the record of our intentions – it's just the record of our accomplishment. And the intention is the real thing for the future. I hope that I can persuade people that we should be confident enough to take back the ground that the orthodoxy beginning with Jevons and Menger has taken away and do so with confidence that we can explain the world better than they can.

I just want to explore the teaching a little bit more. What are you trying to do when you teach a course? What's your objective?

My first objective is to disrupt people's thinking because I know as an economist no matter where they come from they have a bunch of received ideas dominated by neoclassical economics or monopoly school economics and I need to break those down. I try to persuade them that it's not a question of adding on to those ideas but really starting differently. So, I spend quite a lot of time doing that. In that process I want them to see that ideas have theoretical roots. So, I'm not necessarily saying abandon the ideas that you have, but understand where they come from so if you choose them you choose the root too. And that is a difficult task. Usually the first half of the course people are resistant to that because they've come, they're on the left, they know there's Milton Friedman and there's Keynes, and they know which side they're on. But my object at the beginning is to say "well, let's step back and ask the question and perhaps Friedman is right about some things and Keynes is right about other things". But we can't add Friedman and Keynes together because they come from different theoretical roots, so what do we do with that? And that I try to say is that it opens up a space for a way of seeing what questions they address and how they can be addressed in the different framework. And that's the least popular part, I have to say, because that requires commitment to a framework which most of the left doesn't share. So even though people may be persuaded by it, eventually they end up working with another professor who says exactly the opposite. So they shift over. They do their dissertations in ways that are different from what they themselves believe. Others take the position that theory is just a device to further some progressive agenda, so given your agenda you look for the theory that

230　*Anwar Shaikh*

supports it. This instrumental approach is sometimes tied to the notion that it's really just a rhetorical device. So they reject that notion that theory has to be a guide to analysis and you have to be consistent in its applications and implications. As you can imagine, I'm strongly opposed to such fall-backs. I noticed that in one of your lists of questions you asked if economics is akin to poetry. Absolutely not, in my opinion. It's a failure of imagination to think that it's all about rhetoric. Galileo was wonderful with rhetoric. But if that's all he was, he'd be a second-rate poet. He uses rhetoric to argue in favour of his extraordinary theoretical framework. That is profoundly different. He fundamentally changed the way people look at the heavens, and rhetoric was just a tool. Rhetoric is no more sufficient than math. Math is also just a tool. It is in fact a rhetorical tool in much of modern economics. But math in itself has no meaning for social science. Its meaning is attached to its theoretical use, and its limitations are also manifested there.

Might we just explore the question about poetry briefly? I suppose there's a step back from claiming economics is poetry to recognising its poetic elements or artistic elements. You've talked about beauty. Is beauty an important part of persuading somebody?

Yes. Rhetoric is absolutely important as a means of persuasion. But you can persuade people to be followers of one person or another, of Darwinism or Creationism. And people do it very well on all sides, but that doesn't tell you the substance of their positions. Rhetoric and emotion play a big role in that argument. Beauty plays a big role too. But that's not enough. There are people who believe that general equilibrium theory is very beautiful. I don't. It certainly has an elegant structure and the subject is very important, but I find the underlying story to be quite weak. The mathematics disguises the weakness of the argument. Mathematics is the Latin of the neoclassical liturgy. Telling your story in Latin may make it sound more arcane and more mysterious to some people, but that is all. So, elegance and rhetoric are aspects you really have to ask about the underlying story. If you told Newton's story of the heavens badly it would still be a fantastic story. And if you told the Church's story of the heavens, well, it would still be the wrong story. That is my problem.

Humbug **[Shaikh, 1974] – there's an artistic element to that, isn't there?**

I confess there is an artistic element! I was originally going to write "Bullshit" but I knew it would not get published! So "Humbug" came to me. Vela Velupillai once asked me where the word "humbug" came from, and I realised that when I was growing up people would say something like "that man is a complete humbug". I wrote the Humbug paper because Joan Robinson asked me to look into the question of the empirical fit of aggregate production functions, and the paper came in response to her support and encouragement. The word itself is something that you could perhaps find in Oscar Wilde or Bernard Shaw. That paper got me into a lot of trouble, a lot of trouble! It basically excised me from the profession for a long time. But I had already found this project, and so that kept me going. If I had any hope that my original paper would somehow gain me fame, it was a good thing it did not because I might have been tempted to sort of do that again and again, which I could certainly have done. But I have only followed up on it a couple of times, and only on request. And even then only because I didn't want that argument to die. But to show that something is wrong is not to show what's right, and I understood that from the beginning. And so I didn't want to spend my life complaining about orthodox theory – that's something too many clever people do. You can show that the math is nonlinear, the attractor is unstable, clever things like that. I've never been tempted by that. I like math and I certainly studied it, but for me it always has a purpose. In any case, I was saved any temptation along those lines when that avenue was closed off. Solow's response turned out to be disingenuous: he accused me of not realising that the capital coefficients in my data were negative. But what he didn't mention is that with the same regression the capital coefficients in his own data were also negative – as was pointed out by John McCombie. I simply didn't pursue that line after my request to respond to Solow was turned down by the journal editor.

14 Victoria Chick

Victoria Chick is Professor Emeritus of Economics at University College, London, where she has held a position since 1963, having obtained her BA and MA from University of Berkeley. She is a co-founder of the Post Keynesian Economic Study Group and an honorary life member of the Association for Heterodox Economics. Her main research interests are in macroeconomics – in particular monetary policy – and the work of John Maynard Keynes, though she has written on a range of topics, including economic methodology (Chick, 1998; Chick and Dow, 2005) and economics education. She is the author of numerous books and articles in these areas. Her books include *The Theory of Monetary Policy* (1977) and *Macroeconomics After Keynes* (1983). She has been recently instrumental in the compilation of a two-volume set marking the 80th anniversary of the publication of Keynes's *General Theory*, called *The General Theory and Keynes for the 21st Century* (Volume 1) and *Money, Method and Contemporary Post Keynesian Economics* (Volume 2, Dow, Jespersen and Tily, 2018a/b).

Victoria Chick was interviewed by Andrew Mearman at University College, London, in August 2017.

How did you become an economist?

Like many economists, by accident. I didn't take my undergraduate studies very seriously, and I certainly didn't take economics seriously until I fell into one class that was really fun, in which we were enjoined not to read anything. We came in every day and constructed microeconomics from scratch by ourselves, guided obviously.

By?

A chap called David Alhadeff, of whom you probably have never heard, at Berkeley. It was an experiment that he was running to see whether that would work or not. It worked for two of us and the rest fell by the wayside – couldn't cope – but I was one of the two who benefited. It was enormous fun, though I never worked so hard in my life. It was a good game to play and all the kinds of serious reasons for doing something, like I wanted to change the world and make it better and all that, didn't figure really. It was just an accident.

Victoria Chick 233

So it was sort of fun?

It was fun, yes, exactly.

The approach sounds fun, but was there anything about the material that was attractive to you?

That's a hard one to answer off the cuff. Not really, no more or less than anything else. The educational spectrum in a place like Berkeley was very broad: you had to do a laboratory science and something from arts and letters, so I was accustomed to a wide range of material and not really saying to myself "oh, this is boring stuff, and that's wonderful". I just took it all on board.

Was there anything about what you were discussing that was intrinsically interesting?

This was already late in my undergraduate career, and then there was the Eisenhower recession, so I decided to do graduate work. I can remember walking into the graduate reading room and thinking "I feel at home; I feel at home for the first time in my life". But that wasn't really to do with economics, I suppose, as much as being an academic. I still found the suggestion, when it was made to me, that I become an academic frightening: what, me? I couldn't imagine myself standing up in front of groups of students, but I learned how and have always felt at home in this activity.

What about it felt welcoming?

I was always an intellectually curious kid, and here I was amongst a lot of other people who were equally intellectually curious, whereas my family had no intellectual pretensions whatsoever. Most of the people that I had known as a child thought that reading books for kicks was a bit weird; you read them if you had to. All of a sudden everybody was doing it, and it was interesting and satisfying and I was comfortable doing it.

Sandy Darity (chapter 3, this volume) said he decided to become an academic because he enjoyed the debate, but not debate for its own sake. He chose economics because of what the debates were _about_. So, was it academic first for you and then economics?

Couldn't say, it was all an accident really.

So there was never a moment.

If you land on your feet after an accident you stick with it.

Yes, but you mentioned the Eisenhower recession.

Well, it just meant that there were no jobs available. There's a correlation, which everybody knows, that if there's an economic downturn you get more graduate students. The opportunities for women anyway were diabolical.

I guess the question still is "why economics then?"

Well, I was already in it by that time.

Do you remember why you chose to major in economics? Was it just that class that you did?

Well, yes, and stimulating people. There was, at that time, a great variety of ways of thinking, in that department [Berkeley]. That [variety] was entertaining. There were good characters around on the staff.

You talked about variety. Would you use the word "pluralist" to describe it?

I wouldn't describe it as pluralist in the way that Alan Freeman means, for example, where one takes a very considered view of different schools of thought. But different schools of thought were around and were more or less tolerated. There were some pretty severe strains in the department; George Papandreou, later Prime Minister of Greece, was brought in to knock some heads together and get people talking to one another again and things like that. From a student point of view, if you're not involved in the politics of a department but just listening to what people have to say, there was a wide variety of things being said, and that was fun. There were eccentrics like Abba Lerner, Tibor Scitovsky – really interesting people, yes.

Some of our interviewees have suggested that they did not have a "long struggle to escape" a way of thinking because they were already in a department in which difference was tolerated and where variety was normal. Others had to choose consciously to rebel against this mainstream. It sounds as if you're more the former.

Well, yes and no. I've thought about this quite a lot because I can't actually answer the question which it throws up. So much of economics is statics or comparative statics and equilibrium and all that, but I could never really think like that. Most people get socialised into thinking like that and find it hard to get out. I've certainly taught all kinds of things in that framework and all the rest of it, but when I was trying to puzzle something out I would always have to let it run sequentially: first this happens, then that happens from which you discover some rather interesting things. I remember taking apart somebody's article on the optimum quantity of money and I said, "you say that such and such is an optimum. Do you realise that to get there banks would have to give away all their revenue, not just their profit but their revenue, for the entire period of the transition, and that's completely unrealistic". And he said, "well, I'm not trying to be realistic". That was very much one of the attitudes at the time: he got a publication out of it, for which he was widely lauded, yet it didn't make any sense at all, but to him that didn't matter. I had a different view of what one should be doing. But it was because I had examined the proposition from a sequential point of view that I found this out, which most people wouldn't bother doing.

At least you were able to have a conversation with this person and say, "do you realise that this is what you're assuming?"

... which is to say "you've done something really stupid" – which, of course, endears me to people.

How did he react then?

I told you, he said, "I'm not trying to be realistic". That was a very early example of something which is now endemic. He was ahead of his time, far. The mathematisation of economics, to the extreme that's been going on while I've been in this business, wasn't happening then. People had serious discussions about serious topics, realistic topics. They would take some small problem and formalise it and so on – that was fine, but it was contained in a larger argument.

Malcolm Rutherford has talked about how, in between the world wars, there was a genuine pluralism between neoclassical and Institutional Economics in the US and a focus on real things. Then gradually that ebbed. Presumably you're talking about a period of time where that transition was already underway.

It was underway but it hadn't gone very far. When I say "tolerated", again, I pointed to some strains. Variation was much better tolerated at LSE, when I came to LSE. I don't think people fought over approaches to economics in quite the way that they were doing at Berkeley – but the spectrum wasn't as wide either. There was no Marxist or Communist. People will think that's very strange, because of the reputation that the school had, but it's true. So the range was narrower, and people were more civilised in the way that disputes were dealt with.

You've mentioned David Alhadeff as being influential because of the way he taught that class. Who else influenced how you thought about economics?

Well, Howard Ellis taught me money and banking; he was terrific. I don't know if you've read his *German Monetary Theory* [1937]. It's a wonderful book. And Abba Lerner, as I said, and Tibor Scitovsky. A chap called Philip Bell, that you probably wouldn't have heard of, who spent a couple of years here and was very much influenced by James Meade; he wrote a book on the sterling area, just when the sterling area was falling apart. He was a good technical thinker as well. David Landes, historian. It's quite a good roll call. And then Minsky appeared, of course. Everyone concentrates on the fact that I had classes with Minsky, but he was only one of a large number of really quite superb characters.

Was it the things they told you, was it the way that they thought, or was it just their approach?

All those things.

How did you develop your particular contribution to economics?

I don't know. That was an accident too, I'm pretty sure.

What would you say your particular contribution is?

I think there are three areas where I've had something to say. One is money, one is macro and particularly Keynes, and the third is methodology. Now, when I got the job here [UCL], in 1963, I was Tony Cramp's empire of one. Tony Cramp taught monetary economics. I had specialised in international money, but that teaching was already covered, so I moved aside from international money to national money. I'd had tuition from Richard Sayers and Alan Day at LSE. There was an interesting little fracture in the pluralist structure at LSE, in that the people who taught on the degree course Economics Analytical and Descriptive thought that anybody who studied monetary economics was completely batty: "why would you do that?" This was part of a Keynesian confusion that maintained that Keynes said nothing about money, and I can't think of anything further from the truth. Samuelsonian Keynesianism, or bastard Keynesianism, was the orthodoxy of the day, if there was one. There was variety, but that was the mainstream. Things change! So that will impinge on something further down the line when we talk about heterodoxy and orthodoxy. Orthodoxy used to be Samuelsonian Keynesianism.

Could you say more about your own contribution.

Oh, yes. Why these three areas? Well, I've explained money. Then I taught macroeconomics – very conventional IS-LM style macroeconomics – but I started tinkering with it, again in this kind of sequential way. Instead of taking IS-LM at face value as a simultaneous equation system, I began to say, well, if there's saving, where does it go? And if there's investment, how is it financed? In other words, the connection between the two curves. Eventually the whole thing just fell apart in my hands. If you push any system, which involves compromise, as that system does, very far, it's going to collapse. So I thought, well, that's interesting, let's go back and see what Keynes had to say. This is a path-dependency exercise that I'm explaining here, full of accident but not entirely. It's an internal critique story, isn't it? So the internal critique sent me back to look at *The General Theory* again. Poor Minsky had tried to explain *The General Theory* to me but I didn't get it at the time.

Was that your first exposure to *The General Theory*?

I first read it when I was a graduate student. I'm not sure I read it as an undergraduate; I don't think so. I have a wonderful copy that I bought new for $3.75, hardback. I do remember that Minsky's exam paper was full of questions about expectations. But, because the assumptions behind neoclassical macroeconomics, assumptions of perfect certainty or perfect knowledge, weren't explained, I didn't know why this was so exciting. It took a long time to work that out.

Then the third area: it was really Sheila [Dow] that started me off on methodology. I began actually figuring out some of the methodological problems for myself, with the question of statics being so unsatisfactory as a central problem. But she was already well into methodology, so she was a big influence in getting me to go into depth.

So the origin of the first area of contribution was that I started off in international trade and international money and then those got pushed aside in favour of domestic money; the second was an internalist critique and the third was a personal influence.

Do you remember why international money and trade?

Probably the whole question of the sterling area and international reserves, the role of the dollar, Triffin. It was a hot topic at the time.

We've talked about mathematisation and the shift in economics. You've written about formalism in particular. Did you ever dabble in formalism?

It depends how formal your formalism is. You have to have some degree of formalism, but the formalism can be expressed in words just as easily as in mathematics. Actually, you can be pretty formal in words. I don't feel comfortable

238   *Victoria Chick*

expressing complex ideas in mathematical terms. You keep coming back to the early stages of my career: so much of international trade theory is taxonomic; you have to go through case studies one after the other and then see if you can find a pattern. The modern equivalent would be simulation studies, I guess. That approach is quite different from finding some summary generalisation, or at least you're reversing the process: you might find a generalisation out of a taxonomic approach, but you don't start there. That was more or less the way things were being done when I started doing them.

This is not easy to think through. On the domestic monetary side, Richard Sayers, the Radcliffe report, Tony Cramp, to some extent Harry Johnson, though he was important on the international side as well – the way of thinking of these people, though very different one from the other, all impinged quite a lot. Richard's wonderful book, *Modern Banking* [1938], which is, like Howard Ellis's book, an absolutely landmark exploration of how the monetary system works, involves no maths whatever. What it does involve, and this becomes important as I gained experience, was knowing your institutions inside out. Richard was one of the last people who actually went and asked bankers what they did and embodied that in what he wrote. He knew the institutions of the British monetary system thoroughly. You mentioned earlier the blend between Institutionalism and neoclassical economics. I don't think Sayers was neoclassical. He would have just said, "I'm an economist"; there wouldn't have been this question of "what kind of economist are you?" He was part economic historian, too. He would have thought that it was impossible to understand anything in economics without knowing your institutions. The other people who know this full well are development economists; if you try to apply theory which is developed for the developed world to an underdeveloped economy, there are pieces missing, there are things that don't work or work differently, and they have to be taken into account. So, it was perfectly natural to a person like Sayers or Cramp to know their institutions, comparative institutions as well. There was a whole group of former students of Sayers who were employed around the country – Hull and Sheffield and places like that – who I got to know as external examiners and so on, who would specialise in comparative monetary systems. There was always a comparative money paper for students of monetary economics at LSE.

You describe Richard Sayers as one of the last to know their institutions well. In light of the recent major crash, is this something we need more of?

The Independent Commission on Banking, which reported about six years ago, was charged with recommending how to re-regulate the banking system, and yet it did not understand that banks create money out of whole cloth. They described the banks – as most textbooks do – as intermediaries. Now, that is pathetic. The fact that banks create money, not pass it on from savers, was an absolute commonplace of knowledge in monetary economics when I was an undergraduate. It didn't get lost; it was buried. I don't know in whose interest that was, but it was buried, I'm sure intentionally, and had to be recovered. This is now well underway: there was that wonderful book that NEF [New Economics Foundation] published by Josh Ryan-Collins and friends. Then the Bank of England came out and said, "oh yes, of course we've always known that". Dennis Robertson said, didn't he, "highbrow opinion is like a hunted hare, if you stand in the same place long enough it'll come back 'round".

Let's move on to heterodox economics. We've invited people to be interviewed because we consider them to be heterodox economists. How do you feel about that label?

I accept it, even though, as I've told you, heterodoxies and orthodoxies can change places at any time. But at the moment I'm a heterodox economist because the current orthodoxy is what it is.

Were you ever orthodox?

Well, no, no, I don't think so, because of the question of statics. Interestingly, that's not a theoretical answer; it's a methodological answer. That may be not orthodox in any camp, and I wasn't. Although I taught bastard Keynesianism in the form of IS-LM and so on, the minute I started interrogating it I didn't believe it.

Is there anything about being not orthodox that appeals *per se*?

No, no, it's just the way it is; I don't set out to be eccentric, I just am. It's the rest of the world that's mad, you know – they all say that, don't they? Just before we do move on, I don't think it's really very helpful to say heterodox and orthodox. I accept it because that's the way it is, okay, but I don't think it's very good to do this. It's a shorthand. We need shorthands of various kinds. We can't say neoclassical anymore because they've become like an octopus and occupy a lot of other territories. So, it's a shorthand we're using; that's all there is to it. But I've already pointed to the fact that it's an unstable designation: it can change, so it isn't satisfactory.

Are there any other drawbacks?

I think that there's a danger that if you do accept it you automatically put yourself on the fringe, but you're there anyhow as far as the mainstream are concerned. All the best people are on the fringe really; it's a very nice place to be. Like my reading room in the library at Berkeley – it's congenial, there are nicer people. I think there's a good reason for that. Mainstream economics

240 *Victoria Chick*

teaches you that self-interest is what motivates everybody, and then they go on to act it out, which my lot don't. It's a very interesting thing, that if you go to a Post Keynesian seminar, people wait for the speaker to finish and then ask their questions. If you go to a mainstream/neoclassical seminar, people are interrupting all the time. Nobody sets the rules in either case, but you can tell immediately what kind of a seminar you're in by the way people behave.

So why does that happen?

I think in the neoclassical seminar there are all these people wanting to show off how clever they are: got to ask good questions, can't wait or take their turn, and they speak out, interrupting the speakers, which is quite rude, because getting their point across is the really important thing to be doing. It's their point, not the speaker's point, that counts.

What's driving people to want to get their point across?

Well, self-interest: if you tell people that self-interest is the name of the game, they'll act like that.

So you don't think it's the sociology of the profession, the sort of competitive pressures therein?

Well, yes, but where does it come from? Most Post Keynesians that I know are very cooperative; they're not competitive. We're sitting here having a cooperative conversation, not a competitive one.

No. I'm just trying to think of some counterexamples.

I would love to see somebody actually take this on from a serious, sociological point of view. I think it is a very important point. It's just something I observe and have given some superficial reasons for, but you could really explore this to quite a great depth, I think.

What is heterodox economics? Is there anything else you wanted to elaborate on beyond what we've already discussed?

I think the whole methodological foundation is what divides different schools of thought. I don't think it's to do with theory and I don't think it's to do with policy, although the theories and the policies do differ. I think that the real bedrock that differentiates the schools of thought is methodological in every case, including within heterodoxy. Just take one very obvious example, the question of perfect knowledge, which is so useful; it's so tractable; it makes it easy to construct all kinds of models. So the job of theorising is simpler, but it's not the way the world works, so almost immediately you're out of contact with what you're trying to explain. Or take the proposition that in the long run money doesn't affect anything real. Once again, that proposition is going to lead you into some very strange places, which don't mirror what goes on in the economy. When I say mirror, that's probably not a very good metaphor because it isn't a mirror – or it's a distorting mirror – in every case. The question is which distortions you find more useful and which ones you don't, or which emphases you think are important and which ones are less important to you, and every school of thought has different sets of priorities. But there's a great divide, I think, between basing your theory on an idea that you have perfect knowledge and, therefore, the ancient Greek notion of rationality (which depends on having perfect knowledge) instead of the kind of rationality that we all mean when we speak about it in everyday life: using information available to you to the best of your ability and drawing some reasonable conclusions.

I once gave a lecture to a group of undergraduates in Sicily about the methodological foundations of *The General Theory* and mainstream economics. Because it was a group of undergraduates they wanted a translation; the translation actually allowed them enough time to think about what I was saying. I began to realise that they were not only with me, they were ahead of me; they'd figured out what I was going to say. It was really exciting because the whole room was on the same wavelength, just because it was slowed down enough to be able to do that. The next day on the plane somebody hailed me and said, "I was in your lecture yesterday". So we traded places so that we could sit together and she said, "I've never heard anybody say anything remotely like that"; she was tremendously excited. I think there's a tremendous potential there to get students to understand why it is that people differ in their theories, so that you don't have the kind of bickering that I've witnessed in Berkeley when nobody actually sits down and says, "why do you say that?" A great many of these methodological matters are unexamined. Now, I understand exactly why mainstream economists don't examine them, because if they did they'd realise that they were on a hiding to nothing. That's why they pooh-pooh anything to do with methodology: it's dangerous for them. But, when I remember that excitement in that room in Sicily and the woman on the plane the next day, you realise that there's terrific potential there in a genuinely pluralistic approach, because once you get down to the methodological foundations you can determine pretty quickly what you can agree on and what you're not going to agree about.

What is a genuinely pluralistic approach? Having a proper conversation?

Yes, it's a conversation where you're not two ships passing in the night but you're actually getting down to this question, why do we differ? Why have we taken these two different approaches? If we go far enough down into the methodology, is there a common foundation or not? There's one school of thought that says Post Keynesians really ought to try to speak mainstream language in order to get them on side or get them to understand and so on. But honestly, if you have one group of people basing their theory on perfect knowledge of the future and the other saying the future is uncertain, there is no way that they can possibly agree. You either have perfect knowledge or you don't. So, you're really wasting your time, and the way that you waste your time is to operate at a level which is too high up the food chain on the theoretical level or the policy level or something like that. Suppose, for example, you want to talk to a Marxist, and the Marxist says, "why do Post Keynesians ignore class?" And Post Keynesians will say, "well, what do Marxists have to say about the rate of interest?" That's working at a level which is too far up the food chain. They're both concerned with systems which evolve where behaviour changes over time. The question is, how are you going to describe that system? What kind of compartmentalisation do you make in order to make the problem of explanation tractable? If it's just a matter of cutting it up one way rather than another you can say both are helpful, provided you agree on the fundamental shape of the economic system. You might have a different time horizon in which things operate and then, for example, you could say, well, one of them will work in the short run and the other over a longer time horizon; then you end up respecting each other's position. But, if your methodological foundation is diametrically opposed to the other or one excludes the other, as in this question of perfect certainty versus the existence of uncertainty, then there isn't a hope in hell of agreement or complementarity, and it's just as well to find that out.

I suppose the danger with finding it out is that you find a reason to stop talking to that person.

Well, so what?

Well, then the conversation ends.

Yes, so what?

Isn't that part of the problem that we've got, that mainstream economists ignore what heterodox people have got to say?

They'd do it anyway. I think we should just go away and do our own thing. I think that conversation with them is an utter waste of time. It's a pity, but unresolvable.

You stressed perfect knowledge or certainty as a dividing line, so I'm just trying to work out whether there's a core, a key methodological distinction. It could be that, but you also talked about statics as opposed to dynamics or statics as opposed to sequential thinking. You've obviously also written about open systems as a defining characteristic of heterodox economics. I suppose I'm coming back to the earlier quotation about whether or not one is *trying* to be realistic. Is that another difference?

Yes.

Maybe some people care more about that than others do?

I think you could find people in the heterodox camp who didn't care all that much about realism either. I think it's not a sharp dividing line, and I think you can find mainstream economists who are concerned with realism. They may not be going about it in quite the right way, but they're concerned about it. He isn't quite mainstream, or certainly not today's mainstream, but my favourite example is Tobin. Now, Tobin's heart was in the right place, but his mind had been completely taken over by the wrong sort of methodology for the job. He wrote once about comparative statics and said that it would be "impossibly puristic" – his words – not to apply comparative statics to change. As you know, it really shouldn't be applied to change. But he saw this as a minor matter which should just be slurred over; it wasn't a serious issue. Now, if you do apply comparative statics to change, you can actually end up with the wrong answer, like the example of the optimum quantity of money that I gave at the beginning, or I can give you an example from Tobin's own stuff. It's an example of an unwillingness to go down and really dig and say, "should I be doing this? Is this method applicable or isn't it?" that is in the way of what I want to call true pluralism. Contrast the situation at Berkeley where they were always operating at the level of theory or policy, never methodology. That's why they fought. There are a lot of examples that both of us can point to where particularly Post Keynesians and Marxists have a lot to say to one another. Institutionalists I would take for granted in the same way that Richard Sayers did: institutions are just part of the furniture. How can you possibly live in a house without any furniture? It's essential to understanding the structure of theory to understand the institutions that existed when that theory was put together. I've talked a lot about that so I think I don't have to elaborate on that here. All of that is very, very fruitful and I think that's where we should spend our time, not trying to convince neoclassics to listen to us. Forget it.

What about Austrians?

Problematic. As you know, there are a couple of ideas which are worth having, mixed with – how do I put this, even to myself? – as a group they exhibit a personality which I find very difficult to engage with. It's a huge generalisation to make, but I'm going to make it because I don't know what else to do. You wouldn't have been in the audience at LSE when Skidelsky was debating with a couple of Austrians and, honestly, they were so unpleasant – the Austrians, I mean. Even when they fell into error and Skidelsky corrected them, they refused to accept it and repeated the error. I find this difficult to deal with. If you take somebody who, because she was teaching a course in pluralist economics, learned Austrian economics and can talk about it sensibly but doesn't have the personality that usually goes with it – that is to say she doesn't believe in it – I'm talking about Ioana [Negru] – you can have a very interesting conversation about Austrian economics. This is getting into sociology and psychology big time, and I shouldn't really go there.

Well, we can go back to the ideas then. You said there are a couple of ideas worth having: which would they be?

I think the idea that there is a way in which order comes out of potential utter chaos in ways which are very surprising is a very useful idea: it's called emergent properties in other people's language and is worth serious study. But then this gets all bound up with what I think is a very false dichotomy, between individualism and collectivism, as the words are usually used, whereas you want some mix of the two. They fall too sharply onto one side of what I, as I said, consider a false dichotomy, and that makes it very difficult to take things very far.

Another view, though, is that what stops Austrians being full members of the heterodox camp is that they have been, in policy terms, quite influential and quite powerful. But also politically the mainstream tend to be associated with what might be called more right-wing ideas and most heterodox people tend to be associated with what might be called more left-wing ideas. Do you think there's anything in that?

Well, yes, and the anti-collectivist stance, the Austrians, is a perfect example of exactly that and why most people who will allow themselves to be called heterodox these days find it difficult to deal with Austrians. It's also part of their personality: they're rather abrasive about any form of state intervention, without considering that they'd be in a pretty bad pickle if we didn't have any: no police force, no army, no state education, and on we go.

It does: it reinforces the idea that the distinction between mainstream and heterodox is messy and, as you said, it changes as well over time. But even at any point in time it's not clear.

No, no, if it were clear we'd probably be in dead trouble, because our theories would be too crystallised and too definite and not having enough ragged edges. Because what we're trying to explain is so complicated, those ragged edges, I think, should be there and theory should be messy because – let's go back to fundamentals – we have partial knowledge, very, very restricted knowledge of what it is we're trying to explain. So it's hardly surprising that we don't, each of us, subscribe to the same vision of the economy, that we emphasise different things, that the boundaries of our explanations are ragged. I think that's perfectly normal.

The next question is about what are the problems of mainstream economics. How would you assess the proposition, then, that another difference between heterodox and mainstream is that heterodox economists would accept the usefulness of ragged edges but mainstream economists would not?

Mainstream economists tend to like to be tidy, but they aren't, in what they actually do. It would be terrible if they were because they couldn't grow any further. Just imagine that there were rigid borders around mainstream economics. Once you reach the border that's it: no growth, no development, no nothing, no jobs for anybody, finished, perfection. Do you like it? I don't, and I wouldn't if I were a mainstream economist. I'd want some ragged edges, open-endedness, some place for something to develop.

Indeed, the history of thought is full of examples of exactly that: where things have developed because someone developed part of a ragged edge and said something that, at the time, was quite radical and now isn't.

Yes, exactly. Before the interview, we were talking about music and it's so interesting that within my lifetime – okay, my lifetime has been rather long but even a shorter lifetime than mine would have seen, say, Stravinsky sound very radical at one point and now sound almost neoclassical. Our entire perception has radically changed over time because we're used to his idiom and because other people have done things which are more radical – a whole range of different things which put his music in a very different perspective now than what it was when I first heard some of it in the late 1950s. There's a completely different feeling about it.

246 Victoria Chick

Let's go back to a little bit more about you, as an economist. What have you been trying to achieve as an economist?

It's like the first question you asked, how did you become an economist? And I said, by accident. In some sense my whole career has been a series of accidents. I've just followed my nose really. Opportunities present themselves, or people ask me to do things. I don't think about it much; I just think, oh, that's interesting, I'll do that, and follow my nose. It portrays me as a very hapless kind of person; well, perhaps that's not unfair. But I never, for example, thought "where do I want to be in ten years' time?" That just never enters my head. I was very lucky in so many respects: getting the job here, for example. Somebody said to me in the hallway at LSE, "did you know there was a job going at UCL?" And they said, "I think the deadline's pretty close", so I went racing off and found the advert. Then I went to see Richard Sayers and asked if he would give me a reference, and he said, "in principle, yes, but I've never heard you give a paper". "As it happens I'm doing one tomorrow. Are you free?" "Yes". That's accident, every bit of it. In a way I just wanted to contribute and I want to entertain myself as well. If something turned out to be uninteresting I would drop it. If it doesn't entertain me, why should I think it would be interesting to anybody else? Now, the inverse doesn't follow: if it does entertain me it doesn't have to entertain other people, but I'm damn sure that if I think it's boring, so will others. People said, "who did you write *Macroeconomics after Keynes* [1983] for?" I said, "myself". It's been like that.

What have you been trying to achieve?

To say interesting things.

Are you trying to influence society in what you're doing?

Well, in so far as I think that those aspects of economics, macroeconomics, and money are pretty fundamental, and we did have a financial crash to illustrate the fact that it's important to get these things right, then what I've been doing has implications for policy, so yes. But I don't set out to think, "now, I want to move society in this particular direction; what kind of theory do I need to offer a push in that direction?" It's not the way I think and it's not the way I operate. I operate by accident all the time, very often reactively. People ask me to do things. Somebody last autumn said he was putting together a conference on systems analysis and would I please talk about Keynes as a systems theorist? I thought, well, yes, open systems, I've done quite a lot on that. But I knew that systems theory has developed technically rather a long way away from the simple things that I had been writing, so what could I possibly tell these people? Then I started thinking about the fact that every macroeconomist had to be some kind of systems theorist, right? So we can go all the way back. I began to contrast Marshall and Walras with Keynes and I thought, well, yes, the way that you actually compartmentalise within the system can lead you either to good results or bad results. Now, that was new to me, and I thought it really interesting. Sheila [Dow] and I never touched on it in all that work we did on open systems. We knew you had to cut the system up and we explained temporary and partial closures and all that business, but never that it was rather crucial how you did it and that there were good ways and bad ways to do it. Now, it's just because this chap asked me to write something. I didn't plan that, nor did I have any idea, when I started writing, what was going to come out and that it was going to be interesting, at least to me.

The other areas that you work in have got great policy importance and policy relevance and particularly over the last ten years, lots of impact; and yet, some would say that is not true about methodology.

I think methodology has, too, for the reasons that we've already gone through.

So, though there's a policy relevance here, you would say that's not something that's driven you to look at it. Is it another accident?

Well, it's been either internal critique or a response to requests from other people or some other kind of gradual uncovering of an idea or emergence of an idea. I hope it's an evolving system. I think it is; I've no doubt actually that it is. So no, there are people who have this ultimate goal and then find the theory to match it, but I haven't done it that way.

Is looking for research funding something you ever had to engage in?

No, no, by the time I had enough standing to be in the running for research funding, the mainstream had got hold of all the levers of power and they're just not going to fund the kind of work that I do, I reckon. The only funding I ever got was for the Post Keynesian Economic Study Group, and that was because Philip Arestis, my co-founder, is so optimistic. I looked at the application form and crumpled in a heap; he just filled it in.

Can I ask you about teaching, then? One of the first things you mentioned was about being exposed to an unusual approach where it wasn't about reading or a curriculum.

Working it out.

Is that something that you've ever been able to do in your own teaching?

Up to a point. You can only do that in seminars; you can't do it in lectures. I had lunch with somebody I taught in, it must have been 1965, recently, and I asked her, "is it my imagination, or did we used to sit around a table and think things through?" She said, "yes, we did do that; we thought from first principles". Then she said, "not everybody did that". So, I guess it wasn't an absolutely standard approach, even then. But what I wanted to do, above everything else, was to get students to think for themselves. This whole debate about curriculum change, to me, is not only one about what you teach but how you teach – to encourage students to be self-reliant and able and confident enough to think for themselves. It's not easy, and you know this much better than I do because you've gone into the whole question of teaching in a very systematic and serious way, whereas I've just experienced it, so to speak. You start out with students who expect you to be the expert and them to be passive recipients of your expertise, and I just can't stand that way of teaching. To me, it's not what teaching should be for or should be about; it's not the style in which you should do it. My objection, for example, to the CORE [Curriculum Open-access Resources in Economics] project is at least as much one of how it's taught as what is taught. It's an improvement over an awful lot of what is being taught in most places, but it's still: "here it is, learn this"; you can follow up a few steps and so on; that's good but, again, the student is led by the hand through those steps. You want a student who can go to the library and follow some footnotes and chase something up and be curiosity-driven and able to fulfil that curiosity without being taken by the hand and led anywhere. That, to me, is what teaching should be about. I don't actually care terribly much what they learn as long as they learn that, because then they can go on learning for the rest of their life.

That basically answers the next question about your goals of teaching. Can you think of any examples of how you've put this into practice?

Oh, I've tried an awful lot of things, not all of which have been successful. I've tried sitting at the back of the room and appointing a student to chair the seminar; they'd all turn around and look at me instead. I should have left the room, but they'd just pack up and leave, I suppose. It got harder and harder to get students to participate, I think because there's so much rot in the schools now, all exam-driven and goal-driven rather than, as that former student said, sitting around the table thinking from first principles without an exam in mind. It's not immediately obvious to the student what they're doing it for, and they're now so exam-driven that they're asking that question "will this help in the exam?" all the time, so it has become more difficult to do a decent job than it used to be. It's not just that we used to skim a very thin layer of very good cream, even the cream these days is not very self-reliant, and it's a terrible shame. So you wonder where on earth these Manchester [University] people [who formed Post-Crash Economics] came from that were so resourceful.

Their book *The Econocracy* [Earle et al., 2016] is good.

It's a great book. They're wonderful people; I love them, and they're wonderful to me. I spoke at their inaugural meeting up in Manchester. There were three or four of us. They also asked a member of the department to speak in favour of the current curriculum, and he was full of this stuff about heterodox economics being like phlogiston theory and snake oil. He proceeded to shoot himself in both feet. You could see that the students were stifling their laughter; they were polite. But he really wrecked his own case, and you just wonder what it was in Manchester that made their protest work so beautifully. Fantastic.

Finally, we've discussed a number of creative elements in economics, including its relation to music, uncertainty, accident, and open-endedness. So, can economics be thought of as poetry? I realise I've asked you a very leading question.

A leading question and I'm not much good on poetry; is it the poetry of Dryden or E.E. Cummings? You see the point I'm making?

Yes.

How much order is a good amount of order? I don't know; I don't find this question easy. Would economics make good music? Well, in parts, like a curate's egg, but some of it's pretty cacophonous. Poetry is more likely to be open-ended and have ragged edges than music, so it is a better analogy, possibly. Music does typically have a beginning, middle, and an end and they usually are in that order, unlike Godard's films, and you'd be pretty disturbed if that were not the case, whereas poetry gets away with more or can get away with more. One of the interesting things about, shall we say, old-fashioned poetry and non-modern poetry is that poets were always saying that the constraints under which they worked liberated them. The forms were very tight, very closed: 14 lines and a certain rhyming scheme, for example, but they found that liberating. Now, I wonder if there's any parallel with economics in that. I think there must be, up to a point, but then that point is reached and it has to be an open system because the economic system itself is open. The economy is an ongoing thing; it's going to evolve; it's going to change, and the only thing that you can use a closed system for is a very limited part of that system. It's like looking for your keys near the lamppost.

It's nice to have a lamppost: it does illuminate a certain fraction of what you're trying to explain, but you have to realise that there's more out there. Whereas, old-fashioned poetry doesn't aspire to that; it wants something, which is self-contained and beautiful in itself for its form and its limited content. Modern poetry, by contrast, is very often full of ragged edges, open-endedness, and ambiguity, and its meaning may not be clear. You think about it and you can maybe come up with five different explanations. (Actually I'm talking my way into this.) I think both systems, closed and open, are useful in economics. The little closed model that tells you quite a lot about very little is good because it does tell you quite a lot, and then the open-ended system allows you to try to fit what you've learned from doing that into a larger system. You really can't get away with one without the other in economics. Poetry is an exercise for its own sake, in a way, so it can do whatever it likes. I don't think economists are quite so free, at least if they want to have any impact on what it is they're ...

If they're trying to be realistic.

If they're trying to be realistic.

I suppose the other aspect of the question is about the process as well, not just the outcome. You might contrast the scientist narrowly (stereotypically) defined and the poet narrowly defined and conclude that actually the economist may be more like the poet, creative, intuitive, or at least has strong elements of those things.

Should do, anyway. In the very first stage of abstraction you have to decide what are the important features of what it is you're trying to explain. That's a judgement, and as you go on you continue to exercise judgement. When you finish you should exercise judgement as well. I am going to tell my favourite Tobin story. He wrote a paper exploring the question: "does an economy with money grow faster or slower than one without?" Very interesting question – not that we've ever had economies without money, but still it's an interesting, abstract kind of question. What he did was to set up a comparative static exercise with an economy with capital and money on the one hand and an economy with capital, only capital, on the other and the same rate of saving in both, keep "other things equal". In the economy without money all the saving goes into capital accumulation, and in the economy with money some of it is diverted into idle balances, so you get the conclusion that the economy without money grows faster than the economy that has money. Now, that's where you should exercise judgement that this is nonsense, okay? He published the thing and people cite it. All right, we're both laughing; it's partly the way I tell the story, of course, but it is absurd, you know it's absurd. So the proper thing to do is to ask "what is it about the way I pose this question that has brought me to this ridiculous conclusion?" And we know what the answer is: the role of money was only as an asset. There is nothing to do with how it's created and nothing about lending, financing investment, and allowing an economy to grow and all the rest of that, which is the obvious way to ask the question about economies with money growing. They grow faster because money is diverted from consumption to investment by the banking system. But to do that you have to have time in your model because lending takes place at one point and is paid back at another. Comparative statics just gives you the wrong answer. So judgement has to be exercised at the very beginning: how to set the thing up? And it has to be exercised at the end: does what I've come up with make any sense? So the process should have been that Tobin came up with this answer and then said, "there's something wrong here, let me do this again". Tear up the poem, throw it out and take another approach. But he didn't.

Not just him.

No, no: he's just my straw man.

Which is another good metaphor. Thank you.

15 Edward Fullbrook

Edward Fullbrook is founder and editor of the *Real-World Economics Review*, executive director of the World Economics Association, and a Visiting Professor at the University of the West of England, Bristol. He is the author of *Narrative Fixation in Economics* (2017) and of the forthcoming *Duck or Rabbit: Boolean Political Economy*, and editor of eight collections of academic economics essays.

Edward Fullbrook was interviewed by Sebastian Berger via email in September 2017.

How did you become an economist?

It's a story of two conversations. *The General Theory of Employment, Interest and Money* was the first book I ever read with pleasure. I was 22. From age 5 to 16 the school system had me classified as borderline mentally retarded. My luck changed in my penultimate year of high school when a non-conformist English teacher gave me the chance to pretend I was not mentally deficient. She also taught me how to write a sentence, after which, inflated with fantasises of normality, I taught myself how to read textbooks and take exams and soon became academically proficient and for a long time thereafter very neurotic. As an undergraduate I cut classes as often as I attended them and waited till the night before an exam to open the textbook. Sometimes I only managed a C, but in economics it was always an A, and that was the only reason I had for becoming an economics graduate student.

Till then mine had been an all-American, all-textbook education. The textbook genre requires its authors to pretend to know it all and talk down to their readers. Reading *The General Theory*, I encountered for the first time an author who was openly struggling to understand what he was writing about. I too was struggling and so I — and what could have been more preposterous — immediately identified on an existential level with John Maynard Keynes. It meant that for the first time ever while reading a book my resentments and fears from my educational past receded to the background. And when they did the most astonishing thing happened. My brain started giving me an intensity of pleasure that, except for sex, I hadn't thought possible. So it was that an intellectual was born.

I had read the whole of *The General Theory* before I opened Alvin Hansen's *A Guide to Keynes* [1953], the book we had been assigned to help us understand the original work. Reading it was a shock. Either Hansen was in some way corrupt or when it came to economics one of us was rather more intelligent than the other. Given my history, the second possibility was extremely worrying. But my emerging new self was saved when a fellow grad student loaned me a copy of Joan Robinson's *Introduction to the Theory of Employment* [1937]. It both confirmed my reading of Keynes and offered me one that was much deeper. Because of that and because Robinson's brilliance made serious inroads against my inherited sexist bigotry, she along with Keynes became one of my first two intellectual heroes.

Not long after my intellectual birth, a conversational experience and its aftermath turned me off economics — and I thought forever. Having from five onwards been marginalised at school, I had compensated by outside of school organising my peers in games, fort-building, expeditions, clubs, teams, a league, hell raising, and minor pranks. These organising inclinations continued into my twenties, and as a graduate student I gathered some of my new peers into a discussion group. Once a month we would meet with a case of beer and a guest professor in one of our basement apartments. One month our guest was a young professor whom I liked and who was soon to make millions off his textbook. Halfway through our case of beer someone asked him, "What do you do if after you've been working on your dissertation for a year or longer you discover that the data you've collected doesn't support your hypothesis?" "You reselect the data" was his answer. "How do you do that?" The professor volunteered to hold a short series of seminars to show us how. When the time came for the first one, I couldn't make myself go. My peers came away from it enthused. Likewise for the second and third. I decided economics was not for me.

With a backpack half full of books — I was reading widely and seriously now — I set off to see the world. Sixteen years and many adventures and misadventures later, I found myself living in Cambridge, UK. One day walking on a back street near the centre, a shop window caught my eye. It was a photographer's shop belonging to the widow of Frank Ramsey, the philosopher, mathematician, and economist who back in the '20s died at the age of 26. The shop window was full of old black-and-white photos, and soon I was recognising faces from the Bloomsbury Group: Virginia and Leonard Woolf, Duncan Grant, Keynes, and others. One photograph was larger than all the others and the longer I stood there, although I didn't recognise the subject, the more I found myself looking at it: a woman in her early to midtwenties in an oddly patterned dress sitting on a sofa with her legs folded under her. It wasn't that she was particularly good-looking but rather that there was more character in her face than you would expect in someone her age. Eventually I leaned down to read the small print on the bottom of the frame: "Joan Robinson".

A few nights later I was at a chamber music concert. It had yet to begin and I was watching people taking their seats. An elderly couple, entering arm in arm, caught my eye. The woman sitting next to me appeared to recognise them, so I asked her who they were. "They're famous economists: Piero Sraffa and Joan Robinson".

A month later I was at a dinner party. Sitting opposite me was an Indian woman who was a Cambridge English don. We mostly talked literature until we got to the cheese course when she asked what I "read" in university. "Oh", she replied, "I too did a degree in economics. After my undergraduate degree in English I decided to get one in economics before going on for my doctorate in English". She said she still kept up her economics contacts and occasionally had "econ evenings" and would invite me to the next one.

I had zero interest in economics, but when a few weeks later I received the promised invitation I thought it might be interesting as a social occasion. So, more than a little nervous, I went along.

I was the last to arrive. Entering a large sitting room, there in an arm-chair directly in front of me was Joan Robinson. The gathering had been forewarned that an odd American was coming, and I had barely crossed the threshold when the great woman, with the whole room listening, asked me a question about the current state of the American economy. She did so with the kindest possible face, but I had not read anything about any economy for over a decade, and I froze. Thankfully, Sita, the hostess, covered for me and dinner was served.

After dinner – by now I had had a couple of glasses – I decided I had to make something of this once-in-a-lifetime opportunity to engage with one of my heroes. Joan – there was absolutely no edge to the woman so it already seemed natural to think of her as Joan – was in the armchair again, and I sat down on the floor facing her at her feet. I began by asking her what it was like being a student at Cambridge back in the '20s. After recalling the lectures of the literary critic I.A. Richards, she moved on to Wittgenstein and Sraffa and their weekly one-on-one discussions over tea. It was one of those discussions – and in her raspy voice she repeated Sraffa's account of it – that led to Wittgenstein's famous turn from belief in a world comprised of atomistic sets of propositional facts to one where meaning depends on the anthropological setting in which propositions are conveyed. At this point Sita, who was now sitting on the floor beside me, sought to bring the whole room into the conversation by making a broad and potentially contentious statement about the meaning of Wittgenstein's *Tractatus* [1922]. I still had not read the book, but had read one or more books about it, and suspecting it was likewise with Sita, I decided as a way of becoming friends with her to argue against her. It was immediately obvious that she liked my challenge and soon the whole room of economists was debating the meaning of *Tractatus Logico-Philosophicus*. And, bizarrely, something was about to happen that would change the course of my life.

As the debate continued it occurred to me that perhaps no one in the room had really read the *Tractatus*. Joan Robinson stayed out of the debate and, although I was still sitting at her feet, I now had my back to her. Then suddenly from behind me her loud raspy voice broke into the conversation. Here are her exact words:

> "The world is all that is the case. The world is the totality of facts, not of things. The world is determined by the facts, and by their being all the facts. For the totality of facts determines what is the case, and also whatever is not the case. Those are the first four propositions of the *Tractatus*. I've never been able to understand them".

With her eyes turned away from us and into her thoughts, she tried to explain what she couldn't understand. She was not arguing; she was making a confession. Except for maybe herself, the singularity of her behaviour was lost on no one in the room. It was a magic moment for me — the relaxed integrity of her intellect was so plain to see. And such a contrast to the outcome of my conversation 16 years before. I wasn't yet in a position where I could change my life's course, but in time I was, and if it hadn't been for that evening with Joan Robinson and the *Tractatus* I would never have become an economist.

Please tell us how you developed your particular individual contribution.

I am not aware of having made a "particular individual contribution" to economics. If I am known at all in economics I suppose it is for the efforts I have made to make the individual contributions of living economists working outside the neoclassical tradition better known and to bring them together so as eventually to free humanity from the enforced limitations and illusions of that tradition.

So how then did I come to develop this subversive pastime? Like most of the good things in my life, it was a fortuitous accident. One hot summer night in 2000 I was — as we used to say — surfing the internet when I came across a site called Autisme-Economie, recently started by French economics students. Beyond its elegant short manifesto it consisted mostly of articles, some quite long, from French newspapers detailing their rebellion against the neoclassical curriculum.

A week later I was in Cambridge, UK, for a small economics conference. My paper went down well, but I had two failed and humiliating conversations over meals. The conferees, mostly from the States, were both demoralised and conversationally obsessed by the cleansing that was taking place in economics departments — especially by the dropping of economic history and the history of economic thought. When I, an unknown to them, tried to give them encouragement by relating the success of the French students — by now the French minister of education had ordered an investigation into the state of the economics curriculum in French universities — I found myself immediately regarded as a quasi-lunatic. They could not believe that such a thing could have happened, not even in France.

256   *Edward Fullbrook*

For therapy in the days that followed I wrote the first issue of what became the *Real-World Economics Review*. Political correctness has never been one of my virtues, and it was called the *Post-Autistic Economics Newsletter*. It really was written as therapy, as I had no intention, or so I thought, of anyone reading it. But one night sitting at my desk with my second glass and an email list of 99 economists – most of whom had been with me at Cambridge – and an anonymous Hotmail address and then another glass, I clicked twice and off it went. Five minutes later Paul Ormerod subscribed, with James Galbraith soon to follow. Within a week there were over 200. Today 26,507.

We have chosen to speak to you as we consider you a heterodox economist. Would you label yourself as a heterodox economist? What do you think Heterodox Economics is?

I don't like the label "heterodox", at least not for myself and for the people and the ideas I work with. Why? Because I see it as a label for losers. In parliaments there is always the party or parties in opposition, but I do not know of any political party that has named itself such. One could work with a private definition of "heterodox economics", but as used in the public realm it is essentially a negative term, referring to all economics that does not qualify as belonging to today's orthodoxy (i.e., not broadly speaking neoclassical economics). So then what is neoclassical economics? Arnsperger and Varoufakis's 2006 paper "What Is Neoclassical Economics?" is the best answer I know of.

Careers aside, there are two reasons for doing economics and both have been important to me. One is the purely intellectual pursuit of gaining understanding of economies. It is the same basic lust that drives a physicist or an anthropologist or someone who pursues creativity in one of the arts. Except after the fact – and then only marginally – the term "heterodox" does not really pertain to this category of pursuit.

The other reason for doing economics is because what the leaders of society come to believe or pretend to believe constitutes a true description of how economies work can have an enormous impact, for better or for worse or even horrendous, on billions of human lives. And this is where the orthodoxy/heterodoxy divide comes into play, and those economists who find themselves on the heterodoxy side may want to find a label for themselves that does not concede perpetual defeat.

Whereas I do not like to hear economists who are not neoclassicists refer to themselves as heterodox, it is a point scored in our favour – or would be if we also didn't use the term – when one of today's mainstream economists describes us as heterodox because it is an implicit confession that they subscribe to orthodoxy – something no real scientist would ever do.

I have explained elsewhere how identification with the heterodox label acts as a barrier to bringing some cohesion and thereby worldly influence to the stories non-orthodox economists tell the world. By definition, each heterodoxy has a major quarrel with orthodoxy, with each having its own point of divergence, and from which, even if it was not the origin of its founding, it now forms its primary self-identity. As a consequence not only does each heterodox school begin in isolation from other ones, but its primary point of reference remains the neoclassical mainstream. Historically there has been little interchange between different branches of heterodox economics, instead where inter-school exchange has taken place it has been mostly between neoclassical economics and individual heterodox schools. Upon reflection this is not as surprising as it sounds. Because the members of the various schools come to identify themselves in terms of their points of divergence from the dominant school, they retain a working awareness of the common ground, usually quite large, that exists between them and neo-classicalism. Between heterodox schools, on the other hand, their common ground is their outsider status, so that their commonality relates mainly not to economic ideas but to the position of those ideas and their holders in a socio-cultural-economic structure. It is my experience that nearly all heterodox economists are more conversant with neoclassical economics than they are with any heterodox school other than their own [Fullbrook, 2010a].

What are the problems of mainstream economics?

Like "heterodox economics", I am uncomfortable with the way "mainstream economics" is used. Today's mainstream economics was not always the mainstream, nor will it be the mainstream forever unless in economics history has come to an end. And I don't believe it has. In any case, I am committed to seeing that it hasn't. What are the problems with today's mainstream? To answer entails answering, at least in part, the question: what should be tomorrow's mainstream economics?

Many books have been written in answer to these questions. Here is my own succinct list. The ethos of scientism (as defined by Popper) rather than that of science prevails in today's mainstream. In consequence today's mainstream tends to function as a system of belief – an orthodoxy – rather than as a system of exploration. Scientism's prevalence is so overbearing that most economists seem ignorant of how real science operates. Today's mainstream is in significant part ruled by ideological devotions rather than by the pursuit of truth and understanding.

As practised in many elite institutions, the economics profession is financially corrupt to a high degree, with many of its leading academic voices spending their careers in the revolving door between the academy and One-Percent money. The level of financial corruption in the economics profession needs to be substantially reduced. Its empty formalism – when disconnected from ideology and One-Percent incentives – makes it incapable of dealing except superficially with the real world. Its conceptual subordination of the Earth ("natural resources") to the economy makes it a threat to human survival.

What are you trying to achieve as an economist? Do you seek to influence society? If so, how?

I see two primary things one might seek to achieve as an economist: earn a living and increase human knowledge and make it known. I am not seeking to earn a living as an economist, and as a "heterodox" one this gives me an obvious existential advantage. It means I don't have to worry about being cleansed from a faculty or blacklisted from employment elsewhere and thereby risking destitution for myself and my family because of offending the belief system of other economists. The employment situation in economics today is that if one is not in my fortunate situation, then one has to be brave to be a non-orthodox economist. Of course it shouldn't be like that, but it is and strangely it is a reason for optimism. I think that today a significant proportion of neoclassical economists would opt for something else if they thought it would be safe for themselves and their families to do so. This implies that in our profession's future there lies a tipping point.[1]

I need to unwrap a little the notion of advancement of knowledge. For me there are two kinds of knowledge: temporal and eternal. The former includes knowing what's showing this week at the Orpheus and what the trade balance for Germany was in 1988 and what are the chances of improved employment opportunities for non-whites in the USA in the coming year. The latter includes the natural sciences and their technological offshoots. To what extent do we find eternal knowledge in economics and is it advancing? Do economists on average understand economies better today than they did a half century ago?

Advancement of knowledge is not just a struggle against ignorance but also, and in our time perhaps more so, against false knowledge. The prolonged struggle for acceptance of Galileo's observation that the Earth orbits the Sun was due not to it being new knowledge but to it contradicting false knowledge that the society's most powerful institutions used to legitimatise their tyranny.

At least a partial analogy holds between that state of cosmology in centuries past and the state of economics today. Knowledge, in my eternal sense, of economies is today significantly greater than what is permissible to teach in schools and universities. Mankiw-type textbooks are in effect institutions of censorship as were the teachings permitted by the Church in the century following Galileo's observation. So for the last 17 years I have seen my primary aim as an economist as one of trying to open up holes in the censorship of economic knowledge.

What are your strategies for seeking research funding?

In recent years I have attempted to obtain funding from billionaires for the World Economics Association. That I should have tried is a bit ironic – or perhaps just naïve – because it was my encounter in Paris with a billionaire and one of his cronies that motivated me to start the WEA. The billionaire was Peter Thiel, and I have written elsewhere [Fullbrook, 2010b] (https://rwer.wordpress.com/2010/06/25/the-glass-wall/) about the experience and its consequences.

In 2013 I received an invitation to speak at George Soros's annual INET [Institute for New Economic Thinking] fiesta, this one in Hong Kong. I was about to turn it down when pressure mounted for me to accept, as it was seen as an opportunity to raise funds for the World Economics Association [WEA]. So I booked a flight.

Of course everything was paid for by George, and it was my first and only five-star hotel experience. Most evenings our host made a lengthy but charming appearance on stage as we dined. But my attempts to meet him failed, and the letter that on behalf of the WEA I sent him via the head hotel porter to his door was never acknowledged.

While in Hong Kong I had marvellous support from other members of WEA's Executive Committee, one of whom introduced me to the Chinese billionaire Victor Fung. He showed interest in contributing to the WEA and gave me his email address, but my emails were never answered.

One Hong Kong day in the dressing room backstage as I was about to go on stage, Lord Sainsbury came off. I introduced myself and handed him an information sheet on the WEA that I had prepared for this type of situation. Like Fung, only more so, he expressed interest, but none of my and others' emails and letters came to anything nor appeared to reach the billionaire himself.

After that I swore off billionaires and their foundations, and the WEA progressed solely on the basis of membership fees and the occasional academic-sized contribution. But about a year and a half ago I got the idea of starting a new WEA journal titled *Economic Morality*, and I lined up a large and impressive editorial board from a range of disciplines and cultures. Special funds were needed for this project, and I got the idea of seeking funding from a foundation belonging to a billionaire family with which I had recently had a favourable experience. Some of my colleagues thought it was breathtakingly naïve of me to try this. "No billionaire", one of them said, "is ever going to support a journal titled *Economic Morality*".

I ignored their advice and proceeded with the application and submission. I was led to believe that a decision would be forthcoming. When months passed and still no word, I enquired. A response came within hours. The WEA's application appeared to have been turned down immediately, but they had decided not to inform me. In those months the steam had gone off the project, and I let it drop.

Out of fairness to the billionaire class, I add this as a footnote. I also write on continental philosophy, including three co-authored books on the works of Simone de Beauvoir; 1999–2000 was the 50th anniversary of the publication of *The Second Sex*, and in celebration large open-to-the-public conferences were held in various countries.

260 *Edward Fullbrook*

At one in Cologne I found myself attracted to a middle-age woman, a fellow invitee, because of the humanity and intelligence that showed in her face. The last night of the conference an American scholar made on-stage remarks about Beauvoir and Europeans that I found deeply offensive. At the interval I found a door at the back of the stage that led onto an unlit balcony, and I went out to cool down. I thought I was alone when a woman's voice said, "She shouldn't have said those things". I turned and there in the shadows I saw the face I had come to admire. I confirmed her feelings and that was that. About a year ago I learned that she is the richest woman in France.

What do you enjoy most about teaching? What do you seek to achieve in teaching? How do you put this into practice?

I've done very little teaching in my life, but there is one "teaching"-related experience that looms large in my memory. It was 1966 and America's war in Vietnam was raging, and I was an activist in Berkeley in the Peace Movement and in the newly born New Left. I had a bedsit and shared a kitchen and bathroom with a random economics graduate student who introduced himself to me as a Keynesian. At the time, Berkeley and Harvard were the top two places in the US for getting a PhD in economics, and my neighbour had finished his coursework, passed his comprehensives, and was near to submitting his dissertation.

Because we had little in common, when we conversed we usually, although I was no longer interested in it, talked economics. One evening we were in his room when he made a statement about *The General Theory* that I was sure was mistaken. "Give me your copy and I'll find the passage", I said. "I don't have a copy". "Well, I've got one. Come, let's go check it out".

He followed me into my room, and I found Keynes's book on my shelves, a fat black hardback. I had only begun to look for the relevant passage when the Keynesian grabbed the book away from me and, closing it, turned it so as to read the spine. Then he opened it to the title page, thumbed the table of contents, and then literally threw the book down on a coffee table and without saying a word returned to his room and slammed his door. After that he avoided me and a couple of weeks later moved out. About six months later I ran into him on campus. He looked very happy. He had passed his orals and had accepted a tenure-track job at a good university.

The notable economist McCloskey referred to economics as poetry. What do you think about that?

Although McCloskey's comment puts poetry in a dismal light, it reminds me of a passage from Camus's *The Myth of Sisyphus*, a book that influenced my youth:

"All the knowledge on earth will give nothing to assure me that this world is mine. You describe it to me and you teach me to classify it. You enumerate its laws and in my thirst for knowledge I admit that they are true. You take apart its mechanism and my hope increases. At the final stage you teach me that this wondrous and multi-coloured universe can be reduced to the electron. All this is good and I wait for you to continue. But you tell me of an invisible planetary system in which electrons gravitate around a nucleus. You explain this world to me with an image. I realize then that you have been reduced to poetry: I shall never know. Have I the time to become indignant? You have already changed theories. So that science that was to teach me everything ends up in a hypothesis, that lucidity founders in metaphor, that uncertainty is resolved in a work of art. What need had I of so many efforts? The soft lines of these hills and the hand of evening on this troubled heart teach me much more. I have returned to my beginning. I realize that if through science I can seize phenomena and enumerate them, I cannot, for all that, apprehend the world" [Camus, 1955, p. 15].

Note

1. It used to be that numerous *Real-World Economics Review* subscribers, especially ones in the US, made a point of changing their subscription email address from their institutional one to their personal one because, as some explained, they feared that if it became known among their colleagues that they read the *RWER*, then their careers might be in jeopardy. Today, with 26,000 subscribers, that seems no longer the case. Today even the economics editor of *Time* magazine, the venerable Rana Foroohar, is a long-term *RWER* subscriber and whose writing sometimes appears substantively influenced by her reading of it.

16 David Dequech

David Dequech is Professor of Economics at the University of Campinas, São Paulo, Brazil. He has held visiting positions at Stanford University, Max Planck Institute for the Study of Societies, and Université Paris Nanterre (Paris X). He has been associate editor of the *Journal of Economic Behavior and Organization*, *Review of Social Economy*, and *EconomiA*, as well as a member of the editorial board of the *Journal of Economic Issues* and *Estudos Econômicos*. He obtained his PhD in Economics from Cambridge University in 1999, supervised by Geoffrey Harcourt. Amongst his most significant publications are "Expectations and Confidence under Uncertainty" (1999) in the *Journal of Post Keynesian Economics*; "The New Institutional Economics and the Theory of Behaviour under Uncertainty" (2006) in the *Journal of Economic Behavior and Organization*; "Economic Institutions: Explanations for Conformity and Room for Deviation" (2013) in the *Journal of Institutional Economics*; and "Some Institutions (Social Norms and Conventions) of Contemporary Mainstream Economics, Macroeconomics and Financial Economics" (2017) in the *Cambridge Journal of Economics*.

David Dequech was interviewed by Danielle Guizzo in São Paulo in April 2017.

How did you become an economist?

When I was 14, I enjoyed reading encyclopaedias a lot, and when reading about history in one encyclopaedia, I learned about a conception of history in which the economy plays an important role – an example of that is the materialist conception of history in Marxism, but I am talking about a more general idea of how the economy is important in the development of history. In an entry about Marxism, I learned the names of some writers like Maurice Dobb and Eric Hobsbawn. Soon after that, I was in a bookshop here in Brazil, and I came across some books by Hobsbawn and Dobb; I bought them and started reading these works, which I enjoyed a lot. I was interested in economic and historical issues from that age.

And that is very interesting because you have a BSc in History as well, not just in Economics ...

The process of how I became an economist is similar to how I became a historian, at least in terms of my undergraduate degrees, because I was interested in Economics and History at the same time. When reading about Marxism I was attracted to the idea of a "utopia" in society with the ideas of social justice, little inequality, and no poverty – and this was at a moment when I was a teenager growing up – so I became very concerned about poverty and inequality not only in Brazil but also in the world in general.

Do you think your family had an influence on that, or was it mainly your decision?

No, it was a personal decision. My family is quite conservative; my father – who is now retired – was an engineer, and my mother was a housewife, so they were not academics. On the other hand, they bought a lot of books and encyclopaedias, so in that sense they had some influence, but my particular interest in economics and history did not have to do with them. It was a thing of my own.

It mainly had to do with my readings, not only in economics and history, in other subjects as well, and my concerns with inequality, social justice, and poverty. Only later on did I come to realise that other people came to economics because of that, with similar concerns. In my case, when I was 14 I started thinking about taking both degrees, in Economics and History. Sometime later, when I was 17, I started reading some philosophers, for example [Karl] Popper's *The Poverty of Historicism* [1957] and Bertrand Russell's defence of scepticism [*Sceptical Essays*, 1928], and I began to think more critically about the Marxist view of history and its belief, or at least the belief of some Marxists, in a predetermined end to history. In a way, I started thinking about uncertainty about the future, but I did not know about it at that time; I did not use that kind of wording at the time.

I also became less optimistic about the chances of transforming the communist utopia into reality. By the way, by the time I was 19 I had completely lost any hopes of that utopia becoming reality.

In any case, I was still interested in understanding social reality. Then at 18 I started taking Economics and History as an undergraduate. I completed both degrees at roughly the same time, but I enjoyed Economics better, because I thought it was more rigorous, and it had more theoretical content. That is why I decided to pursue my graduate studies in Economics and not in History.

How was your decision to become an academic and to pursue a PhD?

I was quite young when I started talking about going to graduate school, but I do not remember exactly when. The main reason was because I like to learn, and I still love my career because of that – I love to learn. Perhaps

264   *David Dequech*

another factor was that I come from a family of entrepreneurs on my father's side, and I grew up with my father saying that "the Dequech people don't work for other people". In a sense, having an academic career was a way of being my own boss. I like the autonomy that academia allows us.

How did you decide to go to Cambridge and pursue your studies there?

I went to the University of Campinas to do my Master's degree in Economics, and at that time in Brazil there were not many economists at the University of Campinas nor in what we may call "the heterodox community" of economists in Brazil that had gone abroad for their PhDs. For some time, I did not have any role models in the form of people who had gone abroad and come back to Brazil.

However, there was one event that was decisive in my final decision to pursue the PhD abroad: Fernando Cardim de Carvalho, who was a Professor in [the Federal University of] Rio de Janeiro, went to Campinas for one semester to teach a course as a visiting professor, and I took his course and enjoyed it very much. He was my role model as someone who had gone abroad and come back to Brazil. I was already fond of Post Keynesian macroeconomics, because the Macroeconomics course that we took in Campinas at that time was (and still is today) a Post Keynesian Macroeconomics course. I learned more about Post Keynesian Macroeconomics and liked it.

Carvalho had studied with Paul Davidson, whose work I had already started getting to know and to like, so I decided to go to the US to study with Davidson. My initial choice was not Cambridge – I had considered it, but due to personal issues I had initially decided against it.

I went to the US. Paul Davidson had moved from Rutgers University to the University of Tennessee. Cardim de Carvalho had studied with Davidson at Rutgers, but when I started thinking about going to the US, Davidson had already moved to the University of Tennessee, which had a department with a long tradition of heterodox economics, particularly Institutional Economics along the lines of Veblen, Commons, and others. However, things changed after I applied, and then later on I went to Cambridge.

In what sense did they change?

Several things led me to think that going to Cambridge would be a good idea. First, the Department of Economics at the University of Tennessee had taken an orthodox turn; the heterodox people lost political power in the department. When I applied, the head of the department was Anne Mayhew, and by the time I arrived there, they had lost power, and the department was taking a more mainstream direction.

The second thing was that I started reading more things for my PhD project, and it was a literature on Keynes, conventions, and similar issues, in particular Rod O'Donnell and Tony Lawson, who had connections with Cambridge and were writing about that, and later I learned about Jochen Runde's work as well as, in addition to still other people in Cambridge working on those issues. So, I decided it was a good idea to go to Cambridge, and I am very thankful to the National Council for Scientific and Technological Development [CNPq, in Brazil] for granting me a scholarship to go to the US and later to Cambridge.

So, you had a first contact with Post Keynesian Economics whilst in Brazil, and not after going to Cambridge?

No, it was in Brazil. Actually, it was because of that contact that I had decided to go to the US. The institutionalists were not very well known in Brazil during the late 1980s; it was not a strong tradition in Brazil. But Cardim de Carvalho had told me about institutionalists at the University of Tennessee, and I started reading about that. I came across Geoffrey Hodgson's [1989] chapter on the missing link between Post Keynesianism and Institutionalism [in a book edited by John Pheby], and his move to Cambridge was another factor that attracted me to Cambridge. When I arrived there, I had already had some contact with the things I wanted to work with in my PhD dissertation.

Were there any intellectuals that really influenced you?

Not one in particular. I think that an important characteristic of my work is the combination of different influences. Some people were influential in my career as a student still in Brazil, such as Mario Possas (I was a student of his in Campinas, and I think he is one of the very best Brazilian economists), and Fernando Cardim de Carvalho. As for the classics, Keynes and Schumpeter. And so many others among the contemporary economists and other social scientists.

So, you planned to go abroad for your PhD and then go back to Brazil?

Yes, that was the idea. And I had the moral and legal commitment of returning, after being awarded a scholarship funded by the Brazilian government. I had never lived abroad before my PhD. Things changed a little bit after I lived in the US and in the UK.

I enjoyed life in the developed world. When I left in the late 1980s, Brazil had serious economic and social problems, such as very high inflation. So, I started thinking about finishing my PhD, coming back to Brazil to fulfil my commitment, and maybe going back and getting a job abroad, which I never ended up doing.

Please tell us how you developed your particular individual contribution.

I have worked on several different topics over the years, and I hope that I have made some specific contributions in my articles about different topics, but thinking about my work as whole, I believe there are two important characteristics in it. First, my insistence on emphasising the importance of institutions while, at the same time, keeping adequate room for behaviour and thought that does not conform with existing institutional rules – for example, the introduction of innovation. For my Master's degree, I took a course on Post Keynesian macroeconomics, and that was when I started learning about Paul Davidson, Hyman Minsky, and others. The Microeconomics course was very much oriented by the neo-Schumpeterian perspective. In Macroeconomics, in particular in the Post Keynesian literature and the literature on Keynes, an argument was beginning to be developed, according to which emphasising uncertainty in Keynes's sense does not prevent one from developing an economic theory, in particular a theory that incorporates the hypothesis of rational economic behaviour. More specifically, the argument was that in situations of uncertainty (in Keynes's sense), rational behaviour may be – or, in more radical versions, must be – conventional behaviour. But on the microeconomics course, we read Schumpeter and neo-Schumpeterian authors, and they emphasised innovation. When reading the argument that rational behaviour has to be conventional behaviour, I raised the question "what about the Schumpeterian innovator?" I raised this question because I would not like any theory to imply that innovative behaviour is not rational or is less rational than conventional behaviour. This is how I started thinking about my PhD dissertation, and how both the Post Keynesian and the neo-Schumpeterian approaches were present since the beginning. I wanted to study institutions, but I also wanted to leave room for non-conforming behaviour like the introduction of innovations. And I started combining different approaches. The second general characteristic of my work, exactly my conviction that in order to deal properly with several important issues in the economy we need to combine different contributions from different approaches, even different disciplines.

We have chosen to speak to you as we consider you a heterodox economist. Would you label yourself as a heterodox economist?

I do consider myself a heterodox economist, actually in more than one sense, but in order to explain that I would need to define heterodox economics. Regarding the labels of Post Keynesian, Institutionalist, and so on, I think it is necessary to combine contributions from different approaches, but I am not just any one of these kinds of economist or social scientist in particular. I am comfortable with these and other labels as long as they are used in combination.

What do you think Heterodox Economics is?

In recent decades, it is not only neoclassical economics that has been part of mainstream economics. I define neoclassical economics as the school of thought based on the assumptions of rationality, in the sense of utility maximisation, and equilibrium, as the state in which the economic system is or tends to be. Therefore, if we define mainstream economics and neoclassical economics as I did, mainstream economics in recent decades is not comprised only of neoclassical economics.

Additionally, I define orthodox economics the same way as Colander, Holt, and Rosser [2004b] do, as the most recent dominant school of thought, and the most recent dominant school of thought (orthodoxy) is neoclassical economics.

All this leads us to potential problems regarding heterodox economics. One can define heterodox economics either as "non-orthodox" or as "non-mainstream". Many people use both definitions at the same time, without realising that mainstream economics is not only neoclassical economics. The problem is that some approaches that have managed to gain some prestige and influence in academia do not accept one or both of those defining assumptions of neoclassical economics – they are heterodox in the sense of non-neoclassical, but they are mainstream.

I consider myself a heterodox economist in the sense that I am not a neoclassical economist, and I defend ideas that (depending on the context considered) do not have prestige and influence in academia – and the context taken by the majority is the US.

And in that context, how would you classify the case of Brazil, because it seems to be a bit different, as you claim for the case of Post Keynesianism in your *Review of Political Economy* article in 2012: "while other developed countries such as France, Italy, the Netherlands and Japan offer better conditions for non-neoclassical economics in general, the presence of Post Keynesianism in particular does not seem strong. In this general picture, Brazil is a sizeable exception, but it is a developing country with little international weight in academia, especially in the social sciences".

That article refers specifically to the case of Post Keynesian economics, but I can talk about a more diverse set of ideas. I do think that the Brazilian case is different, and it is an example of pluralism and tolerance towards ideas that are not part of the American mainstream. Ideas that are marginalised in the US, that are not part of mainstream economics there, are taught in the main Brazilian universities, are published in the main Brazilian journals, receive the main Brazilian awards, and get funding from the main Brazilian research foundations. I am an example of this tolerance and of the acceptance, in Brazil,

268 *David Dequech*

of ideas that are marginalised abroad, because I teach at one of the most prestigious universities in Brazil, I have published in prestigious Brazilian journals, I have won prestigious awards in Brazil, I have been funded by the main research foundations, and I have even worked as an Economics coordinator in one of these foundations.

So, if we apply the concept of mainstream economics that I defended [2007] to the Brazilian case, I am a mainstream economist – which complicates things, but also makes them more interesting.

And why do you think Brazil is a place that allows this pluralism to take place?

That's a very good question. I have thought about that question, but I must confess that I am not very interested in pursuing a profound answer, which would require us to study Brazil's historical process. In part, it has to do with the fact that Brazil is a developing country with lots of problems, but that does not explain everything.

The strong presence of heterodox economics in Brazil also has to do, in part, with the fact that during the military dictatorship, from the mid-1960s to the mid-1980s, the University of Campinas – which was in the 1960s a recent university, but, together with the University of São Paulo, became one of the two most prestigious universities in the country – had a Department of Economics (later the Institute of Economics) in which there were heterodox economists, and that was not so easy to see in other universities, because of the military dictatorship. Why did that happen in Campinas? Because the first President of the University had a good relationship with the military, he was reliable from the point of view of the military, who then tolerated the presence of left-wing faculty members, not only in the Economics department but also in other places, including in Physics, Medicine, and so on. Several people that were exiled during the earlier phases of the dictatorship came back to Brazil and joined the University of Campinas because there was room for political dissidence, let's say, at that University, essentially because of the reliability and the good relations of the President of the University. This is an important part of the explanation, because back then, the University of Campinas had a graduate programme in Economics that attracted several people interested in ideas that were different from the *status quo*, including a political position against the military dictatorship. That was the place that was more progressive and with left-wing people. It was a kind of institutional monopoly granted by the military, and it happened to be in a young university that soon became nationally prestigious (otherwise heterodox economics would have had more difficulty in becoming part of the Brazilian mainstream).

What also happened was that some people who had studied at the University of Campinas started going to other universities in Brazil, so that department played an important part in the early history of heterodox economics in Brazil, essentially because of the institutional monopoly granted by the military and because of the prestige of the university as a whole. The origins of heterodox economics in Brazil go back a bit further in time, mainly to the early years of the United Nations Commission for the Economic Development of Latin America and Caribbean [ECLAC] and the presence of Brazilian heterodox economists there, starting with Celso Furtado.

Another very important factor that explains why heterodox ideas have more space in Brazil than in other countries is the tolerant attitude of some neo-classical economists, especially when the National Association for Graduate Programs in Economics [ANPEC] was created, including the support of the Ford Foundation for different varieties of economics, as the Ford Foundation did not want to associate itself too much with the military regime.

What are the problems of mainstream economics?

Before talking about the problems, let me say that mainstream economics has good qualities from the sociological/institutional point of view, which are prestige and influence in academia. In this specific sense, it is non-mainstream economics that has a sociological/institutional problem. On the other hand, mainstream economics does have its problems, both intellectually and insti-tutionally. As I said before, mainstream economics is a diverse set of ideas, but if we need to find one single unifying trait of mainstream economics, it is the methodological rule that one needs to develop mathematical models if one wants to be rigorous. It is a restrictive association of rigor with mathematical formalisation. I think there is a problem with that: very often, mainstream economics chooses the method at the expense of the subject matter; it does not study things that are very relevant in economic reality because it does not have the method to do it, or at least to do it in what is considered an adequate way. So, I think there is a very serious problem, and it is a subversion of what science should be. We should adjust the method in accordance to the subject matter and not the opposite.

I think this is well represented in a joke about economists: two people are walking down the street at night, and someone tries to reach something in their pocket and drops a coin, but it is a dark, poorly lit street. One of them is an economist. The economist goes closer to a street light and starts to look for the coin there. However, the person who had dropped the coin says, "but I dropped the coin here!", and the economist replies, "yes, but it is dark there; here we have light". I think this represents well how economists look for things with the method that they think must be used instead of searching for the method that is appropriate to find "the coin".

Another thing that I consider quite problematic in mainstream economics is the neglect of what I call the "profound motivational and cognitive influences" of institutions on individuals. And I think that this has to do, in part, with the first problem, because it is difficult to formalise mathematically this kind of influence.

In addition, mainstream economics, from the late 1970s until 2008, from my personal point of view, became too conservative in terms of politics and

270 *David Dequech*

in terms of favouring the ideology of free markets – I do not want to use the term "neoliberal" here, which is quite controversial. It is undeniable that in that period there was a change in terms of political outlook, even though we should not suggest that mainstream economics is unified around a single political position.

Mainstream economics also has a big problem from an institutional point of view: it is not sufficiently pluralist. It therefore marginalises valuable alternative approaches and it makes it difficult for more alternative ideas to develop within it.

What are you trying to achieve as an economist?

I am trying to give my modest contribution to improving our understanding of economic reality – my own understanding and, hopefully, the understanding of other people, such as my students and the people who read my work. This has to do with what I said before: I like to learn and I started to study Economics and History because I wanted to understand reality better, and this is what I am still trying to achieve these days.

Do you seek to influence society? If so, how?

Well, I do not have any illusions of grandeur or self-importance. I don't try to influence society in any big way, but the main way I think I can influence society is by contributing to people's understanding of reality. I think this is important because we, as professors, have students that will graduate from university and will live their lives as employees, entrepreneurs, members of government, parliament, and so on. If they have a better understanding of economic reality they may do a better job as citizens. So, I hope to give a small contribution to forming better citizens who understand economic reality better. If I do my academic job well, I will play my political part well. I believe this should be the very first mission that politically engaged academics should pursue.

To complete my answer, I was and I am still concerned with social issues such as inequality, poverty, and so on, but as I said I lost any illusions of any big, utopic transformation of society (for example, I do not think communism is a viable alternative). I oscillate between nihilism and social democracy. Politically, I would classify myself as a social democrat. I differ from the Austrians, for instance, regarding the role of the State.

Do you think that heterodox economics provides a more appropriate instrumental for this task?

Like mainstream economics, heterodox economics is also a very heterogeneous group of ideas, even more so. I would not say that heterodox economics as a whole contributes to a better understanding of reality; it depends on what kind of set of ideas we are talking about.

Would this perhaps apply to the idea of institutions, or recognising uncertainty?

I do not find much that unifies heterodox economics. There are a lot of useful contributions from many different streams of heterodox economics, including the Austrians from whose political position I differ substantially.

What are your strategies for seeking research funding?

This is a very easy question for me to answer, as I do not have any particular strategy, and actually I am happy to say what I said before: Brazil is a country that has tolerance for different economic approaches, and in general I have had no difficulty to get funding from federal or state agencies. I have had a very successful history of funding applications. To explain by contrast, in the United States, as David Colander reports, there are people who are sympathetic to non-mainstream ideas but develop projects that are more aligned with the mainstream in order to get funding, and I do not have to do that. I do not have any particular strategy. Something that does help, but does not apply to all cases, is to present projects that are already in progress so that I know better what I am writing about.

So you do not have pressure to seek funding?

I know that in many universities in other countries professors are assessed under these terms, but in economics in Brazil, or at least in my university, this is not common and it does not happen in my department. But even if it did happen, it would not be a problem for me as a heterodox economist in Brazil. If I worked in a different country, a strategy not only to get funding but also to promote my career and the sort of ideas that I like, perhaps would be trying to approach other disciplines than economics.

In more general terms, I would say that the future of non-mainstream and even heterodox economics more generally lies outside economics departments, and I wish there were, in very prestigious, rich, and powerful universities, interdisciplinary departments where economic issues could be studied from the kinds of perspectives that I like. I know lots of people in sociology departments and business schools who study economic issues and write very interesting works. It would be good for heterodox economics and for the development of heterodox ideas if that kind of thing happened. I wish that happened after 2008, when the failure of mainstream economics became more apparent. So far it hasn't. Actually, I had the opportunity to talk to Professor Craig Calhoun (then director of the LSE) in an event at the São Paulo State Research Foundation, and I asked him a question about that after his presentation. Even though I do not remember the exact answer, I remember him saying it would be difficult to convince people to create these interdisciplinary departments.

What do you enjoy most about teaching?

In one sentence, I would say teaching *and* learning. I do take a lot of pleasure out of, hopefully, helping my students think more properly about what they are studying. I also learn a lot from my students and from their questions, because they force me to think about things I have not thought about, and that happens a lot. Through their questions and comments, they also force me to improve my ideas, so I learn a lot from them and I enjoy this. I love my job, I love learning, and I love teaching my students and learning with them, but I also take comfort in the idea that I contribute a little bit to their learning.

Do you follow a certain teaching philosophy, or do you engage in certain pedagogical practices?

I do have some ideas about how teachers should teach, and I try to follow that. I also have my own style. In terms of pedagogy, I try to do some things that I find useful. First, I prepare rather detailed notes, and I distribute them to the students in advance, because I want them not to spend much time taking notes in class – I do that to both undergraduate and graduate students. Then, they can bring these notes whether in printed paper or in their laptops, and the notes will make it easier for them to follow the discussion in class.

I come to class with a presentation that was prepared based on those notes, but I also try to stimulate the students and ask them questions, and I think that is a very important part of teaching and learning. I also like using humour as well during class to make students feel more comfortable.

Do you stimulate them to engage in critical thinking?

If I can describe my teaching philosophy, I think that the most important mission I have as a teacher is to contribute to stimulate rigorous and critical thinking. As it may be implied by what I said before, I do not think that rigour comes only with mathematisation. Whenever mathematics is useful, I try to use it, or even if I do not support a particular approach that I am teaching, but the approach uses mathematics (which is very common in economics), I try to stimulate and help the students to think critically and rigorously, so if there is maths, they need to know how to use it.

However, rigour comes also from thinking about the scope and limitations of the use of mathematics, and this is something I try to discuss with my students. When we do use mathematics – for example, I teach undergraduate macroeconomics and I use [Olivier] Blanchard's textbook, which, like other textbooks, has mathematics – I try to explain to them the method we are using and discuss the scope and limitations of using mathematics. Rigour does not always require using mathematics, but we always need to be careful about the assumptions that we make. I often try to call the students' attention to that, and I try to stimulate them to think more rigorously by sometimes contrasting what they said to a different statement which in my view is more rigorous, so I try to bring them closer to that kind of thinking.

In order to help them think more critically, I do two things that I find very important: one is to contrast the idea that we are discussing with reality; the other is to contrast that idea with different ideas or approaches in economics or in other disciplines.

What do you seek to achieve in teaching? How do you put this into practice?

What I want to achieve is to help students understand economic issues better; this is the general objective. However, some things, like thinking rigorously and critically, go beyond economic issues.

You do have an extensive list of student supervisions, especially graduate level. Would you apply these principles and goals to them as well?

Yes, absolutely. There is also one thing that I do with my students both in class and during supervisions, which is to turn their questions into different questions, the Socratic method. Paul Davidson is someone who does that, and when I sent him some papers that I wrote, he would write down questions on the margins of my papers. I think that is a good method; it is not the only method, but I like using it.

Do you think that your graduate supervisions could have an impact within the heterodox community in Brazil?

Again, I do not have illusions of grandeur, but I could say that we all have some impact on the community through the students that we teach and supervise. I do think that I have an impact in the community here. I have been working at the University of Campinas for 17 years, and when I started working there no one else published articles in international journals in Economics. In the Brazilian heterodox community at that time, very few people did. In this sense, I do have the impression that I served as a role model. The role model that I personally did not have, I think that I played that part a little with some of my students, even students who have not taken my modules or have not worked under my supervision. They know, for example, that I studied abroad and that I publish in international journals.

Publishing abroad is something that I must emphasise, because there has been a major change in Brazil in the last 10 to 12 years, under the incentives of the Ministry of Education, which assesses graduate programmes in Brazil. In addition, even before those incentives, I think I have served as an example to heterodox people in Brazil and students who want to be heterodox economists and to publish in good international journals.

274 *David Dequech*

There is another thing: most of my work is theoretical, but I am convinced that even people who work on the Brazilian economy, or any applied issues, must try to publish their articles in good international journals, either mainstream journals or more alternative journals.

Essentially, I think that is important because whatever empirical work that one does, it needs to have some theory, and there are some empirical methods, either qualitative or quantitative, that are common to different countries. There is not a theory just about Brazil, or an empirical method that is only applicable to Brazil or to any other single country, so I think it is good for the academic development of Brazil that people publish abroad.

The notable economist McCloskey referred to economics as poetry. What do you think about that?

I think that narrative is a very important thing in economics, and I do think that the way one presents his/her ideas is extremely important. It can make a difference in persuasion, and we need to persuade other people, which can be a very difficult thing to do.

I do not want to go into the methodological discussion of rhetoric *versus* realism, as I am not very well informed to do that, but I think I know more or less what people talk about when they refer to the art of economics and the art of economic policy. I also think there is something beautiful in phrasing, argument, and so on. There is some beauty in economics, and even mathematicians like to talk a lot about beauty. For example, someone who is deservedly known for writing beautifully is George Shackle, and sometimes Keynes does that too.

I do not see much poetry in economics, but my answer tries to separate narrative and persuasion from beauty and poetry. I know some people talk about the art of economics, and I think that some people mean that economics is not precise as natural sciences and so on, and that we need some intuition and good sense. Indeed, I think we can talk about art in economics, as there is some skill that one can find in some artists or artisans that one can refer to, at least metaphorically, which can be useful in economics.

On the other hand, economics as an academic discipline or as a social science is very different from literature, music, painting, sculpture, et cetera. Artists do not need to be rigorous in their ideas in an academic way. Economics, as a social science, deals with a form of rigour that is different from what exists in the arts, humanities, and literature.

17 Ulrich Witt

Ulrich Witt is Director Emeritus of the Evolutionary Economics Research Group at the former Max Planck Institute of Economics in Jena, Germany, and Adjunct Professor at Griffith Business School, Griffith University, Australia. He obtained his PhD in Economics at the University of Göttingen in 1979 and his Habilitation at the University of Mannheim in 1985. Afterwards he held numerous positions as professor of economics including at the University of Mannheim, the University of Southern California, and the University of Freiburg. He has served as editor in chief of the *Journal of Bioeconomics* since 2012. In his research he pursues a naturalistic approach to evolutionary economics that enriches economics with insights from biology and psychology. Amongst his most significant publications are "The Evolution of Consumption and Its Welfare Effects" (2017) in the *Journal of Evolutionary Economics*, "Propositions About Novelty" (2009) in the *Journal of Economic Behavior and Organization*, "On the Proper Interpretation of 'Evolution' in Economics and Its Implications for Production Theory" (2004) in the *Journal of Economic Methodology*, "Imagination and Leadership: The Neglected Dimension of an Evolutionary Theory of the Firm" (1998) in the *Journal of Economic Behavior and Organization*, and "Innovations, Externalities, and the Problem of Economic Progress" (1996) in *Public Choice*. Several of his most frequently cited papers have recently been reprinted in his book *Rethinking Economic Evolution – Essays on Economic Change and Its Theory* (2016).

Ulrich Witt was interviewed by Sebastian Berger via phone online in September 2017.

How did you become an economist?

Well, I belong to the 1968 generation, and at that time it was quite natural to develop an interest in what would nowadays be called political economy. When I finished my school education, I had to choose a field for studying at the university, and I wanted to choose something that is related to political economy. There were actually only three choices: sociology, law, or economics. Sociology was not very attractive because I anticipated that I would not have learned much that I could use for professional life after studying. Law was something that I initially found quite interesting. But I soon noticed that whenever I was involved in exams in the first two semesters I somehow failed to exactly reproduce the text that the professors wanted to hear. I found that somewhat arbitrary. So I switched to economics where the models in the exams that you typically have to do as a freshman had a clear solution that was unique so that it was easy to find orientation as to what is wrong and what is right. I only recognised much later that the price for this alleged uniqueness are idealisations that lead away from economic reality. Having clarity basically means you have clarity about fictions.

There's a nice story about the Nobel Prize winner in Physics, Max Planck, the inventor of quantum theory, who once was asked why he quit studying economics after one semester. He answered that he had gotten the impression that things in economics are too complex to really allow you to ever gain a clear insight. He had recognised that after only one semester. I needed eight or nine semesters to understand that, and when I recognised it, it was too late to make a change. So I became an economist.

Were there any teachers or topics in high school that aroused your interest in economics?

Not really. My elder brother had had some influence. He had studied economics already when I entered the stage where I had to make a decision, and he was a devoted Marxist. He always tried to provoke me with his radical pleas for class struggle and stuff like that, which I found exaggerated. But he stirred an interest in me in finding reasons for opposing his radical views. So this may have contributed to my interest in economics.

What influences were decisive for making the transition into a professional academic career as an economist?

My education as a student of economics at the University of Göttingen was not very impressive. The economics department was dominated by mainstream economists and competed with the department for agricultural economics next door. I later met people in the US who knew the agriculture economics department, but I never met anyone who recognised the economics department where I had studied. I have been brought up with the usual standard textbooks that I had a hard time to find interesting. During my studies I actually developed a critical attitude, not so much towards particular theories or their political interpretation but with regard to the scientific standard of the theory. I was influenced by the critical rationalism of Karl Popper and his German disciples. That made me critical of the lacking empirical content of the mainstream teaching, which I saw as a consequence of all the idealisations. They were motivated more by the desire to create a model that can be solved than by the desire to understand how the economy works. Particularly in microeconomics the basic approach is heavily inspired by classical mechanics, which I also found unsatisfactory.

However, I did not engage in working out any criticism until I started my dissertation. The topic of my dissertation was pretty much the result of the fact that my professor, who offered me a position as a researcher, expected me to do research on the theory of market processes, tâtonnement models, and the like, within the framework of general equilibrium theory. That was of course a clear challenge given my view that most of this theory is actually only idealisation, inspired by ideas not coming from carefully observing the economy but borrowed from Physics. As so often in economics, mathematical metaphors are exploited to make sense of economic phenomena. So I started studying tâtonnement and non-tâtonnement models and general equilibrium theory which, with the level of training I had received before, took me quite some time. After two years or so I realised that, if I wanted to oppose this kind of approach, I needed to come up with an alternative where this theory has its weak point: it should actually be a theory about learning behaviour of the market participants, but tâtonnement and non-tâtonnement models do not address learning, because an extension by learning hypotheses would make them too complex to solve them analytically. Thus, in order to do better, I had to switch to a different methodology and run numerical simulations of market processes with learning.

At that time, doing numerical simulation meant that you would use Fortran as a programming language, punch huge stacks of punch cards, and reserve several hours of computing time at the central UNIVAC computer of the university. Competing for computing time with astronomers, physicists, and other scientists, I was always referred to the weekend because my project was not considered first priority. But I did eventually get my results, and they confirmed my expectation that all proofs of existence, uniqueness, and stability of the general economic equilibrium in mathematical economics are in vain. Once you allow a little more realism in the assumptions, such as entering learning behaviour, what you get is an outcome of the market process that depends on unforeseeable influences such as on what the experiences are that people make on their learning path. It is no longer clear what market equilibrium results nor whether you get one at all. In order to characterise the market process in more general terms, it is then necessary to find a different rationale for discriminating between all the possible developments.

This was the point where I thought that something like natural selection would perhaps make the trick. That was the beginning of my involvement with evolutionary economics. I introduced what you would call today agents in agent-based modelling in order to compare their simulated behaviour. They were modelled in a way so that different kinds of learning hypothesis were represented in their behaviour – for instance, reinforcement learning or some form of cognitive extrapolation learning. I populated the programme market with these agents who had different learning theories as instruction for how they would proceed, and I then observed which of them survived in

278 *Ulrich Witt*

the competitive market process. This was the way I arrived at working with the nucleus of an evolutionary approach. I published my dissertation in 1980 at a time when such simulations and evolutionary arguments were simply off the beaten track. A few journal articles that also came out of the dissertation project stirred some curiosity among a few economists, but it was difficult to publish that stuff at that time because it was so unusual.

I also ran an experiment in which I tried to evaluate these models of learning behaviour by comparing it with the learning behaviour of test persons. This was called "gaming" at that time. That is, I exposed some test persons to exactly the same simulated market environment and explored how they adapted to that environment. In this way their observed learning could be compared directly to the learning hypotheses I had programmed into the simulated agents. That experimental work was also hard to publish, because it was not yet fashionable. I actually published it in a journal *Behavioural Science*, which was not an economic journal. After these experiences I had learned my lesson and never returned to simulations and experiments in my later work.

How did that influence your decision to write your Habilitation or proceed to a higher-level academic career as Professor of Economics in Germany?

At those times you had to write a second dissertation in Germany as a precondition for a university career. I had moved in the meantime as a researcher to the University of Mannheim, which had a more ambitious economics department; in fact, it was one of the leading departments in Germany. The exchange with colleagues and the professors there convinced me that, if I wanted to continue working on the idea of evolution in the economic context, I would first have to create a theoretical foundation by means of my Habilitation thesis. Thus, I began developing a theory of economic behaviour informed by what you can call a Darwinian world view. This was an attempt to draw on hypotheses from sociobiology, behavioural ecology, and the behavioural sciences and psychology in order to build up an individualistic foundation for evolutionary economics. It was Darwinian because it started from the hypothesis that humans inherit certain parts of their behavioural repertoire that evolved during the phylogeny of the humankind under natural selection pressure. By considering the ancestral selection conditions, it can be reconstructed what parts of the behavioural repertoire these are and how they now influence the choices economic agents make. That kind of reasoning was quite in line with developments in sociobiology and evolutionary anthropology at that time. However, my interdisciplinary approach faced some opposition in the department in Mannheim because some influential people considered it too far away from economics. Nonetheless they graduated me with my second dissertation in 1985, which was the ticket to become professor later on.

I published the thesis as a book in the German language as it was required at that time. That meant, of course, that it didn't get a significant distribution since the market for German books of this kind is simply too small. I submitted a proposal for an English translation of the book later to Cambridge University Press, where it was accepted for publication. But the acceptance came exactly at the time when I was appointed full professor at the University of Freiburg. I had to build up my curriculum, and I never managed to find enough time to translate the complete book within a few years after getting the contract from Cambridge University Press. When I eventually found the time, I had gained the impression that there had been so much development in the meantime that I actually would have to write a new book, which I never did.

How did you develop your particular individual contribution?

Looking back at that time, I think I had a promising research agenda, but it was ahead of its time. Now you find similar ideas in the Anglo-Saxon literature for instance in the writings of authors like Bowles and Gintis who focus similarly on the role of evolved human nature for understanding economic behaviour. My earlier contribution had been published in German, so nobody really took notice of it when the topic attracted attention in the Anglo-Saxon literature. Not even German scholars did. Since they prefer to cite English sources. As a matter of fact, I got very few citations for my Habilitation thesis.

So just to clarify, would you consider this line of work of the Habilitation your main contribution?

I think it was seminal for my way of interpreting evolutionary economics. It was from the very beginning following the idea that it is not by formal analogy to the Darwinian theory that an evolutionary approach can transform economic theory as most of the proponents of neo-Schumpeterian evolutionary economics believe. Simply invoking a selection model and then having the feeling you are on the evolutionary side was not my cup of tea. I wanted to really understand human behaviour in the economic context as behaviour that was to a certain extent directly or indirectly shaped by evolution and then to go on and explain what difference that makes with regard to the economic implications and compare that with the mainstream approach. A major difference concerns the theory of preferences, which became an important part of my further work. The mainstream doesn't have a theory of preference, except for a few assumptions about formal properties of preference orders such that they imply a certain shape of the utility function. These formal assumptions are postulated in the form of axioms without any empirical support. Supporting the assumption of transitivity of preferences,

280 *Ulrich Witt*

for instance, is empirically much more problematic than it appears on first sight. This has been made a major point of criticism in behavioural economics. But behavioural economics only explores whether and when people make inconsistent choices and doesn't explain what choices they make. That is, behavioural economics doesn't explain the content of preferences, while I try to explain that content and where it comes from. In part it is inherited and in part it is learned by mechanisms which are also inherited. Preferences are, of course, also influenced by cognitive processes. Hence, this is a fairly complicated theory of preferences. It took me years to understand it. I had the privilege, however, of having doctoral students who helped me develop the theory.

We have chosen to speak to you as we consider you a heterodox economist. Would you label yourself as a heterodox economist?

Yes, I do. But that begs the question of what is heterodox economics? I sometimes gain the impression that everyone who disagrees with the mainstream considers himself a heterodox economist. If we can agree on that kind of definition, I'm certainly belonging to the group of heterodox economists. But the heterogeneity in this group is enormous. So I prefer to label myself more specifically as an economist who is interested in an evolutionary approach to economics.

What do you think heterodox economics is apart from an opposition to mainstream economics? And, how do you define mainstream economics?

I prefer to actually call it canonical economics because it is the version which you'll find in almost all micro- and macroeconomic textbooks reproduced. That is in my view a fairly coherent teaching canon used as a brainwashing device for raising young economists. People who prefer a different approach, a behavioural approach, say, or a Post Keynesian, or an evolutionary one, disagree with some core elements of this canon, and that's why they call themselves heterodox economists. But they basically only agree in rejecting the canonical textbook version. They don't agree at all about what the alternative should be, because they focus on different aspects for which they formulate alternatives.

Do you hold any alternative vision for heterodox economics? Do you propose some kind of integration of the various strands?

I'm not sure that this would be a good idea. Economists have the problem that their explanatory domain, the reality about which they formulate theories, is extremely complex and multifaceted. It therefore depends strongly on what you emphasise in this domain, what you consider important, when it comes to drawing up a theoretical alternative. We are talking about the future when we consider the possibility of merging all these different, and partly incommensurable, views on various aspects of the economy. I am sceptical that merging them into a coherent alternative programme is possible. We will perhaps arrive sometime in the future at the idea that a consilience with the sciences would be useful, an idea suggested by the biologist E.O. Wilson. The sciences actually offer an interpretation of human behaviour, and economic agents are humans, after all. So starting from a scientific theory of behaviour may pave the way for a more solid interpretation of economics. The question then is, of course, what kind of aggregate hypotheses can be derived from such an interpretation and whether and in what way they would differ from canonical economics. I think that is something we will only know if enough research is being done, provided there will be resources available for that kind of synthesising research – which may not be the case because canonical economics is not interested in these kinds of questions.

What are the problems of mainstream economics? You said something about it before, but is there something that you would still like to add?

Well, mainstream economics has many faces as well. In my view the main problem is its hard core: the combination or synthesis of optimisation calculus and equilibrium thinking. If you describe the behaviour of many agents as simultaneously maximising their objective functions, you need an equilibrium condition to solve the model, unless you have a model with explicit dynamics. But that is rarely the case because differential and difference equations are not the most popular way of putting theories in economics. Also simple comparative statics models make their living from equilibrium conditions as a formal necessity. This has somehow become second nature for many economists so that they now believe the economy is an equilibrium phenomenon. I fear that's awfully wrong. The economy is an unfolding phenomenon. It always changes. And if it happens to reach an equilibrium this is at best a temporary equilibrium. It is sooner or later disrupted not by that fact that there's an earthquake or that an asteroid has hit the earth. There aren't so many events of that kind. It is disrupted by the fact that people are not content with their status quo and therefore come up with innovations (i.e., thinking up something nobody has thought of before). Innovators disrupt the existing interactions by doing something not thought of as being possible, acceptable, legitimate. If you ignore this kind of disturbance, you will never understand that the economy is an unfolding or evolving system.

As you see, I approach the main problem of canonical economics from my evolutionary perspective. However, I understand that somebody who is doing Post Keynesian economics, say, and who would probably share the view that the interpretation of equilibrium economics is somehow mistaken,

282 Ulrich Witt

may nonetheless draw different conclusions. There are differences in dealing with economic equilibria between an evolutionary approach and a Post Keynesian approach. That is what I mean by the heterogeneity, or in part even incommensurability, of positions in the heterodox camp in economics. We shouldn't create the illusion that the heterogeneous positions can easily be forged into a coherent alternative to the canonical approach.

What are you trying to achieve as an economist?

I am committed to developing a consistent evolutionary interpretation of economic behaviour and then deriving the implications from that at all levels of the economy. One implication is, for instance, a very different theory of economic welfare. Economists give almost all their policy advice on the basis of a welfare theory that is static. But if people learn, they also learn new preferences, and that causes static welfare theory serious troubles. I guess most applied economists have never thought about that. But if you start thinking about it you will find that the welfare foundation of much of the policy advice that is given is not sound. If you want to really have a better foundation, you can start with an evolutionary approach as I do and then work through to the differences that such an approach makes. That is quite a bit of work, of course.

Do you seek to influence society? If so, how?

No, I don't really seek to influence society. It would be an illusion to believe there is such an option for an academic doing basic research. All you can do is contribute to society's opinion formation at a very basic level perhaps comparable to the remote influence of the debate on social philosophy. I do think that the implications of the approach I suggest are potentially quite significant for society. But I have learned that, if somebody is interested in these implications, then perhaps students and young scholars. They often want to get ideas that differ from those they usually hear, and who listen to the implications that perhaps change their grasp of the economy in which they live. I have tried a couple of times to offer the results of my work to journalists. But I found out that they considered them too complicated. They are interested in political economy arguments that are straight and simple. That's what you have to offer if we want to have an impact on economic policymaking.

What are your strategies for seeking research funding?

I could afford to have a relaxed attitude in this regard, because I was lucky to be a member of the Max Planck Society that endowed me with a permanent funding. I could, but didn't have to, apply for additional research funding. However, I basically got along with what I had.

May I then ask you to elaborate a little bit on what you did with the research funding?

We had the opportunity from around 2005 onwards, if I remember correctly, to create a doctoral school in Jena, a joint venture of the University of Jena and the Max Planck Institute of Economics in Jena. This doctoral school educated some 70 or 80 doctoral students over the years, and my share was perhaps some 15 or 20 among them. That was a quite exceptional situation. Once you have reached a critical mass in a place, it is not so difficult to get additional funding. I personally did not apply for extra money, but several of my colleagues at the university did, and they benefited from this critical mass. The school was generously funded by the German Research Foundation.

Would you say that you have been able to promote your orientation within Economics through building a school or some kind of tradition that is now carried on by a younger generation as well?

Well, that is actually not really the case because the Max Planck Institute of Economics was closed in 2014 and for that reason there is no real tradition that carries on. Many of the doctoral students we educated and who continued a career in academia moved on to different places all around Europe. Some of them have gotten their own professorships in Germany, but I think it is not really a coherent school that formed and that is now carried on.

Would you be able to say something about the reasons or the circumstances of the closure of the Institute?

I think it was a consequence of the fact that the work we have been doing in Jena was not much appreciated by our mainstream colleagues. When the directors of the Institute retired almost at the same time, they saw an opportunity to change the agenda for the Institute. But Jena had gained a reputation over the years as a heterodox place, and there were no prominent mainstream colleagues who were interested in joining the Institute in such a place. If, in a multidisciplinary research society with considerable competition for resources between disciplines, one discipline doesn't come up with a very definite proposal as to how to use the resources, you risk that they will go to a different discipline. And that's exactly what happened.

What do you enjoy most about teaching?

I always enjoyed engaging in what may be called a Socratian dialogue, that is, having small groups in which you can really engage in a dialogue about the problems, finding out how students see them. Sometimes you can learn from unspoilt views, and students sometimes have these unspoilt views which you don't have any longer after thinking about things for years. Such a format gives you an opportunity to really exchange arguments with your students. You can try to convince them of what you have been thinking about for many years, not just confronting them with these ideas. I had the privilege, later in my career, of doing mostly postgraduate teaching and then I usually had small groups in which this was possible.

What do you seek to achieve in teaching? How do you put this in to practice?

I try to achieve exactly what I described as developing an evolutionary view in economics and trying to discuss about what alternatives to canonical economics are available and where they lead us.

How do you introduce economics? Do you teach neoclassical as well as alternative approaches?

In the last years I taught postgraduate courses on diverse areas in economics, but always from the point of view of an evolutionary approach. So, I was fortunate to be able to leave behind the teaching of the hard-to-believe gospel I had to do for a decade earlier in my career.

Do you have an ideal of mindset or an understanding that comes out of your teaching?

I basically want to make an intellectual offer, a proposal for how to explain economic reality, and what I can accomplish with making this offer depends on the students.

The notable economist McCloskey referred to economics as poetry. What do you think about that?

That's a provocative statement. I think it is made to induce people to reflect on economics and to learn to appreciate that economics is more than poetry. First of all poetry is much about aesthetics, the beauty of the language and images told. It's also about fiction that wants to elicit emotions in you. Economics, in contrast, is the dry business of developing intellectual tools and applying their logic to make sense of the real economy. Perhaps McCloskey wanted to pinpoint the fact that in economics you can have very different views of the same phenomenon and you can describe them differently. But these are not arbitrarily thought-up descriptions, at least not always, as you would perhaps believe if you think economics is poetry. Controversial as they may be, these are usually serious attempts of reducing an extreme complexity of the object space to something that you can deal with on the basis of analytical conjectures and refutations, as Karl Popper once put it. You have to be selective in emphasising certain aspects while leaving out others, and that depends on what you want to explain. There is a certain amount of discretion you exercise as researcher, or arbitrariness, if you want. But this arbitrariness is subject to critical contests as a principle of scientific culture, as heterodox economists have always claimed. It only breaks down when something is claimed to be a priori true. Unfortunately, some elements of canonical economics are claimed to be a priori true. But in general I do not agree that economics is poetry, or that it is all entirely arbitrary modelling, as it can indeed also be found particularly in mathematical economics.

18 Concluding thoughts

Our interviews aimed at understanding better heterodox economics via a wide-ranging set of questions on the biographical dimensions of heterodox economists, their understanding of heterodox economics and its differences from mainstream economics, their aspirations and social epistemology, their teaching practices, and their attitude towards poetry. We will let the reader decide whether all of the open questions we posed in the Introduction have been answered, and where future research is needed to explore them and novel questions that emerged during the project. We would aver, tentatively, that several questions can be answered, and we offer the following thoughts about the characteristics of heterodox economics and heterodox economists revealed in the interviews. We are aware that for some readers, our conclusions will be too cautious; yet for others, we will have gone too far. Due to the several methodological caveats outlined in the Introduction, we offer these thoughts not as final universal answers but as grounded interpretations, suggesting that the issue of heterodox economics requires further exploration. Of course, the usual disclaimers about our own predispositions apply: our interpretation is not the only possible one.

The main question of the book is: what is heterodox economics? In turn, this begs questions about whether heterodox economics is defined intellectually, sociologically, psychologically, or as something else. How are heterodox economists different from the mainstream and from each other? Is it associated with membership of a specific group? What can we say about heterodox economics and economists, and what can we *not* say?

From our interviews, the emergent picture echoes extant literature in many ways; however, it stresses some elements of that literature relatively more strongly than others and reveals new aspects. Heterodox economics is a multifaceted, layered object comprising complex groups of similarly complex individuals. Thus, heterodox economics defies simple definition.

Nonetheless, we can see that clearly it has a strong sociological aspect: *heterodox economics is a community*. That community emerges in various ways, but to a considerable degree as dissent against the dominant power of mainstream economics, characterised as having an excessively narrow, perhaps dogmatic approach to science and engaging in discriminatory behaviour towards alternative economic perspectives. Heterodox economics is a pluralist community with a diversity of origins, purposes, and standards for economic reasoning, ranging amongst others from history and philosophy of economics, to modelling, community organising, and policymaking. Heterodox economics can therefore be likened to a *eudaemonic bubble* that enables the flourishing of its members.

Whilst heterodox economics is a community that reaches across most continents, it differs from the kind of transnational thought collective of a Mont Pèlerin Society (MPS) (Mirowski and Plehwe, 2009) with its ideologically tightly controlled membership and secretive meetings. The social epistemology also seems to differ from the MPS as heterodox economists are primarily academics who seek to influence society via academia. While policymaking, media, activism, and community organising are explicitly adopted strategies to affect societal change, they seem secondary and not coherently orchestrated or theorised by the community.

The interviews show that *heterodox economists share a* kairotic *experience*, that is, a moment at which individuals make a significant and usually irrevocable decision to reject mainstream economics as a way to understand economic phenomena. The reasons for this *kairos* are opaque and may reflect the being of the entire person; hence they may differ for each interviewee. The *kairotic* decision seems, though, to be associated with a desire for one or several of the following: radically open questioning and debate, critical free thinking, genuine holistic understanding, sound relevant science, pursuit of a core concern, and tolerant inclusiveness. The *kairos* is thus thoroughly creative and provides the much-needed openness for new economic thinking that aspires to change the vectors of economics. Thus, *heterodox economics is not merely about resistance, dissent, and opposition to mainstream economics*. It is also not homogeneous in style, ranging from open radical opposition and martyrdom to less conflictual styles that seek compromise and discussion, or subtle infiltration and subversion to undermine the mainstream.

Nevertheless, in terms of economic theory, we find considerable agreement on the weaknesses of the mainstream. Most prominently, mainstream economics is seen as underplaying the role of power in the economy, thereby also failing to understand *its own power* and its consequences in terms of the suppression of heterodoxy. We also, though, uncover some key positive shared elements within heterodoxy which serve to distinguish them from mainstream economists. In terms of teaching, although overall our respondents did not demonstrate direct knowledge of learning theory or the philosophy of education, we can infer a basic commitment to liberal or critical education via references to criticality, creativity, and autonomy. We can also see a clear commitment to the kind of pluralism in teaching that does not preclude heterodox approaches. In terms of their views on economics as poetry, the answers indicate that most interviewees feel comfortable relating economics to the arts or humanities and that they see no fundamental gap between them. In terms of politics, it seems that most interviewees are left

288   *Concluding thoughts*

of centre, given several references to social and ecological activism and left-wing politics.

Crucially, our interviews allow the inference that *there is something like a common denominator or an ontological and methodological core to heterodoxy*. Most interviewees view the economic process as open to and interrelated with cultural, social, psychological, political, financial, geographical, bio-physical, and ecological factors. Furthermore, several interviews suggest that economic phenomena are open to interpretation as they manifest themselves. These aspects imply that a plurality of methods are needed to further the understanding of economic phenomena. Heterodox economists seem to sympathise with a practical, perhaps even case-based approach that is grounded in concrete economic phenomena and real-world problem situations. In this approach certain principles (e.g., entropy law, open systems, social provisioning) have been derived and gained wider acceptance as tools for analysis. Moreover, in this approach the following concepts have gained wider acceptance: class, gender, institutions, social metabolism, metabolic rift, instability, fundamental uncertainty, ecological distribution conflicts, cost-shifting, entropic degradation, domination effect, exploitation, and power asymmetries. We might aver, then, that heterodox economics adopts more of a conflictual view of the economy as opposed to the "harmony view" of neoclassical economics.

Though many of our interviewees moved from mathematics or science into heterodox economics, this does not entail that heterodoxy rejects mathematical and statistical methods. Rather, it suggests that heterodox economists use such methods – indeed any methods – in a philosophically informed way. This is consistent with a tentative consensus in our interviews that mathematical methods *per se* are not objectionable but that the mainstream *insistence* on them is both discriminatory *and even leads to inferior science*. Our interviews suggest that heterodox economists employing mathematical and statistical methods are better able to communicate with the mainstream and are generally, though not always, more accepted by them. Indeed, several interviews claim that the ability and willingness to employ mathematical or statistical techniques are strongly correlated with scientific credibility expressed in top-level publishing, success in terms of research funding, or policymaking for the highest levels of government. For instance, heterodox macroeconomics often allows the navigation of the middle ground of the spectrum, which encompasses mainstream and heterodox economics. In this respect, Keynes's economics seems to function as a bridge to the mainstream. This indicates that a potential common ground with mainstream economics is the ideal of science that employs adequate mathematical methods when appropriate. The fact that heterodox economists favour doing this in a philosophically informed way suggests they are simultaneously open to other, more interpretative dimensions of economic phenomena that cannot be captured adequately through mathematics. One source of tension here, though, is the argument that mathematics is inconsistent with the above-mentioned ontology held by heterodox economists. In this way, some heterodox economists

Concluding thoughts 289

(for instance, Lawson) accuse their colleagues of committing the same methodological errors as the mainstream.

Overall, though, one finding which emerges from the interviews is that *heterodox economists advocate pluralism*, based on the openness of economic phenomena. It underpins objections to mainstream exclusion of heterodoxy, as the foundation for better economics aligned with the complex nature of reality, and at the core of good teaching of economics. Thus, at the heart of heterodox economics is a commitment to pluralism. There is little suggestion, contra Garnett (2006), that heterodox economists are practising strategic pluralism; that is to say, our respondents seem to genuinely value pluralism and do not advocate it for convenience; it is not just employed strategically to create space for their own work. This matters because it means that heterodoxy could obtain a position of power, perhaps in an economics department, the economics profession of a given country, or even on the governmental level and still be essentially heterodox. In the case of Brazil, for example, the national context is more favourable to heterodox economics than in, say, the UK, US (Guizzo et al., 2018), or even Germany (Heise and Thieme, 2016). This means that, as discussed in the Introduction, the definition of heterodox economics involves a mix of intellectual and sociological characteristics. Thus, significantly, we would contest some previous interpretations of heterodox economics. For example, Colander, Holt, and Rosser's (2004b) definition of heterodoxy is based on its sociological position at the fringe. Dequech (2007) argues heterodox economics can only be identified sociologically (i.e., with no clear intellectual definition).

Crucially, pluralism and the common denominator condition one another, and pluralism ends where it becomes inconsistent with affirming the above-outlined understanding of the economic process. This vision resonates with "structured pluralism" (Dow, 2004). The kind of pluralism espoused by heterodoxy is different from the pluralism advocated by the mainstream, which fails to integrate many of the dimensions mentioned above. Second, heterodox pluralism is not *relativism*, or an "anything goes". Indeed, there are severe problems with pluralism understood as relativism. Neoliberal economists have argued that in a relativist world only the Market, never human beings, can function as the arbiter of Truth. This is the fundamental epistemological challenge posed by neoliberalism, also called "agnotology" and Will to Ignorance (Mirowski, 2013). Consistent with this view, a recent commentator on the political economy of Truth (Kakutani, 2018) argues that the Left's strategy of breaking the cultural hegemonies of the post-WWII era sowed the seeds for the climate deniers, doubt creators, and anti-scientific, anti-establishment populists who now mimic this strategy. Ironically, the movement in economics was the opposite: from more to less pluralism. Nevertheless, heterodox economics' espousal of more pluralism in economics seems to avoid relativism due to the shared understanding of the economic process as outlined above. This reflects the understanding that the seat of Truth is the human being. However, while our interviews are littered with

290 *Concluding thoughts*

references to Truth, we could not explore in enough detail how heterodox economists understand Truth and what this implies for their economics – the above remarks on the grounded approach notwithstanding.

One implication of this pluralism, and one which emerges from the interviews, is that *the relation between heterodox and mainstream economics is complex.* Thus, a simple dichotomy may capture it badly. This follows for several reasons. First, both heterodox and mainstream are complex and multidimensional. As stated in the Introduction, we left it open to our interviewees to interpret what they mean by "mainstream". The answers of our interviewees suggest that most interpret the mainstream as *conceptually* largely synonymous with neoclassical economics; but also, whilst there was some commonality in this regard (for instance, on behavioural economics), our interviews expressed variety in what else might be included as mainstream. Significantly, as well, the mainstream was often defined sociologically, in terms of its structures and behaviour of its members; however, again, interviewees' responses were heterogeneous. Second, rather than being utterly different, there is something akin to a continuum between the extreme positions of mainstream and heterodox. Indeed, on this there was fruitful dissent amongst our set of interviewees regarding the boundaries of heterodoxy. This indicates ragged edges and grey areas of meaning structures which could be crucial for understanding heterodox economics.

Third, as well as lateral continua, say at the level of theory, both heterodox and mainstream economics reflect hierarchies from within and without the discipline. So, within mainstream economics there is a hierarchy of US universities in terms of whose graduates dominate the discipline. More significantly, there is a hierarchy in other dimensions. For example, there is a pecking order in academia, with maths and "hard" sciences at the top and approaches associated with arts and humanities, including philosophy, at the bottom. In economics, then, influences and methods from maths and physics, and to a lesser extent biology, tend to have prestige. Thus, these methods are insisted upon and rewarded. Thus, whilst some heterodox economics falls foul of some mainstream theoretical tenets, by adopting mathematical formalism, they gain acceptance. Analytical Marxism is one example. By aping natural sciences, experimental and some behavioural economists also achieve prestige. Post Keynesian economists doing advanced econometrics may also gain some traction. However, by stressing methodology and philosophy, many heterodox economics merely compound their blasphemy.

The above discussion suggests that there is no simple dichotomy between mainstream and heterodox. Nonetheless, as discussed above, heterodox economists experience a *kairos*, a point at which they eschew mainstream economics. That suggests that, despite there being a complexity, including gradations of mainstream and heterodox, there is some point at which heterodox economists commit themselves to a different path. Hence our findings support previous research (Wrenn, 2007) that there is a threshold in the continuum between the extreme positions of mainstream and heterodox economics. Past this point, an individual becomes heterodox; they may also then ally themselves with others who have traversed the threshold – and against those who have not. This may explain what appears to be a polarisation in economics.

Again, though, things are not that simple. Take, for instance, the issue of the label "heterodox". For example, we have the strange phenomenon that some interviewees are perceived by us as clearly heterodox (Fullbrook, Martinez-Alier, Sent) while they reject the label. On the one hand they express ideas that are consistent with the core concerns of many heterodox economists; on the other hand they criticise alternatively the label's negative connotation, strategic disadvantages, and lack of specificity. One of them even denies the need for heterodoxy because of sufficient pluralism in the mainstream.

For others, though, the rejection or acceptance of the label is more about what it conveys about their attitude. Many adopt the label as it captures their self-image as one engaged in resisting the unwarranted authority of the ruling elite. This could bolster the heterodox economist in their struggle; however, it could also deepen feelings of disadvantage, becoming a "label for losers" (Fullbrook, this volume). A great danger then is that heterodox economics becomes an increasingly self-ghettoised sect of people who are stuck in a double-bind of resentments. This would be unwise, not least because it would not be an attractive home to those young economists formulating their own career paths, for whom pluralism, rethinking and *recapturing* economics is a positive project. However, our sample of interviewees suggests that being heterodox and "successful" as an economist is not a contradiction.

Yet, many do use the label. This suggests perhaps an emotional or psychological aspect of heterodox economics that is linked to experiences and the above-mentioned *kairos*. Our respondents report that heterodox economists experience exclusion, bullying, discrimination, repression, and injustice in different degrees and forms, going as far as attempting to terminate or prevent their careers as academic economists. This would support Lee's (2011) notion of heterodoxy as being akin to blasphemy. One might say that in relating the stories of their own path to heterodoxy, interviewees are revealing some scarring from their experiences. Clearly, many subjects had negative experiences in their training and subsequently in their professional careers. Some express concern that others have been treated unfairly. Some therefore may see heterodox economics as a better environment, a place in which constructive conversation can happen, in which mere self-justification is unnecessary. Considering though the recent emergence of resistance movements in economics, such as "new economic thinking", "degrowth", "rethinking", "reteaching", and "pluralism", the question arises whether the community of heterodox economists and heterodoxy as a label can attract the next generation of alternative economists.

In summary, then, we do believe that our research allows a better understanding of heterodox economics. We are aware, though, that many points require further research and greater depth. Given the wide range of our

292 *Concluding thoughts*

questions, we often could not go into enough detail on each topic. There are questions we could not answer.

When we began the book, we focused a lot on the archetypes which appeared in existing interviews. We were intrigued as to whether the archetypes which appeared in mainstream interviews would be evident in ours. While mainstream interviews suggested some heroism allied with the self-image of the scientist, would we find something different, perhaps more poetic (but perhaps still scientific) in the heterodox economists? At this point, we cannot claim to have reached firm conclusions. As noted above, many of our interviewees attached themselves to science in a way similar to what mainstream economists have done. We might tentatively suggest that the archetypes manifested in the heterodox conversations point to an additional one not found in the mainstream interviews: The Great Mother archetype. This may be unique to heterodoxy as per the significant and substantive roles of nature, nurturing, and provisioning; however, this claim requires much more substantiation.

Further, we were unable to address the question of whether anyone can use the label "heterodox" if they so wish. This is relevant to, for example, economists from the Austrian school, who share with many heterodox economists a scepticism about *inter alia* mathematisation, equilibrium theorising, and statistical modelling. We also could not resolve if heterodox economists do use the label strategically (for instance, instead of "political economist") and what this implies, except that we have found that our interviewees do guard the term "economist" closely: they have not surrendered the discipline to the mainstream. Finally, we are aware that our sample of heterodox interviewees were senior, well-established, "successful" economists and that this brings costs as well as benefits. For, although our book does capture a moment in the history of economics, it allows us to say little by way of forecasting. For instance, we do not know how younger heterodox economists, or even aspiring, nascent economists view the term "heterodox". And, does heterodox economics need a more coherent social epistemology and strategy for achieving social change? How can the common denominator be further elaborated, and is this desirable? These and other questions are topics for another volume.

Bibliography

American Economic Association's Committee on the Status of Women in the Economics Profession (CSWEP) (2017) *Annual Report*. Available at: https://www.aeaweb.org/content/file?id=6388 (accessed 20 February 2018).

Arestis, P. and Sawyer, M. (eds.) (2001a) *A Biographical Dictionary of Dissenting Economists*. Cheltenham: Edward Elgar.

Arestis, P. and Sawyer, M. (eds.) (2001b) "Anwar Shaikh". In: Arestis, P. and Sawyer, M. (eds.) *Biographical Dictionary of Dissenting Economists*. Cheltenham: Edward Elgar, pp. 590–598.

Arnsperger, C. and Varoufakis, Y. (2006) "What Is Neoclassical Economics? The Three Axioms Responsible for Its Theoretical Oeuvre, Practical Irrelevance and, Thus, Discursive Power". *Real-World Economics Review*, no. 38, July 2006, pp. 2–12. Available at: http://www.paecon.net/PAEReview/wholeissues/issue38.pdf.

Auerback, M. (2016) "Capitalism: Competition, Conflict, Crisis". *Institute for New Economic Thinking*. Available at: https://www.ineteconomics.org/perspectives/videos/capitalism-competition-conflict-crisis (accessed 17 July 2018).

Ayres, C. (1936) "Letter to Joseph Dorfman". Joseph Dorman Collection. Butler Library: Columbia University.

Backhouse, R.E. (2000) "Progress in Heterodox Economics". *Journal of the History of Economic Thought*, 22 (2), pp. 149–155.

Berger, S. (2018) "Towards a Poetic Economics: Studies in Ezra Pound's Poetry with a Hammer". In: Luefter, R. and Preda, R. (eds.) *A Companion to Ezra Pound's Economic Thought*.

Berger, S. (2016) "Social Costs and the Psychology of Neoclassical Economists". In: Gräbner, C., Heinrich, T. and Schwardt, H. (eds.) *Policy Implications of Recent Advances in Evolutionary and Institutional Economics*. London and New York: Routledge.

Bieri, H., Moser, P. and Steppacher, R. (1999) "Die Landwirtschaft als Chance einer zukunftsfähigen Schweiz oder Dauerproblem auf dem Weg zur vollständigen Industrialisierung der Ernährung?" Zürich: SVIL-Schrift, Nr. 135.

Binswanger, H.C. (1994) *Money and Magic: Critique of the Modern Economy in the Light of Goethe's Faust*. Chicago: University of Chicago Press.

Blaikie, P. and Brookfield, H. (1987) *Land Degradation and Society*. London: Methuen.

Boulding, K. (2011) *Interdisciplinary Economics: Kenneth E. Boulding's Engagement in the Sciences*. Edited by Dolfsma, W. and Kesting, S. London and New York: Routledge.

Bowmaker, S.W. (2010) *The Heart of Teaching Economics: Lessons from Leading Minds*. Cheltenham: Edward Elgar.

294 Bibliography

Bridges, A. and Hartmann, H. (1975) "Pedagogy by the Oppressed". *Review of Radical Political Economics*, 6 (4), pp. 75–79.

Camus, A. (1955) *The Myth of Sisyphus*. New York: Alfred A. Knopf.

Card, D. and Krueger, A.B. (1994) "Minimum Wages and Employment: A Case Study of the Fast-Food Industry in New Jersey and Pennsylvania". *American Economic Review*, 84 (4), pp. 772–793.

Carson, R. (1962) *Silent Spring*. Boston: Houghton Mifflin.

Carvalho, F.C. (1983) "On the Concept of Time in Shacklean and Sraffian Economics". *Journal of Post Keynesian Economics*, 6 (2), pp. 265–280.

Carvalho, F.C. (1992) *Mr Keynes and the Post Keynesians: Principles of Macroeconomics for a Monetary Production Economy*. Cheltenham: Edward Elgar.

Carvalho, F.C. (2003) "Decision-Making under Uncertainty as Drama: Keynesian and Shacklean Themes in Three of Shakespeare's Tragedies". *Journal of Post Keynesian Economics*, 25 (2), pp. 189–218.

Carvalho, F.C. (2015) *Liquidity Preference and Monetary Economies*. London: Routledge.

Cedrini, M. and Fontana, M. (2017) "Just Another Niche in the Wall? How Specialization Is Changing the Face of Mainstream Economics". *Cambridge Journal of Economics*, 42 (2), pp. 427–451.

Centre for Bhutan Studies and GNH Research (2015) *A Compass Towards a Just and Harmonious Society: 2015 GNH Survey Report*. CBS: Thimphu.

Chang, H-J. (2014) *Economics: The User's Guide*. New York: Bloomsbury Press.

Charusheela, S. (2007) "The Diaspora at Home". *Cultural Dynamics*, 19 (2–3), pp. 279–299.

Charusheela, S. (2009) "Social Analysis and the Capabilities Approach: A Limit to Martha Nussbaum's Universalist Ethics". *Cambridge Journal of Economics*, 33 (6), pp. 1135–1152.

Charusheela, S. (2010) "Engendering Feudalism: Modes of Production Debates Revisited". *Rethinking Marxism*, 22 (3), pp. 438–445.

Charusheela, S. (2010) "Gender and the Stability of Consumption: A Feminist Contribution to Post Keynesian Economics". *Cambridge Journal of Economics*, 34 (6), pp. 1145–1156.

Charusheela, S. (2011) "Response: History, Historiography, and Subjectivity". *Rethinking Marxism*, 23 (3), pp. 322–327.

Charusheela, S. (2013) "Intersectionality." In: Figart, D. and Warnecke, T. (eds.) *Handbook of Research on Gender and Economic Life*. Cheltenham: Edward Elgar, pp. 32–45.

Chick, V. (1977) *The Theory of Monetary Policy*. Oxford: Basil Blackwell.

Chick, V. (1983) *Macroeconomics after Keynes: A Reconsideration of the General Theory*. Cambridge, MA: MIT University Press.

Chick, V. (1998) "On Knowing One's Place: The Role of Formalism in Economics". *Economic Journal*, 104 (451), pp. 1859–1869.

Chick, V. and Dow, S. (2001) "Formalism, Logic and Reality: A Keynesian Analysis". *Cambridge Journal of Economics*, 25 (6), pp. 705–721.

Chick, V. and Dow, S. (2005) "The Meaning of Open Systems". *Journal of Economic Methodology*, 12 (3), pp. 363–381.

Ciccone, R., Gehrke, C. and Mongiovi, G. (2013) *Sraffa and Modern Economics*, Volume 1. London: Routledge.

Coats, A.W. Bob, Backhouse, R.E., Dow, S.C., Fusfeld, D.R., Goodwin, C.D. and Rutherford, M. (2000) "Roundtable: The Progress of Heterodox Economics". *Journal of the History of Economic Thought*, 22 (2), pp 145–148.

Colander, D. (2000) "The Death of Neoclassical Economics". *Journal of the History of Economic Thought*, 22 (2), pp. 127–143.

Bibliography   295

Colander, D., Holt, R. and Rosser, J.B., Jr. (2004a) *The Changing Face of Economics: Conversations with Cutting Edge Economists*. Ann Arbor: University of Michigan Press.

Colander, D., Holt, R., and Rosser, J.B., Jr. (2004b) "The Changing Face of Mainstream Economics". *Review of Political Economy*, 16 (4), pp. 485–499.

Darity, W. (1988) *What's Left of the Economic Theory of Discrimination?* Chapel Hill: University of North Carolina Press.

Darity, W. (1998) *Persistent Disparity: Race and Economic Inequality in the United States since 1945*. Cheltenham: Edward Elgar.

Darity, W. and Goldsmith, A. (1996) "Social Psychology, Unemployment and Macroeconomics". *Journal of Economic Perspectives*, 10 (1), pp. 121–140.

Darity, W. and Mason, P. (1998) "Evidence on Discrimination in Employment: Codes of Color, Codes of Gender". *Journal of Economic Perspectives*, 12 (2), pp. 63–90.

Davis, J. (2009). "The Nature of Heterodox Economics". In: Fullbrook, E. (ed.) *Ontology and Economics: Tony Lawson and His Critics*. London: Routledge.

Davis, J. (2014) "Pluralism and Anti-Pluralism in Economics: The Atomistic Individual and Religious Fundamentalism". *Review of Political Economy*, 26 (4), pp. 495–502.

Deléage, J-P. (1991) *Histoire de l'écologie: Une science de l'homme et de la natura*. Paris: La Découverte.

Dequech, D. (1999) "Expectations and Confidence under Uncertainty". *Journal of Post Keynesian Economics*, 21 (3), pp. 415–430.

Dequech, D. (2006) "The New Institutional Economics and the Theory of Behaviour under Uncertainty". *Journal of Economic Behavior and Organization*, 59 (1), pp. 109–131.

Dequech, D. (2007) "Neoclassical, Mainstream, Orthodox, and Heterodox Economics". *Journal of Post Keynesian Economics*, 30 (2), pp. 279–302.

Dequech, D. (2012) "Post Keynesianism, Heterodoxy and Mainstream Economics". *Review of Political Economy*, 24 (2), pp. 353–368.

Dequech, D. (2013) "Economic Institutions: Explanations for Conformity and Room for Deviation". *Journal of Institutional Economics*, 9 (1), pp. 81–108.

Dequech, D. (2017). "Some Institutions (Social Norms and Conventions) of Contemporary Mainstream Economics, Macroeconomics and Financial Economics". *Cambridge Journal of Economics*, 41 (6), pp. 1627–1652.

Dimmelmeier, A., Heussner, F., Pürckhauer, A. and Urban, J. (2017) "Making the Incommensurable Comparable: A Comparative Approach to Pluralist Economics Education". *European Journal of Economics and Economic Policies: Intervention*, 14 (2), pp. 250–266.

Dobusch, L. and Kapeller, J. (2012) "Heterodox United vs. Mainstream City? Sketching a Framework for Interested Pluralism in Economics". *Journal of Economic Issues*, 46 (4), pp. 1035–1056.

Dow, S. (1990) "Beyond Dualism". *Cambridge Journal of Economics*, 14 (2), pp. 143–157.

Dow, S. (1993) *Money and the Economic Process*. Cheltenham: Edward Elgar.

Dow, S. (1996) *The Methodology of Macroeconomic Thought*. Cheltenham: Edward Elgar.

Dow, S. (2002) *Economic Methodology: An Inquiry*. Oxford: Oxford University Press.

Dow, S. (2004) "Structured Pluralism". *Journal of Economic Methodology*, 11 (3), pp. 275–290.

Dow, S. (2009) "History of Thought and Methodology in Pluralist Economics Education". *International Review of Economics Education*, 8 (2), pp. 41–57.

Dow, S. and Rodriguez-Fuentes, C. (1997) "Regional Finance: A Survey". *Regional Studies*, 31 (9), pp. 903–920.

Dow, S., Jespersen, J. and Tily, G. (2018a) *The General Theory and Keynes for the 21st Century*. Cheltenham: Edward Elgar.

296   Bibliography

Dow, S., Jespersen, J. and Tily, G. (2018b) *Money, Method and Contemporary Post-Keynesian Economics*. Cheltenham: Edward Elgar.

Dunn, S.P. (2009) "Cambridge Economics, Heterodoxy and Ontology: An Interview with Tony Lawson". *Review of Political Economy*, 21 (3), pp. 481–496.

Earle, J., Moran, C. and Ward-Perkins, J. (2016) *The Econocracy: The Perils of Leaving Economics to the Experts*. Manchester: Manchester University Press.

Ederer, S., Hein, E., Niechoj, T., Reiner, S., Truger, A. and van Treeck, T. (eds.) (2012) *Interventions: 17 Interviews with Unconventional Economists*. Marburg: Metropolis.

Ehrlich, P.R., Ehrlich, A.H. and Holdren, J.P. (1977) *Ecoscience: Population, Resources, Environment*. San Francisco: WH Freeman.

Eichner, A.S. and Kregel, J. (1975) "An Essay on Post-Keynesian Theory: A New Paradigm in Economics". *Journal of Economic Literature*, 13 (4), pp. 1293–1314.

Ellis, H.S. (1937) *German Monetary Theory: 1905–1933*. Cambridge, MA: Harvard University Press.

Escobar, Arturo. (1994) *Encountering Development*. New Jersey: Princeton University Press.

Ferber, M.A. and Nelson, J.A. (1993) *Beyond Economic Man: Feminist Theory and Economics*. Chicago: University of Chicago Press.

Feynman, R.P. (1965) *The Character of Physical Law*. Cambridge, MA: MIT Press. Penguin edition, 1992.

Foucault, M. (1972) *The Archaeology of Knowledge and the Discourse on Language*. New York: Pantheon Books.

Francis. (2015) *Laudato si* (online) Available at: http://w2.vatican.va/content/francesco/en/encyclicals/documents/papa-francesco_20150524_enciclica-laudato-si.html (accessed 13 July 2018).

Freeman, A. (2009) "The Economists of Tomorrow: The Case for a Pluralist Subject Benchmark Statement for Economics". *International Review of Economics Education*, 8 (2), pp. 23–40.

Freire, P. (1970) *Pedagogy of the Oppressed*. New York: Continuum.

Friedman, M. and Schwartz, A.J. (1971) *A Monetary History of the United States (1867–1960)*. Princeton, NJ: Princeton University Press.

Fullbrook, E. (2010a) "How to Bring Economics into the 3rd Millennium by 2020". *Real-World Economics Review*, no. 54, 27 September 2010, pp. 89–102. Available at: http://www.paecon.net/PAEReview/issue54/Fullbrook54.pdf.

Fullbrook, E. (2010b) "The Glass Wall". *Real-World Economics Review Blog*, 25 June 2010. Available at: https://rwer.wordpress.com/2010/06/25/the-glass-wall/.

Fullbrook, E. (2017) *Narrative Fixation in Economics*. London: College Publications.

Fullbrook, E. (n.d.) *Duck or Rabbit: Boolean Political Economy*. Forthcoming.

Garnett, R. (2006) "Paradigms and Pluralism in Heterodox Economics". *Review of Political Economy*, 18 (4), pp. 521–546.

Garnett, R.F., Jr., Olsen, E.K. and Starr, M. (eds.) (2009) *Economic Pluralism*. London and New York: Routledge.

Georgescu-Roegen, N. (1971) *The Entropy Law and the Economic Process*. Cambridge, MA: Harvard University Press.

Gerber, J-F. and Steppacher, R. (eds.) (2011) *Towards an Integrated Paradigm in Heterodox Economics: Alternative Approaches to the Current Eco-Social Crises*. London and New York: Palgrave Macmillan.

Gerber, J-F. and Steppacher, R. (2014) "Some Fundamentals of Integral Economics". *World Futures*, 70 (7), pp. 442–463.

Bibliography 297

Gerber, J.-F. and Steppacher, R. (2017) "Basic Principles of Possession-Based Economies". *Anthropological Theory*, 17 (2), pp. 217–238.

Guha, R. and Martinez-Alier, J. (1997) *Varieties of Environmentalism: Essays North and South*. New York: Routledge.

Guizzo, D., Mearman, A. and Berger, S. (2018) "'*TAMA*' Economics under Siege in Brazil: The Threats of Curriculum Governance Reform". Mimeo.

Hansen, A. (1953) *A Guide to Keynes*. New York: McGraw-Hill.

Harding, S. and Norberg, K. (2005) "New Feminist Approaches to Social Science Methodologies: An Introduction". *Signs*, 30 (4), pp. 2009–2015.

Healy H., Martinez-Alier J., Temper L., Walter M., Gerber J.-F. (2012) *Ecological Economics from the Ground Up*. New York: Routledge.

Heise, A. and Thieme, S. (2016) "The Short Rise and Long Fall of Heterodox Economics in Germany after the 1970s: Explorations in a Scientific Field of Power and Struggle". *Journal of Economic Issues*, 50 (4), pp. 1105–1130.

Henderson, W., Dudley-Evans, T. and Backhouse, R. (eds.) (1993) *Economics and Language*. London and New York: Routledge.

Heterodox Economics Directory (HED) (2016). "Your Guide to Heterodox Economics". Available at: http://heterodoxnews.com/directory/#entry-5 (accessed 13 August 2018).

Hirsch, C. and DesRoches, C.T. (2009) "Cambridge Social Ontology: An Interview with Tony Lawson". *Erasmus Journal for Philosophy and Economics*, 2 (1), pp. 100–122.

Hodgson, G.M. (1989) "Post-Keynesianism and Institutionalism: The Missing Link". In: Pheby, J. (ed.) *New Directions in Post Keynesian Economics*. Aldershot, UK and Brookfield, VT, USA: Edward Elgar, pp. 94–123.

Hornborg, A., McNeill, J.R. and Martinez-Alier, J. (2007) *Rethinking Environmental History: World-System History and Global Environmental Change*. Plymouth: Altamira Press.

James, C.L.R. (1938) *The Black Jacobins: Toussaint L'Ouverture and the San Domingo Revolution*. London: Secker and Warburg.

Jevons, W.S. (1865) *The Coal Question: An Enquiry Concerning the Progress of the Nation, and the Probable Exhaustion of Our Coal-mines*. London: Macmillan.

Jo, T-H., Chester, L. and D'Ippoliti, C. (eds.) (2017) *The Routledge Handbook of Heterodox Economics: Theorizing, Analyzing, and Transforming Capitalism*. London and New York: Routledge.

Kakutani, M. (2018) *The Death of Truth: Notes on Falsehood in the Age of Trump*. New York: Tim Duggan Books.

Kapp, K.W. (1961) *Toward a Science of Man in Society: A Positive Approach to the Integration of Social Knowledge*. The Hague: Martinus Nijhoff.

Keynes, J.M. (1921) *A Treatise on Probability*. London: Macmillan.

Keynes, J.M. (1930) *A Treatise on Money*. London: Macmillan.

Keynes, J.M. (1931) *Essays in Persuasion*. London: Macmillan.

Keynes, J.M. (1936) *The General Theory of Employment, Interest and Money*. London: Macmillan.

Keynes, J.M. (1964) *The General Theory of Employment, Interest and Money*. San Diego: Harcourt, Brace, Jovanovich.

King, J.E. (1995) *Conversations with Post Keynesians*. Cheltenham: Edward Elgar.

Klamer, A. (1983) *Conversations with Economists*. Totowa, NJ: Allanheld and Rowman.

Klamer, A., McCloskey, D.N. and Solow, R.M. (1988) *The Consequences of Economic Rhetoric*. Cambridge: Cambridge University Press.

298 Bibliography

Koppl, R. and Mongoivi, G. (2012) *Subjectivism and Economic Analysis: Essays in Memory of Ludwig M Lachmann*. London: Routledge.

Lakoff, G. and Johnson, M. (1980) *Metaphors We Live By*. Chicago: University of Chicago Press.

Lavoie, M. and Godley, W. (2001) "Kaleckian Models of Growth in a Coherent Stock-Flow Monetary Framework: A Kaldorian View". *Journal of Post Keynesian Economics*, 24 (1), pp. 277–311.

Lawson, T. (1997) *Economics and Reality*. London: Routledge.

Lawson, T. (2003) *Reorienting Economics*. London and New York: Routledge.

Lawson, T. (2006) "The Nature of Heterodox Economics". *Cambridge Journal of Economics*, 30 (4), pp. 483–505.

Lawson, T. (2009) "The Current Crisis: Its Nature and the Course of Academic Economics". *Cambridge Journal of Economics*, 33 (4), pp. 759–777.

Lawson, T. (2013) "What Is This 'School' Called Neoclassical Economics?" *Cambridge Journal of Economics*, 37 (5), pp. 947–983.

Lawson, T. and Pesaran, H. (eds.) (1985) *Keynes' Economics: Methodological Issues*. London: Croom Helm.

Lee, F.S. (2007) "Making History by Making Identity and Institutions: The Emergence of Post Keynesian-Heterodox Economics in Britain, 1974–1996". *History of Economics Review*, 46 (1), pp. 62–88.

Lee, F.S. (2009) *A History of Heterodox Economics*. London and New York: Routledge.

Lee, F.S. (2011) "The Pluralism Debate in Heterodox Economics". *Review of Radical Political Economics*, 43 (4), pp. 540–551.

Lee, F.S. (2012) "Heterodox Economics and Its Critics". In: Lee, F.S. and Lavoie, M. (eds.) *In Defense of Post-Keynesian and Heterodox Economics: Response to Their Critics*. London: Routledge, pp. 104–132.

Lee, F.S. and Lavoie, M. (2012) *In Defense of Post-Keynesian and Heterodox Economics: Response to Their Critics*. London: Routledge,

Le Guin, U. (1980) "The Dispossessed". *Bicicleta* (Barcelona), no. 31, pp. 47–50.

Leijonhufvud, A. (1968) *On Keynesian Economics and the Economics of Keynes: A Study in Monetary Theory*. New York: Oxford University Press.

Martinez-Allier, J. (1973) *Los huacchilleros del Peru*. Lima: Instituto de Estudios Peruanos.

Martinez-Allier, J. (1977) *Haciendas, Plantations and Collective Farms*. London: Frank Cass Publishers.

Martinez-Allier, J. (1990) *Ecological Economics: Energy, Environment and Society*. Oxford and New York: Blackwell.

Martinez-Allier, J. (2002) *The Environmentalism of the Poor: A Study of Ecological Conflicts and Valuation*. Cheltenham: Edward Elgar.

Martinez-Allier, J. and Jusmet, J.R. (2015) *Economía ecológica y política ambiental*, 3rd ed. Madrid: Fondo de Cultura Economica.

Marx, K. (1967) *Capital*. Volumes I–III. New York: International Publishers.

Mata, T. (2004) "Constructing Identity: The Post Keynesians and the Capital Controversies". *Journal of the History of Economic Thought*, 26 (2), pp. 241–259.

McCloskey, D. (1983) "The Rhetoric of Economics" *Journal of Economic Literature*, American Economic Association, vol. 21 (2), pp. 481–517.

McCloskey, D. (2012) "Happyism". *New Republic*, 8 June 2012. Available at: https://newrepublic.com/article/103952/happyism-deirdre-mccloskey-economics-happiness (accessed 13 July 2018).

Mearman, A. (2011) "Who Do Heterodox Economists Think They Are?" *The American Journal of Economics and Sociology*, 70 (2), pp. 480–510.

Mearman, A. (2012) "'Heterodox Economics' and the Problem of Classification". *Journal of Economic Methodology*, 19 (4), pp. 407–424.

Mearman, A. (2017) "Teaching Heterodox Economics and Pluralism". *Handbook for Economics Lecturers*. Bristol: Economics Network.

Mearman, A. and Philp, B. (2016) "The Association for Heterodox Economics: Past, Present, and Future". In: Jo, T. and Todorova, Z. (eds) (2016) *Advancing the Frontiers of Heterodox Economics: Essays in Honor of Frederic S. Lee*. London: Routledge.

Mearman, A., Guizzo, D. and Berger, S. (2018a) "Whither Political Economy? Evaluating the CORE Project as a Response to Calls for Change in Economics Teaching". *Review of Political Economy*. DOI: 10.1080/09538259.2018.1426682.

Mearman, A., Guizzo, D. and Berger, S. (2018b) "Is UK Economics Teaching Changing? Evaluating the New Subject Benchmark Statement". *Review of Social Economy*. DOI: 10.1080/00346764.2018.1463447.

Mirowski, P. (1990) "The Philosophical Bases of Institutionalist Economics". In: Lavoie, D. (ed.) *Economics and Hermeneutics*. New York: Routledge, pp. 74–110.

Mirowski, P. (1994) "What Are the Questions?" In: Backhouse, R. (ed.) *New Directions in Economic Methodology*. New York: Routledge.

Mirowski, P. (2013) *Never Let a Serious Crisis Go to Waste*. London and New York: Verso.

Mirowski, P. and Plehwe, D. (eds.) (2009) *The Road from Mont Pèlerin: The Making of the Neoliberal Thought Collective*. Cambridge, MA: Harvard University Press.

Mirowski, P. and Sent, E-M. (eds.) (2002) *Science Bought and Sold: Essays in the Economics of Science*. Chicago: University of Chicago Press.

Mongiovi, G. (1990) "Keynes, Hayek and Sraffa: On the Origins of Chapter 17 of the General Theory". *Économie Appliquée*, 43 (2), pp. 131–156.

Mongiovi, G. (1996) "Sraffa's Critique of Marshall: A Reassessment". *Cambridge Journal of Economics*, 20 (2), pp. 207–224.

Mongiovi, G. (2002) "Vulgar Economy in Marxian Garb: A Critique of Temporal Single System Marxism". *Review of Radical Political Economics*, 34 (4), pp. 393–416.

Mongiovi, G. (2012) "Orthodoxy, Heterodoxy and Post-Keynesian Economics: Notes on Taxonomy". In: Lee, F.S. and Lavoie, M. (eds.) *In Defense of Post-Keynesian and Heterodox Economics*. Abingdon: Routledge.

Mongiovi, G. and Petri, F. (1999) *Value, Distribution and Capital: Essays in Honour of Pierangelo Garegnani*. London: Routledge.

Moura, M.L. (1932) *Love One Another and Do Not Multiply [Amai-vos e não vos multipliqueis]*. Rio de Janeiro: Civilização Brasileira.

Musgrave, A. (1981) "'Unreal Assumptions' in Economic Theory: The F-Twist Untwisted". *Kyklos*, 34 (3), pp. 377–387.

Navarro, M.G.M. and Martinez-Alier, J. (2001) *Naturaleza transformada: estudios de historia ambiental en España*. Barcelona: Icaria Editorial.

Nelson, J. (1992) "Gender, Metaphor, and the Definition of Economics". *Economics and Philosophy*, 8 (1), pp. 103–125.

Nelson, J. (2018) *Economics for Humans*, 2nd ed. Chicago: University of Chicago Press.

Popper, K. (1957) *The Poverty of Historicism*. London: Routledge.

Robinson, J. (1937) *Introduction to the Theory of Employment*. London: Macmillan.

Rodney, W. (1973) *How Europe Underdeveloped Africa*. London: Bogle-L'Ouverture Publications.

300 *Bibliography*

Royal Economic Society Women's Committee (RES) (2017) *Royal Economic Society's Report on the Gender Balance in UK Economics Departments and Research Institutes in 2016.* Available at: http://www.res.org.uk/SpringboardWebApp/userfiles/res/file/Womens%20Committee/Publications/WomensCommitteeReport_2016SurveyResults.pdf (accessed 20 February 2018).

Russell, B. (1928) *Sceptical Essays.* London: George Allen and Unwin.

Samuelson, P.A. and Barnett, W.A. (eds.) (2007) *Inside the Economist's Mind: Conversations with Eminent Economists.* London: Wiley-Blackwell.

Samuels, W. (ed.) (1990) *Economics as a Discourse: An Analysis of the Language of Economists.* New York: Springer.

Sahlins, M. (1972) *Stone Age Economics.* London: Routledge.

Sarkar, S. (1983) *Modern India.* London: Macmillan.

Sayers, R.S. (1938) *Modern Banking.* London: Humphrey Milford.

Shaikh, A. (1974) "Laws of Production and Laws of Algebra: The Humbug Production Function". *Review of Economics and Statistics,* 61 (1), pp. 115–120.

Shaikh, A. (1994) *Measuring the Wealth of Nations: The Political Economy of National Accounts.* Cambridge and New York: Cambridge University Press.

Shaikh, A. (2016) *Capitalism: Competition, Conflict, Crises.* New York: Oxford University Press.

Shaikh, A. (2017) "Book Lectures". Available at: http://realecon.org/videos/ (accessed 13 July 2018).

Shanin, T. (1983) *Late Marx and the Russian Road.* New York: NYU Press.

Sent, E-M. (1998) *The Evolving Rationality of Rational Expectations.* Cambridge: Cambridge University Press. Available at: https://ideas.repec.org/b/cup/cbooks/9780521571647. html.

Snowdon, B. and Vane, H.R. (1999) *Conversations with Leading Economists: Interpreting Modern Macroeconomics.* Cheltenham: Edward Elgar.

Snowdon, B. and Vane, H.R. (2005) *Modern Macroeconomics: Its Origins, Development and Current State.* Cheltenham: Edward Elgar.

Steppacher, R. (1976) *Surplus, Kapitalbildung und wirtschaftliche Entwicklung – Zur Relevanz der Physiokratie und der institutionellen Ökonomie für das Problem der Kapitalbildung in unterentwickelten Ländern.* Liebefeld, Bern: Lang Druck.

Steppacher, R. (1989) "Das keralesische Gesundheitsparadoxon und die Frage der landwirtschaftlichen Entwicklungsperspektive". In: Seeland, K. (ed.) *Gegenseitiges Verständnis als Entwicklungsprozess, Beiträge zu Theorie und Praxis der Entwicklungszusammenarbeit.* Konkrete Fremde, Grüsch: Verlag Rüegger, pp. 175–206.

Steppacher, R. (1996) "Die sozialen und ökologischen Kosten der Marktwirtschaft – Zur Aktualität von K. William Kapp". *Globalisierung – Arbeit und Ökologie, Widerspruch, Beiträge zur sozialistischen Politik,* 31 July 1996, pp. 95–102.

Steppacher, R. (2008) "Property, Mineral Resources and Sustainable Development". In: Steiger, O. (ed.) *Property Economics: Property Rights, Creditor's Money and the Foundations of the Economy.* Marburg: Metropolis, pp. 323–354.

Stiglitz, J. (1994) *Whither Socialism?* Cambridge, MA: MIT Press.

Thornborrow, T. and Brown, A.D. (2009) "Being Regimented: Aspiration, Discipline and Identity Work in the British Parachute Regiment". *Organization Studies,* 30 (4), pp. 355–376.

Tyler-Miller, G. (1986) *Environmental Science.* Belmont, California: Wadsworth.

Tyson, K., Darity, W. and Castellino, D. (2005) "It's Not 'a Black Thing': Understanding the Burden of Acting White and Other Dilemmas of High Achievement". *American Sociological Review,* 70 (4), pp. 582–605.

Ura, K. (2004) *Deities, Archers, and Planners in the Era of Decentralisation*. CBS: Thimphu.

Ura, K. (2018) *The Unremembered Nation*. Forthcoming.

Vernadsky, W. (1924) *La Géochimie*. Paris: Libraire Félix Alcan.

Walsh, V. and Gram, H. (1980) *Classical and Neoclassical Theories of General Equilibrium*. New York: Oxford University Press.

Weintraub, E.R. (2007) "Economists Talking with Economists: A Historian's Perspective". In: Samuelson, P. and Barnett, W.A. (eds.) *Inside the Economist's Mind: Conversations with Eminent Economists*. Malden, MA: Blackwell, pp. 1–9.

Williams, E. (1944) *Capitalism and Slavery*. Chapel Hill: University North Carolina Press.

Witt, U. (1996) "Innovations, Externalities, and the Problem of Economic Progress". *Public Choice*, 89 (1–2), pp. 113–130.

Witt, U. (1998) "Imagination and Leadership: The Neglected Dimension of an Evolutionary Theory of the Firm". *Journal of Economic Behavior and Organization*, 35 (2), pp. 161–177.

Witt, U. (2004) "On the Proper Interpretation of 'Evolution' in Economics and Its Implications for Production Theory". *Journal of Economic Methodology*, 11 (2), pp. 125–146.

Witt, U. (2009) "Propositions about Novelty". *Journal of Economic Behavior and Organization*, 70 (1–2), pp. 311–320.

Witt, U. (2016) *Rethinking Economic Evolution: Essays on Economic Change and Its Theory*. Cheltenham: Edward Elgar.

Witt, U. (2017) "The Evolution of Consumption and Its Welfare Effects". *Journal of Evolutionary Economics*, 27 (2), pp. 273–293.

Wittgenstein, L. (1922) *Tractatus Logico-Philosophicus*. London: Kegan Paul.

Wrenn, M. (2007) "What Is Heterodox Economics? Conversations with Historians of Economic Thought". *Forum for Social Economics*, 36 (2), 97–108.

Zein-Elabdin, E.O. and Charusheela, S. (2004) *Postcolonialism Meets Economics*. London: Routledge.

Index

A Monetary History of the United States
  (Friedman and Schwartz) 42
Acción Ecológica 167–8
Acosta, Alberto 166
Alhadeff, David 232, 236
Alternative Economic Strategy 135
Althusserian concept of power 74
American Economic Association 75
American Economic Review 43, 164
*American Economic Review Papers
  and Proceedings* 118
anarchism 161
Anarres 161
Andalusia 156–7, 161
Anguelovski, Isabelle 172
anti-Malthusian argument 52–3
Antonopoulos, Rania 226
Archer, Margaret 149
Arestis, Philip 46, 214
Argentina 41–2
Aristotle 163
Arrhenius, Svante 162
Arrow, Kenneth 5, 176
Asimakopulos, Tom 38, 39
aspirational selves 15–16, 102
Association for Economic and Social
  Analysis 71, 72
Association for Evolutionary Economics
  (AfEE) 11
Association for Heterodox Economics
  (AHE) 3, 10, 11
Association for Social Economics
  (ASE) 11
Atlantic slave trade 52
Atlas of Environmental Justice
  168–9
Auerback, Marshall 214, 221, 228
Austrian economics 2, 11, 22, 145,
  189–90, 194–5, 244

Autisme-Economie 255
Ayres, Clarence Edwin 1
Ayres, Robert Underwood 157

Babylonian Approach 19–20
bad research 58–9
Bank of England 18–19, 26–7, 217
Baran, Paul 156
Bardhan, Pranab 66
Barker, Clarence 19
Basu, Kaushik 68
Baumol, William 187, 193, 201
Beauvoir, Simone de 259
Becker, Gary 208, 217, 219–20, 223
Becker, James 187
behavioural economics 198–9
Behavioural Science 278
Beinart, William 168
Bell, Philip 236
Berger, Sebastian 24
Bergmann, Barbara 7
Betinho (Herbert de Souza) 45
Bhaskar, Roy 149
Bhopal gas tragedy 69
Bicicleta 161
Bieri, Hans 104, 105
Binmore, Ken 5, 6
Binswanger, Hans Christoph 104
biopiracy 167
Black Jacobins (James) 52
Blaikie, Piers 158
Blair, Tony 217
Blanchard, Olivier 5, 272
blasphemers 57
Blinder, Alan 201
Bloomsbury Group 253
Blumer, Herbert 56
Boettke, Peter 195
Bolin, Bert 162

Bonilla, Heraclio 160
Borgstrom, George 160
Borras, Jun 157
Boserup, Ester 52
Botwinick, Howard 222
Boulding, Kenneth 157
Bowles, Sam 76
Brandeis University 118
Brasilia 18
Brazil 41–2, 265–6, 267–9
Brazilian Keynesian Association 43
Brock, William 5
Brookfield, Harold 158
Brunner, Karl 5
Buddhism 85

Calhoun, Craig 271
Cambridge Economic Policy Group 136
Cambridge Growth Project 134, 136
Cambridge Journal of Economics 153, 190, 197, 223
Cambridge Realist Workshop 150, 155
Cambridge Social Ontology Group 155
Cambridge Society for Economic Pluralism 151
Camus, Albert 260
Canadian International Development Agency 91
capital stock 51
capitalism 2–3, 131, 138, 148, 154, 165, 203–4, 211–12, 214, 215–16, 219, 223, 224
Capitalism 209
Capitalism, Nature, Socialism 167
Capitalism and Slavery (Williams) 52
capitalist economy 40, 51
Carabelli, Anna 147–8
Cardim de Carvalho, Fernando José 33–49, 264, 265; academic biography 33; becoming an economist 33–4; on Brazil and heterodox economics 41–2; contribution to economics 38–9; doctoral programme 35–6; on economics as poetry 48; education 34, 35–6; going back to Brazil 36–7; as a heterodox economist 39–41; influence on society 44–5; Keynes's influence on 37–8; on mainstream economics 42–3; strategies for seeking research funding 45–6; on teaching 46–7
Carson, Rachel 167
Cartesian-Euclidean way 24
Cattaneo, Claudio 161

CEDES 41
Cedrini, Mario 4
Centre for Bhutan Studies 83
Chamberlain, Edward 218
Charusheela, S. 66–81; academic biography 66; admission into economics in Delhi University 67–8; becoming an economist 66–7; contribution to economics 69–72; on economics as poetry 80–1; education 67–9; goal as an economist 59, 77–8; graduate studies 68–9; on heterodox economics 73–4; as a heterodox economist 72–3; influence on society 78–9; parental influence on 67; on problems of mainstream economics 76–7; strategies for seeking research funding 79; on teaching 79–80; on women's studies 74–5
Chayanov's rule 160
Chester, Lynn 4
Chick, Victoria 194, 232–51; on Austrian economics 244; becoming an economist 232–4; contribution to economics 236–7; on economics as poetry 249–51; on Eisenhower recession 234; on formalism 237–8; goal as an economist 246; on heterodox economics 239–41, 243; influence on society 246–7; influences on 236; on mainstream economics 234–5, 242, 244; on pluralism 234, 235, 241–2; on problems of mainstream economics 244; strategies for seeking research funding 247; on teaching 247–9
Christodoulopoulos, George 226
Circle of Vienna 163
Classical and Neoclassical Theories of General Equilibrium (Walsh) 187
Clifton, Jim 223
climate change 162
Clower, Robert 5
Club of Rome 52–3
Cobb-Douglas production functions 150
Colander, David 5, 200, 271
Cold War 9, 85
Collaborative Online International Learning (COIL) 79
Collected Writings (Keynes) 38
Colletti, Lucio 36
Comisiones Obreras 161
commodity extraction frontiers 165
Communist Party 223
competitive socialism 164

304 *Index*

consciousness, raising 103, 109
consumer microeconomics 221
cooperative economy 40
Corbera, Esteve 172
Correa, Rafael 166
Costanza, Bob 162
Cramp, Tony 236
creativity 108
Cripps, Francis 135
critical realism 149
critical thinking, teaching 185, 272–3
Cuadernos de Ruedo ibérico 157, 160
Curriculum Open-access Resources in Economics (CORE) 248
cutting-edge economists 5

Daly, Herman 9, 157, 162, 163
Darity, William 49–65, 232; academic biography 49; on bad research 58–9; becoming an economist 49–50; contribution to economics 51–3; credibility 54; on economics as poetry 64–5; as an economist 56; as a heterodox economist 54–5; influence on society 59; interest in equality and poverty 50–1; on mainstream economics 57–8, 59; papers on mathematical models 51–4; on political economy 55; strategies for seeking research funding 60–3; on stratification economics 55–6; on teaching 63–4
Davidson, Paul 35, 36, 38, 39, 194, 264, 266
Davis, John 147–8, 176
Day, Alan 236
De Marchi, Neil 176
de Souza, Herbert (Betinho) 45
Deaton, Angus 136
"Decision-making under Uncertainty as Drama" 48
Del Bene, Daniela 168
Déleage, Jean-Paul 171
Delhi School of Economics 68, 69
Delhi University 67
Denis, Andy 2
depth psychology 98–9
Dequech, David 2, 3, 43, 262–74; academic biography 262; becoming an economist 262–3; contribution to economics 266; on economics as poetry 274; first contact with Post Keynesianism 265; goal as an economist 270; graduate degree 263–4; on heterodox economics 267, 270; as a

heterodox economist 266; influence on society 270; influences on 265; on institutions 271; on pluralism 268–9; on Post Keynesianism 267–8; on problems of mainstream economics 269–70; strategies for seeking research funding 271; on teaching 272
Development and Capitalism (Pellegrini) 156
D'Ippoliti, Carlo 4
Dispossessed, The (Le Guin) 161
dissenting economists 5
Dobb, Maurice 152
Dobusch, Leonhard 4
Dochula Druk Wangyal Temple 83
Domar, Evsey 166
double truths 15
Dow, Sheila 17–32, 237; academic biography 17; on Austrian economics 22; Bank of England experience 18–19, 26–7; becoming an economist 17; on being an outsider 25; book and publications 17; contribution to economics 19–20; on economics as poetry 31; exposure to wide range of views in economics 19; goal as an economist 27; as a heterodox economist 20–2; influence on society 27; interest in Babylonian Approach 19–20; interest in town planning 18; on Kuhn 28; on mathematics 31; strategies for seeking research funding 31–2; on student movements 30–1; on teaching 29–30
dowry 70
Drewermann, Eugen 103
Duesenberry, James 58–9
Dupré, John 176
Dutch Science Foundation 182–3
Dynamic Stochastic General Equilibrium (DSGE) 42

Easterly, William 5
Eatwell, John 188, 189
eco-development 109
eco-integrative 105
Ecologia Politica 167
ecological distribution conflicts (EDCs) 164–5
Ecological economics 160–2, 163–4, 166
Ecological Economics from the Ground Up 164
Ecological Economics (Martinez-Alier) 161–2, 168
ecological footprint 160
ecologically unequal exchange 160, 166

Econocracy, The 138, 249
Econometrica 117, 118
econometrics 180
Economía ecológica y política ambiental 164
Economic Morality 259
Economic Policy Institute 124
economics *see* Austrian economics; Ecological economics; heterodox economics; Keynesian economics; mainstream economics; Marxian/Marxist economics; Post Keynesian economics
Economics and Philosophy 116
economics as poetry 31, 48, 64–5, 80–1, 92–3, 109–10, 128, 153, 172, 185, 205–6, 230, 249–51, 260–1, 274, 284–5
Economics for Humans (Nelson) 123, 124
Economics: The User's Guide (Chang) 127
economists: heterodox *see* heterodox economists: interview books 4–5; Keynesian *see* Keynesians; Marxist *see* Marxists; Post Keynesian *see* Post Keynesians; as scientists 6; training of 24–5
Ecoscience (Erhlich et al) 171
eco-socialists 167
EcoTrust 125
Ehrlich, Alexander 208–9
Ehrlich, Anne 171
Ehrlich, Paul 171
Eichengreen, Barry 5
Eichner, Alfred 39, 196, 197
Ellis, Howard 236, 238
Elvin, Mark 168
Encountering Development 71
enlightenment 122
entrepreneurial economy 40
Entropy Law and the Economic Process, The (Georgescu-Roegen) 161, 172
Environmental Science (Miller) 171
environmentalism 167–8
Environmentalism of the Poor – A Study of Ecological Conflicts and Valuation (Martinez-Alier) 167–8, 168
equality 122
Escobar, Arturo 71
Essays in Persuasion 65
eudaemonic bubble 287
European Association for Evolutionary Political Economy (EAEPE) 11
European Research Council 169
European Society for Ecological Economics (ESEE) 11, 169

externalities 166
extractivism 166

Farmer, Mary 133
Fazzari, Steven 46
Federal Reserve Bank 61
Federal University of Rio de Janeiro 43, 47
Feminist Economics 123
Feynman, Richard 20
Fine, Ben 147
Fischer-Kowalski, Marina 157
Fluminense Federal University 36, 44
Fondo de Cultura Económica 158
Fontana, Magda 4
Ford Foundation 61, 125
formalism 237–8
Foucaultian concept of power 74
Frank, Robert 5
Franklin & Marshall 72
Freire, Paulo 47–8
Frenkel, Roberto 41
Friedman, Milton 4, 25, 42
Fromm, Erich 103
Fullbrook, Edward 252–61; academic biography 252; becoming an economist 252; contribution to economics 255–6; on economics as poetry 260–1; goal as an economist 258; on heterodox economics 256–7; influence on society 258; strategies for seeking research funding 258–60; on teaching 260
Fung, Victor 259
Funtowicz, Silvio 172
Furtado, Celso 41

Galbraith, James 256
Galbraith, John Kenneth 2, 65, 196
Gandhi, Indira 69
Garcia Lorca, Federico 161
Garegnani, Pierangelo 35, 36, 191, 193
Geddes, Patrick 157, 162
gender studies 75
General Theory of Employment, Interest and Money, The (Keynes) 6, 35, 38, 40, 43, 237, 241, 252–3
Geneva Institute 107
Georgescu-Roegen, Nicholas 9, 97, 98, 157, 161, 172
German Monetary Theory (Ellis) 236
German Research Foundation 283
Germany 258
ghazal 81

306   *Index*

ghost acreage 160
Giampietro, Mario 172
Gintis, Herbert 5, 6
Global Development Environment
    Institute 123, 125
global financial crisis 1; characteristics
    of 1–2
Gödel's incompleteness theorems 131
Godley, Wynne 143, 227
Goethe 104
Gokhale Institute of Politics and
    Economics 105
González de Molina, Manuel 164
Goodwin, Craufurd 177
Goodwin, Neva 125
Gordon, Robert 6
Gram, Harvey 187, 188
Grant, Duncan 253
Great Depression 7
Great Mother archetype 7, 292
Green movement 161
Griffin, Keith 84
Grinevald, Jacques 96
Grinnell College 50
gross domestic product (GDP) 7
Gross National Happiness 83, 85, 88–9,
    91, 93
guano 160
Gudynas, Eduardo 166
Guevara, Che 159
Guha, Ramachandra 167
Guide to Keynes, A (Hansen) 253

Haberl, Helmut 157
Habilitation 97, 105, 278–80
Haciendas, Plantations and Collective Farms
    (Martinez-Alier) 160
Ha-Joon Chang 127
Haldane, Andrew 26–7
Hamermesh. Daniel 5
Hamlet 48
Hands, Wade 176
Hansen, Alvin 253
happiness 85–6
"Happyism: The Creepy Science of
    Pleasure" 92–3
Harding, Susan 115
Harris, Marvin 208, 209
Harrod, Roy 166
Harrod-Domar model 166
Hart, Oliver 136
Harvard Divinity School 118
Hayek, Friedrich August 145, 188

Hecksher-Ohlin model 224
Heilbroner, Robert 209
Hein, Eckhard 2
Heinsohn, Gunnar 104
Henry George School of Economics 229
heretics 57
heterodox economics 2–3; Charusheela's
    views on 73–4; Chick's views on
    239–41; as a community 286–7;
    creativity in 108; critical/oppositional
    attitude of 3–4; definition of 178;
    Dequech's views on 267, 270; dialectics
    in 148–9; as a eudaemonic bubble
    287; first known use of ther term 1–4;
    Fullbrook's views on 256–7; integration
    of approaches in 100; literature 1–4;
    vs. mainstream economics 7–9, 22–3,
    290; Mongiovi's views on 191–2;
    multiple ontologies 22; Nelson's views
    on 119–20; open systems in 243;
    pluralism in 289–90; on problems of
    mainstream economics 256–7; scope of
    100; Sent's views on 178–80; Shaikh's
    views on 214–16; sociological definitions
    of 3; Steppacher's views on 100; Ura's
    views on 87; Witt's views on 280–1
heterodox economics directory (HED 1, 2
Heterodox Economics Newsletter 11
heterodox economists: common
    denominators 288; interview books
    4–5; kairotic experience of 287; label
    291; *vs.* mainstream economists 7–9;
    organizations 11; pluralism 289–90;
    risks of 102; self-labelling 3, 10
Higgs-Boson theory 138
Hildebrand, 222
Hilferding, Rudolf 36
History of Ecology (Déleage) 171
Hitler, Adolf 215–16
Hodgson, Geoffrey 265
Holdren, John 171
Hopkins, Barbara 2
Hornborg, Alf 160, 164
How Europe Underdeveloped Africa
    (Rodney) 52
Hughes, Alan 135
Human Development Index 163
Humbug (Shaikh) 230–1

Ibase 45
incommensurability of values 163–4
Independent Commission on
    Banking 238

Index 307

INET 125
Initiative for New Economic Thinking 226
Institut Universitaire d'Études Developpement (IUED) 96
Institute for New Economic Thinking (INET) 146, 259
Institute for Women's Policy Research. 124
Institute of Development Studies 97
Institute of Environmental Science and Technology 161
Institute of Social Ecology 166
Institutional Economics 235
Institutionalism 120
Instituto de Estudios Peruanos 160
intellectual defence 101
interested pluralism 4
International Confederation of Associations for Pluralism in Economics (ICAPE) 11, 22
International Development Research Centre 91
International Initiative for Promoting Political Economy (IIPPE) 147
International Monetary Fund (IMF) 18
International Panel on Climate Change (IPCC) 162
International Society for Ecological Economics (ISEE) 162
international trade 237
interview questions 11–13
interviews: Cardim de Carvalho, Fernando José 33–49; Charusheela, S. 66–81; Chick, Victoria 232–51; Darity, William 49–65; Dequech, David 262–74; Dow, Sheila 17–32; Fullbrook, Edward 252–61; Lawson, Tony 130–55; Martinez-Alier, Joan 156–72; Mongiovi, Gary 186–206; Nelson, Julie 111–29; Sent, Esther-Mirjam 173–85; Shaikh, Anwar 207–31; Steppacher, Rolf 94–110; Ura, Karma 82–93; Witt, Ulrich 275–85
Introduction to the Theory of Employment (Robinson) 253–4
IS-LM style macroeconomics 237
Italian Communist Party 36

James, C.L.R. 52
Jansson, Ann-Mari 162
Jayaraman, Nityanand 169
Jevons, William Stanley 162

Jevons Paradox 162
Jo, Tae-Hee 4
Johnson, Harry 238
Johnson, Mark 116
Journal of Business Ethics 123
Journal of Economic Literature 197
Journal of Economic Methodology 23
Journal of Economic Perspectives 118
Journal of Economics and Finance 55
Journal of Peasant Studies 157, 169
Journal of Political Economy 118
Journal of Post Keynesian Economics 39, 48
Julius Caesar 48
Jungian depth psychology 12
justice 122

Kahn, Richard 188
kairos 287, 291
Kaldor, Nicholas 135, 225, 227
Kalecki, Michal 194, 196, 209
Kallis, Giorgos 161, 170, 172
Kant, Immanuel 122
Kapeller, Jakob 4
Kapp, K. William 95–8, 104–5, 157, 163, 164, 165
Kapp Foundation 98, 104, 105
Kapp Prize 98, 104
Katzner, Don 71
Kazanas, Katherine 222–3
Keen, Steve 2
Keller, Evelyn Fox 115
Keynes, John Maynard 35, 37–8, 65, 135, 154–5, 227, 252–3
Keynesian economics 34–5, 166, 192, 221; cross model 205; military 216; Samuelsonian 236; *see also* Post Keynesian economics
Keynesians 39, 41, 135, 146, 260
Kirman, Alan 222
Kirzner, Israel 187, 204, 221
Koppl, Roger 195
Kregel, Jan 35, 36, 38, 46, 197
Krishna, T.M. 169
Krugman, Paul 25, 43, 193
Kuhn, Thomas 28

La Géochimie (Vernadsky) 157
labour theory of value 36
Labourers and Landowners in Southern Spain (Martinez-Alier) 157
Lacerda de Moura, Maria 161
Lachmann, Ludwig 188, 194–5, 204
Lakatos, Imre 179

308 *Index*

Lakoff, George 116
Land Degradation and Society (Blaikie and Brookfield) 158
Lange, Oskar 164
Late Marx and the Russian Road (Shanin) 160
Laudato si 169
Laughlin, Robert 220–1
Lavoie, Marc 192
Lawson, Tony 22, 130–55, 193, 265; academic biography 130; on Austrian economics 145; becoming an economist 130, 140–1; Cambridge Growth Project 134, 136; contribution to economics 133–4; credibility 136–7; on critical realism 149; on dialetics 148–9; on economics as poetry 153; on heterodox economics 146–7; as a heterodox economist 141–2, 144–5; influence on society 154; on mathematics 130–1, 137; on misuse of mathematics 132, 139; on ontological terminology 137; on physics 138; on political economy 147; on power 154; on problems of mainstream economics 139; on psychology of mainstream economics 140; relevance in heterodox economics 135; on Stock-Flow-Consistent modelling 142–4; student politics as an influence 131–2; on teaching mathematics 150–2
Le Guin, Ursula 161
Lee, Frederic 3, 7, 39, 57, 192
Lee, James 10
Left parties 223
Leijonhufvud, Axel 35
leisure class 56
Leontief paradox 224
Leontief Prize 157
Lerner, Abba 234, 236
Levy Institute 47
Levy Institute of Bard College 226
Liebig, Justus von 160
liquidity preference theory 35
Loasby, Brian 22
Lomborg, Bjørn 171
London School of Economics 236
Los huacchilleros del Peru (Martinez-Alier) 159
Love One Another (More) and Do Not Multiply (So Much) (Lacerda de Moura) 161
Lucas, Robert 5

Macbeth 48
macroeconomic theory 38
macroeconomics 199–202, 215, 217, 266; IS-LM 237
Macroeconomics in Context 123
Magdalen College 82
Maiguashca, Juan 160
mainstream economics 42–3, 57–8; definition of 178; difference with non-mainstream economics 193–4; *vs.* ecological economics 163–4; *vs.* heterodox economics 7–9, 22–3, 290 on incommensurability of values 163–4; intellectual defence in 101; lack of realism in 101; on mainstream economics 234–5; power and 77; problems of 23–4, 76–7, 88, 101, 139, 162, 180–1, 244, 256–7, 269–70, 281–2; psychology of 24, 59, 139–40; as a science 213–14
Malloy, Mary 222
Malthusian argument 52
Manchester University 249
Mankiw, Nicholas Gregory 5
March, Hufg 161
marginal efficiency of capital 225
Marglin, Stephen Alan 7
market failure 166
Marshall, Alfred 190, 247
Martinez-Alier, Joan 156–72; becoming an economist 156–8; contribution to ecological economics 160–2; contribution to economics 159–60; on ecological distribution conflicts (EDCs) 164–5; on economics as poetry 172; goal as an ecological economist 164–8; on heterodox economics 162, 170–1; influence on society 164–8; on problems of mainstream economics 162; professional success 170–1; strategies for seeking research funding 168–70; on teaching 171–2; undergraduate education 158–9
Marx, Karl 199, 209–12, 214, 214–16, 222, 225
Marxian/Marxist economics 34, 35, 36, 54, 54–5, 72, 74, 78, 95, 192, 192–3, 193
Marxist *Monthly Review* 222
Marxists 2, 3, 20, 22, 55, 71, 72, 74, 146, 192, 195, 222–3, 242, 243, 263, 276

Index 309

Masjuan, Eduard 161
mathematics 8, 31, 137, 235; good
economic practice and 180; misuse of
132, 139
Max Planck Institute of Economics 283
Mayhew, Anne 264
Mazonne, Andrew 229
McCloskey, Deirdre 5, 31, 64–5, 80–1,
92–3, 109, 116, 128, 153, 172, 185,
205–6, 260–1, 274
McCloskey, Donald 116
McNeill, John 164
Mearman, Andrew 1, 2, 3
memory blocks 15
Menger, Carl 145
Mephistopheles 104
Metaphors We Live By (Lakoff and
Johnson) 116
methodology/methodological issues
13–16
microeconomics 199–202, 217, 221, 266
Microeconomics in Context 123
military Keynesianism 216
Miller, G. Tyler 171
Minsky, Hyman 9, 36, 38, 40, 236, 266
Miranda House 68
Mirowski, Philip 15, 176
Mises, Ludwig von 145
Mishkin, Frederic 5
Modern Banking (Sayers) 238
Modern India 70
Modern Macroeconomics (Snowdon and
Vane) 227
Modigliani, Franco 5, 38, 51, 193, 194
Moncloa Pact of 1978 161
Money and Magic (Binswanger) 104
Mongia, Nandita 69
Mongiovi, Gary 186–206; on Austrian
economics 189–90, 194–5; becoming
an economist 186; on behavioural eco-
nomics 198–9; on economics as poetry
205–6; goals in intellectual work
204–5; on heterodox economics 191–2;
influences on 189; on intellectual
history 199; on mainstream economics
191, 193–4; motivations in research
190; on neoclassical economics 191;
on teaching macro and micro principles 199–202; on teaching Marxian
economics 199
Mont Pèlerin Society (MPS) 287
Mooney, Pat 167
Moore, Jason 165

Moser, Peter 104, 105
Mumford, Lewis 157
Munda, Giuseppe 172
Murra, John 159
Musgrave, Alan 200
Myrdal, Gunnar 98
Myth of Sisyphus, The (Camus) 260

Naredo, J.M. 157
National Council for Scientific and
Technological Development (CNPq,
Brazil) 35–6, 265
National Research Council 46
National Science Foundation 61, 62, 125
Naturaleza transformada 164
Negru, Ioana 244
Nell, Edward J. 188, 189
Nelson, Julie 74, 75, 111–29; academic
biography 111; becoming an economist 111; contribution to economics
115–17; on credibility 118; denial of
tenure 118; on economics as poetry
128–9; *Economics for Humans* 124; on
enlightenment concerns of justice and
equality 122; on equality 114; family
background 115; feminist work 115–17;
goal as an economist 121–2; graduate programme 112–13; grants 125;
on heterodox economics 119–20; as a
heterodox economist 119; influence on
society 123; on Institutionalism 120;
move to University of Massachusetts,
Boston 118; PhD programme 113;
political work 123; on post-modernism
122–3; on poverty 112; on problems of
neoclassical economics 120–1; strategies for seeking research funding 125;
on teaching 125–7; transition into
academic world 114; transition into job
market 114
neo-Austrianism 21
neoclassical economics 74, 87, 88, 143,
217; definition of 178; justification for
103; pluralism 235; problems of 102,
120–1
neo-Malthusian movement 161
neo-Ricardians 38, 39
neo-Schumpeterian 266
Neurath, Otto 162, 163, 164, 166
New Cambridge School 135, 136
New Economics Foundation 239
New Republic, The 93
New School for Social Research 186

310   *Index*

New York Times 43
New York University 187
Nietzsche, Friedrich 12
non-cooperative economy 40
non-governmental organizations (NGOs) 45
non-orthodox economics 40
Nordhaus, William 193
Norgaard, Nicholas 6, 157
Norrie, Alan 149

Ochoa, Ed 226
O'Connor, James 167
O'Donnell, Rod 147–8, 265
Odum, H.T. 157
oikonomia 163
On Keynesian Economics and the Economics of Keynes: A Study in Monetary Theory 35
"On the concept of time in Shacklean and Sraffian economics" 39
On the Shoulders of Giants 15
Onaran, Ozlem 2
O'Neill, John 162
one-percent money 257
ontological terminology 137
Ormerod, Paul 256
Oxford University 84

Pacific Sociological Review 56
Pantaleoni, Maffeo 192
Papandreou, George 234
Paris Agreement (2015) 164–5
Parrinello, Sergio 35
Pasinetti, Luigi 51
pedagogy 12
Pellegrini, Lorenzo 156
Pheby, John 265
Philips, Paul 19
physics 138
Pigou, Arthur 193
Pigs for the Ancestors (Rappaport) 160
Planck, Max 276
Plehwe, Dieter 15
pluralism 4, 108, 177, 181–2, 234, 235, 241–2, 268–9, 289–90
Podolinsky, Sergei 157, 162
poetry, definition of 92–3
Polanyi, Karl 160, 163
political ecology 166
political economy 55, 147
Pollack, Robert 75
Popper, Karl 179, 257, 263, 276, 284
Possas, Mario 265

Post Keynesian economics 34–5, 44, 74, 142, 144, 147, 217, 264–6, 264–7, 265, 281–2; *see also* Keynesian economics
Post Keynesians 2, 3, 20, 22, 34–5, 36, 44, 48, 54, 135, 146, 147, 192, 193, 194, 214, 217, 242, 267–8, 290
Post-Autistic Economics Newsletter 256
postcolonial feminism 72
Post-Crash Economics 249
Post-Jungian archetypal psychology 12
post-modernism 122–3
poststructuralist feminist theory 72
poverty 112
Poverty of Historicism, The (Popper) 263
power 77
Prager, Jonas 188
Prebisch, Raúl 41
Prebisch-Singer 68
Preiswerk, Roy 97
Prescott, Edward 6
Progressive Labour Party 223
psychology 5
pure math 18

Quarterly Journal of Economics 197

Rabin, Matthew 5
Radboud University 178, 180
Radhakrishnan, R. 71
raising consciousness 103, 109
Raj, K.N. 66
Ramsey, Frank 253
Rappaport, Roy 160
rational choice 221
Rawls, John 122
RE Stats 118
real business cycle theory 47, 57
Real-World Economics Review 256
rebound effect 162
Rees, Bill 160
relative income hypothesis 59
Reorienting Economics 146
Research Council of Switzerland 97
research funding 31–2, 45–6, 60–3, 79, 90–1, 125, 168–70, 182–3, 247, 258–60, 271, 282–3
"Reserve Army of Labour, The" 214
Resnick, Stephen 69, 70, 76
Rethinking Environmental History 164
Rethinking Marxism 78
Review of Economic Statistics 117
Review of Economics and Statistics 114
Review of Political Economy 197, 204, 267

Revolutionary Communist Party 223
Ricardians 38, 39, 151, 224
Ricardo, David 199, 221, 224
Richards, I.A. 254
Riskin, Carl 209
Robertson, Dennis 239
Robinson, Joan 35, 160, 188, 192, 196, 218, 253–5
Roca, Jordi 161, 164
Rodney, Walter 52
Rowthorn, Bob 135
Royal Economic Society 43
ruling classes 210
Runde, Jochen 265
Russell, Bertrand 263
Rutgers University 35, 39
Rutherford, Malcolm 235
Ryan-Collins, Josh 239

Sahlin, Marshall 160
Sainsbury, Lord 259
Samuelson, Paul 5, 38, 51, 193, 194, 206
Samuelsonian Keynesianism 236
Sanchez, Jeannette 166
Sanz de Santa Maria, Alejandro 71
São Paulo State Research Foundation 271
Sargent, Thomas 5, 173–4, 176
Sarkar, Sumit 70
Saro-Wiwa, Ken 167
Sawaya, Rubens 47–8
Sawyer, Malcolm 7, 214
Sayer, Andrew 149
Sayers, Richard 238, 243, 246
Sceptical Essays 263
Schabas, Margaret 115
Schlüpmann, Klaus 161
Schumpeter, Joseph A. 266
Schwartz, Anna 42
scientism 256–7
Scitovsky, Tibor 234, 236
Scott, Jim 168
Second Sex, The (Beauvoir) 259
Second World War 85
Self 102
self-interested behaviour 58
self-labelling 3, 10
Selves 12
semi-structured interviews 14
Semmler, Willi 225
Sen, Amartya 66
Sent, Esther-Mirjam 173–85; academic biography 173; becoming a historian and philosopher of economics 174–5;

becoming an economist 173–4; contribution to economics 175–7; on economics as poetry 185; goal as an economist 181; on heterodox economics 178–80; influence on society 182; on pluralism 181–2; political career 175, 183; on politics 174; on problems of mainstream economics 180–1; strategies for seeking research funding 182–3; on teaching 183–5
Shackle, George 22, 39
Shaikh, Anwar 207–31; academic biography 207; becoming an economist 207–8; on economics as poetry 230; on Gary Becker 219–20; on heterodox economics 214–16, 222–3; Humbug 230–1; influence on society 216–17; influences on 208–9; on mainstream economic models 213; on mainstream economics 213–14; on Marx and Marxism 209–12; on problems of mainstream economics 221–2; on teaching 228–30
Shanin, Teodor 160
Shapiro, Nina 46
sharecropping 157
Shiller, Robert 225
Silent Spring (Carson) 167
Simon, Herbert 175, 185
Simon Fraser 19
Singh, Ajit 135
Skidelsky, Robert 244
slave trade 52
Smith, Adam 224, 225
Smith, Yves 124
socialist calculation debate 162, 164, 166
Socialist Labour Party 223
Socialist Workers Party 223
socio-environmental conflict 165
sociological definitions 3
Soddy, Frederick 162, 163
Solow, Robert 5, 38, 193
Soros, George 146, 259
Spanish Civil War 161
Spash, Clive 157
Spivak, Gayatri 70
Sraffa, Pierro 34–5, 188–9, 190, 196, 225, 253
Sraffians 2, 20, 24, 36, 39, 54, 151, 181, 191, 192–3
St. Antony's College 159–60
St. Stephen's College 82
statistics 83, 84, 180

312   *Index*

Steiger, Otto 104
Steppacher, Rolf 94–110; academic biography 94; as an academic economist working in academia 96–7; becoming an economist 94–5; career options 97; contribution to economics 97–9; on depth psychology 98–9; early influences on 95; on eco-development 109; on economics as poetry 109–10; family background 95; goal as an economist 102; on heterodox economics 100; as a heterodox economist 99–100; influence on society 104; Kapp's influence on 96; on Kapp-Wiechert tradition 103; on neoclassical economics 102; PhD dissertation 95; on politics 106; on problems of mainstream economics 101; publications 98; on raising consciousness 103; strategies for seeking research funding 105–6; working for Kapp Foundation 98
Stiglitz, Joseph 40, 193
Stock-Flow-Consistent modelling 142–4
Stockhammer, Engelbert 2
Stohler, Jacques 95
Stolcke, Verena 156, 157, 159
Stone Age Economics (Sahlin) 160
stratification economics 55–6, 58
Strauber, Ira 49–50
student movements 30–1
Svampa, Maristella 166
Swiss Association of Industry and Agriculture 105
Swiss National Research Fund 105

Taylor, John 5
teaching: critical thinking 185, 272–3; enjoyment of 29–30, 46, 64, 79–80, 91–2, 106, 125–6, 171–2, 183–4, 202, 260, 272, 283–4; goals in 46–7, 63, 63–4, 79–80, 92, 107–8, 127, 171–2, 184, 201–2, 229–30, 248–9, 284; good teacher 126; mathematics 150–2; pedagogical practices 272; personal relationships with students in 107; philosophy of 106–7, 272; pluralism in 108; in practice 108; professor's opinion 203; strategies in 184; student supervisions 273–4; techniques 127; textbooks 127; tools 127
Temper, Leah 168
Tetlow, Katherine 103
Thames Papers in Political Economy. 10

Thiel, Peter 259
Third World Scholarship 82, 84
Tobin, James 5, 7, 38, 243
Toledo, Victor 157
Tonak, Ahmet 227
Tooke, Thomas 215
town planning 18
Tractatus Logico-Philosophicus 254–5
training 24–5
transitional justice 160–1
Treatise on Money 135
Treatise on Probability (Keynes) 39, 135
Trump, Donald 102
Tufts University 125

UNICAMP 159
Union for Radical Political Economics 219
Union of Radical Political Economics (URPE), 11
United Nations Commission for the Economic Development of Latin America and Caribbean (ECLAC) 166, 269
United Nations Development Program, 84
University of Barcelona 156, 158
University of Basel 104
University of Campinas 34–5, 37, 264, 268
University of Edinburgh 83, 84
University of Glasgow 19
University of Göttingen 276
University of Hawaii Women Studies Department 73
University of Jena 283
University of Manitoba 19
University of Mannheim 278
University of Massachusetts, Amherst 69, 71
University of Massachusetts, Boston 118, 125
University of Nevada, Las Vegas 78
University of North Carolina 59–60
University of Notre Dame 177, 180
University of São Paulo 34, 268
University of Tennessee 265
University of Washington 73
University of Wisconsin, Madison 112–13
Ura, Karma 82–93, 85; academic biography 82; becoming an economist 82–3; contribution to economics 85; on economics as poetry 92–3; education 82–3;

goal as an economist 88–9; on happiness 85–6; on heterodox economics 87; as a heterodox economist 86–7; influence on society 89–90; influences on 84; on problems with mainstream economics 88; social vision 89; on statistics 84–5; strategies for seeking research funding 90–1; on teaching 91–2

van den Bergh, Jeroen 172
Varieties of Environmentalism (Martinez-Alier and Guha) 167
Veblen, Thorstein 56, 58, 95, 98, 103, 143
Veneziani, Roberto 2
Verhulst curve 161
Vernadsky, Vladimir 157
Via Campesina 166
Vickrey, Bill 208
Vietorisz, Thomas 188
village fair paradigm 40
von Mises, Ludwig 164, 166

Walker, Ralph 84
Walras, Leon 162, 247
Walsh, Vivian 187
Wangchuck, Jigme Singye 85
Weber, Max 164
Weintraub, Roy 15, 176
Whither Socialism? (Stiglitz) 40

Williams, Eric 52
Witt, Ulrich 275–85; academic biography 275; becoming an economist 275–6; contribution to economics 279; on economics as poetry 284–5; goal as an economist 282; Habilitation thesis 278–80; on heterodox economics 280–1; as a heterodox economist 280; influence on society 282; influences on 276–9; on mainstream economics 280–1; on problems of mainstream economics 281–2; strategies for seeking research funding 282–3; on teaching 283–4
Wittgenstein, Ludwig 254
Wohlstetter, Philip 78
Wolff, Richard 70
women's studies 74–5
Woolf, Leonard 253
Woolf, Virginia 253
Wordly Philosophers, The (Heilbroner) 209
Wordsworth, William 92–3
World Bank 159
World Development 118
World Economics Association (WEA) 258–9
World Health Organisation 50
Wrenn, Mary 4

Zein-Elabdin, Eiman 72